"David James Keaton is a monomaniacal genius, splicing words together in the tailmost room of your movie-saturated snake-brain, and *The Last Projector* is his masterpiece. It is insane, anarchic, and fucking brilliant. I can't wait to read it again."

—Benjamin Whitmer, author of *Cry Father*

"Quite simply, David James Keaton is a twisted genius, and you read his work at your own risk, risk of a neural or moral meltdown... Keaton's stories are like secret maps to murder swamps where the bodies are buried by the serial killers who comprise Keaton's fan clubs... Say you are a mad scientist and you want to make a monster writer of the future, well, first you dig up the corpse of Kafka, get some DNA, then you do the same with David Foster Wallace, then toss some Stephen King and Woody Allen into the mixture. Add a pinch of Poe and Robert Parker, shake the test tube with vigor and presto you have David James Keaton. His writings are as sickly exuberant and gargantuan as gothic dirigibles, tall tales of teleportation into urban myth and mystery, post-truth, anti-reality, they break every rule of regular fiction and good taste."

—Chuck Kinder, author of *Honeymooners*

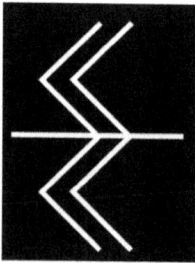

A Broken River Books original

Broken River Books
10765 SW Murdock Lane
Apt. G6
Tigard, OR 97224

Interior design by J David Osborne

Scenes from *The Last Projector* were originally broadcast in drastically different form in *Dogzplot, Indiana Crime Review, Dirty Noir, Pulp Metal Magazine, Shotgun Honey, Slut: Pure Slush Vol. 1, Yellow Mama, A Quick Bite of Flesh, PANK, Uncle B's Drive-In Fiction, Grift*, and *Hell.*

ISBN: 978-1-940885-27-8

Printed in the USA.

PRAISE FOR DAVID JAMES KEATON
&
The Last Projector

"A brutal headcase of a novel, dealing with the muck collecting under rolls of celluloid and DVD trays, the symbiotic relationship of on-screen smut and technological progress and life struggling to keep up with art, even as art grows bloated, uncontrollable and finally collapses in an orgy of self-destruction... manages to maintain the reader's interest even to the bitter end... sheer madness."

—*Albedo One Magazine*

"I want to know where David James Keaton buys his pants. There must be some kind of specialty store to buy trousers with enough roominess for him to stuff his immense balls into. *The Last Projector* (at a whopping 500-plus pages) maintains the sure hand and immense voice of someone well into a long and legendary career. And this is his @#$%&!ing debut. Ridiculously entertaining and well-paced, crossing genres at points with subtle flair that you won't even notice at first, this is the opener for a huge new voice."

—Todd Robinson, author of *The Hard Bounce* and editor-in-chief of *Thuglit*

"The Most Anticipated Book of 2014. Hell, it's the most anticipated book since this podcast has existed."

—*Booked. Podcast*

"Imagine Harry Crews' grit-filled world head-butting William Gaddis' dense, rollicking literary hopscotch and you're firmly entrenched in David James Keaton country. His thrilling debut, *The Last Projector* is the bubbling, epic story of how wonderfully screwed up America is."

—Patrick Wensink, author of *Broken Piano for President*

"Wickedly outrageous. The writing is fluid in ways it's not supposed to be — a plot point picks up and reverses itself, a girl morphs from one look to another to another in the telling, not a magic thing, just in the narration. There are great meandering conversations about movies, and strange, sick setpieces. It feels like stream of consciousness but it's only partly that, because [Keaton] is smart and funny and he knows what he's doing, and there are nudges in the text to let you know he's having fun all along. He really is."

—Carolyn Kellogg, *The Los Angeles Times*

"That thing called 'voice' authors are said to have? Keaton's are legion. That 'Tap, tap, tap' you may hear issuing from this book? I wouldn't open it up without a quick 'Klaatu barada nikto' for good measure. This book is a monster - dense, visionary, apocalyptic, reality-challenging, and flat-out entertaining."

—Jedidiah Ayres, author of *Peckerwood* and Godfather of the "Noir at the Bar" reading series

"The kind of multi-layered narrative that challenges readers as much as it entertains them. A wild debut novel that pushes against everything standard crime fiction is known for and emerges on the other side sporting a smile and shaking the debris of the fourth wall off its shoulders. Harry Crews' weirdness is here, along with Elmore Leonard's knack for dialogue and a playfulness that brings to mind Cuban giant Guillermo Cabrera Infante. Perhaps the most impressive thing about this novel is that it's Keaton's debut. A powerful and strange narrative that demands attention."

—Gabino Iglesias, *Full Stop*

"A great deal of humour, wit and invention. A novel this strange is almost critic-proof and I couldn't say which genre it belongs in (perhaps its own)."

—*Crime Fiction Lover*

"A literal smorgasbord of a novel, loaded with grease and fat and enough madness to choke a goat. Richly braided with dialogue and so many cultural zingers it should be registered as a weapon."

—*Shock Totem*

"Seriousy, half this thing is about dogs walking, dogs showing up, dogs that may or may not have attacked someone, tattoos of dog bites, etc. Don't get me wrong, I like dogs…except poodles. Fuck poodles. They have a guy here with a breakfast tattooed on his head. Who does that? What he's done, which I've decided to call "incest-friendly, overcomplicated, pooch-obsessed porny shit," is an assassination of a plethora of genres that no sane author would ever attempt."

—Hatebino Hateglesias, *The Literary Haters Ball*

"Some books define categorization, and then some books like *The Last Projector* actually wriggle free from your grasp like greased up marmosets furiously doing the Sprocket's dance. Underneath all this ornate dressing and psychedelic framing is a story about identity, regret and the peril and untrustworthiness of memory. All this existential digging and the book's other ruminations on gritty and brutal topics like rape, murder and insanity might be excessive and depressing if not for Keaton's knack for Altmanesque dialogue and angular, swift prose."

—*DigBoston*

"It's refreshing and playful and yet thoroughly exhausting. It's cliché to call something Lynchian, but there are elements of a Lynchian logic yet the story resembles more of the screenplay of a reckless John Carpenter movie. I'd call The Last Projector a psychedelic mystery.

—*Dead End Follies*

"There are plenty of "what the f*ck" moments in *The Last Projector,* but overall Keaton manages to balance out the weirdness with his distinct, hilarious voice and craft an intensely engaging plot."

—*LitReactor Bookshots*

"David James Keaton is a mad genius. This is his first novel but it's less a novel than an experience. It's David Foster Wallace and David Lynch co-directing a video-game adaptation of a musical adaptation of a sci-fi horror fantasy porno. It's getting over heartbreak by going to the cinema alone and taking communion with the silver screen while enveloped by the darkness."

—*Pulp Chronicler*

THE LAST PROJECTOR

by
David James Keaton

BROKEN RIVER BOOKS
PORTLAND, OR

To my mother,
for her ceaseless encouragement and love, as well as her
tremendous patience when I always wanted to watch a movie

"She has a view of Niagara that nobody has
And Basin Street, known as the birthplace of jazz
And on a clear day you can see Alcatraz!
You can learn a lot from Lydia…"

—Groucho Marx "Lydia the Tattooed Lady"

I.

Tap Tap Tap – Doing Everything but Actually Doing It –
Captain Redbeard Waves the White Flag – Dreamcatchers
Equal Dogcatchers but Daydreamcatchers Save Lives – No
Sleep till Krypton – The Oldest Tricky Shit in the Book
Is Her – Double Wishbone Suspension – Larry Catches
Something – Three Minutes

"A black eyed dog he called at my door
The black eyed dog he called for more
A black eyed dog he knew my name
A black eyed dog he knew my name
A black eyed dog, a black eyed dog
I'm growing old and I wanna go home
I'm growing old and I don't wanna know"
-Nick Drake "Black Eyed Dog"

Larry was late to the porn set as usual. He blamed that stretch of road near the baseball diamond. He would slow way down, drive with one knee, elbow hanging out the window as he combed the unruly white hairs of his beard with his fingers to start the day with a bit more confidence. His morning routine typically peaked with him spraying mouthwash out the window of his car at the same four-way stop, then tearing ass down the on-ramp to valiantly joust some morning traffic, pointing a finger over the lip of his Styrofoam cup to pretend it was a lance.

But today, something big was blocking his way.

Larry stomped the brakes, then peered through his steering wheel, cup squeaking between his teeth, a drop of coffee stinging his nose, finding himself staring down some red-faced, steel-worker-looking bastard. Just standing there, right in the middle of the road, actually squeezing Larry's hood ornament in a furry fist the size of a catcher's mitt. Larry assessed the serious muscle mass on this beast by the way his car creaked under the weight, and, squinting harder over the wheel, he could make out what was either the end of a Marine Corps anchor tattoo or a devil's pointy tail peeking out of the sleeve of his sweat-stained flannel. Larry should have revved the engine, stabbed the horn, done something, anything to coax the man out of his way. But he was paralyzed. Larry

1

felt like this fucker was gripping his necktie instead of his car, like he was frozen in his own headlights.

He waited, waited, nervous foot hovering over the gas.

Larry hated it when he locked up like this. It wasn't uncommon, and quite a liability at his job. It always made him think of hitting pause on a videotape, and how, if left unattended, the tape would begin to stretch and tear, forever marking the spot on the movie with an EKG ripple of white static across his television screen. He sometimes had to visualize his finger pressing "play" on an imaginary VCR in order to start moving again.

But this time, the man hit the magic button for him. As if grabbing his goddamn vehicle at an intersection and stopping it dead didn't already have Larry's attention, the monster was now knocking on the heavy glass of his headlight with the knuckles of his other meaty paw. Larry felt the sound deep in his chest.

Tap, tap, tap.

Then the red-faced bastard released the steel hourglass logo on his Grenada's nose and came around to Larry's window with whatever bullshit he was gonna bark already working around his mouth like too much bubblegum.

"Can I help you?" Larry tried, all friendly.

What came out of the man's mouth was a riddle for the ages:

"Why the fuck you spit green on my fuckin' grandma every day, cockfucker?" bleated the red bastard.

"Huh? What? No, I just..." he bubbled out of the corner of his mouth, drooling a little green.

"Every day she says she watches you spit on her house." Impossibly, the bastard's face grew even redder. "What the fuck you got against my grandma's house, motherfucker?!"

Larry looked at the house in question and stifled a laugh. No way he was spitting that far and hitting grandma's house. No way. Wait...

Oh. That house. The one with the Virgin Mary statue in the front yard.

The sculpture was a skinnier representation of Mary than the ones he was recently starting to notice on the bodies at work, a serene visage turning up regularly on more and more tattoos, creeping dangerously closer to the naughty "bathing suit areas." But those renditions were pink, plump, usually bowing and bending with the movement of the muscles below Mary's noble form. This statue was a different kind of Mary altogether. Hard, sinewy, as if the sculpture had been crafted to be a weapon, kind of like an unexploded bomb that had stabbed the ground decades earlier but never went off, never even tipped over. Her body was triangular, broad-shouldered, coming to a point at her feet, probably in order to jam her into the hardest soil and still maintain maximum stability. Looking at her now, he was suddenly struck by her profile. She reminded him of something else he'd seen at work lately: smaller, plastic Marys that his crew would roll out on a TV tray when the men's tanks were exhausted, like orderly rows of pink and purple Fisher Price surgical tools.

Yes, Stone Mary's silhouette was exactly like a vibrator, specifically those bunny rabbit deals. There was no denying it. In his business, where the band played every possible "instrument," Larry had seen some crazy dildos before: Hello Kitty, Strawberry Shortcake, Cthulhu, Mickey Mouse, Minnie Mouse, chainsaws, revolvers, coffins, even one molded after the Pope, big pointy hat and all. He'd even seen a line of Virgin Mary urinals once at a rinky-dink Creation Museum in Alabama, palms out like they were daring you to piss on them. Few people believed him about the urinals because he couldn't wrestle one loose from the wall, but it was true. He was seeing her everywhere.

But he'd never seen a Virgin Mary vibrator before. It was a shame, too, because, built to the right dimensions,

3

those clasped hands locked forever in prayer were positioned perfectly for clitoral stimulation.

If he ever got past this sputtering tower of asshole blocking his path, Larry was honestly considering a call to the U.S. Patent Office.

Today, however, he noticed Mary was leaning a bit, and he suddenly remembered why. Larry had gotten drunk a few nights back and left his car at the neighborhood bar to hoof it the short three blocks back home. And on the way, when he saw her growing in the distance all righteous and proud and stone-faced, head tilted forever in reverence, he couldn't help picking up his pace until he was at a dead run. Then, before he could talk his buzz out of it, he lowered his shoulder and uprooted the statue from the yard. Tucking her under one arm and never slowing, he circled every base at the baseball diamond across the street, then shamefully ran back to screw her into the wet earth from where he'd snatched her, positioned under that umbrella of pink flowers where she seemed to grow taller every day, finally saying good night with a gentle, first-date kind of kiss on the gray stone apple of her cheek.

He'd always tried to show Stone Mary the utmost respect, even that night. Any other drunk fuck would have smashed her ass on the street like a Halloween pumpkin. But not Larry. *Just who does this orangutan think he is?*

Mouth still dribbling, Larry decided to ask him.

"Listen, just who do you think..."

And that's when the red bastard punched him in the mush. Not particularly fast, but hard and heavy, like a lumbering freight train with no caboose any time soon. Larry's mouth ballooned like he was blowing a fish face on a window, then it helplessly rode along that prodigious big fist until it eventually ran out of arm. Larry squawked when the force of the blow popped his bottom lip against his teeth like a hot dog left boiling too long in the pot.

4

The last bit of green mystery mint foam sprayed the steering wheel, and for a second Larry thought that's what his blood looked like, though yellow would have seemed more appropriate. Then things started to clear, and the world began to straighten itself back out. Until a screech like a strangled cat came from deep in the dash.

Did he punch my car, too? Larry wondered.

That's when he saw the black tape curling into the ashtray like a submissive puppy's tail and realized that the red bastard had actually hit Larry so hard it had somehow made his stereo choke on his brand-new cassette, The Cult's *Electric,* his recently anointed, unofficial soundtrack to morning commutes. Not even a week old, he'd only been able to listen to "Love Removal Machine" 47 times. Only approximately 984 "baby, baby, baby"s.

You can't say "baby" that many times without catching one, Larry laughed to himself, rubbing his face way too hard and remembering something his ex-wife once said. *And you can't talk with mouthwash in your mouth, so you better get some more.*

But the bastard was long gone before Larry's eyes stopped watering, and he forgot about his vomiting dashboard and focused his anger on Mary instead, wishing he'd spiked that bitch on the asphalt like a touchdown that drunken night he kissed her, wishing he'd watched her detonate between his stumbling feet, on the faded binary code of lines and reflectors that divided the highway.

Larry stared into the dead eyes of the statue another minute or two, heartbeat eventually slowing in his fish lip, waiting to see who would blink first. Then he checked his watch and headed to work, twisting a bit of blood into his beard and slipping lower, lower, lower in the driver's seat with every turn.

* * *

"I'm gonna honk at that cop."

"Don't do it."

"Why not? He won't know it's me. Look at all these cars."

"He might."

"Nah, it'll be like in the movies when someone in the crowd yells, 'We will never yield!' and the villain is all like, 'Who said that?!'"

"That was never in a movie."

"I'm gonna honk."

"Don't do it. Honking is an imperfect weapon. Lots of collateral damage."

"What the hell is he doing blocking both lanes?"

"Huh?"

"Look, there's a trailer with the construction arrow on the left, so why is he matching speed in the middle lane? This is idiotic." Pause. "I'm gonna honk at him."

"Have you ever honked at a cop?"

"Nope! But now's my chance. I'm in the middle of five fucking cars. It'll be like shouting, 'I am Spartacus!' He'll have no idea who did it."

"I'm just saying…"

He honked.

The noise caused every car near the flashing arrow to hit their brakes simultaneously, including the cop. Then the cop was slowing, slowing, slowing until he was right next to them.

"Isn't it amazing how a cop behind you makes you automatically itemize everything in your trunk?"

Then he was behind them. With the flashers on.

"Oops."

"What was that all about?" the police officer asked them after they'd all pulled over.

"Wasn't me," the boy said.

"Where are you going?"

"What does that have to do with anything?" the girl asked.

"Step out of the car, please, sir. You, too, ma'am."

The big bear buster of a cop peered over his sunglasses at her.

"So, where are you going?" he sighed.

"To get a desk lamp."

"License and registration, please. You, too, ma'am."

The cop looked at their photos a while.

"This doesn't look like you, Mister... Gray? Adam Gray? Or do we got an 'Adam Henry' here?" he laughed. "How old are you in this picture?"

"Huh? 23."

"And now?"

"What? It says it right there." Awkward silence. "29?"

"And you, Miss Blue?"

"And me what?" she muttered. Then, "Wait, what did you call me?"

"How old are you?"

"Did you say 'Blue?' My name's not 'Blue.'"

"Oh, sorry, 'Amber.' I was looking at 'eye color.' But wouldn't that be interesting if your name was Blue and his was Gray?" he laughed.

"My name *is* Gray," Adam mumbled. "Why would that be funny?"

"You know, like the Civil War! Match made in hell…"

The cop studied them as their engine ticked away the seconds. Then he moved in close, and Amber smelled a cloud of something around him like piss and strawberries.

"I'm 21," Amber finally said, nervous now.

"Sir, what's in that bag in your back seat?"

"Cat food."

"But her shirt clearly has a dog on it."

They both looked at each other then back at the cop.

7

"It sure does, 'Detective,'" Adam said with a sprinkle of smartass.

"I have five dogs of my own," Amber said carefully. "You know, the little yappy kind."

"I see. Good luck with that."

The cop handed back their licenses, then stood back and waited until they noticed he'd given them each the wrong one. It took a minute.

"Next time, yield."

The cop started walking away.

"And stop sticking your tongue out when they take your picture, boy!" the cop barked suddenly, startling them both. "Oldest trick in the book! Right up there with dogs on your shirt."

"The oldest trick in the book was when the caveman pulled his dick out of a hat," she mumbled. "The very first hat, of course."

Then he was gone.

The boy and the girl gave each other's fake I.D.'s an extra long look. The boy thought their tiny plastic cards suddenly seemed like a list of reasons why they would be an unlikely match, and he was angrier than he thought possible. The girl didn't think this at all and simply waited for the boy to give her license back. They'd picked the names for a joke, and she loved how they sounded out loud in the mouth of a cop.

And if anyone checked the video on the officer's dashboard camera, they both mouthed the words at the exact same time:

"Let's follow him."

Larry had been directing hardcore pornographic features for nearly a decade, never quite getting enough commercial work on the side to leave it behind completely, never convincing anyone with clout to read one of his "real" scripts. Although he'd earned some *AVN* awards along the way, he couldn't bear the idea of hitting the Vegas ceremonies to accept one in person, not since he discovered his then-future wife was nominated for the industry's coveted Noble Piece Prize. He promised his producer, Damon, he'd attend the next year's awards since the summer of '84 marked the five-year anniversary from when *Adult Video News* first started pretending this business was something respectable. Supposedly, there was going to be some sort of Lifetime Achievement Award handed out to him and a couple other grizzled vets, and he would have to pretend it was both a surprise and anything but an embarrassment. He couldn't think of anything worse.

"Larry" had been directing under his fake name since 1979, for fear that it would keep him from more legitimate work when he finally, inevitably, blew up.

He was 47 years old.

As he lurched from light to light, driving as low in the seat as he could while still seeing the horizon, he thought of everything he should have told the Virgin Mary's red-faced grandson:

How he's sorry, but he's out the door in the morning too fast to spit in a sink like a normal person. How if he tries to spit while cruising more than 15 miles an hour, it will mist back through the window all over his mug. How spitting away from the Virgin Mary's house and out his passenger window would look like he was aiming for that park, as if he was trying to hose down those kids laying lime on the ball diamond every morning. Or scare those two girls always balancing on the seesaw. Seriously, did the Virgin Mary want him spitting at freakin' kids on a playground? Seemed like the surest way to end up on a sex offenders' registry.

He simply had no choice to do what he did if he was going to stick to his obsessive routine of swishing that mouthwash in each individual cheek precisely fifty times (twice as many as recommended on the bottle), originally a way to appease his wife that it would kill any "AIDS juice" he carried home from a shoot. But still he swore he'd never mourn the countless opportunities for conversation he was missing in the world, specifically in his own parking lot, for example, because of this compulsion, not the least of which was a new girl in his apartment building who'd tried to talk to him but hurried past when he smiled too wide and started drooling and leaking from the alcohol burn. To be honest, he'd considered breaking his routine the next time he saw the new girl, and would probably swallow if he got the chance again. Swallowing would be a small price to pay.

"Is the Virgin Mary that fucking stupid?" Larry didn't say when he had the chance. "Didn't she notice my spit was coming out in colors not found in nature? Hell, my spit's purple some days after those big-ass gumballs…"

"Purple, eh?" Mary's grandson might have shrugged in response, likely fascinated with spit and big bubbles. "Let's watch yours turn red!"

Bloosh. Fist like a canned ham. Arm like a freight train. Right in the goddamn grill.

Larry drove on. And when he finally found the morning's clandestine set at the sound guy's stepdad's brother's beach house, it felt like a party he was crashing (sometimes they put a blue balloon on the mailbox to signify a "blue movie," a heads-up for late crew additions or an emergency location switch, and today there was a big birthday bunch of them chasing each other around in the breeze). But all four of his actors were already restless. Four was usually the magic number for these fly-by-night features, but this quartet was loitering around in robes like royalty, slamming doors, slamming coffee, power drinks, milk, and tequila.

No, not tequila, Larry remembered. The gold bottle one of the girls was recklessly spinning around her palms was empty, now just a prop being refilled with apple juice. She was trying to imitate newbie sensation Tom Cruise from *Cocktail,* which was still "Coming soon to a theater near you!" even though it had been pushed back indefinitely due to the death of a stunt bartender. But the poster action was all they needed to ape to make it the newest movie to get the porn parody treatment from every studio (or more likely imitating Tom *Cooze* from *Cock Tales* [the first copycat to hit the shelves], a dexterous actor who was actually much better at spinning bottles than fucking). Larry made a mental note to retrieve the bottle before she broke it and went over budget.

"When he pours, he reigns!" was the tagline for the real movie. They didn't even need to change that for a porn version.

Larry slumped into his director's chair, one he'd stolen from a previous campsite shoot because of its long foot rest and cup holder, *not* because it was painted like an American flag (missing about five stars), and he sighed loud enough for everyone to hear. He was already tired and not one foot of film was in the can. He looked around the set, trying to get into the scene, already changing things up in his head to make the movie better. The day before, he'd insisted the patio furniture be dragged into the living room and covered with Visqueen and sheets, giving it the look of a crime scene. Like in a movie. Larry was always thinking.

A crime scene? And a tequila bottle? Hmm. Inspiration was now tickling his head like raindrops. This would be a great opportunity to make the film more of a…

"Dyed your beard, eh, boss? Looks good!"

It was Glengarry, half of his two-man crew (not counting "talent," of course), greeting him with a huge tangle of electrical cords over his shoulder like a fireman

11

hauling hoses. Older than everybody, Glengarry's given name was "Glen," making his nickname actually more cumbersome than the real thing, but Larry had anointed him, mostly because he couldn't stop talking about the David Mamet play he'd caught last time he was in New York, how much it reminded him of the "weight of his own job," how it "shook him to his very soul." Also because he had a bit part in Larry's *Death of a Salesman* meets *Caligula* epic *Glen, Gary, Glen, and Ross.*

Today, Glengarry was moving faster than usual, only stopping to chalk the name of this week's movie onto the clapperboard that he balanced on his knee. Even though they'd always done shit so cheap that Larry claimed they were one disappointing turnaround from making porn with flip cartoons in the corners of *TV Guides,* Larry insisted on starting with the "clap" every time. Mostly because of the easy jokes.

"Where do you need me, Redbeard?"

Larry just ignored him. Taking the hint, Glengarry started to turn away, and Larry stopped him with a police hold on his upper arm meat to spin him back around. He took the clapper away to read it. On the slate, his perfect movie title, the one he'd spent a good 45 minutes thinking up in the shower, had been changed into something artless and ugly:

"Fuck Your Mother."

"Get Damon on the phone," Larry sighed, then mumbled, "Fuck *your* mother?"

"Come on, boss. It doesn't matter what it's called. We recycle half these scenes anyway."

"'Come on' nothing. That is the worst title of all time. It sounds like someone's gonna be fucking their own mother."

"No, boss, it's like the insult, you know? Mom jokes. You know, like, '*Fuck* your mother!'"

12

Larry had argued hard to get the name he wanted for this flick. *Dr. Strange Gloves* he'd called it, the story of an obsessive compulsive cured through intercourse. And their latest producer, an uninspiring car dealer from the Valley with the unlikely name of Damon Gold, mercifully got the joke at first. But Kubrick's *Dr. Strangelove* had that colon in the title. And they started fighting over what came after their colon during a particularly heated bout of Marco Polo at one of the pool parties Damon loved to throw for his underlings.

"Came after the colon?!" Damon cackled. So many jokes.

How I Learned to Stop Worrying and Love the Blondes was what Larry had been dead set on for the subtitle because it was so close to the original. *How I Learned to Stop Worrying and Love the Twat* was the car dealer's unfortunate brainstorm.

During their heated debate in the pool (also heated), Mr. Gold had pushed Larry around like a rubber ducky, verbally and physically. He was a small man, but seemingly super-powered ever since he'd moved out west from Denver, where, in a cruel second-act twist, he now suffered from sleep apnea due to the high altitude. But Larry thought he might as well have come from Krypton the way he dominated any room below sea level with sheer force of will. And in a piss-warm swimming pool? Forget about it. Motherfucker dunked people two at a time until they raised the white flag in surrender. Or at least agreed with him. Sometimes, he'd use his free hand to play Solitaire with floating, plastic-coated playing cards.

In the end, Larry had to stay underwater for three minutes with Mr. Gold palming his head in order to impress him enough to cut a deal. The super-powered car dealer had laughed and pointed out his accomplishment to everyone, "Yep, he held his breath till he got his way, just like a fuckin' baby in the bathtub!"

13

"Listen, G.G.," Larry said, squeezing Glengarry's upper arm less affectionately than his boss had squeezed his head. "I know what that half-ass title's supposed to mean, but…"

"Dude, you should be honored!" Glengarry squawked. "He just wants to make the most money we can. It's because Damon loved the script that he changed it, man, especially *this* scene. This is gonna be a good scene."

No one had to tell Larry this was gonna be a good scene. He fuckin' knew it was a good scene. That's the one thing that kept him going, besides dreams of one day directing commercials full-time. Knowing he could always squeeze in just one… good… scene. It's what kept him sane while he squandered his talent, the knowledge that just one of the scenes in his movie would be so good that the viewer might forget they were jerking off for half a second and actually start caring about a character.

Glengarry waited patiently, spinning two bulbs in his palms and singing a Peter Gabriel song that wasn't even out yet, but still somehow getting the lyrics wrong.

I hold the light… I hold the light…

This particular scene depicted an eager young man, "Bobby Bee Jay," knocking on the door of the requisite bored housewife, informing her that the stall in the boys' bathroom at the high school was sporting some new graffiti that advertised, "For a good time, call T.J.'s mom." The twist, of course, what had always previously been perceived as an insult, was actually put there *by* T.J.'s mom.

"Genius!" Damon Gold had thundered when he first read it.

And to make the point that this wasn't a coincidence, the subsequent scene would then cut to a shot next door, where another lucky teen (hopefully not conspicuously tattooed and in his early 30's) would be looking for the author of "For a good time, call *Bobby's* mom" at the exact same time. Then T.J. and Bobby would both ride these "moms" (no choice but for the moms to be in their late teens/early '20s tops) all the way out the back door, where they would then be horrified to see each other... and then all decide to finish each other off in the pool anyway. Now that was some twists!

"You're like Hitchcock up in this bitch!" Glengarry had positively squealed as he stole a shot of apple juice. Larry let him get away with a lot more than the other guys on the set after Glengarry had moonlighted months earlier on Larry's "real" movie without getting paid one red cent.

A real movie. Yes, Larry was trying his hand at a real movie on the sly. It had a name that sounded like porn, but it was as real as movies get. And as of last weekend, all edited and ready to roll. Not that there was anywhere to roll. But that was another story altogether. Today, he was making adult films, and he was taking it seriously.

Larry was proud of *Strange Gloves*, he couldn't lie. Even if he hadn't thought of a way to force a doctor, or gloves, into the damn thing yet, if he could make one person release their grip and think back to the graffiti on their own high-school restroom walls with longing, he'd done his job. A man's job. An artist's job!

He sighed and plucked the script out of Glengarry's back pocket, then let him scurry away. As he thumbed through the screenplay (all fifteen pages of it, his longest yet), he found the guts of his story missing, the touching fable of a boy suffering from OCD and the Isotoners that stopped him from touching, "really touching," another human being.

"Are you kidding me?" Larry said to no one as he read.

"Yeah, Damon did some edits," Glengarry shouted back as he whipped his extension cords to shake the knots out. Then he stopped, and ran back to Larry, ducking in close and spitting on his fingers as he reached for Larry's

15

beard like a mother working her kid's cowlick at the bus stop.

"What the fuck are you doing?" Larry jerked away.

"You really don't want to be Captain Redbeard, man," he whispered. "You ever read that comic strip? He loses every time!"

Larry moved away, nervously tugging his beard, then his nose. Then he scratched his elbow. He was wound up. Way up. He felt like today was gonna be the day for something, anything. Maybe a bunch of anythings. Battles brewing around every corner, but he didn't know which one to choose. Oh, well, Damon once said you couldn't make an omelet without breaking some eggs. But he also said things like, "You can't have 'popcorn' without 'cop porn'!" Which was ridiculous.

"Come on, boss. *Please!* We don't have this house very long!"

Larry closed his eyes, scratching one elbow, then the other, until his fingernails almost flipped back. Then he scratched himself all over like mad. His hives were back, and his arms itched like a motherfucker. Sometimes it was so bad he would scratch the buttons right off his sleeves so they'd flap around with his frustration to ensure people took him even less seriously.

You can't be around them that long, his ex-wife had warned him once. *You're gonna catch something.*

"Are you fucking kidding me?!" Larry screamed, spiking the script like a rotten football.

The explosion of paper was entirely too small to satisfy anyone.

The first time Billy saw Bully was about three fake names ago for both of them. She was with her boyfriend, and he really didn't think twice about her. The second time he saw her, she was sitting with her bare feet in a fountain at a dog park, wearing a tight black T-shirt (tight and black was always his weakness), with the telephone number for a no-kill dog shelter stretched across her chest. In that moment, Billy thought she could have a "Slaughterhouse Help Wanted" sandwich board over her body and still receive the same fawning looks from the passers-by. Something about black eyes nested in black curls that just sucked you in. She asked Billy to help her out of the fountain, and when he grabbed her hand, she started thumb-wrestling him instead.

He obsessed about that thumb for a good 48 hours.

The third time he saw her was at the local poetry slams she hosted, where she sat directly across from Billy at a long table, complaining loudly about how her dogs hated, *hated,* her boyfriend. She failed to notice Billy's hand on her chair leg, pulling her away from this kid and closer to himself inch by inch. But the boyfriend did. He told her they were going home, and he used a name that confused Billy, seeing how he'd lifted her wallet an hour earlier.

The new name on Bully's fake I.D. was "Amber," but for the first fake license Bully ever got, she'd tried naming herself "Any Luck." Most people misread it and called her "Amy" anyway, and even after Billy and Bully carefully picked their latest names based on the abduction lingo of "Code Adams" and "Amber Alerts," out of habit, she still worked hard to get everyone to call her "Any."

"You know, like when someone stumbles onto you working on a lost cause?" she'd explain. "Like you're trying to unplug a toilet, and they go, 'Any luck?!'"

But even weirder than all this was her real name, "Tully," which was Irish as fuck but only lasted until she was five and started to speak. And because she'd started so late, she skipped baby talk altogether and jumped headfirst into profanity, where she'd since happily remained.

One time, Bully's little brother revealed that her nickname was a mispronunciation of "Boli," which was

17

short for "Bolita," which was Spanish for "Little Ball," which was something her grandma called her. Her little brother paid for that with a cracked tooth.

Whatever her name was that week, did Billy have any luck with Any Luck? No, he had about as much luck with her as she had making her favorite names stick. But it didn't matter. He would keep on trying, and calling her "Bully." Everyone called her "Bully" now, and that name rose right to the top. And really, Billy couldn't imagine calling her anything but. She was the smallest bully he'd ever met, but he loved it when she pushed him around.

The third, fourth, and fifth time Billy saw her was with her boyfriend at the slams. The sixth time Billy saw her was when his first real progress was made, at the last slam of the semester, when Billy brought T-shirts for everybody. It was something else to do instead of secretly tugging on her chair when no one was looking. Billy even got one for her boyfriend, and this battery-powered shirt was the impetus of a strange arms race at the readings that expedited the demise of the group.

This particular shirt he'd purchased for Bully's boyfriend, some smug, spiky-haired hipster who refused to make eye contact, had been advertised online as a "Me-Qualizer," and it had an LED display of an American flag across the chest that rose and fell to the music or, he hoped, would display the ferocity of her dogs' contempt for the kid when they were at her apartment and Spike was making his moves. Billy tried to be subtle, getting the more innocent spin-off "Bee-Qualizer" T-shirts for everybody else in the group, shirts with a happy swirl of bumblebees dancing to ambient sounds (one of hundreds of variations in the popular line of patented See-Qualizer Wear, a name Billy thought was kind of idiotic since you could "see" a normal equalizer, whether you were wearing it or not). The shirts were a huge hit. It made the normally shouty-but-morose poets step it up a bit, cracking smiles when the loud response of the crowd lit up their chests instead of their faces.

"Equalizer." Billy loved that word.

But Billy's plan backfired a little bit, after it became clear what he was up to all along. For the next slam, Bully bought herself a "Pee-Qualizer" in protest, the shirt where cartoon puppies urinated in an arc up to her shoulders when certain audio levels were reached, much like the fountain at the Bellagio Hotel in Las Vegas (there were many other possibilities for shirts that gauged emotions, but she had no interest in the much classier "T-Qualizer," since it didn't feature critters pissing to the beat of the music). And after she showed up on the 4th of July wearing her boyfriend on her arm again *and* that particular T-shirt, tight and black of course, the spiky-haired human accessory had no choice but to trade up shirts himself a week later.

It was his last mistake. The "Zeee-Qualizer," or "Tanzfruedig Sprengstoffspürhund!" (which Billy later discovered translated to the baffling "dance-crazy, explosive-sniffing dog"), the rarest in their line of battery-powered clothing, featured a spiraling red swastika.

The spiky-haired boyfriend probably should have put the battery in to test it out before he got to the bar because he quickly discovered that getting your ass righteously kicked while wearing a T-shirt that flashed to the beat of your pummeling was pretty much the most embarrassing thing that could ever happen in front of a girl. And, lucky for Billy, it was also the quickest way to lose one for good.

So Billy wasn't too shocked when he offered to get more supplies while setting up for the final open-mic night (the desk light they used to illuminate the poets got smashed in the brawl), and she said she'd tag along with him. He reset his watch to noon when she got in his car, figuring he had about three hours to get her interested. He worked better with self-imposed deadlines.

19

"Bully for me!" he couldn't help whispering when he walked around to get her door.

He'd made it an hour before he pulled that stupid power play with the cop and the horn, so he cranked his watch back to start over.

"I hate when they do that," Billy said as he sat in his car, stewing. "You'd think they'd try a little harder after what happened on the South Side."

"What happened on the South Side?"

He didn't answer the question yet. He was pouting too much to enjoy spinning a story. "I wasn't ready to tell you that stuff about me," he grumbled. "And cops know that tricky shit. That's why they ask so many questions."

"What tricky shit?" Bully asked, half-smiling at his efforts to impress, but never looking at him when he did it. He looked at her another second before pulling back into traffic. She wasn't even his type anymore. That was the crazy part. She'd dyed her hair that morning, now suddenly an icy little blonde, something out of Hitchcock. Even her eyes seemed lighter. Steel-blue and dilated. Foot always tapping impatiently. You'd think those pupils would mean you could get a good look into her head, but damn if it didn't always seem the other way around. If she stood in a line-up with the rest of his black curly-haired ex-girlfriends, someone would protest, "Get that albino jackrabbit out of there!"

"It was subtle," he explained to her. "But everything that cop asked was geared to show how incompatible the two of us would be in a relationship. There's too much shit on a license."

"Really? I think he was just being an asshole. My hair color on there probably says 'Any.'"

"And what was all that about an 'oldest trick in the book?'" he muttered. "Glorified dogcatchers, all of 'em…"

"Oh, that. Well, it's common for ex-cons or terrorists to stick their tongue out in their driver's license photo to distort their features and make them less recognizable."

"Come on. Even when third graders do it?"

Instead of answering, she started digging through her purse and came up with a stack of cassette tapes, buried under some 8-tracks. He hadn't seen one of those since forever.

"What are those for?" he asked.

"You just reminded me! I use 'em to get people to come to the poetry readings. Like advertising. I leave them everywhere: bushes, gas pumps, drive-thrus. Call 'em 'Tape Bombs.' Or 'Luck Bombs.' Like a photo bomb? You know, like when you fuck up someone's picture."

"What's on the tapes?"

"Just the last few people we had at the readings. The best of the bunch, which ain't saying much…"

"Did you see that cop's tattoo? On one of his forearms, it read 'In God We Trust, But…' something."

"But what?"

"Exactly. His other sleeve was rolled up. I couldn't see it. I think that's where the answer was hiding."

She looked around his car, disappointed and suddenly bored. "So, what's all this then?"

She flicked the tangle of necklaces, air-fresheners, and feathers that hung off his rear-view mirror. The motion erased his new smile.

"Huh? Oh, it's a dreamcatcher."

"A what? A dogcatcher?"

"No, you know, dreamcatcher? A circle? Bunch of shit hanging off of it? Catches dreams."

"Right," she snickered, going back to her purse.

He felt like she was judging the authenticity of his dreamcatcher, or even worse, its size. He was frustrated, as he mistakenly assumed everyone knew the ratty little counterfeit versions hanging from rear-view mirrors were at least *daydreamcatchers,* and they did help your concentration while driving, as important as turn signals as far as preventing traffic fatalities.

He wanted to bring up the boyfriend, find out if the T-shirt competition had vanquished him for good, maybe talk some passive-aggressive shit about him disguised as helpful brotherly advice. But she put out this vibe that made him want to steer clear of the subject. Of all subjects actually. And the more he thought about the cop asking those questions, screwing up his moves before he even made them, the angrier Billy got.

Right then, Billy thought maybe he could kill one for her. Or at least convince her he could do it. Maybe she'd like that. He checked his watch again. He still had a couple hours with her as a captive audience in the passenger's seat. It might be enough to convince her. Then he remembered that incident on the South Side again, and he thought maybe it would be much easier to get her to imagine murdering a police officer, too. Easier than it would be to imagine being his girlfriend.

Once someone gathered the pages back up, Larry tried to get the blue vein on his forehead to sink back into his brain while he blocked out the rest of the scene. Around him, his cast mingled, impatient but still groggy from partying the night before, all four of them with their bathrobes open but still over their shoulders, the same robes they'd stolen from their last shoot at the Ritz-Carlton.

The robes always cracked him up. It made Larry feel like a cult leader. Until the robes came off anyway. Then every tattoo would ruin the fantasy.

He hated the tattoos. Always with the tattoos lately.

Nothing against tattoos as a concept, he'd tell himself. It's just that they were a distraction. And they fucked up his movies. And there seemed to be so many of them these days. How could you believe what you were seeing on the screen was real (and by real, he meant "fiction") if space monsters, jagged signatures, and the smiling faces of strangers inked all over the bodies shook you right out of the illusion? In real movies, a bit of tattoo peeking out of a collar or shirt-sleeve was a little dose of character, a bit of sympathetic mileage or free characterization, like a wandering eye, a broken nose, or a chicken-pox scar on someone's forehead. It could be incorporated into the story fairly easily.

But not in porn. In porn, the entire body was visible.

It could be an all-nighter to fix the continuity. On those nights, he wished he only had sleep apnea.

"Places!"

They dropped the robes.

Impossibly, it was worse than he remembered.

For hours, they drove behind a shimmering lake of heat they never seemed to catch.

"How long do you think before he notices we're back here?" Bully asked.

"Not for a while," Billy said, then reconsidered. "At least not till he gets off the highway."

"Why are we following him again?"

"Again?" Billy almost jumped.

"No, I mean tell me again while we're following him so that... never mind."

Billy felt like he was losing her, so he told the story, the one he'd been saving. He unloaded it all at once, in an ugly brick of words that actually made the car squeak from the weight.

"So there was this cop who was driving home from a bar on the South Side, and these other two guys, big dudes, were walking across the street and stepped in front of his car. So this cop, also big but sloppy big, started running his mouth to these two guys to impress his wife, a woman who I know little about but will consider a dumb fuck for marrying a cop. So she's in the seat next to him, I forgot to tell you that, dutifully impressed with his display of plumage. The cop is drunk, by the way, a regular occurrence on his days off, but we don't find that out until later. So, one of the two legitimately big dudes gets tired of the cop talking shit and walks over to the car… and punches the cop right square in the mouth. Big dude doesn't know he's a cop, and he finds it so easy, this particular punch, that he decides to special-deliver about ten more into this cop's mailbox before the bastard can do anything about it. The cop tries to roll up his window at one point, as if it's the weather blowing in on him, as if it's a literal rain of fists that he's happened upon…"

Billy cranked the handle of his window for effect, winding himself up to talk even faster:

"…then the big dudes are gone, the cop is stunned, and the wife is still stupid. The cop's fuming now, bleeding a bit, feeling ashamed that his wife saw all that, feeling like a fucking *citizen* of all things, God forbid. So he pulls into a nearby parking lot and scurries back to his trunk to get his gun. Then he leaves his betrothed in the car and runs down the street to make his drunken arrest, and the wife hightails back to the bar they were getting sloppy at earlier to try and get other off-duty cops to come to the rescue. The inebriated cop is stumbling up and down the street with his bloody nose and his gun and comes across this kid all by himself, minding his own beeswax and walking home. This kid has nothing to do with anything, of course, and not even a drunken fuckin' cop could reasonably claim he resembles a dude who would ever punch someone in the face once, let alone ten times, but for some reason, the cop decides he'll have to do. Now, if I was to take a moment of vacation in this idiot's brain, I would guess he thought an arrest would redeem him with his idiot wife, but who knows. So he runs at the confused kid and screams for him to put his hands in the air. The kid complies, protesting a bit. Then the cop is grabbing one of the kid's hands on the back of his head when the gun goes off and blows a hole through… hold on. Is that car gonna let us get over?"

Billy's neck cracked like knuckles as he leaned back to look for a hole in traffic.

"Guess not. Anyway, what was I saying? Oh, yeah. Gun goes off. Blows a hole through the kid's hand. But it could have been his head, right! You thought it was his head, didn't you? But drunk cop still handcuffs the kid because he's gotta maintain appearances and stick to his story, of course. And the kid is on the ground with the cop's knee in his back, trying to get a hold of his own bleeding hand, when the other cops from the bar finally arrive, see this fiasco, and call for an ambulance. Long story short, the kid is still arrested, but of course the kid is cleared of all charges because, guess what? Cop was drunk. Did I mention that? And even though his court date is pending over this shit, the cop's already back to work apparently, as if this wasn't enough reason to lose your fucking job. So, here's what I want to do. Ready? I want to send a series of postcards to this cop and claim I'm the dude who punched him in the face ten times. And I kind of want us both to do this postcard thing, if it's okay with you, for the rest of our lives."

She didn't answer, but he could tell it was the most romantic thing she'd ever heard anyway.

"Oldest tricky shit in the book?" he joked, hoping for something.

And when she smiled, he finally took a breath and the car's shocks raised back up.

"'Betrothed' means 'engaged,' by the way," she said.

But she was all in.

Billy had so much swagger now, he would go home right after this and dust off the seat of his dirt bike and maybe exceed the speed limit on some of those back roads without stop signs. Maybe.

"How funny does the word 'cop' sound when you say it too many times?" she giggled. "Hold on, what does this have to do with…"

"Okay, I wasn't gonna say it, but that cop who pulled us over, the one I honked at… that was the same cop."

"How do you know?" she laughed.

"What do you mean how do I know?"

"How do you know?"

"Same blue shirt."

Larry took a different route home that night. The drive was so uneventful, he almost wrote it down so he'd remember it. His new way enabled him to barely slow at a new crossroads, an intersection without any stop signs at all to hinder him, and 100% fewer red-faced bastards. It felt like a second chance, but the lack of stop signs was even more exciting. Besides potentially reducing the opportunities of him being punched in the mouth, he hoped it also meant less chance of drivers performing that infuriating four-way Mambo of, "Are you going? No? Okay, I'll go. Wait. No? Fine, I'm going. Okay, you go… Argh!"

Larry swished his mouthwash a little bit longer on this new route, too, which was fine by him. He had a tiny travel bottle of Scope tucked next to the driver's seat for the way home, originally his wife's idea. After work, his mouth was much more sensitive, and he relished the heat, the sting. He wished he could blame this fetish on his germophobic ex-wife (*You're gonna catch something*), just like when she would yell and he would absently pick at the deep itches around his elbows until he was sure they were bleeding. But he'd grown to enjoy both. And if his elbows were bloody, he didn't need to know.

Okay, maybe his elbows freaked him out a bit these days. Invisible and numb. One of the few places on your body you'd have to break a bone to ever get a peek at it.

Anything could be growing there, he thought.

To distract himself, he slapped in Captain Beefheart's debut, *Safe as Milk*. A 20-year-old Ry Cooder on guitar? Impossible. Larry had no choice but to listen to older tapes like this lately, as every time his stereo ate a new one, he ended up going back a decade into his personal soundtracks. He didn't like to be reminded of music he liked when he was young man. It never made him feel nostalgic, only mortal. It also reminded him of his previous job, which was enough mortality for a lifetime.

He gargled some more, nervous now, like someone watching a cat play with a balloon of bumblebees. He'd heard once that stereos only ate your tapes when it was humid outside. That might explain it. He lived on a part of Florida Street that even real Floridians considered swampy. Humidity was terrifying enough. He thought about creeping things growing on his elbow again before he could stop himself.

Then he shook it off, turned up the music, and slowed down a bit as he neared the new crossroads, tipping his head back for a last-second gargle.

Safe as Milk, my ass, Larry thought, then went to crank up the window a little bit for extra protection against the blowback. For years, after he first got his license, he used to drive with an elbow hanging out, like everybody else. Then some snarly little dog jumped up and snapped onto his arm like a gator. For months after that, people would mistake the wound for one of those horrible spider web tattoos, the kind white-trash sported like associate professors flashing the patches on their new tweed jackets. He'd just started hanging his elbow out again and felt weird with the window up too high. And there was the itching…

A dirt bike was coming up fast. It looked like it was going to arrive at the intersection at the exact moment Larry did. He sighed, realizing that even without a stop sign, he'd have to do that stupid stutter-step dance of vehicles after all. But without a blinker on the bike, Larry decided the kid on the bike probably wasn't turning. In fact, the kid didn't seem to have a headlight either, just a tiny, red-reflector-covered boombox that was duct-taped to the handlebars. He cocked an ear and heard it belting out Billy Squier's "Who's Your Boyfriend," which the kid was in the process of turning up louder. Billy Squier competing with madman Don Van Vliet?

Seriously, kid? Larry smiled at this sad little Battle Of The Bands where youth really stood no chance at all, especially when Larry was armed with a 20-year-old Ry Cooder on guitar.

So Larry took the initiative, having been taught the dangers of idling too long the previous morning at the Virgin Mary's house. He hit the gas and the volume, then rolled down his window to spit some music and mouthwash before the wind had a chance to give everything back.

He was shocked to see the kid give his handgrip a snake bite and gun his engine at the exact moment the green fluid vaulted Larry's swollen lips and arced across the white line. The spray caught the rider full in the face, filling the poor whelp's nostrils and washing up over his aviator glasses like a steaming, toxic wave. Larry flinched right along with him and almost said, "Sorry," but decided to crush the accelerator instead.

He glanced up at the rear-view to see the kid hanging off the side of his bike, hacking and hawking at the ground, desperately trying to clear his nose and his eyes, yelling protests not quite indecipherable, then awkwardly tripping over his kickstand in a tangle of anger to finally pitch over into the drainage ditch on the side of the road.

Aw, man.

Ashamed, Larry turned his mirror away from the scene, vowing to start bringing more Styrofoam cups into his car as spittoons, more tiny bottles. There was suddenly way too much collateral damage from his rituals to keep a clean mouth, and he was starting to worry about all the shit lists he'd end up headlining if this kept up.

He tapped the mirror, unable to force a laugh as the kid bumbled and fell one more time.

Fuck it. Shit lists roll downhill, too, right?

In the back, Jack is mumbling to remember his training as he treats her injuries and prepares to rationalize the worst thing he's ever done.

"Systolic blood pressure eighty-nine. Injecting point one milligrams Vecuronium. Applying cricoid pressure, preparing to intubate..."

His partner is singing The Flaming Lips' "Mr. Ambulance Driver" with the tape as best he can, which isn't very good, even against a tuneless demo bootleg.

"'Cause I'm wishing that I was the one that wasn't gonna be here anymore... the only one that isn't here anymore..."

Then he stops, squeeze bladder and mouthpiece in his hand as he steadies himself and stares. The girl is bloody, beautiful, more naked than not, just half a belly shirt and one leg of her blue jeans remain. Frowning, Jack raises her knee to look closer, accidentally bumping the driver's elbow, who jerks it away as if burned. To the driver and amateur crooner, Jack Grinstead has always been a conspicuously quiet but bullish Yankee import, a partner who has never quite gotten used to the position of the patients in the backs of these British boxes:

head by the doors, feet up by the driver, everything opposite of how they did it back in the States.

Personally, Jack always thought these things made no difference at all. Until today.

He raises her other knee, drying blood crackling perceptibly. This sound startles the driver, reminding him of biscuit wrappers crinkling in movie theaters, a pet peeve. He finally turns around, now as hungry as he is irritated.

"What the hell, man? Come on, we just crossed Pritchatts. We'll be there in three minutes. Just make sure she's immobilized. Hey, are you listening?"

Jack ignores him, instead crossing the victim's legs at her ankles and closing his eyes. Another hard turn, and he bumps his head on a shelf. He's taller than most Brits, but short as shit back where he was born.

Jack is slowly understanding that something must have happened after the crash. It had taken them a long time to get there. Longer than usual. Their ambulance was on the lift when they got the call. Anywhere in the world, the vast amount of time that lapsed before anyone was on that scene would have been inexcusable. But in Birmingham, it was utterly inconceivable.

This was why Jack had transferred here in the first place, to join the West Midlands Ambulance Service, specifically to be a first-responder for Category-A life-threatening emergencies. It was the only reason he packed up his entire life and travelled 3,000 miles across the pond, and also the biggest secret he had in his life. Until today.

In Birmingham, paramedics ride motorcycles. Yes, motorcycles. Instead of a goddamn ice-cream lorry like this, his adopted countryside provided an unusual combination of crisis and speed that was intoxicating for Jack. Sometimes he even imagined arriving at a scene fast enough to catch the first drop of blood in the palm of his leather glove before it kissed the ground.

But after only a week on first-responders, he was unceremoniously kicked off, demoted, sent back to riding in the "bucket" with the knowledge he was getting to the scene of the crash second, third, sometimes last. He may as well have been riding in the boot.

And Jack knew why he'd been shamed, even if they'd never admit it. Sure, his brain may have traded some minimal life-saving instruction for a mental map of every alleyway of this fucking shire, but he was sacked simply for being faster on a Honda ST1100 than anyone else, before or since. The higher-ups placed the blame squarely on his transition from film school to paramedic, specifically his inability to shake movie myths out of his brain, but Jack had no time to humor this. The competition around Birmingham was fierce. Amazingly, five hospitals surrounded the golf course where the girl was found. Priory, Calthorpe, Queen Elizabeth, Edgbaston, Moseley Hall. It was a miracle she wasn't flung directly into an emergency room.

The girl had been thrown fifteen feet from her car, the majority of her clothes left behind in the jagged teeth of the windscreen. And that's where she stayed, half a snow angel in a sand trap, for twenty minutes at least. No bikes. None of those crazy "blues and twos," sirens with a sound so ugly they scared away wildlife and rubberneckers alike.

She should have been surrounded. It should have been the goddamn London Parade before his partner even stopped bleeding singing.

Normally, Jack would have complained about a mob of limeys saying, "bleeding" much too cavalier around a crime scene, especially when they weren't talking about blood. And they usually had all the time in the world to gather around and get in the way. Until today. She had been lying there alone for a long time.

Plenty of time for something else to happen.

If he had still been allowed on a bike, Jack would have been there first. He should have been there before the first ant crawled across her arm. He could have been there and back again. He had no doubt.

He would have made the difference.

Jack inhales deep and makes a decision. Soaking a cloth with alcohol, he begins to pull her leg free from the torn tube of denim and raises her knees high. He begins to clean.

He's convinced himself he's doing the right thing. He has no doubt about the action he's taking. Jack has traveled across the planet but found one thing to be universal in small towns. Scorn. He wouldn't allow any of these things to happen to her.

Another bump, and the driver turns his baseball cap around in frustration. Jack freezes, crouched with his hand under her knees, eyes locked on a team logo, one of those slow, baffling sports the Brits loved. The leering, slobbering bulldog watches his actions with interest.

Jack checks his watch and quickens his pace.

"Don't worry," he whispers. "Three more minutes and it never happened."

As he pulls up her shirt, he finds a large five-pointed bruise marking the side of her stomach.

He spreads his fingers to cover it. It fits him like a glove.

The siren starts to stutter and warble again, so the driver punches the dashboard and jiggles the switch.

The siren barks once then returns to normal.

II.

It's the Worst Cop of all Time! – The Man Who Loved Breakfast – Billy Squier Plans His Revenge – Do the Münster Mash – The Boy Who Cried "Important Movie You Must Watch This Instant" – A Willful Suspension (of Balls) – No, It's Still a Crime, Dude – Toronado Warning – Pizza Pizza Party Party – Spiders Snag the Emesis They Always Wanted

"I'm the dog that ate your birthday cake"
—Sparklehorse "It's a Wonderful Life"

"What the fuck is all over your boots?" Bully asked Billy, then she glanced up and recoiled, "And your face! Gross."

"Man, don't get me started," Billy sighed. "I have no idea. I think some asshole spit at me from his car while I was out Baja-ing around. But I can't be sure."

"What the fuck do you mean, you can't be sure?" Bully asked in disgust.

"It was green."

"The fuckin' car was green?"

"No, the spit."

"What?"

"That's what I'm saying."

"Weird."

They followed and followed their cop, followed him home to get his address, followed him back to work to fight crime or whatever. Drove everywhere he drove, got gas when he got potato chips, until the sun threatened to come up and chase them away.

"Get this," Billy said. "I was on my way to pick you up tonight, after that asshole spit on me, and they've got half the highway blocked off. You know, down by the on-ramp? A chunk of rubble had slid down the hill, and there were three cops standing there staring at it, two of them texting their fucking girlfriends, the other one leading a dog around in circles. On the van, it said 'Bomb Sniffing Unit.'"

"Wait, there was a bomb?"

"No! That's my point. Bunch of assholes pretending they're in a movie or something. Calling in the cavalry for a shrub that tumbled off a cliff."

"Doesn't everyone pretend they're in a movie?"

"Yeah, but we're doing it right."

They sat in Billy's car across the street from the cop's cruiser, engines ticking, waiting for the heat fog of his rant to clear the windshield.

"What was his name again? Bigby?" Bully asked.

"No, 'Bigbee,' like Big 'B,' or something." He noticed she was writing this on an envelope. "But any combination and the letters will probably get through to him."

"How come the back window of his car says K-9 and no dog ever goes in or out?"

"That's a good question."

"And why is it 'K-9' instead of 'canine' anyway?"

"It's from a Prince song."

"Nice," she smiled. "You know, I hate those smug K-9 cops, acting like they got this magic bond with an animal no one will understand. Meanwhile you know how they haul those dogs around? There's no car seat for a dog, you know. They're in a goddamn metal box. If you ever see a car chase on TV and you can read 'K-9' on the back of the car, what you don't see is the dead dog when the chase is over."

"No shit?"

"Seriously, K-9 plus 'car chase' equals 'Get me a new dog' back at the station."

"You know what I hate? When cops are always quoting movies without realizing it. The other day I'm watching this crap cop show, supposed reality show, and this fuckin' idiot yells at the spectators standing around the arrest,

'Can't you see there are guns here!' Yeah, saw that movie, too, fuckface."

"Ah, yes," she said. "I call that their Chuck D Rapper Voice. Can't be a cop without it. But what I hate hate *hate* is how they're always saying 'vehicle' instead of 'car.' Like they're already practicing for their big debut in court. But that posturing omits crucial info! Like, what is it? Truck, car, unicycle, rocket pack, or what?"

"And they're always yelling at the crowd," Billy said as Bully sat forward, excited. "Hey, maybe you wouldn't draw a crowd if you didn't have a fucking camera crew, am I right? And of course they're all acting hardass like the movies with their line, 'You have the right to remain silent!' Do they even say that for real?"

"Uh, you realize Miranda rights sound like the movies because that's something they really do, right?"

"Huh? Yeah, of course. But what's amazing is they constantly mangle movie quotes but nail those Miranda rights every time. Sometimes I pray I'll get arrested, just so I could interrupt them. First they'd go, 'You have the right...' And I'd go, 'To a hospital!' And they'd go, 'Uh, no, the right to an attorney.' Then the other cop would be like, 'What's this guy's problem, Joey? Make him an offer that he should seriously consider!' Dipshits."

"No, I mean that reading someone their rights is only gonna *sound* the same because..."

"Okay, okay, back to our cop. Here's how I imagine the guy," Billy was practically bouncing in his seat. "Okay, every morning he lines up his bacon and eggs like a frown..."

"Wait! Let me go first," she insisted. "His name is... Dwayne Robert 'Bob' Bigbee, but going through the academy, the other cadets anointed him shit like 'Bigbeak,' 'Bigbleed,' 'Bigbleat,' 'Bigbleep,' 'Bigsleep,' 'Bigsweep,' 'Bigsheep,' 'Bigfreak...'"

"Very nice."

"And the worst nickname he always detested was 'Biglittlebopeep.'"

"Perfect. No 'Bighorn?'"

"What?"

"It's a kind of sheep. Bighorn might sound tough, but he's a glorified Bigsheep."

"Doesn't sound tough. Just noisy. Anyway, this was all before civilians started misreading his name tag. And his superiors all call him 'an enigma wrapped in an idiot' behind his back."

"Yes, yes. That is our Officer Bigbee! The kind of man who once went to a vending machine and kicked the shit out of it before he even pressed a button. 'That way, no matter what chips fall,' he tells his new rookie partner, he could be sure it didn't give him 'what he wanted, but what he *needed.*'"

"Wait, what was his name again?"

"Bigbeep or some shit."

"I think I'm in love."

Me, too, he thought.

When the cherries started flashing on the roof of the cop car, both their hearts hiccupped, and the cruiser tore off around the corner. Billy pulled out, then inched up over the speed limit to give chase. He turned about three corners tops before he found a circle of police cars around a pizza-delivery man, red square bag in hand, standing in the middle of the road. The pizza man was wearing a large metal collar like a dog, hands palms up. He was shouting something at the officers, then suddenly sat crossed-legged on the yellow line.

"What the fuck?" Billy and Bully both said at the same time.

"I can hear it ticking!" the pizza man was shouting in despair, sometimes with his head between his knees. "Why aren't you trying to get it off of me?!"

The cops just mingled around him. One of them kicked at the pizza bag. Officer Bigbeep even took a step backward. Then the collar must have stopped ticking because every cop flinched at once… then the collar fired off a small poof of confetti, and every blue shirt hit the deck.

Their favorite cop was now halfway under his car. After a minute or so, the officers finally approached the pizza man, laughing nervously. The pizza man brushed the confetti from his hair and started to stand when a cop put a knee in his back and started to cuff him. But Bigbee didn't join the dogpile of arresting officers. He crawled out from under the car and made a big beeline for something else in the road. Then, just like the seasoned sleuth they'd hoped he was, Bigbee began to study the two pizzas spilling out of their boxes, hanging grotesquely out of the red bag. He sniffed that road pizza like it was the answer to everything.

"That's the training kicking in," Billy giggled.

And right when Bigbee seemed sure no one was watching him, he pulled a slice from a crumpled box like a greasy orange tongue and stuffed it into his pocket.

"Wow," Bully hissed. "That's our hero."

"Okay, I don't want to overstate anything, but I think we've happened upon the worst cop ever to wear the uniform."

"Worst cop of all time," Bully said. Then, "Let's kill the fucker."

"Let's scare him, you mean?"

"Yeah, that's what I said. Let's scare the fucker."

Eyes closed, head pounding on the set of yet another movie, his third in as many days, Larry heard another four bathrobes drop together like the gentle thud of snow off a rooftop. He slowly opened one eye, then the other.

It was the moment he always dreaded before a shoot. And he could have sworn it was even worse than the time before, which, at the time, had been the worst time yet.

Larry had worked with all of these actors for years, but he could have sworn their tattoos were multiplying every 24 hours. Like poison ivy, or an angry friction rash. There was no other explanation. In the '70s, you'd never see a tattoo staining your film, unless you were using the hoary "sailors on leave" in your plot. And even then, it would probably just be a faded green lizard on the arm, or a little "Semper Fi" on the shoulder. Sure, back then there was always that one girl who grew out her bush to mythic proportions and turned it into Willie Nelson's beard with some ink of him from the nose up, like a beatnik "Kilroy Was Here." But other than those exceptions, tattoos in porn usually signaled "prison" to the viewer, which was tough on their concentration, as well as blood flow.

But more ink had started creeping onto his set lately, and no one else seemed to show the slightest concern. Larry was starting to think it was that movie *Tattoo* with Kinsky and that Bond girl, whatever her name was, that might be to blame. It had just come out on video. Or maybe it was the colorful Ray Bradbury bibliography Carl was carrying on his back in the movie *The Illustrated Man.* But that flick had been out awhile. Maybe it was all those "Z's" on Fletcher Christian's neck in *The Bounty*? Or that glimpse of "death" on the toes of the Night Rider in *Mad Max*? And what about the proud eagle adorning Fenix's chest in the brutal *Santa Sangre*? Or maybe it was Harry "The Story of Love and Hate" Powell's knuckles in *Night of the Hunter*. Maybe Snake Plissken's cobra in *Escape from New York*. Maybe it was that leering devil on Lee Umstetter's groin in *Weeds*. Maybe it was Woody Woodpecker in *Raising Arizona*. Maybe it was that little fucker from *Fantasy Island*. Maybe…

Or maybe it had something to do with this line of work.

Maybe that's what happens on a movie set like this, when you fuck so much without offspring, he wondered, eyes crawling from body to body, crew starting to worry. *Rather than fertilize an egg, you'll just hatch a chopper-riding Grim Reaper on your pectoral muscle instead.*

He'd been sorta prepared for the skin doodle apocalypse today, however, because he already knew he'd be dealing with Head Breakfast's tattoos on this shoot. "H.B." as they called him was so named because of the Denny's grand slam breakfast inked across the top of his bald cranium. Hey, what could you do? Motherfucker loved breakfast. His real fake name was Freddy, but how could you call him that when he had goddamn Eggs Over Easy, sausage links, and a side of flapjacks forever staining his dome? And everybody agreed you didn't bother asking him about it, as Larry made the mistake of doing more than once. Freddy had no explanation, except that he honest to God loved breakfast like no one had before or since, or before the since.

People would say, "Hey, remember that book, *The Man Who Loved Women*?"

"Yeah, the movie with Burt Reynolds?" most people would ask right back, or "Yeah, the movie by Truffaut?" as Larry would have said to score points back in film school.

"Well, swap the word 'women' with 'breakfast.'" Or, "You ever see *When a Man Loves a Woman*?"

"We get the point, dude."

"Would a breakfast tattoo on someone's head make a woman (or man) hungry if he went down on them?" Glengarry once asked Larry. "Might be worse to have a sandwich. Bad form, you know? But swirling toast around those egg yolks? Nasty. Maybe he should have put a crossword puzzle up there instead…"

But besides his head tattoo being kind of hilarious, it was also easily covered up with a skully cap and forgotten. Head Breakfast was something else entirely. A quirk. An anomaly. Larry could forgive the kid. But everywhere else, it was an epidemic. Larry could not believe he was the only one who found it unusual that every one of his performing monkeys was sporting a veritable road map of bullshit across its tanned, sinewy hide. Time to read them all?

Indecipherable Chinese characters and their even more confusing cartoon characters, lightning bolts and Frankenstein bolts, lower-back sunrises and sunsets, gift-wrap bow above the ass crack, tombstone or two on the hip bones, every phase of the moon, a man on the moon, the man in the moon, all the pretty insects (some asshole even had a fly tattooed on the head of his cock once, causing Larry to ask, "Why? No, seriously, why?" Then he shouted "Cut!"), and all the scary spiders, the essential Virgin Mary, of course, this one on a motorcycle, even an ashtray right above the left cheek, 'cause Christ knows *that* joke never gets old, even if she does, and all the weapons you could think of, usually covering the L5-S1 rupture scars that ran down to their tailbones (more bad backs than warehouse workers in this business, and Larry never understood why workman's comp didn't cover it), gold porn "stars" everywhere like grade-school stickers, all the trendy music-scene bullshit like nautical everything and those swallows everyone called "sparrows" by mistake (particularly funny considering the industry), a noble tree that turns into a goldfish or a tidal wave, whichever is more Zen, and finally, without fail, the ol' stand-by, a tribute to some dead family member, who may not have said it out loud but was certainly relieved in the afterlife that their last wish to be immortalized as an angry rash of cherry blossoms next to their niece's vulva had been granted.

How the fuck was no one seeing this shit? Larry would wonder.

But all of those skin scribblings may have been ignored. If it wasn't for the names.

Sure, getting punched in the face very first thing in the morning was gonna throw off your day. So he expected every little thing to get on his nerves before he burned the first foot of film.

But those fucking names.

Not their porn names. Not the real fake names. Those were all suitably ridiculous. The tired joke among civilians is that your porn name is the name of your first pet plus the name of the street you grew up on. Wrong. Maybe a decade ago, back in the swingin' dick '70s. Now it was much simpler. Now, at least for the men, it was a name that sounded like genitals, then whatever rhymed with that.

And Freddy Frigg, forever known as the Head Breakfast, was a good example. The "Frigg" part being particularly unusual because it represented only getting to third base.

But the other kid, Cuban, Italian, Greek or some shit (broken English falling all over his movies like dead leaves, just another example of the ridiculous surge of cheap Middle Eastern men in porn, satisfied to be paid in chickens and track suits), he just went with "Joe Fuck." That one made Larry smile a little. Either something was lost in translation, or he just got lazy. He was a pain in the ass on top of it, sometimes a little too rough on the ladies, thinking it was cute ("Joe Fuck should be in jail, not in porn" was the most common reaction from the neighborhood adult vendor), but worse, without fail, asking the girls in the scenes with him, always in that horribly distracting accent, "Are you coming again? Are you coming again already?" Typically when they were never close to begin with.

43

Maybe if Joe loved women as much as, say, Freddy loved breakfast, he might have a chance at getting this done for the females. But, sadly, working in the porn industry, with the women consistently blurring the line between real and fake orgasms for the sake of the scene while the men had no disconnect from the moment at all, it made fuckwits such as Joe the worst sexual partners in history. Coins flying everywhere when they dropped their pants too fast.

But they were pros at doing what Larry and Damon needed them to do, when they needed them to do it. And he saved the day in *Romancing the Bone, Rocky Whore Picture Show, Lawrence of a Labia,* and one day, God help us, in *Kindergarten Cock.* See, few things were as frustrating as all the tight close-ups and angles when a money shot threatened but never came. When there was the crescendo but no orgasm, it was as traumatizing as a lost sneeze. It reminded Larry of when Journey's "Lovin', Touchin', Squeezin'" came on the radio with no "City of the Angels" afterwards. Or when they split up those two Zeppelin songs off *Physical Graffiti.* Actually, that might be worse.

And the only thing worse than that, Larry decided, *is when the LP on the radio is skipping and a DJ is forced to change it halfway through. Thank Christ for cassettes.*

Then Larry remembered the punch that broke his stereo's jaw, and the black tongue that now rolled out of its mouth sometimes. Maybe *that* was the worst.

But for the women, their monikers were usually just those fake real names they'd give you at a party anyway, when you were trying to chat them up. Always a lot of alliteration, and usually something cute, something that sounded a lot like the name of a car. And today, the two girls Larry was eyeballing in the stable, preening and pointlessly flirting with their co-stars (has there ever been more wasted effort than that?), were known in the business as "Suzie Starrr" and "Roxy Renault."

Plus there was the copyright issue. Larry was convinced that as his adult films inevitably crossed over into the mainstream, displaying tattoo artists' distinctive work without compensation might become more of a concerning gray area. Not as concerning as the gray area around Joe Fuck's urinary meatus, but still its own harbinger of a future problem.

Larry couldn't fault them for it. Hell, he'd changed his name, too. At least twice. Ironically, his last fake real name (all three parts of it) was a lot like a noble, bearded director's name, just waiting to adorn a tasteful, understated, Oscar-bait kind of poster. Something with a rose on it. Which meant it sounded more like a porn name than anyone.

Lawrence Bridge Kensington III. The third? Yeah, probably. His real given name, Jack Grinstead, was too loaded with history to bear. And people always thought he was saying, "Just grin instead!" Way too heavy with memories that name, just like the job he'd carried on his shoulders along with it. His character arc was so backwards, it sounded sideways. He went from America to England to America, from Jack to Lawrence to Larry, from "paramedic" to "professional student" to "pornographer." And all of them were the most natural journeys of his life.

No, aliases weren't the real problem. It was the real names his performers had written on their bodies that were the real problem.

He thought of the movie hidden in his car, a real movie on a reel. The movie he'd always wanted to make. Not some 8 millimeter bullshit. 35mm. Big, beautiful 35mm, wrapped around one of those brushed-steel, 15-inch Goldberg reels. This movie was mostly true and filmed on a shoestring budget, mostly Damon's shoestrings to be honest, even though Damon had no earthly clue. All

Larry had to do was ride along with some friends on their day jobs to get a real movie done. It was the '80s when he started, the season of the Cinéma Vérité, a style that suited cheapjack filmmaking. If he could find the right distributor, he would no longer be the only one to ever see the film with a light bulb behind it. Hell, if he could find the right projector.

Someone was tapping his shoulder. It was time to pay the bills. He opened his mouth to say it, but today Larry actually feared the word that was every director's best friend. He'd been on set for five minutes, and the pulse that still lingered in his split lip told him he wasn't gonna be able to keep it together for long, not after that bastard's alarm clock at the stop sign.

He feared the word today because it felt less like a friend and more like someone flicking his earlobe in church, daring him to fuck up everyone's sermon. And when he finally said the word, it hung out there in the air between him and his lens, taunting him so bad he almost tried to suck it back through his teeth like spaghetti.

"Action!"

"Well, before we do that, you know, before we do that other thing, I think we should start thinking about the dog."

"What do you mean?"

"I mean, it's a cop dog. It's probably been tagged or numbered or tattooed or got a microchip in it or something. That's how they keep track of 'em, you know."

Billy and Bully sat on the curb, sometimes staring at each other's shoes, sometimes hypnotized by the glow of the restaurant's back door and the flurry of plate-scraping dishwashers in the steam.

Billy curled his leg to wipe the green toe of his boot on the back of his jeans, and shook his head when the sticky glaze didn't come off. He would have curled his tail if he had one.

"You still got that spit on you? Nasty."

"It's not my fault."

"What?"

"I don't know, maybe they're evolving," he shrugged.

"Who?!" Bully was little, but she was loud as shit.

"Them. Us," Billy stood up to be more dramatic. "Maybe human beings spit so much that it's turning into something else, something like glue you can't just wipe away..."

"Shut the fuck up and sit down. How much longer do we have to wait?"

Billy looked at his Nelsonic *Space Attacker* game watch and started pressing buttons until Bully slapped it down.

"I'm bored. I'm going to get him."

"No!" Billy pleaded. "Just wait, please. He's doing us a favor."

"Fine," Bully said, slumping in defeat. She took a deep breath. "Okay, let's go over it again. Pretend we've already stolen the dog, and Officer Bigbeep..."

"It's Bigby."

"How are you spelling that? Like Big-Bye?"

"Huh?"

"Nothing. So Officer Bigby is chasing us through these alleys right now. Where the hell would we hide?"

"A movie theater? Like in the back row, trying to keep the dog quiet. You know, just like Oswald."

"Right. Just like Oswald and, uh, his dog," Bully scoffed.

Billy pouted.

"You know, you shouldn't feel safe in a movie theater."

"Why not?"

"They fuck with people's heads," Bully said. "People react different, but most lose their shit. That's why they had to invent drive-ins. You can't put too many people in a room to watch a movie together. They'll fuckin' explode. They had to move that action outside."

"Bullshit."

"No shit. Have you ever heard how you're not supposed to yell, 'Fire!' in a crowded theater? That's nothing compared to yelling, 'Movie!' in a fire."

"You're high," Billy laughed, starting to turn away.

"No, wait! I have a theory!" she said, smiling and grabbing.

"Of course you do."

"Okay, think about it for a second. What's the worst thing you've ever experienced in a movie theater?"

"You. Talking my ear off."

"No, seriously."

"Well, it's a matter of opinion."

"No, never opinion!" Bully stomped her foot. "There are right answers."

"What is it?"

"I'll just say this, if we are ever in a ticking-time-bomb type situation, or a lit fuse or the gas tank on a car is gonna blow, whatever you do, no matter how tempting it is, no matter who may be watching, do *not* walk slowly away from the explosion."

"What?"

"I can't tell you how much I'm worried this is gonna be a problem in movies some day."

The thing about Bully that Billy sometimes forgot was how she could see the screen of a nearby drive-in from her bed. This meant she silently watched about a hundred movies a year. That's a lot of movies to ponder in bed every night. Expectedly, patterns began to emerge. And theories.

"What are you talking about?" he sighed.

"In the movies! Haven't you seen this? There will be an explosion, and someone walks away from it trying to be cool. I saw it in *Apocalypse Now* last week, and thought that was annoying enough on the beach with the cowboy, but then I saw it in *Get Mean* last night, and was like, 'Come on!' Then, the other day, I take my little brother to see *The Adventures of 'Reno' Williams*…"

"Ooh! Is it good? I heard it was good."

"Yeah, it's all right. Except the part where he walks away from the explosion."

"I think you need to stop using a drive-in as a nightlight. Or be more forgiving."

"It's gonna be a problem," she nodded. "This walking-away-from-fire thing is infectious. And it's fucking up my sleep, not good." She got up on her toes to grab Billy's face in her hands, deadly serious. "Trust me on this." Then she grimaced at something green on the tip of his nose and let him go.

"You're nuts," he decided.

"Point is, there's no way we're hiding in a theater. The drive-in maybe…"

"I think you've had enough of the drive-in. What's showing at the Butch Cassidy tonight anyway?"

"Butch Cassidy is dead. The only one left is The Spotlight Kid, remember?"

"Whatever."

"Well, last night at The Spotlight Kid, it was still the Rowdy Roddy Double Feature, *Hell Comes to Frogtown* and *They Live*."

"You wanna sneak in?"

"Why would I bother to sneak in?" she scowled. "I've seen 'em three times each."

"Oh, I don't know. To actually *hear* a movie for once? It might be a whole different experience."

"Maybe," she said, unconvinced.

Billy allowed a rare three minutes of silence between them. Then:

"I still think you're scared of cops," he declared.

"I fear no man."

"Okay, how about *besides* men?"

"I only fear one thing these days."

"What's that?" Billy was on the edge of his curb waiting to hear it.

"If you must know, I believe that insect populations have based their growth on a constant culling from car windshields," Bully explained. "And one day soon, they'll all learn to fly just three feet higher over the roads that circle our planet. And as a result... we will be forever covered in them from head to toe."

She loved talking about bugs. And it was times like this when Billy was reminded how much he loved her.

Then the summer locusts in the chestnut trees suddenly seemed deafening. Billy frowned, scared, trying to remember if they'd started out soothing or if he was just noticing a continuous shriek. Maybe their call was like those new alarm clocks that got louder and louder, supposedly to ease you into the waking world. He'd heard that the panic they'd induced in consumers necessitated a recall, and now he knew why. Once, Bully swore she was involved in the class-action lawsuit against the company that made them, and hopefully the settlement would at least pay for the aquarium she'd smashed the first morning it went off. She was full of shit. She loved the sound. They were her Sirens.

Some gravel popped under a shoe, and they looked up to see their back-alley restaurant connection, a hollow-chested dishwasher who was sorta friends with Bully's brother. He stood in the kitchen doorway with a black garbage bag over his shoulder, one headphone plugged into his ear, twirling the other headphone like a lifeguard whistle and grinning. They both hopped up.

"It's okay," Billy whispered to her. "I fear one thing, too."

"Yeah? What's that?"

He angled a thumb back at the cop car across the street.

"I fear looking up one day and seeing a dog's head hanging out the window of every car. Why do people think that shit's normal?" He tried to high-five the dishwasher, who left him hanging.

"Is that him over there?" Bully whispered. "I thought we were following *his* ass!" Then she seemed to process what he'd just said.

"Wait! No fair! I want to change my answer. I take it back. I'm afraid of three things now. Spit turning green forever, you eventually covered in that shit, and bugs learning to dodge cars. And people no longer respecting explosions! And this motherfucker with the bag…"

The dishwasher walked past them, pretending they weren't there, but doing it badly. He dropped his garbage bag on the ground in front of a dumpster, then without a word went back into the restaurant, kicking the brick away from the door and letting it swing slowly closed behind him. They caught a last glimpse of him leaning over a burner, one loose headphone bobbing in and out of a steaming pot of jambalaya.

Billy and Bully ran to the bag like it was Christmas morning, but Bully got to it first to shake it open. Then the bag suddenly jumped and squirmed in her hand, sharp snaps and pops scaring her low to the ground like a cat. Billy took the bag away, laughing as she shook off her embarrassment.

"Asshole," she mumbled.

"He gotcha! How can anyone resist setting mouse traps?" Billy laughed, shaking the bag hard like he was trying to get the final popcorn kernels to pop.

"Not mouse traps, fuckface. Rat traps."

"Same thing."

They walked to her car, a yellow hatchback Mustang, glancing nervously at the cruiser across the street. Bully popped the back, then lifted the flap that hid the spare tire.

51

She dumped the rat traps in with the rest of the junk she'd hoarded, trying not to flinch when the last trap sprung. Tucked in around her tire jack were walkie-talkies, telephone receivers, crumbling Lego structures, a couple gnarly dreamcatchers, all feathers and turquoise with the gas-station price tags still on them, a bunch of D-size batteries, and the keypad she'd torn off her diminutive "big" brother's electronic toy tank, this lumbering thing called a Big Trak that he'd gotten for his birthday. He'd be crying once he noticed it missing.

Billy took the weight of the hatchback from her and surveyed their treasure and the torn notebook pages detailing their plans, trying to smile. When they first thought of this project, Billy thought it was the best idea Bully'd ever had. But now the pile looked ridiculous, comical, crass, like the parts of a fake bomb spread out on a terrorist's table in a shitty movie where a camera wasn't meant to linger too long. Whatever they were building would not withstand scrutiny.

And her schematics were shit. He wished there was a way they could base their contraption on the shark tooth necklace his father had brought home for him from South Carolina when he was little. Simplicity of design. He wore the necklace for about five years, refusing to take it off until it snapped during a hockey game, sticking him in the throat about an inch from his jugular. But up until that savage hip check in the third period, Billy would sleep in that necklace, dreaming of that necklace spinning and those teeth cutting deeper and deeper into his neck, a nightmare that was somehow comforting as well as horrifying. And he never took it off, no matter how deep it stabbed him. To this day, teeth marks still appeared on his throat every summer he got a sunburn.

"It was like you slept under the Chainsaw of Damocles," Bully had whispered in awe when she first saw the ring of tiny white triangles at the beach. This would also be the first and last time she'd kiss him. She started singing a bastard version of a *Rocky Horror Picture Show* song.

"Chainsaw of Damocles hanging over our heads, and I've got the feeling someone's gonna be cutting my meds…"

She squeezed his hand like she was working a toothpaste tube.

"I fucking love our plan," Bully whispered now. Billy's smile stretched until it was genuine. He decided to love it, too.

She slammed the hatch shut and brought him all the way back.

"We'll build this bitch, put it around the dog, let him run back into the police station, and those cops will shit a brick," she said, and clapped her tiny hands. "They'll have a bomb squad around that mutt before you can say, 'Locusts are getting louder.'"

"For real? You think they're getting louder? I was gonna say something."

"Joke."

"Well, you're getting louder anyway."

"So, how about that asshole who spit on you out of his car? Is he the next target?"

"What? Fuck him. I don't need another nemesis."

"More like 'emesis,'" Bully corrected.

"Huh?"

"Look it up."

It's a hot, hazy day. Daytona Beach, Florida, summer of '83. A young man sits on a bench facing the ocean. He's tall but skinny, shoulders hunched out of habit, not insecurity. He wears a trucker cap way too big for his head and aviator glasses that obscure most of his face. The cap, covered in candy-like splashes of paint, features a grinning pig mascot selling its soul for a barbeque smokehouse. High behind the pig is a blank, peeling billboard with the lone, scorched eyeball of a sunscreen company logo. Higher still is the dead concrete screen of an old drive-in theater, patiently waiting for the sun to go down.

Near the beach, someone is cranking "Second Home by the Sea" in their headphones so loud that everyone can hear it, one of the few Genesis songs not on the radio this year, as their self-titled album just landed the previous spring. The young man frowns trying to locate the direction of the muffled music, as well as place it in his memory. Just over his narrow shoulder is yet another advertisement, a toothy cartoon dog shilling for surfboards. Smiling cartoon animals are everywhere today, it seems. Their eyes are watching all while the young man stares straight ahead, unblinking, vacant. Everyone on this beach is leading a dog, their own personal doppelgängers, and every so often an animal shows a curiosity in this young man that is not returned.

One dog passes particularly close to him, a mutt dressed head-to-tail in a purple pimp costume. Still the young man never blinks. He only smiles once while the sun is still up, when someone switches the Genesis song to a strange, all-German version of Peter Gabriel's "Intruder," and he realizes this person must be flying the superfan flag high to dig so deep.

"All Dogs And Their Owners Welcome!" is scrawled on the yellow boards of the young man's bench, but with his arms out, he covers three words to cancel out the owners' invite. He's done this on purpose. The boards of this bench are rotten, almost transparent. Lovers' hearts that were carved too deeply are linked by cracks, like a child's connect-the-dots ready to bring the bench down at any moment. The young man traces one heart with this thumb and wonders if it was one he scratched into a tree trunk as a boy, surviving the rebound down rivers and dissection in the mill, now hoping to finally upend the original vandal.

Everything about this young man suggests blindness. The sunglasses, indifference to a parade of half-naked rollerbladers, drooling dogs chasing balls, and girls chasing their dogs chasing those balls. In his hands, he holds a pot of dirt at an awkward angle, a tiny green seedling peeking from the center of the soil. Sometimes the young, blind man shields it from the sun.

A white American Eskimo runs by him with a dead fish in its mouth, the fish flapping faster as the dog picks up speed, dodging its master.

The young, blind man stares straight ahead.

A small, black-headed Münsterländer chases a bright red ball, and the young, blind man lazily cracks his neck toward nothing. A small, fawn-colored Pug dog trots by wearing a tiny hat with a propeller. Several people turn to laugh. Even the dog in the pimp costume turns toward the pug, seemingly ready to comment. The young, blind man yawns.

Then the Münster's bright red ball pinballs off pedestrian traffic and rolls toward the young man's shoes. The little dog slips and scratches at the sand as it frantically changes direction to lunge. For a moment, the young, blind man seems to be teasing the dog by maneuvering the ball around his feet, just out of its grasp. Then the young, blind man kicks the ball away. Hard. The dog anticipates the kick and catches it easily. With the ball finally locked in its mouth, the Münster runs back to its master, a boy with a prog-rock mix in his headphones, who misses the impressive footwork and unlikely exchange between a young, blind man and a dog he cannot see.

As the dog drops the ball, head cocked in confusion and anticipation, a tall, dark-skinned Hispanic woman walks by the young, blind man, confidence in her hips.

The young man stuffs the ball in his pocket, and the dog nuzzles this bulge, immediately forgetting all suspicion. Then, when the woman is closest, the young, blind man sits up straight and turns his head toward her, nostrils flaring as the Peter Gabriel song climaxes.

"Eindringling kommt... eindringling kommt und legt seine spur... legt seine spur."

"Can you please tell me what time it is?" the young, blind man asks.

The girl ignores him and keeps walking.

He stands to follow, and the dog runs back to his feet.

Tomorrow, he'll be back with his plaster cast, or maybe his badge. Of all his props, the badge is the only one that's real. He doesn't worry about the name on it, since most will see it for the first and last time. Staring at the animal, he thinks of his squad and their secret quota of 50 dog executions a year. Their sergeant, a Democrat, adjusted the limit to 25 if they were chained. He waits for the boy to again be buried deep enough in his music to forget about his doppelgänger, and then he kicks the dog so savagely that it folds over the toe of his work boot with one last air horn of a yelp, sailing high over the head of its master, trailing a tongue now twice its length. Because of the size of his headphones, which bob the boy's his tiny ears like a Dobie, he doesn't realize what's happened until the young, blind man is long gone.

No one remembers what he looked like. The girls either.

Billy was sprawled out in the stones under his dirt bike, staring up into the chrome and oily guts of it all, rubbing off the last flecks of green spittle while he waited for Bully to wander by and assume he was actually fixing something. She was late for their research trip to the video store, and he was gonna give her another hour before he started to get mad, or at least pretend he got mad. He kept his boombox nearby, ready to hit the button on Joe Walsh's "The Confessor" so she'd walk up right when the guitars kicked in to make him look cool. While he counted the minutes in his head, he wiggled his ass to move the painful stones off his tailbone and get comfy. Something his dog used to do.

His old dog. His old dog was big, but he wasn't black, but Billy called him "Shaft" anyway. Kind of mangy, and more *Shaft in Africa* Shaft than *Shaft's Big Score* Shaft, but Billy came up with his own lyrics to go with the original theme song:

"Shaft! Ah-Ahhh! Likes the pussy and the ass… Shaft! Ah-Ahhh! He's a miracle!"

Okay, he had to admit it was more of a combination of Isaac Hayes' "Theme From *Shaft*" and Queen's "Flash's Theme," but it was catchy as shit. Billy loved his monster pooch, a good-looking German Shepherd, the same kind of dog they drafted into the police force, and even though he never got Shaft a collar, everyone in town knew that dog was his. Everyone.

Especially Officer Bigby.

Officer Bigby, or "Bigbeep" as the kids all called him, was one of those insufferable pricks who was up in everybody's business at all times. They first met when he busted Billy for painting a fake registration sticker onto the corner of his dirt bike's license plate.

"That's some wonderful artwork!" he laughed, right before he scruffed Billy's neck like a puppy. After that, Billy seemed to see him everywhere, even when his registration stickers were up to date. And Billy honked every time he saw the bastard.

He was pretty sure it was the same cop. Always the same cop. He didn't care if he was wrong.

Sometimes Billy thought they might be two different guys, since a little recon showed there was both a "Bigby" and a "Bigbee" in that precinct. But with those mirrored glasses and a hat pulled down like a hardass, and that blue-on-blue shirt, it was all the same difference when you came right down to it.

Bigby probably got his nickname just like Bigbee, Billy figured. Here was a cop so lazy he would lay on his horn instead of using his siren every time he pulled someone over. He was like those assholes who couldn't be bothered to use a turn signal because of the effort it required to flick it, saving all their strength for the horn. Billy imagined Bigbeep's greasy sausage thumbs resting on the center of the steering wheel at all times, locked and loaded.

Then came the day that Bigbeep picked up Shaft wandering around town, like he was the dogcatcher or something all the sudden. Shaft was lassoed and driven straight to the shelter. And unlike his namesake who got out of every tight fix, even in Africa for Christ's sake, Shaft was put down within the hour.

An hour? The original *Shaft,* the shortest of the trilogy, was actually longer than the amount of time they waited to kill Billy's dog. And Billy had no idea he'd just barely missed the end of that movie when he came busting through the door at the pound, joking about posting bail and singing his dog's theme song. He even walked up to a cage with another smiley German Shepherd looking a lot like *Shaft in Africa* before it slowly started to dawn on him what was wrong. Fifteen minutes later, he was all fists and feet, flailing in a tornado of brochures detailing how to avoid heartworm, until three cops ran out to put knees into his spine.

Heartworm.

As Billy laid there, fighting to catch his breath under all that weight, one of the brochures a tent over his nose, he had time to read all about heartworms. He had none of the symptoms, but he was pretty sure this word was the perfect diagnosis for what he was feeling in that moment. Something had wormed its way into his heart all right. His brain, too. Something that never left. He wouldn't need to ask the vet for a second opinion.

Veterinarians were fucking worthless anyway, he decided. He'd already suspected they were simply failed doctors, chopping up animals instead of humans because no one could sue for malpractice. But when Bully told him about her cat, detailed the so-called "peaceful" process of animal euthanasia she'd witnessed, sniffling with her head against Billy's chest to hear the beating of his heartworms, Billy made up his mind right then and there what he was now capable of.

Bully's cat's name had been Little Stupid, and, according to her, yeah, that about summed him up. He was little, and he was stupid. But then one day he was suddenly more dizzy than stupid. He may have eaten a piece of plastic, a rubber band or mothball, but with no warning, he was puking up something like dish suds all weekend. Then all week. He puked so much, Bully and her brother considered changing his name to "Wyatt Urp."

"Don't worry. Cats puke," everyone kept telling her. "They're like little vomitoriums," they insisted. "Like Caligula'n' shit," they shrugged. "Nothing to worry about!" they shouted. Then the suds turned yellow, and now they were telling her it was bad news instead of cracking jokes. So she took Little Stupid to the vet.

"Might as well have thrown him in a fucking wood chipper and cut out the middle man," she said.

She told Billy they did blood work first and concluded he was dehydrated.

"No shit, right?"

Then they took X-rays and explained they couldn't find anything else wrong. Then that Tarot reading somehow turned into "bone cancer."

"Let me get this straight, you put the lime in the coconut?" Bully swore she sang these words.

"Why are you singing?" the vet asked her.

"Because you're a witch doctor. Nothing then… boom. Bone cancer. The one thing the X-rays magically can't show you."

Billy agreed it was no accident that fucker picked an ailment no one could prove either way without some insane amount of cash. And the X-rays and blood work had already broke the bank on her summer "mad money." So her family decided to put him to sleep. Bully told Billy they called it "putting an animal to sleep" because calling it "putting an animal through a gauntlet of Death-Row-type limb shavings, fumbling injections, and wheezing, shrieking, strangled death rattles" didn't really roll off the fucking tongue. She told Billy she tried to grab the cat and run out the door at one point when Little Stupid was howling, but the vet and his fake nurses stopped her.

The "vet." Bully didn't need sarcastic air quotes when she said that word. And after her story, Billy already hated vets almost as much as he hated cops. Failed doctors, all. In fact, the previous Veteran's Day, Billy saw signs on telephone poles reminding everyone to "Thank Your Vet For Freedom!" and tore every one of those suckers down.

So, checking the final bill, Bigbeep owed him a dog. And veterinary medicine owed Bully a cat. So, fuck it, they decided they'd charge Bigbeep for the cat, too. It was easier that way. Especially when friends of theirs just started noticing Bigbeep rolling around town with a new, fuzzy partner, all *Turner and Hooch*-style, sniffing trunks and back seats and bonding together while teenagers lined the curbs until they showed enough fear and/or respect to be free to go back to skateboarding.

Bigbeep's new partner was a big, healthy German Shepherd with enough training and shiny leashes and fancy collars and shine in his thick coat for ten scrappier mutts like Shaft. He was a good-looking dog, they had to admit, and he probably didn't deserve anything too bad to happen to him just because he drew the short straw with Canine Selective Services and got paired off with that cocksucker.

But neither did Shaft.

Billy wasn't sure how far they'd go with their plan, but he figured he had to start doing something, right? They'd talked it to death.

He was scratching at the rust on the bike's exhaust like a real grease monkey when Bully pulled in. He quickly reached up to wiggle something that would rattle while she was walking up and totally forgot to cue up "The Confessor."

"What are you doing, dipshit? Quit pretending you're a mechanic."

"The world makes sense under here," he tried. She didn't buy it. "So, what did you do last night?"

"Snuck into the movies."

"Without me!" Billy bonked his head on something metal he couldn't name. "The Double Feature? Come on! That was my idea to go see those flicks!"

"It's always your idea to go see everything."

"What are you saying?" he asked.

"I'm saying you're worse than The Boy Who Cried Wolf. You're more like The Boy Who Cried Important Movie You Must Watch This Instant."

"Was it any good?" Billy asked, still pouting.

"I'm just fucking with you. I didn't sneak anywhere. Why bother? I just watched them from my window."

"You've got to be the best lip reader by now."

"Maybe. Haven't had a chance to try it on lips that aren't the size of a semi."

"What was showing again? 'Rowdy' Roddy Piper's flicks, right?"

"Well, you've seen *Hell Comes to Frogtown,* of course. But *They Live,* though, man. I don't know. You'll either love it or hate it."

Billy detested that phrase. In his experience, if something was ever described as "love it or hate it," it was, without fail, fucking terrible. He'd studied this phrase for a decade, and so far there had been no exceptions to this. And even though she gave him crap about him wanting to see a ton of movies with her, she watched ten times as many every week. It was just another reason he loved her.

"Really. So it sucks," he sighed.

"Nah," Bully shrugged. "It was cool. There were these sunglasses. And if you wore them, you'd see we're surrounded by these alien skeleton assholes, right? But the best part was it turned out there are words and messages all over everything around us *at all times*, but we can't see this without the sunglasses, and..."

"That sounds terrible. John Carpenter made this mess?"

"It was good! All those secret messages were easy to read through the trees. You know what though? You could totally tell it was supposed to be another throwaway Kurt Russell flick. You remember last month when Butch Cassidy had..."

"You mean The Spotlight Kid."

"...when The Spotlight Kid had that Kurt Russell/John Carpenter Triple Feature? *Big Trouble in Little China*, *The Thing*, and *Escape from New York?*"

"Oh, shit, *The Thing*! I can't believe it got pulled as fast as it did. I wanna watch that again right now," Billy said, sitting up. "I can't believe people went to see *E.T.* instead. Did I ever tell you about the rap song I wrote as a tribute? It's called "The Rap's *The Thing*'..."

"'To Catch the Conscience Of the King?'" Bully mocked. "Anyway, like I was saying, it's obvious that Mr. Piper was just some bush-league version of Kurt Russell. Good fight scene though. It lasted fucking *forever*."

"...and I'll sing it for you any time you want. It's my finest moment and the only thing I ever finished and-"

"Nope. Thanks."

"Oh, okay. It lasted forever, huh? How long is the movie?"

"Not the movie! The fight scene!"

"Oh. How long is forever?"

"The big fight in it lasted, no joke... forty-five minutes."

"No way," Billy was skeptical.

"I swear. I would kill to be in a fight like that."

"Who was fighting?"

"Poor Man's Kurt Russell! And that black dude... Keith David? David Keith? Whoever. Question! Why hasn't there ever been a movie starring both David Keith and Keith David? Think of the poster!"

"No idea who you're talking about."

"You know the guys I mean. The black one is in *They Live*, and the other one was that cracker in *An Officer and a Gentleman* who hung himself when that dumb bitch wouldn't marry his ass. So, like, the same guy pretty much."

"Yeah, right," Billy laughed. Bully got worked up about movies sometimes.

"Imagine the money they'd save on advertising," she went on. "They could probably splice their heads together on the poster like that 'Let That Be Your Last Battlefield' *Star Trek* episode. Yo, Hollywood, pay attention!" Bully yelled at the sky. "Keith 'Keeps Roddy Piper From Forcing Him To Wear Sunglasses For Fifty-Seven Minutes' David vs. David 'Still Wants To Marry Worst Woman In Florida After She Lied About Being Knocked Up' Keith. Clear winner: Keith David for the K.O. No, seriously, though. You have to see this movie before we blow ourselves up this weekend. In that two-hour fight scene, he's all like, 'You dirty motherfucker!' and David Keith really does seem genuinely surprised in that moment. I think those two actors were really fighting. That's the key."

"How come people in movies always cough a lot after they get their ass kicked real bad?" Billy asked her. "You don't give someone a cold when you punch them in the face."

"I think you're used to too much WWF bullshit. You need someone to tap out to know it's over."

"No, I just…"

"Tap tap tap!" she snapped, rapidly slapping his chest like a wrestling mat.

"…just when I got my ass kicked three years ago, I just crawled under a car."

"I believe it," Bully said, kicking at his shoes. "You crawl under shit like a tick."

At that, Billy finally pulled himself the rest of the way out from under the bike, wiping his hands on his thighs like he guessed blue-collar dudes did at the end of their workday.

"All fixed!" he exclaimed, clapping no puffs of dirt into the air. "So, did you get the goods or what?"

"Yep." Bully pulled a bright yellow plastic card from her pocket. It read "Wooly and Wily Video" and sported a gorilla with sunglasses cracking a video tape over a furry knee.

"Perfect. Let's go to work," he said.

"Real work this time," she laughed, boxing at his lilywhite hands.

"Action!"

Larry was punching one of his actors in the ear, blood flowing freely from his own split lip all over again, and he was quickly realizing that you never pick a fight with a naked man. Naked people fight harder. Especially if they're hard. Then they're damn near invincible. He remembered something one of his gym teachers always said whenever they played Shirts versus Skins in basketball. It had something to do with being vulnerable:

"Skins always win!"

His gym teacher was right. The confusion of bodies in basketball made stripping down necessary, but Larry always wondered why someone didn't try it in other sports, too. Skins in baseball, with all those cleats and bats, would mean victory guaranteed, right?

"What the fuck is going on here?!"

It was Stevey, the other producer, the one who signed Larry's checks. He was holding the corner of his sunglasses, but he was too horrified to take them off. Joe Fuck had Larry pinned under one knee, rabbit-punching him in the forehead, fire-engine red cock and balls nodding in enthusiasm with every shot.

Larry shouldn't have been surprised at his resolve. Joe Fuck always went the extra mile. "Mile" meaning "7 to 9 inches," depending on the weather. Maybe not as big as some. Hell, some of his regular actors were so long that not only did they actually have that old gag about "Wendy" tattooed on their dicks, theirs *started out* saying, "Welcome to Jamaica and have a nice day," but when erect read, "I wasn't really welcome when I first came to Jamaica and I have no reason to go back, but there's the thing, the weather is nicer during the weekend, although you'll be fucking too much to notice on Monday through Friday." Larry guessed they might still read "Wendy" if it was cold enough. Or windy. But God help you if Joe "gave you roses" when he was through, porn slang for inducing a prolapsed rectum.

Larry tried not to think about such things while he was under the guy, and eventually Glengarry and Stevey broke them up, dragging Joe outside to the pool to cool off and sending Head Breakfast over to Suzie to keep him up to at least quarter-mast. She was pulling double duty as the fluffer that week for the promise of an extra hundred bucks and two tickets to Gustavo Dudamel.

Larry plopped down Indian-legged on the floor, head pounding like a drum circle, a ridge of knuckle marks rising between his eyes like bread dough.

"Larry, what happened?"

He wanted to explain to Stevey that he didn't know, that he'd just lost it. He wanted to tell him how he'd been setting up a shot that focused on the chest hair of Head

Breakfast, since hair like that was rare for a porn set, with bodies so often waxed and oily like little sausage casings. In fact, it was H.B.'s uncontrollable pelt that pegged him as just two or three gigs from a regular *Triassic Cock* slot. But Larry had gotten lost looking through the lens at that hirsute motherfucker, looking for the gray, thinking about commitment, thinking about his ex-wife, thinking about how he should get a shot of Suzie running her fingers through all that gnarly shit with her engagement ring until they both got caught.

But instead he decided it was a good time to tell his producer how tattoos were ruining everything, especially ones with names. Stevey was sympathetic, up to a point anyway. But not when he got to the part about the names.

"What names, Larry?"

"You're kidding, right?"

"We've been through this before. There aren't any…"

"Listen, I have to have some control over the reality of this film."

"I know, I know, I know. Come on, I know what you're talking about, Larry. You need a suspension of disbelief, right?"

"You mean a *willful* suspension."

"Huh?"

"Everybody always fucks that up. A *willful* suspension of disbelief and truth sufficient. Big difference."

"What?"

"A willful suspension."

"Hey, can I get a willful suspension of my balls?" a pleading voice called out without an ounce of sarcasm.

"Larry, listen up. No one knows what the fuck you're talking about with this tattoo stuff. Come on, we got cocks falling asleep over here, and…"

"Truth sufficient."

"What?"

66

The sound man's boom started to sag with everything else. Then something was ringing, and Stevey laid a palm on the huge portable telephone holstered to his belt like a six-shooter. They both knew who was calling. Stevey's voice changed, and now he sounded like he was from Krypton, too.

"We're burning time and money, and you still think you're making a fuckin' movie!"

Suddenly, Larry's angry itch was back. He stormed back toward Stevey, scratching and scratching so hard that his fingernails started creasing the fabric of his shirt, gouging into his skin like he was tucking a sheet under mattress corners. Then he stopped, heart like a hummingbird, and rolled up a cuff to stare at the trenches he'd dug into his arms and the stains spreading on his clothes.

But the color was all wrong.

He moved under the Tungsten lamps to get a closer look. Underneath his sleeve was not so much the black-and-red ruin of blood and skin as he expected, but instead a strange blue jelly seeping from his pores, surrounded by angry red hives, like a Zen garden on each side of a river.

You can't be around them that long or...

Bullshit. Sure, they fucked up their backs a lot. And, sure, this AIDS thing was hovering like a thunderhead every year, now that someone in the industry had finally been diagnosed and all fears were realized. They were calling AIDS "the new Ebola," which was cool because the new acronym finally made sense. But it didn't help that Reagan thought of it as a weapon. Plus there was the Hepatitis with that other dude last month. But as far as regular STDs, as far as anyone catching anything, it was unheard of these days.

But how about STTs…

Larry couldn't prove it, but he knew the reason for their luck wasn't because of any sudden awareness, or the big, new stash of rubbers on the sets. And it wasn't because of mandatory testing either.

Larry was convinced it was because they'd long since fucked themselves immune.

"Truth sufficient, Stevey!" he shouted, shamefully covering the strange lesions on his arms. "It's because these people are actually fucking. That's what's confusing everyone. Then you add the names? Forget about it. Maybe they should fake it!"

"Just get it done, man," Stevey growled as he answered his giant phone. Damon's voice jumped out of the speaker and bounced around the walls like someone had side-armed a tennis ball into a phone booth. A sound guy actually ducked.

Honestly, Damon was a lot easier to deal with since he started drinking. Behind his back, they called him Wild Bill Hiccup. A month back, Larry mistook Damon's demand to "add more violence" for "add more violins," and goddamn if Damon didn't end up admitting it made the movie even better.

But today he was yelling, and Stevey dropped the phone when he flinched, and that's about the time Suzie laughed and Head Breakfast's testicle popped out of her mouth a little too fast. He doubled over in pain, and Glengarry flinched, too. He ran for the fridge before anyone had to say it.

"Get him some ice!"

"Get him an ambulance!"

"Get him some breakfast!"

"No, get it *done!*" Stevey shouted, trying in vain to muzzle a phone receiver wider than his palm.

Larry couldn't wait until this was all over, when he could throw some more of Stevey and Damon's money at his crew of hungry, horny moonlighters, for once paying them not to fuck, but to make a real movie in the middle of the night. Like it was his job.

* * *

"Planning a crime isn't a crime, right?" one of them asked.

They had decided to build a neck bomb, just for fun. Just keep working on their scheme as long as they could pay attention. It would be their first secret.

"Uh, probably," the other one answered, blowing on a slice of pizza. Then after a second, "No, I think it's still a crime, dude."

"How many times have you started something but never finished that shit?" It was dark in the car, but this was definitely her asking.

"Every single time," he smiled, teeth shining.

"Why is that such a relief?" she laughed. "We aren't really going to do anything, are we?" He didn't answer.

"Hey, what was Bigbeat talking about with your driver's license picture anyway?" he asked. "You never explained that sufficiently."

"It's an old trick. You stick your tongue out when they take the picture and it accomplishes two things. First, it's disrespectful to the cop who's reading it, and second, it makes your features distorted and less likely to be recognized if your records are ever pulled."

"Do it right now," he said.

"You do it."

He stuck his tongue out and goddamn if she didn't catch the end of it in her teeth like someone had thrown her a grape. Her mouth was salty, delicious.

"Revenge is a dish best served with extra pepperoni," she whispered, kissing him some more. Then she bit.

For the first time in his life, Billy stopped his car in the middle of the highway. It was 4:00 a.m., no cars in sight, with his headlights shining on roads stained red forever with the comet trails of roadkill. They sat in silence, bouncing on the tires once or twice like a shipwreck on the rocks, and Billy waited for Bully to get scared. She never did.

Instead, she moved as close as she could, and they started playing some games, waiting to see how long they could idle there in the road before another car caught them. He felt beached, unable to move, tires replaced by a broken rudder scraping the stones, the sweat down his back like leaks in the hull.

She laughed and asked what happened. Asked if he was wearing one of those invisible-fence collars and had found the finish line. He shrugged and said he'd get zapped if he touched the gas. The he asked if she was "his."

"Almost," she told him, not ready to answer.

So he took her left hand and asked if he could have that instead. She said okay. Then he tapped her knee and asked if it was his, too. "Almost," she said again.

He slipped a hand between her legs, felt a finger slip up to the knuckle in warmth before she squeezed. He thought he was long past "almost," but she pushed him out easily without using her hands. Then she tortured him even more by unzipping his jeans and smiling at the red face peeking out to greet her. It shook, nervous and swollen. She thought it looked a lot like a toddler trying not to sneeze.

All his life, people told Billy he always got what he wanted. And it was mostly true. Billy usually got what he wanted, but he rarely got to keep it. He asked how far she'd go, said they had to hurry before there was another car. She wouldn't answer.

"But tell me this," she asked. "What's really going on with your guy?"

"Who?" For a second, he thought she was talking about the boyfriend with the electric t-shirt.

"Officer Bigfeet. Why do you want to kill a cop so bad?"

"You mean scare a cop so bad."

"Yeah, that."

"I don't know. Because I wasn't ready to tell you those things about me when he pulled us over. Because he just read it *all* to you off my license. I can't explain it. You ever read a story where they list too much stuff too early and you start skimming? That's what happened to us yesterday. And you tuned out."

"Why would you put accurate information on your fake I.D.?"

"It's an art form."

"You're serious," she said, backing off a bit, zipper clinking.

"I'm completely serious."

"Listen, I'm sorry Officer Bigleak spilled the beans and ruined your imagined aura of mystery. But the mystery was kinda solved already."

"No, it's not that I want to remain mysterious. It's you, too. I just don't want to know too much about you. Because I will never forget anything."

"What does that even mean?" She was about a foot away from him now, and he wished he had a chair leg to grab.

"I have a perfect memory, but only with anything that in no way is helpful."

"I'm lost."

No kidding, he thought.

He tried to pull her close again, but a car was coming. He looked to the rear-view mirror at the approaching headlights, wincing as he tried to stretch a leg out for the gas pedal. He tried to shift his body quickly enough to line shit up for her hands again, but much like the architectural limitations of the museum that housed the *Santa Maria*, one of the worst disappointments of his childhood, he found his favorite stone-washed jeans painfully relegating him to half-mast.

"You're more dangerous than you know," he told her. "And I'm gonna prove it right now. I'm going to remind you of something that's gonna freak you the fuck out."

"Go ahead and try."

"Remember when you were a baby, and you got your teeth. Then those teeth fell out and bigger teeth came in? Does anyone realize how goddamn strange that is? You're an animal. We're animals. Our childhood was motherfucking Shark Week."

She got a little closer at that, but not close enough. He wanted her more than he wanted those headlights to stop growing. She sighed and zipped him back up, and he put his wrist to his ear, listening for a pulse or the tic of extra time to convince her.

His watch had stopped, but there was no doubt about it. His biological cock was ticking.

Then a big beep ruined everything.

The next day they were together, when they were trying to get Bigbeep's attention, Billy's car horn got stuck. They didn't know it yet, but it would stay on for days.

A horn is an imperfect weapon.

This new development meant three things. First, angry looks from other cars. Second, they couldn't get that close when they were following their cop. And third, they had to talk to each other that much louder.

This was particularly risky in a new relationship. But luckily, they got so used to the noise that they stopped hearing the horn completely. Or at least he did. He was used to horns.

Billy was still convinced they were meant for each other, mostly because it only took her about an hour and a half to successfully ignore this horrible sound coming from under his hood. In fact, neither seemed to be noticing the horns on other cars either. Billy hoped that books would be written someday to theorize how much this sound may have affected their reasoning, especially when things got real bad down the road. He wasn't entirely convinced that the sounds of horns hadn't just become more feeble out on the highway.

It may have worked out if it wasn't for the fact that talking just that little bit louder didn't really suit Billy's voice at all. Never mind that she was ignoring him, as well as the horn. Billy's voice was kinda high already, even without any obstacles. And just like that, she was done.

A sweaty, young couple is having sex as they drive, having finally found a stretch of Bardstown Road without any streetlights, far outside the usual weekender mayhem. The girl, small, olive-skinned, is on top of the driver, arching back to grip the steering wheel behind her. She's seen this in the movies and knows it's what she's supposed to do, hopes it's what he's always wanted her to do. The boy, smaller, homemade tattoo lashes and scratches on his arms, is navigating the roads well in spite of the obstacles. Until he starts messing with the stereo, and this turns out to be one thing too many for his brain and body to process simultaneously. His foot draws pressure off the accelerator as they slow, slow, slow, then quickly speed back up. Over and over. Slow, slow, slow, before he catches his breath and stomps the gas again.

Even though the song hasn't been released yet, somehow they're listening to "Pounding" by The Doves (lately the boy's favorite summer, windows-rolled-down song) but the music is fading completely now, along with the car's momentum.

She sighs, knowing they wouldn't be having this problem if he'd just left Animals *playing instead. It was a typical Pink Floyd concept album, basically just three songs, but none less than ten minutes, plenty of time for a kid his age to hold his concentration and finish.*

But he got sick of the dog song, and they'd gotten into an argument over the album before she'd even begun wrestling with his blue jeans, him shouting something about the "irrational bile towards disco was directly proportional to the inexplicable reverence for '80s music," her wearily explaining that Animals *came out in '73 and was "conceived a decade before she was conceived."*

The difference between this boy and her fiancé was clear to her in this moment. Unlike her betrothed, they always smiled when they argued.

Eventually, he'd admitted to her he just wanted to fuck to the drums in one particular song. He said he'd been saving it for about a week ago, back when that tornado was threatening.

Actually, there was no tornado. Just the idea of a tornado that would never come.

Just like the boy behind the wheel.

Eric met Jacki Ramirez during a thunderstorm, which wasn't quite as impressive as a tornado, but it was good enough for him. The night they met, there was an argument about tornadoes that went on so long, everyone thought there had actually been one.

Jacki and her friend were on the deck of a bar-and-grill near campus called Café 180, waiting for some ribs to finally come out of the smoker when the rain started stinging their faces sideways, turning the smoker into more of a steamer, and everyone had to pile inside. On the TV screen was the frozen image of a Doppler radar, a big red blob over the entire city of Louisville.

"That's not a good sign," Eric laughed, alone at the end of the brass counter, his arm circling his cole slaw like he was back in a prison cafeteria.

Jacki's friend smiled politely, but kept lingering near the door, waiting for a chance to run and get her car. They both taught at the nearby University of Louisville, and their lunch hour was two hours old. But Jacki took his bait.

"What's not a good sign?" she asked him. "The Doppelgänger Radar? I've seen bigger weather amoebas than that on maps before."

"Not the radar. The television. It's set to the wrong aspect ratio. Why am I trusting these assholes with my food if they don't understand people's heads shouldn't be stretched out to look like footballs?"

Jacki laughed and looked up at the weatherman's elongated, Cro-Magnon skull.

"I like his head stretched out like that," she shrugged. "Makes him look smarter than he did anyway."

Eric scoffed, then took a big bite of slaw, chewing way longer than he needed to.

"Look at you savoring that food," Jacki said. "Who are you kidding? You love this place."

"Ha. Yeah, right. Duct tape on the seats, busted hookah rentals for dumb-ass kids, breakfast burritos as big as sleeping bags? The whole joint smaller than a railway car, meth-addict waitress sleeping against a wall, cranberries in the coleslaw, the only dry-rub ribs anywhere in ten blocks, what's not to love?"

"You seemed conflicted with that list," Jacki smirked, then leaned out the door again. The rain had let up. "Let's make a run for it!"

Her friend's eyes widened at the tornado siren revving up in the distance. She wasn't running anywhere soon. She looked at Eric, then back at Jacki. She wasn't having it. The new friends, impulsive plans, none of it.

"Come on," Jacki gave her a playful shove. "I doubt tornadoes even exist."

"What?!" Three other patrons turned to chime in.

"It's always just wind and rain," Jacki said. "No one ever sees the damn things."

"Naw, you just don't see them in the city, or on streets named after a city. Hollywood Boulevard in Kentucky, for *example? No tornadoes. Pennsylvania Avenue, California? Made of tornadoes."*

The scrawny waitress got involved at this point, face twitching around a speech she was dying to give.

"Well, my grandpa got killed by one, so I'm pretty sure they exist. So maybe you should…"

"Maybe it was just a storm," Jacki bravely went on, and Eric put down his plastic fork.

"Excuse me?" the waitress was livid.

"She's just messing with you, baby," Eric offered. "How about those ribs?"

"We put all the meat away," the waitress said, still staring at Jacki. "We hadn't had a paying customer for an hour, so the owner told us to start closing."

"Bullshit!" a sleeveless guy near the door shouted. "You took my order!"

"Yeah!" a shirtless guy agreed with him. "I earned my ribs! I helped you set the tables, didn't I?"

The tornado siren got louder, and now there was a mob near the door, watching the sky. Eric stood up.

"Fuck it, I'm going to Crazy Mark's Feed Store."

"Nah, fuck that. It ain't as good as the L.A.P.D. Smokehouse, ain't as good as here even, and it's weird."

"Weird how?"

"Like people at other tables think it's okay to talk to everybody? Every time I go, some asshole five tables away starts debating where I should go for ice cream afterwards. If I wanted to talk to strangers… uh, I'd do it."

"I ain't good with sirens. I ain't good with sirens!" A large woman was repeating.

"L.A.P.D. Smokehouse, huh?" someone mused. "I'll have to try that some day."

"How come Kentucky Road isn't used to tornadoes yet?" Jacki scoffed. "I thought around here they were just another form of public transportation."

Jacki's friend stared at her like she'd never met her before. In fact, even though they shared an office on campus, their friendship would end that weekend.

"No such thing," Jacki said again, grabbing a stool.

"Are you kidding me?!" someone else was angry now, too. "Can't you hear the sirens, Miss?"

"Yes, yes, I hear them. But I'm just saying no one ever sees tornadoes. How come they don't cruise down the street in the big cities? Huh? Okay, be honest, who here has ever seen a tornado with their own two eyes?"

About five people raised their hands. The waitress put up both of hers. Eric was already in love.

"Besides you," he said to himself.

"Forget it," she said.

"I ain't good with sirens!" the woman yelled.

"Whoa, you know what I wish?" Eric offered, trying to calm everyone down, actually spinning the waitress' shoulders, who was about two steps from making a grab for Jacki. "I wish these were Toronado sirens instead. You know, to alert us that a sweet, big-ass car was gonna come cruising by any second."

He got half a laugh from someone near the jukebox, but he still felt like a hero because everyone was back to looking at the sky instead of Jacki. He clinked his plate down next to hers, and now she was close enough to him to look down at his half-eaten food like it was her own. She liked this intimacy and counted the cracked pepper and cranberries still in his slaw until she finally spoke again.

"Sorry about that. It's just all those 'people stuck in a diner' apocalypse movies you always see. You know, all the dumber ones near the door, hootin' and hollerin' about sirens and crap? Strangers are always waaaay too excited about storms. I've heard about five sirens since I started at U of L, but I haven't seen a tornado yet. Like ghost skunks on the highway."

"Ha!"

77

"I think that siren is a signal for something else no one knows about..."

"I ain't good with sirens," Eric whispered, giggling, but the large woman heard him. Luckily, she just agreed.

"Me neither!"

"You know what else they always do in those movies?" he asked. "When they only got a few minutes to live?"

Jacki and Eric talked awhile, taking advantage of some alone time while Jacki's friend was cornered by a man with a sombrero trying to explain key scenes from a "little-known cult film called Ghostbusters." He seemed surprised anyone else had heard of it, even more surprised they insisted it was called Ghost Skunk Busters. But when the man was brave enough to pull down the sides of his hat and run for his car, Jacki's friend was helicoptering again and eventually succeeded in pulling Jacki out the door.

"You should wait," Eric said. "Rain's gonna stop any second." Then came the challenge. "But you probably won't."

"Let's go," the friend said, annoyed with all the games, and they ran, hitting a wall of water about as thick and heavy as the octopus strips in a car wash. They made it about ten feet and had to run back inside. But the sun broke through before the water stopped dripping off their noses, and everybody laughed.

"Told ya."

"Why didn't you try harder to stop us!" Jacki said, playfully punching him in the shoulder, really looking at him for the first time. He was a good-looking kid. Average in every way, but this was kind of reassuring. That's when Eric said some words that didn't make her fall in love or anything, but got her interested enough to cheat on her future husband:

"I'm so good at predicting human nature that I should be made an honorary human being!"

Her friend left without her.

When she saw what kind of car he drove, the sirens were still climbing in the distance. He didn't get her door, but she

78

*made up her mind right there on the spot she'd do it, even
before they made their plans.*

Fast forward a week, and Eric's right about the song. It
does have the drums that are perfect for an end-of-the-
world moment like this. But the song is too short, and he's
already started it over twice. He reaches out to hit the rewind
arrow again, hoping to remember more about how they
met, stretching around her long, dark torso with some effort,
getting ready to tell her all excited that he can smell a ghost
skunk out there somewhere, too, and that's when he takes his
eyes off the road.

Suddenly the tires are squealing, and Jacki's screaming,
and two sticky, sweat-covered hands grab the dashboard
for balance, accidentally turning the music up so loud the
speakers crackle.

Then the ass end of the car gets loose of the road. And
when Jacki comes down off the steering wheel and headfirst
into the passenger's seat, her body steers the car so hard off the
pavement that it starts to roll.

And it keeps rolling. And now Jacki is sitting behind the
steering wheel and Eric is flying over that wheel and leaving
the car forever, limp and flailing like a broken rubber band
over a child's thumb. His jeans, still bunched around his
ankles and trailing behind him, flutter in the wind like
an outboard motor, stuck on the bottom row of safety-glass
canines he's left behind.

Then the car stops rolling, upended in a ditch, and Jacki,
bloody and dazed, pinned to the driver's seat by the crumbled
dashboard, stares out past Eric's clothes and the gaping hole
in the windshield, straining to reach his bare feet high above
the car. She blinks at his body, confused, wondering how long
he'll be flying. Then her vision starts to fade, and she focuses
on his toes, still visible in the dark, wiggling fifty feet in mid-

air, as she listens to his song one more time before she passes out.

He never comes down.

Later. The hissing wreck glows red from the tail lights, one cracked headlamp flickering a rescue beacon up into the trees. Enough time has passed for the song to change from "12" back to "1" again, even play the hidden track, but the music is strangled, popping out of the blown speakers like cooking oil chasing sausage around a pan.

The sizzle of the music makes this crash seem like an inferno from a distance, so the long shadow of a man and his dog approaches cautiously along the side of the road. The dog, a large blue Doberman, pulls on its leash to pick up the pace, but the man holds tight. His face is hidden under a baseball cap, and he reaches up to scratch the back of his head, the mesh of the cap revealing a rat's nest of unwashed gray.

Seeing no flames, the man ties his dog to a nearby tree, and the Dobie immediately starts scratching the bark to climb it. The man squints up into the dark to see what his dog wants so bad, then the animal is distracted by a nearby strip of bloody blue jeans and works on subduing that instead.

The man walks to the front of the car and cradles the headlamp in two hands, careful with the trailing optic nerve, and aims the beam of light up over his dog's muscular shoulders into the tree, spotlight on the bloody, naked boy twisting in the lower limbs.

The body is bent into impossible shapes, back arched, head looking way too far behind him, one eye open, mouthful of leaves, arms and legs higher than the rest, seemingly swimming for the sky with every gust of wind.

The man watches his dog rip a chunk of blue jeans from the jagged windshield and shake it into submission, and the man scratches the bobbed ears affectionately. Then he looks back to the car and finally notices the girl.

She's slumped over the steering wheel, unconscious but still breathing. The man looks up and down the road again, then takes the steering wheel in both hands and begins to pull. Already damaged, it breaks free in his hands, and the girl sags forward into his arms. He turns his ball cap around, all business now, and he carries her as carefully as a bride, away from the wreckage and down into the ditch, cattails parting for them like a beaded curtain. He gently lays her in the high grass and weeds, then wipes the black hair from her face. Seeing her so close, illuminated in red, he freezes, and his movements change, his curiosity about the crash transforming into something else.

Then the blue Doberman starts barking, noticing the dead boy above them all over again, and there is a hiss of anger from the shadow in the ditch as he tries to quiet everything.

"Shhhhh..."

At this, the pointed ears spring up like antennas, and the dog stares at the dark shapes until its master bends down so far he disappears into the ground completely. The dog whimpers, then cocks its head, ears practically spinning now as the shrieking ambulance siren approaches too late to help anyone.

When the horn finally stopped, or when they just stopped hearing it, Bully was still around, but things were different. So Billy stepped up the planning, desperate to keep her interested.

For reconnaissance, Billy and Bully rented every movie they could find with a collar bomb in it. They hoped this would be the quickest way to learn how to build one. Or, at the very least, build something that might *look* like one.

The first videotape they brought home was *Wedlock* a.k.a. *Deadlock,* starring that melancholy, bleach-blonde bad guy Bully loved so much in *Blade Runner*, a film that had been ripped on by critics for its clichéd, monotone voiceover narration, something Bully was completely unaffected by while watching it from a bedroom window from a mile away.

But fast-forwarding through this flick, they quickly realized its collar bombs just looked like typical, plastic sci-fi props. Sure it would be easy to build one, but such a device would convince no one outside of the universe of shitty science-fiction films it was dangerous.

Next, they checked out *Battle Royale 9: Royale with Cheese*, which popped a neck bomb early on. But all the kids screaming their heads off (figuratively) drove Bully nuts. She couldn't stand that much mayhem while trying to read subtitles, so they ended up skipping to the end. If there were more neck bombs in the middle, they missed them.

Then came *Wild Wild Wild Wild Wild West*, the show from the movie from the show, which, in addition to them deciding it was "real fuckin' dumb," turned out to be false advertising by the clerk. It had actors running around corn fields with devious devices that were more like neck magnets than neck bombs, and Bully couldn't help but talk shit on Will Smith the whole time anyway. To harass her, Billy constantly grabbed the remote control, her shoe, a stray potato chip, even his own testicles, going through a future Fresh Prince's best catchphrase possibilities, like his endorsement deal for the T-Qualizer, "I have *got* to get me one of these tees!" Then maybe squeezing his balls until they turned blue with a resounding, "Welcome to Smurf!" A secret fan of the Smith clan and all their timeless progeny, he'd done this dance before, and it worked better after a shower.

And they had to slap in *Saw XVII*, of course, a series that had run so long, much like *Battle Royale with Cheese* or the *W.W.W.W.W West* movies, it felt like they'd zipped around the sun, stretching out like taffy, both backwards and forwards in time and messing up the chronological order of all sequels and spin-offs forever. They weren't out yet, but Billy was convinced he saw the last of the *Saws* when he was 2 years old, which had to be the '70s, he was sure of it. And he'd be just as convinced he'd see the first one when he was 50. Which was worse than just remembering all 50 of those films.

Billy didn't have the vocabulary yet to define it, but eventually he'd learn what an "anachronism" was just in time to realize there was no such thing, kind of like when he scoffed his way through his first book on Bigfoot. Kind of like when he snickered his way through his first court transcripts by Officer Bigbeep. There was nothing wrong with his recollection and never would be.

Music, movies, and books followed you forward and back. Time was broken when it came to media objects. Occasionally, time could break when it came to music. But time would always be broken when it came to movies.

Fuck books, though, Billy thought. *Especially ones on Bigfoot.*

So, maybe he'd seen *Saw* before, maybe he hadn't. But he knew three things for certain. First, the movie was terrible. Second, this movie had traveled forward or backward in time to give him a gift. And third, that the best gift of all was a simple, practical design for a neck bomb that they could duplicate quickly and trigger easily with any spring-loaded mechanism.

A ring of shotgun shells around the neck.

For the first time, they were quoting *Young Frankenstein* with a high-five and a manic, excitable, "This… could… work!" A couple trips to the corner store for ammo and mouse traps and their brains really started cooking. But they weren't ready yet. Something was still missing.

"More movies!" they cried.

They tried *Escape from New York* since Bully's brother had promised there were some collar bombs buried somewhere in there. *And* some Kurt Russell. This turned out to be a bit of a stretch. The movie didn't really have a collar bomb at all, just these two, tiny, more-hypothetical-than-"microscopic" neck-bomb injections. And the movie forgot about those bombs, too, just like Billy and Bully did. It was like the movie equivalent of a dog's electric fence collar. Unless it zaps, you forget it exists. Not that they weren't into the movie. It had just hit the video stores that Tuesday, and full-size cardboard cut-outs of Snake Plissken were hard to avoid eye contact with, let alone the real-life, eye-patch-wearing imitators at the skate park. In fact, Bully swore she would backhand the next kid she saw in a sleeveless shirt and camo pants (like the punk that rented them these movies actually). She claimed the only thing stopping her from doing this was that she didn't want to risk *actually* putting out some kid's eye and making some fanboy's wet dream come true.

Then they watched *Wanted Dead or Alive,* another one of her brother's suggestions, starring that asshole "guitarist" from Kiss ("Worst guitar player ever," Billy's dad said once. "But not half as bad as the drummer."), and Billy had to groan when he realized it was Bully's favorite bleach-blonde madman from *Blade Runner* playing a hero this time around. Then they both groaned even louder when the "bomb" turned out to be just a grenade the hero jammed in Gene Simmons' ample mouth. "Well, at least his head blew up," they shrugged.

So, gun shy, they went down her brother's list to the next recommendation, *Runaway.* And that's when they realized her brother just had a hard-on for shitty movies starring the asshole from KISS. Plus, to add insult to injury, during the wobbly climax, Simmons' head got injected by all these robot spiders, and for a second the music was winding up and convincing Billy and Bully that he was gonna pop, but then... nothing. She saved a special backhand for her brother after that.

Next was *The Fury*, which was a total bust. They waited till the end when the music was gearing up for the bad guy to burst, as always, and, oddly enough, everything *but* the man's head exploded. It spun around in slow-motion for about a minute to some classical tune, then credits.

Discouraged after wasting so much time, and especially by the off-camera head smashing disappointment of the original version of *The Fly*, (*Return of the Fly,* and *Curse of the Fly* completed the triple feature at The Spotlight Kid drive-in, reflecting off Bully's bedroom window the following weekend), they decided they didn't need to find depictions in movies where a collar actually blew up someone's dome, and they settled for renting any movie they could find where a cranium suffered massive trauma for any reason at all.

Scanners finally made an appearance for posterity. Then *Deadly Friend,* where they couldn't believe the pirate bitch from *The Goonies* got her head knocked off by something as soft as a basketball. Then *The Beyond* with its head twisted off like a piece of taffy, *Chopping Mall* with its clunky robot mall cops and their unlikely head-bursting lasers, *Dawn of the Dead* with the trusty shotgun through the afro, and even those three Nazi stooges at the end of *Raiders of the Lost Ark*, whose rubber heads deflated, melted, and detonated, in that order, and didn't help our heroes in the least.

Bully was licking another envelope addressed to "Officer Bigweek," when Billy noticed her tongue was hanging lower than the last seven times she did this.

"What's wrong?"

"Maybe we should prank call him, along with the postal onslaught."

"There's the bomb."

"Besides the bomb."

"Like what? Like order a pizza? That's the oldest trick in the book."

She didn't get the joke, and his heart sank. It had been sinking a lot lately.

"I don't know," she spit. "It's not you. I think it's just Bigsqueak. He's such a one-dimensional villain. I can't get engaged."

"You mean 'enraged.' We're already engaged, remember?" he laughed.

"I just wish he was the one cop in the world that you *didn't* hate. It would make this more interesting. It would make him special. Me, too."

"Who are you?"

"Forget it."

"Do I scare you?"

"No," she scoffed. "It's like someone's writing about us, but they're being kinda lazy. We need one good cop to make the other cop seem bad. Like in the movies. It balances everything out, get it?"

"Getting sick of the movies."

That night, because they had to, Billy and Bully finally ran into their favorite bumbling bear of a cop out in the world, outside his cruiser. It was inevitable with so many trips to the video store. Forget about the doughnuts, Billy told her. A video store is a cop's best friend. A veritable second home by the sea.

The cop was standing behind them, trying to hide the title *Doppelwängers* from everybody (they'd try to translate that porn name later, "Cocks that have faces just like their owners?"), but suddenly very interested in what was happening at the counter. Shoving everyone in line aside, he intercepted a particularly floppy dollar Bully had just handed to the video store clerk. He'd watched it leave her hand with interest, and now it seemed he was doing some quick math to get the dollar back with his change. This spooked Bully bad. They were close enough to smell him. They expected old pizza, but it was more like rotten oranges.

Billy leaned in and noticed Bigbeep signing the name "Angela." He tried to point this out to Bully, then asked what the big deal was about the money. The cop suddenly turned around, annoyed, before she could answer.

"Did you two know that the life expectancy of a single dollar bill is one year?" he snarled, not recognizing either of them as a threat.

They did not.

"Did you ever wonder about that delivery guy? The one in the road?"

"The one with the neck bomb and the confetti? Hell, yeah. Like what he was doing, how he got involved, whether or not he was in on the robbery." She leaned forward, almost tipping the pizza box. "That's what he did, right? Robbed a bank?"

"No, no, no," Billy interrupted. "I'm talking about the most important detail that has yet to occur to anyone."

"Which is?" Bully asked.

'Which is what was on the pizza that man was delivering."

"Uh..."

"Think about it," he went on. "Whether he was in on the crime or not, someone had to call and order the pizza. According to the chatter on your brother's police scanner, supposedly someone calls in, puts a bomb on the pizza guy at gunpoint, or 'bombpoint,' and then forces him to rob a bank. But what kind of pizza did they order? Did they order one at all? Maybe the pizza guy slapped one together and just so happened to put on a combination of ingredients that have only been ordered once, by one man, ever in the history of pizza. Or a variety of ingredients that were desperately random, suggesting there was never any phone call? See what I'm saying? Maybe the pizza is the key."

"I feel ya. In fact, this is what I think is happening at this exact moment. Our main man, Bigbeep, is trying to reconstruct the pizza the man was delivering that day. It is his only solid clue. That's why he took that slice with him."

"Heck, yeah! How many ingredient combos could there be? Maybe we crack the case right fucking now."

"Well, there's a ton actually."

"Come on, a pizza is a pizza," he said.

"I'm telling you, you'd be surprised."

"There's what? Pepperoni, mushrooms, olives..."

"Pepperoni, mushrooms, black olives, green olives, Kalamata olives, sausage, green peppers, ham, anchovies, bacon, chicken, spinach, onions, broccoli, ricotta, mozzarella, asiago, parmesan, shrimp, tomatoes, alfredo sauce, artichoke hearts, garlic, jalapeños, feta cheese, goat cheese, ground beef, grapes and gorgonzola, curry, yogurt sauce with green onions, hot dogs, tandoori chicken, pineapple, mango, raw potatoes..."

"There's no fuckin' potato pizza."

"...cream cheese, eggplant, salami, arugula, truffles, balsamic soaked figs, prosciutto, sauerkraut, sage leaves, capers and horse, mint mushroom, kale, head cheese, venison, rooster sauce, cilantro, squid, the most common in Japan, and, oh, yeah, ghost peppers, how terrifying is that name?" By the time she got to the end of her list, the pizza slice Billy had been holding was wilted.

"How did you do that?" he asked her, awestruck.

"Well, I used to..."

"Be a cook?"

"No, I used to..."

"Deliver pizzas!"

"No. I used to edit rap dictionaries."

"I was gonna say that next, I swear."

"Rapping about pizza is very popular in the hip-hop community. Believe it or not, there's a rhyme for every ingredient on a pizza."

"Prove it," he said, arms crossed.

"'I wanted extra anchovies, not extra gorgonzola. Pussy so hairy she looked like the Ayatollah. Pizza party, pizza party, pizza pizza, party party.' Bam."

"You win. Hold on, that didn't make any sense."

"Just hand me another piece."

"Piece of the pizza or piece of the bomb?"

"Can we really just continue to do this? You know, without doing it?"

"What do you mean?"

"Pretending to do it. It's fun to go as far as we can, see how close we get to the crime without the crime, but…"

"We'll see. Maybe we're like any movie with a pregnant woman in it," Billy said, "They always go off, no matter what they do."

"You never saw *Fargo*, did you?"

"Nope, too long of a drive." He flipped the limp end of the pizza into his mouth and talked around the bite.

"Rapping dictionaries, huh? No wonder you keep changing Bigbeep's name every six seconds. Make any money at it?"

"A little. That's about all you can get with an MFA, like editing, transcription stuff, some ghost writing."

"Ghost writing! That sounds scarier than ghost peppers. Why didn't you do that?"

"Tried it. Got assigned a biography of a local politician. Problem was he was a religious man."

"Why was that a problem?"

"I never thought I was dyslexic, but I couldn't seem to type the word 'God.'"

"Let me guess, you typed 'dog' instead."

"No, I kept typing 'sog,' 'bog,' 'scrod,' sometimes 'jihad.'"

"Odd."

"Yeah, that, too."

Pizza, rap music, and faith in dogs. Billy would have to write this all down once he replaced his watch battery. These three things were catnip to her, and he thought maybe there was still a chance.

Then the last piece of the puzzle hit them, the light bulb over the head, the elevator ding of inspiration, right around when they'd run out of exploding heads and started resorting to animal explosions in Peckinpah westerns filmed before the ASPCA came to Hollywood. Once they saw *Pat Garrett and Billy the Kid* sharpshooting the heads off those chickens in the opening credits, it was all over.

Yes, *actually* shooting the heads off chickens.

They had their solution. They would stop suspending disbelief. They would stop trying to make it real. They no longer needed to look for answers and inspiration in the imagined technology or prosthetics of a fictional storyline. From now on, they wouldn't creep closer and closer to the Chronocolor TV screen in Bully's basement to try and decipher exactly what special effects wizardry had been used to rupture a dummy filled with sheep entrails or whatnot. They'd only need to go frame by frame on the poor Gila Monster in *The Ballad of Cable Hogue* until they captured a real-life murderer.

Even without their cold noses against the glass, they started to see it:

A tiny spark. A tongue of smoke. Small explosive charges in key points around the fur, feathers, or scales. Angled inward around their throats. And they began to realize this kind of down-and-dirty, basement technology was much simpler than the elegant fiction of most films. And then, also inspired by his old driver's license where he was still wearing that ridiculous shark tooth necklace, and, hell, they'd admit it, even inspired by a preview for *Saw XVIII*, inexplicably shown at the beginning of *Saw XXX*, they settled on a simple, practical design that could quickly duplicate the realism they were looking for: a ring of shotgun shells around an animal's neck, waiting to be triggered with any spring-loaded mechanism. A couple trips to the corner store for ammo to go with the rat traps they'd already secured, and they were pretty much done. They attached a couple screws to the bale on those traps for a firing pin and then high-fived and low-fived each other like those clowns in *Top Gun*.

They even rented a couple porn parodies to celebrate, *Top Buns* (bad) and *Top Nuns* (worse). They didn't excite them at all though. Lackluster titles aside, they just didn't believe anything they were seeing.

But Bully was convinced their invention still lacked one final detail to make it their own. So she provided this missing link with one last mad dash to her car, where she ripped the web of turquoise, twine, and feathers from her rear-view mirror (a birthday gift from Billy, actually) in order to give their collar bomb of eight shotgun shells and rat traps a little more finesse. It was a bit more unwieldy when construction was done, but they were satisfied it looked like the kind of thing you wouldn't want to wake up wearing. Maybe the last thing you'd want to discover on your dog.

As they crouched in the red glow of Bully's taillights, Billy gently draped the finished contraption around his own neck, smiling and pretending to arm one of the traps with a click.

"Does this mean we're enraged?" he asked her, trying not to betray the squirt of acid reflux on his tongue, still green from the mouthwash he chugged on the way over to prepare for any potential smooching. He didn't want to forget about the man who'd spit on him at the

91

intersection, and that great, green yawn he'd passed on to Billy like a gift.

"More like 'engaged,'" she said, then reached up to flick a stray feather nestled behind his ear. He sucked in a breath and vowed to steal every dreamcatcher at every gas station for her and pluck those spider webs like chickens. Then he wondered what spiders had to do with a talisman that supposedly soothed you to sleep.

"Hey, sorry we had to trash your dreamcatcher, baby," Bully purred.

"Fuck it. It never worked anyway."

"And now it will do exactly the opposite, if you think about it," she laughed.

Billy still may have thought he was just going to scare the police officer. But now Bully was hoping they wouldn't stop until they blew that goddamn dog's head sky high.

III.

A Boy with an Unfortunate Tattoo Finds Himself –
Pondering a Dog, Napping – Making Movies on Vacation
(They Don't Know What It Means) – Nine Minutes of
Battery Left Can Lead Us – To a Pinocchio Situation –
Dogs Playing Poker – Little Boy Blue and the Supermoon
Will Tell You – You Can't Make a Head Breakfast without
Breaking Some Eggs – The Falcon Hears the Falconer
Yawning – Catching Bubble – The Ghost of Jim Toad –
Shock Collar

"Didn't take too long 'fore I found out
What people mean by down and out"
-Led Zeppelin "Black Dog"

Larry sat in his car, trying to cool down. He stared at his bloody knuckles as he listened to his tape player struggling to turn the eerie synthesizers of Thomas Dolby's "Windpower" into the lonesome echoes that opened "One of Our Submarines."

"...missing, missing, missing, missing, missing, missing..."

He adjusted his rear-view mirror to watch a neighborhood girl pacing her front lawn in despair. He was confident she had no idea there was a pornographic film being made on her street. But he thought it was likely that she noticed all the film equipment being carried inside, and was trying to get a bit of attention, just in case.

"...a hungry heart... to regulate their breathing..."

Well, he thought that initially. Then he realized she was talking on a cordless phone bigger than Stevey's, tucked up under her pink sweatshirt hood as best she could, frantic hand actions telling Larry she was dealing with a situation where she truly needed somebody's help. Probably waiting on a ride, by the way she stared up and down the street.

But this girl had the look he could spot from a mile away. An attractive girl with a phone pressed against her ear while a crisis unfolded around her, no ink on either arm? It was on his checklist of characteristics for recruitment. She'd be equally vulnerable for a movie or a relationship.

The tragedy was that, until recently, if Larry were to notice a tattoo on the arm of a girl next door like this one, he would normally see dollar signs instead, because, ironically, just as a tattoo artist knew a naked arm would be more likely to be connected to a tough sell, Larry knew pristine skin was the most difficult to talk into getting in front of that camera.

He hated how much he'd grown to detest them. He used to stick up for tattoos. One day, when some asshole walked onto the set and loudly declared tattoos were, "The self-inflicted permanent stamp of the proletariat," he got a temporary stomp from Larry that begat a permanent limp, courtesy of Head Breakfast.

This Girl Next Door was a little short, though (probably too short for decent lighting actually), and he was reminded of his unfortunate detour into dwarf porn. It turned out there was no good reason to ever use a "little person" because their torsos were the same as any normal-sized person. This meant they looked exactly the same in anything other than the widest shots. And who the hell wants wide shots in adult films? David Lean? He remembered long, drunken debates with Damon and how he wished their torsos were the freaky small part of their bodies, how their limbs should be normal length instead ("Then those little Rumpelstiltskins would be spinning gold!"). Larry tried to picture such a creature coupling and silently thanked evolution for denying the world these imps and "The Damon's" "human spider porn" fantasy.

He rubbed the remnants of Joe Fuck's nosebleed onto his steering wheel, peering close under his skin at the black blood that had stained his hand forever. Back before high school graduation, before film school sunk him into debt, before his short-lived (but long story) adventures in the United Kingdom had him boomeranging back to the

United States, he'd landed a temporary job on an assembly line making door hinges. And in this factory, Larry would accidentally pinch some part of his body in his vise at least once a week. On his very first day, he pinched the top of his hand so many times that he tried adjusting every angle of his routine when he directed the teeth to crush and curve the metal plates. But this only made it worse. This caused the vise to pinch him harder out of spite, five times in as many hours, so hard that the blood under his skin never dissolved back into the dermis. Just like the pencil dot on his knuckles that would apparently follow him from Kindergarten to his grave, this crisscross of pinches had permanently tattooed his hand with his body's own ink. These marks might not have been noticeable if it hadn't been for the pattern they'd formed, quite accidentally.

A swastika. Right below his knuckles. The first thing anyone would see if or when they shook his hand. Even worse, the quadruple blood blisters made a *terrible* swastika, and Larry worried that people wouldn't just dismiss him as a racist, but a moron to boot.

His experiences with this symbol drew him to the song "A Boy Named Sue," but he imagined Johnny Cash singing about "A Boy with an Unfortunate Tattoo" instead. Growing up in Southfield, Michigan, close enough to pretend he was from Detroit, Larry liked to think the clusterfuck of markings on his hand forced him to become a little bit tougher. At least until the beatings got real bad. That's when he wised up and tried to get rid of the swastika, borrowing some lotion a secret-cutter ex-girlfriend used on the fake suicide scars across her wrists. He remembered her saying pregnant women used it to get rid of stretch marks on their bellies. But it did nothing for either of them. So, tired as he was of all the leather gloves he wore in the summertime and the drag races the gloves would provoke at every red traffic light, he attempted his own homemade tattoo removal. With a cheese grater.

And it worked. But his hand still itched, even worse than everything else, something that made him suspect a swastika was still buried under there, another sneaky quadruple blood blister, still furious from all those fucking pinches, waiting to seep almost-but-not-quite to the surface to brand him again. For years, the threat of it made Larry afraid to scratch hard enough to satisfy his itching.

"...*missing, missing, missing, missing, missing, missing...*"

Larry knew that with the repetition in this song, his tape player would be eating Mr. Dolby shortly. So he was surprised when his stereo died a quiet death that afternoon without even a last meal. It just sighed once, twice, then a plastic rattle came from deep in the dashboard, like a fan blade slowing on a fingertip.

It was done. Larry closed his eyes. He only had a factory stereo, A.M. no less, and finding anything worth listening to on the dial was close to impossible. He hated A.M. radio, not just because he met an A.M. disc jockey once when he was a little kid, the DJ running his mouth at the bus stop trying to cash in on his minor celebrity, getting in everyone's face with his all-nighter power-drink breath smelling vaguely of an aluminum asshole. Larry chugged Red Bullet himself, when he was just starting porn and pulling all-nighters, but this was due to mishearing their radio spot as "It gives you things!" He cut himself off after the spin-off drink "Red Belly," though, which ended up staining kids' feces bright red and necessitated five more name changes in as many years.

No, A.M. radio was just too muffled to use the static between stations for a game kind of like "hot and cold" (maybe more like Marco Polo actually), where you zeroed in on bursts of music to find your way out of dead spots on the road or the minefield of talk radio. With the A.M. band, you just had dead air and a strange huffing, something like blowing into a baseball glove, when you spun past the stations too fast.

He played with the dials, frowning when he heard another voice that seemed to be speaking directly to him. He started to narrow it down and decipher this voice, but then people were hopping up and down in his rearview mirror, waving Larry into the house. He looked past them for the girl in the pink hoodie, but she was gone. He rubbed the rest of his actor's blood into his jeans, fighting the unbearable urge to scratch his elbows and those scaly, assistant-professor patches of dead skin, now finally tenured and ripe enough to rip free from his arms forever.

Instead he covered his yawn with the old scars on the back of his hand and went back to work.

"Work, my ass. You never had a job."

"I swear I did. See this sunshine? When I first started working up there, the people coming down the hill off the previous shift would drive by trying to wave at me. At least that's what I heard they were doing, because I couldn't see shit through the glare of the sun. It's always in your face on this hill. And because I was blinded, I never waved back. So they all hated me. They thought I was trading their smiles or pleasant nods with this nasty look. You know that squinty face you make when the glare is the worst? Come on."

"I think you thought about it way more than they did," Bully yawned.

"Yawning, too! Did you know direct sunlight makes you yawn? But even on the cloudy days, I'd sometimes yawn at them, and they'd catch my yawn and yawn at the car behind me, who would catch *that* yawn and yawn at the next car in line. I swear I tossed yawns like beach balls at a concert right here on this hill. There's probably still a yawn hanging here. See?!"

Billy put his finger in her gaping mouth.

"That was my yawn from three fucking years ago! Got ya!" She tried to bite it but missed.

"Anyhow, this *is* a job," he told her, pulling down the car's visor.

Billy and Bully cruised behind a supermarket at the top of an industrial park. Idling in a cul-de-sac in the distance, they could just barely make out the "K-9" on the back of a police car. They'd spent most of the day with their favorite cop in the world, never letting him out of their sight for long. At least his car anyway.

Billy turned down his Billy Squier mix, even though he'd been waiting for the perfect time to serve up the guitar opening of "Lonely is the Night." Hopefully, he could time the drums from "The Big Beat" instead.

"Look at that motherfucker. Ever read their user manual? *To Protect and Serve Man*? It's a cookbook!"

"I don't get it."

Silence for awhile. Bully practiced thinking about John Carpenter movies rather than talking about them. She thought about an alternate future where John Carpenter's remake of *The Thing* is so popular that upstart Stephen Spielberg's labor of love, *E.T.,* is considered the biggest flop of the '80s. Carpenter's *The Thing* is so good, it negates arguments for and against remakes all at once, since the world could finally imagine how unnecessary a third *Thing,* the inevitable remake of Howard Hawk's remake, would be. In the future, all of *The Things* are so good that, years after that, Bully will sometimes forget she hid her pornography on a videotape labeled "The Things," and will always be disappointed after she sticks it in. But something about *The Thing* will always make her want to sing. So she will talk instead.

"So…"

"I drove a propane truck for awhile, too," he interrupted her. "You know, the ones with the signs on them saying they could blow up at any moment?"

Bully sighed.

"The weird thing is I never cared," he shrugged. "At least until I saw that movie where they were hauling the dynamite and couldn't hit any bumps. What was that called? *Wages of Fire?*"

"You didn't see that movie. *I* saw that movie. Then I told you about it. *Wages of* Fear."

"No, because seeing that movie made me seek out the remake, *Sorceress…*"

"Oh, my god. I saw that, too, dude. Right out my window. Double feature. One was in French, so I could almost read the whole fucking thing for once. Wait, was it really called *Sorceress*? Because for a movie about a couple of trucks hauling dynamite, that makes no sense at all."

"…and seeing those two movies changed everything about that job. Suddenly, it made sense. It was… wonderful."

Bully stopped yawning and stared at him until they both laughed. He knew she wasn't going to let him get away with saying the word "wonderful" without repercussions. Not on her watch. Not after he forced her to sit through *2010*, believing it would be anywhere near as good as *2001*. Not after he dragged her to that teen holocaust *Some Kind of Wonderful* and she'd slapped him open-handed across the face when the hero wasted his money on stupid earrings.

"You know what we need to give Bigbeep?" she asked after a few minutes.

"What?"

"A motive."

"You think?" He frowned.

"Yeah. He needs one. Me, too, probably."

David James Keaton

"But you have one! We have one. My dog. Your cat. We're gonna strike a blow against vets everywhere."

A few minutes passed.

"What do you think a police dog dreams about?"

"Being bad."

"If a police dog could watch any movie, what would it be?"

"A movie where the dog belongs to the bad guy."

"Yeah, I think so, too."

"You remember the last time I stalked somebody?"

"Yep. That kid who kicked your ass in the ninth grade. You remember how that worked out, right?"

"I told you about that?

"Yep."

"I didn't do shit?'

"Exactly."

"Well, it's not like I'm in a hurry or anything. I looked him up in the phone book, and the cocksucker still lives and works in exactly the same place. He makes it way too easy to stalk. That kills any sense of vengeance."

"I heard he hit you so hard everyone thought you disintegrated?"

"What?! Shut the fuck up. I fell back into some bushes and you couldn't find me for awhile, that's all."

"Someone called 911 reporting a disintegration."

"Stop saying that."

"They were blowing on blades of grass for hours looking for you."

"Obviously, that didn't happen," Billy sighed. Then, "I'd fuck him up now."

"How do you know?"

"Because I was parked outside his house last week, and I watched him throw away his workout equipment. And it was the same chin-up bar I've been using for like eleven years! Get it? Now *that's* a nemesis! Both doing the same exercises for over a decade? We would battle until the end of time…"

"Let's go. He's leaving."

Billy pulled out to give chase in Bully's Mustang, sneaking looks over at her every chance he got. Her wet, blonde hair was suddenly back to black, those dark curls all askew, sour look on her face at all times now. Totally his type after all. She looked like Maggie, actually, not just his first but his worst.

The first time Billy saw Maggie was in math class. She'd just come to their school that morning and already seemed to have a boyfriend. So Billy didn't think twice about her.

The second time he saw Maggie was at one of those underage pool hall hangouts where she was working. Glass City Boardwalk it was called, and she was wearing a black Ted Nugent tour shirt that a teacher had made her turn inside out earlier in the day. It apparently depicted Ted standing on a dead Santa Claus with a shotgun, shouting "Seasons Greetings!" Billy learned this later, when all the kids were squinting at the shadow on her chest of what she was covering up, theorizing on what she'd worn that was so bad. You could see the hints of red, blood or Santa, who knew? But whatever it was, it made the boys stare at her all day, really noticing her for the first time. She fast became the most popular girl in school. At least for that one day.

Then she started talking, and only Billy still followed her around after that. It was the first time he ever called a girl on the phone actually, when he called Maggie. He might have called her a little too much. A typical phone call would go like this:

"I'll stay on the phone with you."

"Why?"

"At least until you get to your car."

"Why?"

"It's common knowledge that more females are attacked when they're distracted and talking on the phone."

"So why don't I hang up and call you when I'm in the car."

"I just told you why! I want to make sure you're safe."

"But…"

"Please, just keep talking to me until you're on the road."

"You're really not kidding are you?"

"Slow down here for a second."

Her voice was high, like a little kid, but she was rude as hell, seemingly belligerent to make up for the high pitch of her vocal cords, and it was tough for people to take. But Billy decided he could take it right after he reached out to shake her hand, and she started thumb-wrestling him instead. He then obsessed about that thumb for a good 48 hours. Wait, this wasn't her Billy was remembering. This was her…

Billy and Bully followed the police car for an hour, staying about six car lengths behind, but getting closer when he would exceed the speed limit like the rest of those slippery badge-wearing motherfuckers they were suddenly seeing *everywhere*. That's when Billy would match speed perfectly just to piss him off.

Bigby was weaving through a residential neighborhood, sometimes slowing to shout out his window, and Billy was excited they might get to see some secret second residence, when Bully punched him hard in the meat of his shoulder to get his attention.

"Slow down here! Pull up next to that house." She cocked a thumb. Oh, how Billy remembered that thumb.

He stopped the car and watched Bigby go. Then he turned to see her tossing something into a random mailbox. She raised the flag. A red flag, of course. He was suddenly seeing those everywhere, too.

"What was that?" he asked.

Instead of answering, she dug through her purse, hands rattling around a stack of audio cassettes.

"What are those for?" he tried again.

"Huh? Oh, I just use 'em to get people to come to Glass City. Like advertising. They let me put a bunch of songs on them and leave them everywhere: bushes, gas pumps, drive-thrus. The name and phone number is on there to get more kids to come. I call 'em Tape Bombs. I drop them all over, and..."

"Yeah, yeah, you said that. You ever drop them into cereal boxes? I'd love to get one for a prize instead of those bullshit stickers."

"I'll do that for ya."

"Wait, where do you drop those tapes again?"

"What are you talking about?"

"I mean, I didn't see you drop a tape just now. That was a piece of paper. Hold on, whose mailbox was that?"

"Nobody's. That paper was just a flyer for movies showing at The Kid. So I can make some extra money. I'm like their papergirl."

Billy drove on, not really convinced. He made a mental note of the next intersection, mapping it so he could come back and retrieve the tape or flyer or whatever and see what was up. But now thinking about a "prize inside," Billy remembered the dream he'd had the night before, the one dream he always had with the red ball rattling inside the tiny skeleton. He'd dreamt about that tiny skeleton at least a dozen times now, never able to get the rubber ball out of the ribcage. Tonight he vowed he'd tell her about if it happened again. He had no idea that everyone in the world hated to hear about other people's dreams.

Later, both their hearts contracted when they thought they were getting pulled over again, but it was just a siren in a song on the radio.

It got them every time.

* * *

Firemen try to untangle the dead boy from the tree while a paramedic strains on his toes to check for signs of life. But the way the boy is arched, his limbs corkscrewed up high and out of reach, both femurs cracked upwards at the pelvis like a doll crammed uncaring into a toy box, there's only one part of the body hanging low enough to reach.

The medic looks up and down the scene, blows a weary raspberry through his lips, then strains up on his toes to squeeze the young man's genitals for a pulse. As he stands there on the ladder, handful of testicles, fingers digging into the big veins at the base of the sack for any sign of a heartbeat, the firemen recoil in horror.

The medic finally lets the balls drop and snaps at the spectators.

"What the fuck is your problem? You, yeah, I'm talking to you," he says to nobody in particular.

"Are you supposed to be here?" someone asks.

Jack Grinstead glares at the firemen one last time, then loads the girl into the back of an ambulance. His partner, Rick, wanders over, wiping his hands to indicate there's no other injury on the scene. They switch places, Jack heading over to the car wreck to peer inside.

"Daaaaamn. Is that really a Toronado?" he asks it.

The speakers still pop and hiss, and the display indicates it's trying to play song number "5" just one more time. Jack backs up and walks to the front of the car, the source of the spotlight on the dead boy. He reaches for a loose headlight and finds a pulse blinking in that instead. He trains it back on the firemen, fighting the urge to shout directions.

"Jack! Come on!" Rick yells, and Jack runs to hop into the back of the ambulance with the girl. After closing the doors, he leans down to study her face, expecting her twitching eyelids to snap open and explain such a bizarre wreck. He reaches for a syringe, but then freezes.

As they drive away from the scene, Jack is framed in the back window of the ambulance, scrubbing the back of his head with both hands as if he's trying to shake loose an idea.

Then he looks directly into the camera, which would have fucked everything up if they weren't already so far away from the car with his crew.

"Take off your fuck faces and put on your cop faces."

Six months before Larry would finally lose it on set and crack the eggs on a Head Breakfast, Larry was standing at the base of a tree at the intersection of Florida Street and Kentucky Road, trying to get his actors into a headspace they weren't used to. The two men were playing the parts of police officers, "Bobby Garcia" and "Joe Stansberries" (one tall, one short), but they were having trouble finding the characters. Without the inevitable sex scene looming, Larry's two moonlighters found themselves with a case of the giggles. They were bullshitting and barely suppressing their amusement as Larry tried to explain how in the next scene, Joe, the shorter cop, would be scanning the trunk of the wrecked car with his flashlight.

"Then you'll say, 'What the hell? A bear chase him up there?'" Larry explained.

Bobby, the big cop, shrugged. He was "Bobby" in real life, too, and he was so big they called him "B.C." sometimes, as in "Before Christ," as in a fucking throwback to the caveman days. Bobby had five long hairs growing straight out of the head of his dick, a horrible detail Larry had discovered late in production and had since made it a point to have a fluffer hit it with the tweezers every time. Tonight, Larry was relieved those five hairs would not be an issue. Cheap and ugly as it was, this was a real movie they were shooting. He was using porn stars, but "No fucking this time!" Okay, they did have that one sex scene

107

David James Keaton

in the car, but it would have been way harder to fake it with a song like "Pounding" coming out of the speakers.

But now it was the part of the movie with all the uniforms milling around, which meant no tattoos. Larry loved it. Disbelief could be suspended indefinitely with a little hint of authority and long sleeves in a movie. And this was all on Damon's dime, though he didn't know it. He didn't even need a script. He was shooting this story from memory.

Larry had been so patient about locations, and holy shit if it didn't pay off with the perfect car wreck, a real car wreck, in the woods for them to frame in the distance. This is why a police scanner was a reasonable expense.

Officer Stansberries leaned back to crack his neck, ready to start complaining. The crew would start calling Stansberries "Small Berries," now, and Larry hoped it would stick for the rest of his life.

"Okay, Small Berries, you'll go, 'Never try to fuck 'em while they're hibernating!'"

They both scratched their heads at this. Then a real fireman walked up to scratch his head and mock them, and Larry realized his crash scene was quickly becoming a head-scratching pandemic.

"Let's try it again!" Larry shouted, and he rolled camera.

"Did you see that faggot squeezing that kid's shit?" B.C. asked his partner, probably in character.

"He was looking for a pulse, dummy."

"Well, it was a hell of a crash. Apparently only that shitty Mötley Crüe drummer can drive with his cock."

"Goddammit, everyone keeps saying that," Small Cop sighed. "Watch the video again. He wasn't really driving the boat. All he did was honk the horn with it. That's very easy to do actually…"

"Okay, let me ask you this…" the Big Cop began, spinning his flashlight beam over his head, then finally tracing a lighthouse beacon back to the headlamp of the wreck.

"Ask me what? Damn. Big ass car. What kind is that? A tornado?"

"*Tor-ah-nay-doe*!" Larry hissed from behind a tree.

"What are the chances of… that?" Big Cop asked, ignoring his questions.

"The chances of what?"

"Of this car getting flipped and smashed to shit but landing so that it puts one fucking headlight on that kid in the tree like he's the spotlight dance on *Soul Train*."

"What are the chances of this being a Toronado?" someone else whispers.

"Hold on," the Small Cop mimed some math in the air between them. "36 to 1?"

"You've been playing roulette again, haven't you? And we just got paid! Oh, shit…"

He stopped talking as his flashlight beam froze on the tree again. Larry crept up to get the shot of both cops leaning in to see the claw marks on the bark. The red and blue strobes of more arriving officers lit everything up a little brighter.

But these cops were not extras. They were real, and they were responding to a complaint of suspicious lights in the woods. Oh, yeah, there was a real wreck, too. Larry got low and ready to use them in his scene as long as he could.

"I wasn't really gambling, man, so I found a roulette simulator, one of those Tomy Pocket Games. Those soothing, clicking little balls really help keep me off the riverboats."

"Why do you keep going to that casino?" the Big Cop sighed. "All that water and cigarette butts makes it smell like open ass."

"Closest legal gambling on Kentucky Road. Unless you wanna drive all the way to Florida Street. They get away with it by being on the water. So it's technically…"

"Atlantis?"

"Hey, I'm up three hundred bucks."

The Small Cop mimed like he was writing a letter in midair.

"'Dear gambler, if you can't look the ball in the eyes when it stops, it's time to stop playing roulette…'"

I looked some balls in the eyes, Larry thought, remembering the flashback.

"Did you know that roulette means 'little wheel'?" Big Cop asked him.

"No shit? So, can *you* look at a ball when it stops?"

"Not only can I look at a roulette ball when it stops, I'd happily watch its entire life leading up to that moment."

"Why?" the Small Cop asked, nodding at the parade of police exiting their cars like he has a good reason to be there in an ill-fitting uniform.

"Because then you'd see the pattern, asshole."

"Bullshit. You'd see a ball being made in a factory. All shiny, happy to be alive, heading for the riverboat. Until some sorry son of a bitch like you bet his car payment on it."

"You know what I mean. It's life on the wheel."

"Oh, 'life on the wheel,'" he laughed, walking away from his partner. "And what does that mean?"

"It means, spin it enough times and you'll see that the ball favors one number over the other. It can't help but do the same goddamn thing, every time. It'll find that exact same slot, again and again."

Real police officers were running up now, looking all authoritative, and Larry captured it all.

"Cut!" he finally yelled. He couldn't believe how good porn stars could act. Maybe they all just needed the chance. He didn't know where some of that casino shit was coming from, but it didn't matter. He was gonna have a real movie to cut and print in no time. "Cut" and "Print," Those were the secret words that a teenage Hitler used in *Boys From Brazil* to command his dogs to kill all three of his fathers and start making movies for real. They were secret words only his Dobermans knew. Larry walked up and scratched the trunks of the trees with his fingernails. His nails were strong from years of scratching himself like he was burying treasure.

Larry had done location hunting for the stateside half of that flick.

The police started shouting to clear out of the woods, and Larry gathered up his buddies hiding in the ambulance, taking the cigarette from the mouth of the one who resembled Larry the most. He was a paramedic now for real, and he'd let them film in his ambulance for peanuts. No, seriously, he loved peanuts. He'd probably do it for free. Larry got the idea when he first heard they had cameras back there, to make sure you didn't do anything wrong.

But this guy also owed Larry, big time. Someone owed someone from back in the day anyway. Larry smiled and turned up the radio to sing along with Dire Straits' "Skateaway." Somebody said something about a real ambulance pulling in, and they moved a little faster.

The medic who wasn't singing would be playing "Jack Grinstead," a name that might have meant something to Larry, but who could remember that many stories? They piled their camera equipment next to the mannequin playing the part of their "girl," not noticing the plastic sheen of her skin was looking an awful lot like real skin all the sudden, and Larry thought about his cops' dialogue and how the roulette ball found the same slot again and again, no matter how many spins.

* * *

In the back of the ambulance, Jack is still hovering over the face of the female victim, checking symptoms and talking to himself as he treats her injuries.

"Systolic blood pressure ninety-nine. Injecting point one milligrams Vecuronium. Applying cricoid pressure, preparing to intubate..."

Jack stops with the rubber squeeze bladder and mouthpiece in his hand. He stares down at her frowning. The girl is naked, except for her blue-jeans covering her uninjured leg. As he starts to work on her again, he seems to be getting increasingly upset. He checks her splints, then, after a moment, picks up one of her hands and checks the fingernails. The driver turns around.

"What are you doing, Jack?" his partner asks, annoyed. "Just make sure she stays immobilized. You listening?"

Nothing.

"Hey, wasn't it your turn to drive tonight, Jack?"

Jack ignores him and pulls back a torn piece of her shirt and looks close. He lays his fingers across a large five-pointed bruise that marks the side of the girl's stomach. There is a black and blue handprint rising on her skin. Jack's hand fits inside the pattern perfectly.

He's seen this hand print many times. Everyone's hands fit inside.

Jack's eyes are wide in horror as he realizes that something else must have happened to the girl after the accident. He knows from experience it's a vulnerable time. Being naked by a fire. He mumbles something incoherently to himself as he continues to study her body. Rick turns up their radio on that Seattle shit he loves and loses interest in Jack completely. After looking nervously around the back of the ambulance, Jack seems to be regaining control.

He makes a decision.

He uses his own fingernails to clean the blood and skin from under her purple nail polish. Then he begins pulling her remaining leg out of her jeans. Rick stops making guitar noises long enough to screw his baseball cap around, and Jack freezes a moment. The cap has the Chicago Fire's Dalmatian mascot on it, and its eyes stare accusingly. But Jack continues to clean her body nervously, periodically checking his watch and picking up his pace.

Suddenly the ambulance jerks to a stop, and Jack almost falls over. Looking to the street over Rick's shoulder, he's relieved to see they're stuck in traffic. Frustrated, Rick starts weaving through the tangle of cars, and Jack grabs a handrail to steady himself.

"Hey, slow down, man."

"What? Wait, did you actually say, 'slow down?' You're fired."

Jack crawls up behind the driver's seat.

"Yeah, man, slow down. You're gonna roll this thing. Haven't you ever played Grand Theft Auto on the Atari 2600? The physics of the fire truck brick and ambulance block are solid. The cop cube is jacked though."

Frustrated by the lack of response, Jack reaches past Rick to the small stereo cassette player duct-taped to the dash and turns it up. The song "Heartbreaker" by The Rolling Stones is starting. It's better than Dire Straits anyway.

"What the fuck are you doing?" Rick is mad, thick finger in his face, and Jack remembers suddenly why they call him Big Rick. He's a big bastard all right. Furry, too. Once when they were heading for the showers at the hospital, Jack saw him tuck his sunglasses into the hair on his chest like it was the collar of a shirt. And sometimes, on site, he lost patience with the crowds that gathered, even when it was law enforcement. Especially when it was law enforcement. Just last week, a ring of officers leaned in too close while they worked on a boy in blue who'd been clipped by a jack-knifing semi, and Rick finally flipped out. He put a meaty thumb on one badge and walked the guy back a step. Big Rick's voice always sounded calm, though, even when he said things like, *"Officer... Basch is it? Your last name sounds like the noise it makes when I punch your mother in the twat." Officer Basch turned white, and then he muttered, "My mother is dead."*

Without missing a beat, Big Rick smiled and explained, "I meant when she was alive."

It took Jack and a couple of brown-shirted sheriffs to break them up after that.

"Don't you like this song?" Jack asks him, fumbling to get better reception. His elbow hits the switch for the sirens and cuts them off.

"Oh, shit. Sorry."

"Hey, they're playing my song, let me turn this shit up..."

Rick glowers and shoves his arm away, then switches the sirens back on. As he slams on the brakes to avoid a collision, Jack returns to the girl, satisfied that he's bought himself some extra time. He yanks on her jeans, then stops.

Jack studies her. She's dark-skinned. Bruised and bloody but beautiful. Jack carefully puts her right foot into her pant-leg, struggling with a splint. He closes his eyes, ashamed and not sure why. He whispers in her ear something like he's whispered it before.

"Don't worry. Nine more minutes and it never happened."

Sunrise is cracking the clouds, and the song "Deep Hit of Morning Sun" by Primal Scream kicks in. Mistaking it for the static between stations, or the even more common sunspot disruptions which have, in the past, broadcast live baseball games a full hour before they've even started, Rick smacks the dashboard as the ambulance's siren starts to stutter and warble.

Jack has heard this song before, too.

Larry was explaining to his "Jack" and "Rick" that they needed to unload the girl in the emergency room dock.

The beauty of using porn guys for a real movie (or porn guys turned paramedics turned unemployed) was that they were so used to aliases, you could give them a new character name and a couple days later there was a good chance they'd roll in with it as the vanity plate on their shitty car.

Pornography always had a cheaper, more effective method of getting into a role (and covering your ass from disapproving family members). And don't get Larry started on the Stanislavsky System. But more on that Catch-22 later.

Larry told them both that Rick would frown when he saw a hand-shaped bruise on the girl's bare stomach. Then Rick would glance up at Jack as an explanation tumbled out of him.

"You'll say something like, 'Yeah, that happened when we were pulling her outta the car. Goddamn cops were too busy cracking jokes and getting in the way. I almost dropped her twice making sure they didn't,'" Larry told them. "Make sense?"

"Sure. One thing though…"

"What's that?"

"We got a Pinocchio situation here, boss."

"What?"

"When did this become a real girl?"

Larry ripped the sheet off their patient.

"Holy fuck."

It was a real girl all right. The girl from the crash. Jack started to panic. Rick started to tell them he thought she was part of their crew. Jack started to go for his throat, saying he knew this kind of shit was gonna happen. He didn't want to lose his job. But he knew Larry would remind him how he got the job in the first place, and he quieted down. Larry told Jack what he would do.

"You're going to do what you'd normally do. You're going to take this girl to the emergency room."

Jack decided that made the most sense, so Larry started directing again.

"You'll go, 'Hey, c'mon, I had no choice! I squeezed to keep from dropping her headfirst onto the road. Don't tell me you've never squeezed someone too hard, you fucking monster!' Or something. Action!"

"Are you kidding?" Jack asked, but he said his lines anyway. Rick was really into it now, too, surprised by the tone and the explanation his character never asked for. Frowning, he turned his attention back to the girl as they rolled her toward the building.

"I just don't want no lawsuit, brother," Jack explained. "I'm already on thin ice. Just let me do all the talking, all right?"

Larry didn't know whether that was directed towards him or the fake medic, but it worked either way. Then Rick shrugged as the automatic doors hissed open, and the girl was suddenly awake, leaning up on her elbows. Jack was so startled he almost ran the gurney into a wall. She looked at Jack, then at Rick. Then back to Larry and his handheld camera.

Then Rick laughed, and Jack knew there was no way Rick didn't understand the implications of this new development. He stared at her some more, scared to ask the questions:

Did you hear what I said? Or do you know what I did?

An old man came around the corner, sipping some hooch out of a jelly jar, and Larry recognized him immediately.

"Jesus Christ. How old are you now? A hundred and a hundred?"

"Shut the fuck up," was the old man's guttural reply. "I got chronic pain, boy."

"Yeah, a chronic pain in my ass."

"Who is this guy?" Rick asked.

"One of our Frequent Flyers from back in the day. Look at him. See how he's happy right now? See how you're happy right now? In spite of anything I say to you, because you're getting something for free. You remind me of those crackheads who have twenty surgeries a year just to get the pills. You want to figure out which ones are in the waiting rooms just to get their hands on another script? Look for the ones who are talking to the fish tank. The ones that are happy to be there. Like you…"

"Damn, Larry, chill out. Old bastard ain't hurting nobody."

Larry rubbed his face to erase the old man from memory. When Larry first decided to cut corners on his movie by having them wait for a real car wreck, he explained to the crew that everything that resulted would be a happy accident.

Happy accident. Two words that went together like chocolate and peanut butter.

He tried to remember everything that happened to him back then so they could keep making the movie. He told everybody to pretend it was tomorrow. Both were easy with the sun coming up.

Hospital. Next day. Jacki Ramirez is being gently sucked into an MRI tube.

"Just like a coffin into a crematorium," she mutters.

"Excuse me?" a technician covered in cartoon Tinkerbells asks her.

"Never mind. How long will this take?"

"Longer if you don't lie still."

"Figures," she scoffs.

When she's all the way inside, machines start humming and clicking around her like insects in a hollow tree trunk. Her tree seems to shrink as the time ticks by, almost closing to a point around her head and feet. She feels like she's being stretched in a Chinese fingercuff, and she hallucinates a bit in her panic, seeing a flash of a dog's mouth, rooting its way up into the darkness between her legs. She shakes it off. Immediately, a stern voice comes over the speaker.

"Ma'am, we're going to have to start again because you moved. Please, remain as still as possible."

"Sorry sorry."

The corner of her eyes water, and she grinds her teeth to keep her eyelids and the ends of the tube open until it's over. Twenty minutes into the scan, she feels calm, even a little ornery.

"Has anybody ever played a practical joke on you?" she asks the nurse. "Have you ever pulled out a dummy instead of a patient?"

"Please, ma'am!"

She's quiet awhile longer, but fifteen minutes later, she can't help but shout:

"Hey, did you know there's graffiti all over the walls in here?"

There's about a 30-second pause this time, then Tinkerbell's voice over the speaker, frustrated.

"Miss Ruiz, we have that machine cleaned regularly. That is simply impossible. What exactly are you-"

"I was kidding. And that's not my name, by the way."

The next half hour is real quiet.

Later, when she's finally out of the electric tree trunk, Jacki's sitting up in her hospital bed watching something called Into the Mild *on the wall-mounted television, trying to turn off the screen but not the sound.*

Jack Grinstead walks in. Awkward half-smiles are exchanged. She recognizes his medic uniform.

"Are you... did I leave something in your truck?"

Jack looks around nervously, cracks his knuckles, tries to work up some courage.

"Not exactly." He looks to the TV for help. "What's this?"

"You've never seen this show?" she says. "It's on once a week. Buncha kids trekking out into the wilderness to try and jumpstart a tour bus. Sometimes bears almost get 'em. Sometimes they eat the wrong shit and almost starve. They're never more than ten yards from a major highway. It's like a terrible game show where nobody wins anything. Good music though. I can't believe I've never heard these songs before."

"Didn't that happen in real life? Some little rich prick die for real?"

"Really? It's gotta happen one day with shows like this. It needs a better title though."

"Like what?"

"Like Educated Young Men Reject College and Everything It Taught Them. *"*

"Nice," Jack says, smiling.

"Or Rich Assholes Burn Dads' Money, Forget Which Seed is Which.*"*

"Ha, yeah, I love it. Or how about just Magic Bus? More Like Roach Motel! Kills Fifth Hippie in as Many Years. *"*

"It makes sense though," she says. "The urge to play a game with no prize. Like philosopher Marshall McLuhan wrote about the radio, 'When you are on the air, you have no body.'"

Jack ponders this, and the injury he erased, and the answers to everything are so close he can almost grab them from the space between them. But then a prime example of the guy they were describing walks through the door with a bundle of "Get Well!" balloons in his arms. Ratty little punk, looking like he'd be perfectly at home on any San Francisco band's album cover, likely the one clown in the photo looking the wrong way, all dramatic.

He stamps past Jack, ignoring him way too hard not to see him, and leans down to kiss her. Jack is amazed to see more irritation than concern for her on the punk's face. He's clearly waiting to have her alone, to accuse, to bully, to find out who she was with in that car. His lips are so tight they're white as marble. Jack watches the blood fill them back up as the punk finally prepares to speak, and he jumps up to stop this from happening.

"So!" Jack interrupts. "Once the first one dies, how many more will die making pilgrimages to the first kid's grave?"

"About 30?" she smiles. The punk finds a spot on the wall to study. Even this makes Jack angry.

"Not enough!" Jack says. "Why doesn't anyone realize that this is not a game?" he asks them both. "Just an awesome horror movie about a killer bus."

"Good question," Jacki says.

"They're all horror movies," the punk says, finally turning for the stare down. "Did you need something, buddy?"

"I'll come back," Jack says.

They both smile at each other longer than they have to, then Jack walks out.

There's no one in the hallway, so he can walk a long time with his eyes closed.

It was later that night, and Larry was filming his latest Jack sitting at a desk in his apartment, staring at a dead television screen. Jack's apartment was a spitting image of the apartment Larry had for all his worst adventures. Larry was telling Jack to pick at the wrappers in front of him and wrinkle his nose at the dog-food smell of fast-food tacos. This was easy. The sounds of partying just outside his door spiked for a moment, then his door opened and a naked girl framed by the yellow glow of the hall light was suddenly posing in the reflection of the TV screen.

Initially, Larry was disappointed there would be nudity in his first real movie, but his elbows weren't itching at the moment, so it didn't really bother him.

"Action!" Larry told them.

"So, she was cheating," Jack said, almost to himself. Luckily, Larry was close enough to get it on his hand-held.

"Who was cheating?" the girl in the TV asked him.

"The naked boy in the tree. The scarecrow. She was cheating with him," Jack mumbled to the shadow on his screen. Larry motioned with his thumb to talk louder.

"No, you're the one who's cheating. Come out and join the party, Jack."

"And that punk in the hospital knew all about it."

"Knows all about what?"

"What if he was the one who-"

"Truth or dare?" asked Naked Girl suddenly, tits bouncing, ice cube popping in her teeth. Jack refused to turn around and face her, happy to keep her trapped on his monitor for now.

"Tell those guys to keep it down," he snapped. "I have a shift in four hours."

That's true, Larry thought.

"Truth. Or. Dare," said Naked Girl, still bouncing, chewing louder.

"I'm not playing."

"Wait, I'm doing it wrong," said Naked Girl, momentarily confused. "You ask me, 'truth or dare.'"

"Just tell everyone to please-"

"Turn around!" Naked Girl stomped a bare foot, but Jack just kept staring at her in the reflection like a pro. He was supposed to consider reaching out and trying to turn her off instead of the television, but, before they began, Larry had resigned to the fact he had no idea how to visualize this.

"Ask me truth or dare!" she pouted.

"Truth or dare."

"Dare," Naked Girl said, smiling, expecting something sexual.

You can take the actress out of the porn, Larry thought. *But you can't...*

"Piss in your hand until it's full. Then drink it."

Naked Girl's smile dropped. Larry's, too. If he had a script, he would have rifled through it.

"Do it for me?"

"What the fuck is wrong with you?" she shouted, walking into the room between him and his screen. Jack deftly ducked his head to avoid her kiss. Something was barking in the hallway.

"Who brought their fucking dog?" Jack asked.

Naked Girl didn't answer, instead crunched the last of her ice cube and swallowed.

"What the hell? You said you had four hours."

She turned to leave, but stopped at the door. Jack reached up to finally turn on the TV. The screen heated up, her outline slowly swallowed by static. Larry moved in close to capture the blizzard of snow on the screen.

"Hey, next time you kiss me, do me a favor?"

"What?"

"Keep the ice in your mouth."

"Why?"

"So your tongue will be cold…"

"Oh, no."

"…and I can pretend you're dead."

Stunned, Naked Girl started to say something, then smiled and exaggerated the motion of biting her tongue instead.

Jack jumped up and walked past her and out of his room, past the dogpiles of half-dressed partiers in the living room, past the low growl of someone's dog, out of his front door and straight across the hallway.

Larry ran after him, desperate to keep him in the frame.

He opened the door of another apartment and entered.

It was identical to the room he just exited, except for stark white walls and a lack of furniture, noise, or televisions sprouting naked, ice-cube munching females.

Jack and Larry walked around a corner to where their bedroom used to be, then they sat down in the middle of the floor.

* * *

Half in the shadows, a dog blinks slowly, love struck, almost intoxicated by the affectionate digging and scratching of a heavy hand into the fur at the base of its skull.

Tom Waits' "Raindogs" creaks its way around an old turntable like a calliope.

"Her long hair black as a raven. Oh, how we danced and you whispered to me, 'You'll never be going back home...'"

Then the master's hand stops and taps the face of a wristwatch impatiently. The dog begins to whimper, convinced it did something wrong and is on the verge of being disciplined. Confused, it runs to a pile of fresh feces and frantically tries to bury it, nails catching on a pile of nearby postcards, which rocket through the shit, one after another. The master's hand moves to his own ears, trying to stay angry, but it wasn't the dog's shit on his floor, and he's also thinking of that popular painting now, realizing this is what would happen if dogs really played poker.

It was getting dark, and when they got to the top of the next hill they both saw the glow of the drive-in through the trees. Bully's drive-in. The Kid. Even with a bronze stripe of daylight still on the horizon, a movie was already playing, and the huge shapes were moving in the distance, giants that moved way too fast and turned a romantic comedy into a monster movie. Billy always wanted to take her there, in a car, like you were supposed to, but she'd never bother if she was getting it for free every night.

On the radio, Saga's "On the Loose" was winding down, and Bully reached out to find something else before he could stab the button on Billy Squier's *Emotions in Motion* again.

She was fast getting sick of both Billys, and if she had to hear that tape one more time... She jammed one of her tapes in, giving him a look that it was her music or nothing from now on.

"What the hell is that?" she frowned, turning up the volume.

She'd hit the A.M. band by mistake, and they could just barely make out a creepy children's chorus.

"Eight more days till Halloween... Halloween... Halloween..."

"You hear that?"

"Is it a commercial?"

"Eight more days till Halloween... Silver Shamrock..."

"No way that's a commercial. I mean, I've heard that in a commercial somewhere, I think. Is this..."

They both looked at each other, simultaneously understanding what they were really hearing.

"It's a song from a movie! The movie in the trees."

"What movie?"

"*Halloween III*," she said. "Tonight only."

"Let me guess, 'Triple Feature,'" Billy sighed, squinting into the distance. "Wait, I thought this was a romantic comedy."

"No, the triple features are only on the weekend, when people can stay up all night. Question though. How can we be hearing voices from the movie coming through the radio? There's no way it broadcasts that far."

There was a heavy thump through the frame of the car, then a muffled bark, and he rolled down his windows.

"What the fuck," she said.

They could barely hear the sound of Officer Bigbeep shouting indistinctly in the woods. After a minute, they were able to decipher the word.

"Is that really the dog's name?" Billy wondered aloud.

Billy looked at Bully eagerly, hoping for admiration or at least shock that he'd already grabbed the animal.

But she didn't give him the satisfaction of eye contact, not even a half-smile for actually going through with the dognapping. Just a change of subject.

"You forgot one pizza, you know."

"Huh?"

"Before, when you listed the ingredients, you forgot one. What if there was *zero* ingredients on the pizza? How freaky would that be?"

"Well, yeah, but that's just a white pizza. Or a Greek pizza. So, you understand there's a dog in my trunk at this moment, right?"

"Of course. You want to name it?"

"Maybe we should feed it. It was sounding a little ragged."

"How about 'Little Beep!'" she said. "Or 'L.B.' for short."

"That sounds like a disorder."

"Speaking of Big Greek, we're not still following him today or..."

"Shhh, I want to hear this."

Billy turned up the radio to decipher more voices.

"He's your emesis," she said.

"Huh?"

"Look it up! Jesus Christ."

"I thought your ex-boyfriend was my nemesis."

"What ex-boyfriend?"

"You know how I'll always remember your boyfriend? Waking up screaming with a dog collar on his neck."

"But if he screamed, that collar would squirt him in the face."

"Do you think he got loose? Those handcuffs weren't that tight."

"Yeah, but his arms were stretched out tight. I can't believe he let me click 'em. Or swallow the key."

"He was always such a martyr."

David James Keaton

"Question. What's the only difference between Jesus and the Karate Kid?"

"Hold on. What name is that cop yelling?"

"I don't know," Billy said, nervous.

"Do you think we should rename his dog?" she asked him.

"We'd need to know its name to rename it."

"Why don't you go find out?"

"No. That's never a good idea with a hostage."

She knew its name. She rarely slept, and she sure loved that solitary recon, so she'd heard Bigby shouting for his dog more than once. He lost his dog sometimes. They all did. And other times he got it mixed up with other dogs. These K-9's were apparently as interchangeable as the assholes on the leash.

Bully got wrist-deep in her bag again, organizing cassettes. She'd brought them instead of the batteries, but they didn't need them anyway. She suspected it was just any old canine and not *the* K-9 in her trunk, just as much as she knew Billy didn't have the guts to do anything to the cop or his dog. There was just no way Bigby named his dog "Hansel."

But she was having lots of fun seeing how far he would go.

When Bigbeep got back to his car, they tailed him some more, but they hung back so far they almost got pulled over by another cop instead. It was a false alarm, but it scared them enough to eject Public Enemy's *Fear of a Black Planet,* realizing for the first time that bass shaking your rear-view mirror with cop-hating tunes made it much easier for a cruiser to sneak up on you. He fumbled it at first, backing off of "Burn Hollywood Burn" and stopping on "Welcome to the Terrordome." Heart pounding in panic, he went back to something a little more high-end instead, safer, shriller. Squier.

"Do you work for them?"

"Who? The drive-in? Sort of."

"What does that mean?"

"It means no."

"Then why are you nailing up posters around town?"

"I didn't nail anything. I'm just sort of doing them a favor, unsolicited."

"But…"

"It'll all make sense later."

"It better."

There was a rustle in the trunk and the dog crawled in a circle, attempting to get comfortable. It had taken to barking when they talked.

"Okay, if we're not gonna rename it, maybe we should at least feed it," he said.

"Why?"

"We have to get it to trust us if we're gonna get our collar on it."

Billy trailed off as he watched her messing with something in her purse, then the something clicked.

"What the hell is that?"

"An answering machine. My brother gave it to me."

"Answering machines don't run on batteries."

She was silent.

"Are you recording the news? Is that what's on your tape bombs? News broadcasts?"

"They got a little bit of everything. News, songs, us. All mixed together like a smoothie."

"Now I'm not so disappointed I never drank one."

"You realize Bigbeep's not your nemesis, right? He's your emesis."

"Huh?"

"I thought you looked that up," she sighed.

"Speaking of, you never did tell me the difference between Jesus and the Karate Kid."

"Holding your right foot about nine inches higher off the ground."

David James Keaton

"Good point," he had to admit.

"You know what I just realized? Either your horn's fixed or we're not screaming anymore."

"Were we ever?"

She squeezed his hand. It was beautiful. It was like fucking Christmas. They drove silently for a while to get the barking to stop. In the distance, they heard Bigbeep yelling out the window of his cop car.

"Hansel!"

"Now that's a good cop. Getting lost dogs out of trees."

"What?"

"Nothing," she giggled.

"Did you put up flyers about a lost dog named Hansel? I'm suddenly sure that's what you're doing."

"How dare you!" she said, slapping his hand. Then, "Probably?"

Billy started to ask why, but stopped himself.

"I'll bet he shoots cats out of trees," he decided.

"Hey, did you see the supermoon last night?" Bully asked after a minute. "Last one of those motherfuckers was fifty years ago."

"Nope."

"Well you missed out. It was so bright, I couldn't see the drive-in. Can you imagine some asshole celebrating their honeymoon on a supermoon?"

"M-o-o-n. That spells 'supermoon.'"

"Hansel!" the voice was a little closer.

"Isn't there a crime somewhere, dude." Billy muttered. "Get to work, supercop."

"I'm telling you, the moon was fucking huge."

"Was it?"

"It was red as a baboon's ass."

"Missed that."

"You couldn't have missed it, even if you didn't look at it."

"Why."

128

"We're 60% water. It affects us no matter what."

"I'm not. I only drink coffee. A ton of coffee. I'm like a bag of coffee covered in skin. I drink water only accidentally. While swimming."

"I've never seen you drink coffee," she frowned.

"All bets are off when there's a supermoon."

"Dogs must be 90% water. That's why they howl at it."

"Maybe."

"Hey, how's your bike?" She didn't wait for him to answer. "Hey! I thought of you the other night. Did you see that documentary on Evel Knievel? Where he tried to jump those sharks? Dumb ass was trying to cash in on *Jaws*."

Billy didn't hear much after her words "I thought of you." He had to bite his tongue to pay attention.

"But Evel didn't even do it really. During rehearsal, he wiped out, ran into the camera guy and put out his eye, then broke both his arms! What a freakin' disaster."

"Whoa, he lost his eye? Like *Escape from New York*?!" Billy laughed.

"No. Pay attention. His cameraman lost his eye. I think he was trying to ride his bike on water or some shit. Who knows. Fonzie jumped the shark pretty easy on *Happy Days* because he was on skis. That's a lot easier on water. We're made of water, you know..."

"What a stupid stunt," Billy scoffed. "That's like saying you're jumping starfish. They're fucking underwater. Who knows what you're jumping. You might as well say you jumped Moby Dick."

She laughed at this. "You know what you never see jump a shark?"

"What?"

"Sharks."

"Very true," he smiled. He smiled more when he got her hand back. It was dry, cold. He loved it. "You know what even Evel Knievel never did?" he said. "Jumped a line of cars *long ways.* Now that would be impressive. Cars lined up end to end?"

She took her hand away. "Why not just get more cars?"

"Because jumping cars longways is like burying people in cemeteries straight up and down," he said. "It's way harder all around."

"Oh. But not as hard as jumping a supermoon."

"Probably right," he sighed.

"Could you do it? With that dirt bike?"

"Are you serious?"

"Would you even try? You wouldn't even try."

"It doesn't matter. Where would you be able to get that many cars to line up?"

She said nothing, but her hand was gone, and her eyes already held the answer. Billy desperately fiddled with the equalizer below her stereo, hoping it worked on her, too.

The dog in the trunk struggled so loud they actually considered what they were doing. For at least a mile anyway.

Determined, Billy had set out earlier that morning, all by his lonesome, to get that dog. He'd found that a "dognapping" was impossible unless the dog was really napping. And by napping, Billy really needed it unconscious. But if there was one thing a K-9 didn't do when it was on duty, it was nap.

Billy had been counting on Bigbeep's dog being as incompetent as its master, only this fuzzy little fucker was all business. Even worse, this new dog seemed to have put a spring in Bigbeep's step. Billy had been stalking him for a while, but watching him with the animal, he was amazed to see Bigbeep practically oozing newfound confidence in his authority. Something in his walk? Maybe something in his moustache. Scientists always claimed symmetry was power.

Billy first tried one half-ass ambush around 8:00, calling in a bomb threat in order to get a bunch of K-9's sniffing around an electrical substation, not really knowing how he was going to knock out the dog when he got there. He'd done some cursory research on tranquilizers, even bought a bag of Milk Bones and some bungee cords for his dirt bike in case he had to strap it to the handlebars, but eventually he'd settled for something a bit more low-tech.

Unfortunately, the bomb squad had already cordoned off six blocks before he could get anywhere near the dog with his hammer.

He'd rode around petulant for awhile, dreaming of stealing the dog, maybe turning Bigbeep into one of those "Unstoppable Revenge Machines" Bully was always going on about. Apparently the best action movies had one. He could have sworn it was the name of a song.

While he'd killed some time, in a futile attempt to get his mind right for any possible adventure, he tried balancing a cap of mouthwash on his gas tank to see how far he could ride without spilling it. All the while, he imagined being one of the old, sweaty South Americans in the movie *Sorcerer*, trying to prove his resolve when it came to hauling boxes of explosives sweating out nitroglycerine. He had a whole case of the stuff. The first and last time he ever used the shit the way it was intended, his window was frozen shut and he ended up blowing it the length of his windshield in frustration, driving the rest of the way to school through a fog of minty haze. He missed looking at the world that way.

He'd made it half a block before the acrid splash hit his chest, the wind running green rivers up his neck like an algae bloom.

It didn't bother him. These days, he was expecting all his planning to detonate in his face at any moment.

He was on his tenth lap around the block when he started looking for the red flag he'd raised on a mailbox, where Bully had dropped her first flyer. He pulled it out. It was an ad for the drive-in, just like she'd said. He was stuffing it in his pocket just as a jingle for The Kid came on the tiny radio he had strapped to the crotch of his handlebars. The only time he could really hear it was when he was idling at stop signs, or peeking into mailboxes, so he didn't catch most of it. But it was certainly a real jingle, not just the voices from the movie they'd marvel over later in the car.

"Come down to The Spotlight Kid for this weekend's Triple Feature of Terror! Terrifying Tots! You're gonna need your own sitter because you'll fall off the edge of your seat!"

"What?" he asked the radio that morning. Then he pulled out the flyer Bully had crammed in the box and looked at it again.

"The fuck?"

It was an ad for a triple feature all right, only they didn't seem quite as terrifying as the screams coming from his speakers. It read:

"She's Having a Baby, Baby Boom, and *Three Men and a Baby.*"

"Baby baby baby baby baby," he sang. "I fell from the sky…"

He'd rode on a little longer, until the flutter of white under the windshield wipers on every parked car finally got his attention. Then he stopped and read one.

"Lost Dog. German Shepherd. Answers to 'Hansel.' He can't find his way home! Report any information to local law enforcement."

No way, he thought. *A fine, German name for a dog though.*

He would never mock it again. It conjured up sniffing trails of breadcrumbs and all that good shit.

He'd finally pulled over, clicking off another promo for the drive-in and thought about the last movie he'd seen, *Close Encounters of the Third Kind*. He thought about people seeing Devil's Tower in their toilets and mashed potatoes and then all converging on the same place. He felt like he was being left behind in some race, so he was very grateful when the inspiration finally hit.

Back when Billy first burst into the pound looking for Shaft, unaware he'd already been put down, there was another German Shepherd in there that looked just like him. Which meant that this dog looked like Bigbeep's dog, too. All those goddamn dogs, really. The big cop dogs. Identical strangers, every one of 'em.

So that afternoon, Billy borrowed his Bully, and her car, then dropped her off at Radio Shack to get more batteries. Then he drove straight to the pound.

And just like he would have done a year ago, he posted bail.

The animal jumped into the trunk like it was made for dogs.

Billy laughed and scratched its ears for a second, before he slammed the lid shut. He knew trunks were really made for sneaking into drive-ins.

Professional until the end, Larry made the mistake of trying one more time to finish the shoot.

Joe Fuck was all business after the apology, so there was hope. Like most of the young bucks, no fluffer necessary, no crew turning their backs for a second, no sweet talking at all. Just *sproing!* Like a toddler's arm finally finding the sleeve in a snowmobile suit. Never mind that the dumb immigrant kept saying "donkey style" instead of "doggy style," Larry actually felt grateful for a second. Then he started to dwell on the implication of their unique skills. Again.

David James Keaton

Punks like him were so into the scene that they never got *into the scene.* Larry called this The Ultimate Paradox of Pornography.

It was a way of thinking few could grasp, as it was directly opposite of the typical acting "methods" he would see bandied about his set by Hollywood wannabes, a tendency more common in the girls than the boys, who usually left their delusions at the door. Actually, any mention of Constantin Sergeyevich Stanislavski around Larry, or specifically the Stanislavski System, would mean a pink slip in that actress's hand by the end of the day. And the fact that Larry used an actual *pink slip* in place of any written notice of termination did little to soften the blow.

He bought slips in bulk, as his cast routinely fucked the lace on the lingerie as ragged as paper snowflakes.

Suzie stayed down on Joe while Larry circled, fighting the urge to make what real directors called the "loser box" in the air with his forefingers and thumbs. Then Suzie started deep-throating Joe with those duck noises that were getting more and more popular these days, the steady stream of saliva rolling off her bottom lip, always coating their indifference with such a convincing façade of *hunger.* It made no real sense really, all that spit. Mouths got so confused with a cock in them, convincing the lips, teeth and tongue that the whole crew was seconds from chewing that shit. That saliva would soak the talent and any and all nearby surfaces. The mouth really did think it was dealing with food.

And the noises. When Larry first heard the sounds coming out of his little organ-grinder monkeys, they were familiar but confusing, and Larry never could quite place the memory. That is, until his car stereo started eating his *Frampton Comes Alive!* tape right on the squawking guitar wanking in "Do You Feel Like We Do" at ten times normal speed.

134

Back in college, one of Larry's film school buddies dropped out to take a closed-captioning gig, even typing out the subtitles for some of Larry's own performers, or so he claimed. Supposedly, he'd been captioning censored versions for hotel skin-flick channels. And sometimes this guy would e-mail Larry to complain about the dark turn Larry's movies seemed to be taking lately.

"Joe Fuck should be in Grenada, not in porn," his buddy complained once. "I mean the country, not your car." Then he went on to explain he'd had to add typing shortcuts to save time while tap, tap, tapping horseshit like that into a weary keyboard all day, and how hitting the letters "GG" used to conjure up "[girl giggling]," but now he had to use "[girl gagging]" because of Larry's band of rutting psychos. "A dark day indeed," he'd told him. Larry heard from the guy only one last time, when he lamented being forced to change his keyboard shortcut "VB" from "[vibrator buzzing]" to "[voice breaking]." He told Larry he quit that same day, but Larry didn't believe him. It wasn't *that* bad.

From Larry's experience, the girls might have voices breaking and tears in their eyes sometimes, but he knew they could encourage the sadistic bullshit that induced it.

But damn it if Joe couldn't perform. He'd heard rumors of fake rubber dicks with squeeze bulbs full of milk that other crews were forced to bring in to wrap up a shoot. He thought of those turkey basters as The Doomsday Button. If porn lost that much integrity, he was out the door. Joe kept the Apocalypse at bay. He could even "Ouroburos" on command, if the female bowed out or got lost on the way. This was Larry's nickname for auto-fellatio.

He looked Joe up and down, like Wile E. Coyote mapping out the meat on the Roadrunner. He had a new tattoo. Smack dab in the middle of his washboard abs and the railroad tracks drawn over them, a bit to the right of the angry rash where his bush used to be. It screamed:

"I Love Fiona."

Unbelievable, Larry thought. Roxy and Suzie sure weren't "Fiona." And neither were their characters. Larry suddenly began to lose his mind watching Joe fucking Suzie with this declaration of "I Love Fiona" inflating faster and larger with each wheezing breath. He couldn't think of a worse distraction for his film.

Until he saw Suzie's tattoo, across her lower back, of course.

"Sammy," it said simply, to anybody listening.

Has anybody seen Sammy? Larry couldn't take it.

"Cut!"

Suzie stood up fast, ejecting Joe like a sprung diving board.

"What did you call me?!" she yelled.

"Huh? No, I said 'cut.'"

Suzie was standing so close to Larry, he could smell the hate coming off of her. She stood there glaring, bare foot tapping his shoe impatiently, nostrils flaring, lip quivering, while the gold charms on her necklace tangled and slung over her shoulder tinkled like coins. She pulled them back over her chest and fingered them nervously, a tiny pair of brass knuckles and a Tweety bird whose square Frankenstein-like forehead gleamed with as much sweat as hers.

"Listen, Suzie," Larry said, as soothing as he could muster. "With this 'Sammy' thing, we got, at the very least, a continuity error here."

"Wha-?" Her eyes darted around, looking for coke. "Who?"

Larry looked her up and down. He remembered the first time a girl showed up to a shoot with an angry red tattoo on her arm, some dead nephew's babyface, fresh from the needle, and how he was so mad that he turned off his camera and made her ride the guy for thirty-five takes just so she'd sweat enough to ruin the new ink on

136

her shoulder. He felt guilty when he saw the splotchy holes in the baby's mug a week later. But he didn't feel guilty about it anymore.

Larry straightened out her necklace, fighting the urge to pull the chain tight above her head so she'd look and listen just once.

"The names! Your names! We got real names, fake names, characters names, and now you got names on your bodies? Just who the fuck are you supposed to be? Do you even know?!"

"What are you talking about?" she yelled, foot tap, tap, tapping, loud as gunshots.

Is her nose bleeding?

Larry thought about how he could remove the blood later, just as they were adding blood in more recent movies. "Computer-generated imagery," they called it. And he knew it would eventually ruin the world of film. He'd argued about it with Damon the week before as they watched the dailies and Damon rubbed Larry's face in one of the "real" movies he was producing. Damon was pointing out where they'd be adding the splashes of red, and Larry tried to explain how computer-generated blood would do more damage to a movie than an actual death on the set. Damon said, "Well, Vic Morrow and those two kids would probably disagree with you about that one," and Larry said, "No, they practically advertised his death when the *Twilight Zone* movie came out. If anything, it did more damage to possible sequels, I'll give you that, but that's time travel you're talking about now."

Damon had seemed to consider his point since he'd made stranger production decisions for even stranger reasons in the past. When they were cutting corners and leaning towards "gonzo" and fewer cinema parodies, Damon had once told him of a dream he'd had about movie sequels, and the "inherent danger" of too many roman numerals marching off a poster and around the sun until they snuck up behind you at every important moment of your life, disrupting crucial memories forever. "Too many sequels make movies... untethered," he'd warned Larry. This had all made sense to Damon, and they retired their roman numerals for a while, even stopped production on *Spurtacus VIII*, just to be safe. Damon took a $3,000 hit with that move, and Larry mourned a script that had pretty much written itself:

"I fucked Spurtacus!"

"No, *I* fucked Spurtacus!"

So Larry pressed on, pleading with him that CGI blood introduced artificiality at the precise moment it can do the most damage to the film, that computer-generated blood was worse than a computer-generated person, that, even in its infancy, the disastrous effects of computer-generated blood on horror and action films could not be overstated, that computer-generated blood is worse than a stuntman missing a punch by a mile but still making a smacking sound, that if they only had a way to look into the future right now, at this moment, everyone would see that he was absolutely right! But they added the fake blood anyway. And Larry knew, if they were going to start faking the fake blood, it was only a matter of time before someone used a computer to fake an ejaculation. And on that day, he'd drop the microphone and quit. Or tell someone to drop the microphone he'd told them to hold.

"Burning daylight, man!" Stevey yelled.

"And we still have to shoot outside in the pool!" Glengarry yelled.

"Come on! What's with you today, Larry?"

"Who's Sammy?" Suzie asked Joe sincerely when she climbed back on.

After a minute, there came that point during the shoot Larry dreaded, the one the actors called "Hands Up," named after the moment on the roller coaster where you clear the big hill, stick your hands in the air and just enjoy the ride. Hands Up represented the moment when they stopped acting, straining for foreplay, trying to make things all sexy, and actually engaged in intercourse. Once the sex started, since the vast majority of them had experienced sex before, of course, from a filmmaking point of view it could be dangerous to let their instincts take over and ride out the rest of a scene. Dangerous because they would essentially stop working. They were on their own time after that. The best way to snap someone out of Hands Up was to stop the scene, pretend you ran out of film, or, a more recent tactic, that the battery had died. But lately Larry just liked to frown at random parts of their bodies as if he discovered something strange and horrible.

This made them panic and try harder all over again.

They resumed filming, and Joe started his tired-ass routine all over, ramming himself down her throat as far as he could go, making her gag, popping it out, making her gag. Larry rubbed his face hard. All the dudes did this now. Every goddamn time.

Then came the part of his act that drove Larry right up the fucking wall. Joe pushed the head of his cock against the inside of her cheek, then began rapping it with his knuckles. Larry had no idea what this was supposed to prove, and he couldn't imagine anyone wanting to see it happen, let alone try it, but Joe must have loved it even more than himself. It was sort of his trademark.

He knocked on her face, harder and harder. The echo now like mortar fire in Larry's head.

Tap, tap, tap. Tap, tap, tap…

They were driving behind the cop when Billy asked her what had changed.

"I don't know. It just seems like we're arguing all the time and…"

"No, jerk. With his car."

139

"Whoa. You're right. The 'K through 9th grade' on his back window is gone!'"

"No, I mean – Wait, what did you mean about arguing though? We don't argue. No, you're right, you're right. We're just in a funk."

"Here. Watch me change our mood with different theme music for trailing this clown. First, here's… the *Scanners* soundtrack."

"That makes me want to lean my head out and catch a stop sign with my face."

"But now here's the change…"

She cranked the radio on the song.

"And now here's… the theme music from *Magnum P.I.*"

"Perfect."

It *was* perfect. And with their soundtrack secured, they followed Bigbeep around the neighborhood in an ever-widening spiral. They couldn't get too close since the horn still honked occasionally for no reason at all. In fact, "No reason at all," was exactly what the mechanic muttered, the third one to give up trying to figure it out.

"So, what's the worst place? You never answered me."

"E-e-e-e-e-rie, Pennsylvania," he sighed. "Such a backwards ass town that the state bird is a pumpkin. As many E's as you can stand to scream. I can't think of a worse place to live."

"How about Pittsburgh?"

"Let's compare. Ready? Go."

"Here. The highlight of my day is feeling my heart skip when I come around the corner and mistake the dark outline of dogshit stations for a human being in the shadows."

"What the fuck is a dogshit station?" he asked her.

"You know, a pole with a box on it. Dispenses bags? Catches dreams."

He laughed.

"You're supposed to drop your dogshit in there," she added.

"Even if you don't have a dog?" He was truly confused.

"No one uses them. It really just serves as a warning not to get within a hundred yards."

"Okay, I can top that. Pittsburgh, Pennsylvania. Spring of '81. Sunny and warm. One day, I'm reading in a camping chair that's painted the colors of the American flag. I'm down by the river that runs past my apartment building, and behind me I hear a child, no more than 10, say, 'Look at that stupid fucking goose!' Then I hear her mother say, 'That's a vulture!' I put down my comic book and turn. It's a kite. With two big eyes painted on it. I broke my lease the next day."

"Are you from there?"

"No, from here."

"Where's here?"

"Same as there."

"Come on."

"So what if I'm from here? People say you have to accept your hometown, know where you're from to know where you're going and all that. Bullshit! That's for people with a city, or a country, not the in-between, not 'burbs, strip malls, not us. The people that exist there, or exist here, they're in-between, too. Unremarkable in every way." He actually sounded proud.

"So why move to another one?"

"Because of its name. You can think of some good rhymes."

"Huh? Okay, you win," she said. "You know why?"

"Because I'm having a good beard day?"

"Because you're having a weird beard day. Like you could grow one. Step on it! You're gonna lose him."

"Who?"

"Officer Bugbear."

"You mean 'Bugbeard'?"

"Turn left," she said, all business again. "And don't smile so much."

"Why?"

"If makes you seem unhinged."

"I'm as sane as the next guy who's trying to kill a cop."

"No, literally unhinged. Like the corners of your mouth will connect in the back and the top of your head will fall off."

"Oh. What a relief. I thought you were saying I was crazy."

"Don't be so self-defecating."

He almost reached for her hand. Then the horn got stuck again, reminding them that they were too close, and he backed off the chase.

"So, I have an idea," Billy said to the first unrequited love of his short life. "When is the next Triple Feature over at the Sundance Kid?"

"In three days. *She's Having a Baby*, *Baby Boom*, and *Three Men and a Baby*. Didn't you read my flyer?"

"Ugh. Seriously? That doesn't sound right."

"That's what's on their poster," Bully shrugged.

"I just can't believe they'd do that. Those are all, like, rated fucking *G*. Who would go to a drive-in for kids' stuff?"

"I know what I saw. So, you never answered me. Would you do that jump? If you had the chance?"

"Maybe."

"When?"

"I don't know. The chance would have to present itself."

"How would it do that?"

"Well, you know those new tow trucks? With the ramps on back instead of the chains?"

"I guess," she lied.

"I would need one of those. If someone parked one of those just right, by a line of cars, I could do it. Out of nowhere, I'd zip in on my bike and fly over everyone's heads. That's the only way it might work. But the timing would be one-in-a-million."

"So you'd do it, is what you're saying."

"Sure."

"You'd leave it up to fate is what you're telling me."

He considered this and they pulled up to Radio Shack and both hopped out. They needed a couple final items. But first Bully reached back in to drag a bag of Dog Chow and a gas can from the back seat to the trunk. Taking the keys from Billy, she popped the lock. A sluggish rustling and thumping began, but she held it open just a crack while she poured the dog food in with a gas can's funnel. The trunk stank like mold from when they'd run a water hose into it earlier that morning. A little like gas, too.

Inside the store, they accosted the teenage suit-wearing clerk like they usually did.

"Question!" Bully shouted. "Where do villains in movies buy their stylish knife holders that they revel in unrolling all dramatic in front of their victims? The Bed Bath & Beyond guy had no idea what we were talking about."

The clerk shook his head. He'd dealt with them a dozen times now.

"I guess he's gonna be no help finding a movie assassin's three-level tackle box with the foam cut-outs for guns either," Billy laughed.

"I told you, you guys should go to where chefs shop," the clerk said. "Those places are wannabe serial killer gold."

"I had a similar experience looking for falconry equipment," offered a nearby browser, unsolicited. He was head to toe in flannel and playing with a plastic robot arm. "I ended up having to go to a welding shop."

143

But Billy was still stuck on the serial killer comment.

"I think you're on to something, man. 'Don't get mad, Mad Doctors! Come to Serial Killer Gold. For all your sinister basement tool needs!'"

Bully laughed, and the shopper backed up a step. Billy tried to keep a straight face.

"But no, seriously, do you have a poster that looks like a decade of newspaper clippings to save time on making a Crazy Shrine?"

Nothing.

"Hey, do you know anybody who will provide a service cutting out all the individual letters from magazines to threaten people, you know, for kidnappings, ransom notes, or whatever? Seriously. Because that shit takes *forever.*"

After the clerk gave up on them, they wandered around, looking for toys with colorful remote controls to scavenge. Billy had his eye on a gas-powered helicopter, but it was three hundred bucks. He tapped it and nodded at Bully. The guy in the flannel had finally left, so Bully went to keep an eye on the clerk, who had gone back into a storeroom to use the phone. His face was visible in the glass sliver of window on the door.

She watched the clerk for a long time, then finally whispered to Billy, "He's not looking. He's on the phone with his girlfriend talking all sexy."

"How can you possibly know this?"

"Are you fucking kidding me? I can read his lips! A decade of watching drive-in movies from a mile away has finally paid off! I'll start the car." Then she headed out.

Billy did one more lap, saw the guy still on the phone, then put the helicopter under his arm and moved for the door. He'd just cleared the threshold and was aiming for their corner of the parking lot when he realized a couple things were different.

Her car was gone. And a police cruiser was pulling into the space she'd left behind.

The officer stepped out and froze. Billy held the helicopter out as if he was going to drop it, then tried to make light of the situation.

"Hey, I've always wondered about something. Are you still littering if you set something down real slow?"

"You betcha." Click.

"One more question…"

"No more questions. Now put down the Space Shuttle and place your hands behind your head."

Space Shuttle? Billy was insulted. Every toy was a "Space Shuttle" after a recent launch. Until the *Challenger* explosion anyway.

Then the clerk came out, setting off the door chimes and the cop looked away. Billy ran like the fucking wind, knowing the back alleys well enough to quickly win the foot chase. He didn't stop running until he got home and back on his bike. And he didn't stop his bike until he got back to her.

"Do you hate all cops?"

"I hate cops, firefighters, paramedics, bounty hunters, security guards… and probably astronauts."

"Come on, what did a firefighter ever do to you?"

"Fuck 'em. They're lucky they're around fire all day. Otherwise, they'd just be a bunch of assholes in stupid hats."

"My uncle's a firefighter."

"Firefighters rely on the cool aspects of fire to act tough. But what if they were fighting, say, bubbles? That's what I thought. Just a bunch of punks who wash their trucks too much."

"Yeah, but you can't die from third-degree bubble. Or catching bubble."

"Catching bubble! I'll bet you fifty bucks that hundreds of kids die every year trying to catch bubbles. You know, tripping over shit, getting balls impaled on fences."

"Fuck that. You're on."

Two thugs, one big, one little (the modern-day, post-Heat versions of thugs anyway, with the business suits, black Isotoners and flak jackets), high-step over the line of bodies like the tire obstacle at a Police Academy, two silver shotguns swinging at their sides. Everyone is doing it right so far, hands over heads, breath fogging the floor, not even a whisper to raise their blood pressure. They hear their partner in the vault wrestling with the last garbage bag. The big thug and little thug always give the middle guy the physical duties, mostly because his size is "just right."

"Answer me this," Little Thug goes on. "You ever had a run-in with a cop before today?"

"Yep," Big Thug says. "I was 15. My brother was 16 and just got his license. We both hopped into my dad's Chevy van, armed with Super Soakers so we could scare-"

"Yeah, you're under arrest," Little Thug laughs.

"No, no, wait. Okay, sure, we wanted to scare some people, yanking open the sliding door and lighting 'em up with a stinky dose of Northwest Ohio egg water. But that's not a crime. So my brother slows down, and I hose this punk on a bike from head to spokes. Which was a fuckin' favor since it was about 90 degrees out. So, yeah, we come home, and we've pretty much forgotten about it, except my brother, who's drinking water out of the end of his barrel at the dinner table. Then there's this knock on the door."

"Busted!"

"Yep. The boys in blue. My dad answers the door, and they tell him about some 'drive-by' and some 'terrorizing of local youth,' and they give him a description of two scrawny whelps, right around our height, wielding, get this, 'pump-action shotguns.' My dad yells for my brother, who's still suckling the end of his gun like a freakin' hamster, and we all step outside. And before we know it, the cop actually has his .38 out, barkin', 'Put the weapon on the ground, son!' My brother and I drop, and my dad laughs, 'Seriously? It's green

and purple for Christ sakes.' The cop sputters some bullshit like, 'Someone could paint a gun to look like a toy, sir!' And my dad snaps. He takes a step too close to the biggest one, and suddenly my dad's on the ground, arm dislocated over his head, three knees in his back. But my brother, who always moved a little quicker than me, God bless him, he gets off one good squirt, super-soaking one of the fucker's legs, right before he's choked out."

"What happened to your dad and your brother?"

"Nothing. Charges dismissed. But here's the worst part. They kept the toys. Even after one of them fired a 'round' into the grass and reported into his radio, 'Weapon discharged, no danger, over.' Right now they're in an evidence locker surrounded by heroin and AK-47s. Breaks my fuckin' heart. I'd walk right into that station if I knew I'd get them back."

"You want to?"

He thinks about it. Then they pull up the bottom of their ski masks to breathe easier. Big Thug slips a boot under the security guard's ribs and flips him over. The guard carefully opens one eye, then the other.

"See this cocksucker?" Big Thug hisses.

"Yep."

"He was chewing gum when we walked in. I think it distracted him." Big Thug kicks him in the kidney. "You got gum?"

The guard stares, coughing through the pain.

"Chew it."

The guard's jaw starts working like a horse with an apple.

"Hey," Big Thug whispers, tugging on his mask, "Do we have to do so much cop bashing? I mean, I know it's all part of the…"

Little Thug smacks his hand away and motions down with his gun.

Big Thug finds the guard on the floor again and laughs. "Blow a bubble."

The guard tries, air and spittle whistling. Big Thug cocks his shotgun for incentive. It's spray-painted green and purple with a water bottle taped to the top.

The guard tries harder, and finally a big pink ball of bubble gum inflates and covers his face completely. Little Thug sees Big Thug's eyes inside the mask, and he realizes what's gonna happen next.

The heat of the blast instantly turns the wavering balloon to sugar and vapor while chasing most of the guard's skull halfway up the wall in a supernova of teeth, blood, and burger.

"I owe you fifty bucks."

A tongue starts to roll back down the wall, end over end before it hits the ground, exactly like those sticky rubber spiders you get from the gumball machine when you wanted something better. Probably because that's where Larry had bought the sticky rubber spider to shoot the scene. He leans in close until it's stuck to the lens of his camera.

On their way back home, out of their uniforms and back in their uniforms, the radio by their knees starts chattering, and they slap a red light on their roof like the cherry on a sundae.

Mike and Mike sit on the curb, splitting a tuna sandwich. Larry is sifting through a handful of bubblegum machine toys.

"How did you like the tongue?"

"I've never seen shit like that in my life," Little Mike says. "That's not how it would happen, would it? Human body don't work like that. You of all people should know this."

"Oh, I don't know," Big Mike says. "We've seen some shit. *I've* seen some shit."

"Like what?"

"Okay, remember that building where I used to live back in Nashville? Like most of those apartments, the building was old as fuck and sagging, but the decks were all new and straight lines, so it was like walking onto a lumberjack contest when you went out back. I was living there with Peggy, and you know how she was a talker, but I don't think we were used to sitting on a deck, smoking, talking smack, because otherwise we would have shown a little discretion about some of the shit we were saying out loud, Peggy anyway. But everyone was out there doing the same thing. Most of the people didn't have a nice, level-headed deck before to pretend they were normal. We were on the second floor, right between all the neighbors. Above us was April and her creepy mom, Brenda, I think. I just called her Doris, because it rhymed with 'Loris.' You ever see those videos of the Slow Loris? Bitch looks exactly like that, but doesn't move nearly that fast. One time, she waddled out and showed Peg her bandages from her last suicide attempt, which invokes sympathy in some, but usually makes me imagine someone holding out a pile of dog shit and saying, 'Look what I almost stepped in!' And April, she was never home. She bartended every night, and most of the time she was hooking up with some barfly and creeping in at dawn, nice and early so she could wake up Garbage Dog."

"Who?"

"I'll get to that fucking monster in a minute. So it was mostly just Slow Doris up there, creaking around, peeking down the steps that connect us since Doris used to steal Peg's cigarettes, too. And her purple lighter, not that we could ever prove it. I shit you not, I ended up threatening the maintenance guy instead when I saw him smoking, might have got him fired since this was in a red state and the poor bastard was black. All I know is he never came back for his hammer, and it was a nice hammer. The Cadillac of hammers. The *pink* Cadillac of hammers.

Oh well, collateral damage. Like he never stole a lighter before. Now, on the ground floor was the main event. Some tall, skinny kid we called Hendrix after we caught him torching a guitar in the burn barrel the day we moved in. Actually, it turned out an ex-girlfriend had torched this guitar earlier, and he was just trying to save it, but all we saw was him waving his hands like a witchdoctor over the flames like Jimi did at Woodstock. And Hendrix, he had this Chihuahua named Tom Joad, which we thought was kind of pretentious until we realized it was named after Springsteen instead of Steinbeck. Tom Joad was a gnarly little rat, yeah, but at least he wasn't Garbage Dog, so we kind of liked him. He was tiny and purple and green around the edges from some homemade mariachi costume Hendrix forced on him in the winter, so Peg started calling him 'Jim Toad' instead, because maybe Tom Joad had a Mexican buddy named Jim? Who can say. Still a hell of a lot better name than anything in *Grapes of Wrath* or the Springsteen song - blasphemy, I know. Maybe not better than 'Green Machine' like I wanted though."

"No way that dog was green. Monkeys can be green, sure, like the one that started the AIDS. But dogs? No way."

"Wait, almost forgot, in the apartment directly above me was Cindy. At least that's what was on the mailbox. We never saw her. And above her are anywhere from two to five assholes, but they don't count either. Frat types, baseball caps. No idea. It just got noisy sometimes, or someone would be out in the back yard navigating the dog shit to play cornhole, and it was always them. They were funny at first, then after the third night we listened to them one-upping each other with finger-banging flashbacks or whatever, we lost interest. One time, I *thought* we were hearing an honest-to-Christ argument, full of passion and hate and betrayal, but, nope! It turned out it was the drive-thru at the McDonald's, right out our alley, about 20 feet away. Actually, it could have been some girl Hendrix just broke up with *working* at McDonald's, yelling out the speaker trying to get his attention. The way the alley is set up, that shit is loud. So I know he heard her. But, yeah, Hendrix was a trip. When we were out there on the deck, we'd hear him down there smooth-talking some female, and the way he laid it on, you'd be surprised to know that this skinny Mac Daddy punk was sporting a mouthful of chrome. Here he was, about a hundred pounds, almost six foot six, voice like Al Green… and braces that filled every inch of his face. I kind of loved looking at him. He was like a James Bond villain, or at least the villain's nephew. Every time I'd see him walking Jim Toad, I'd smile just to get one back and watch his lips work to cover those huge metal chompers. I didn't realize they still made braces out of car parts! Thought that shit was all plastic now, seriously. But he was a cool kid, at first. Okay, he never really said, 'Hi,' but always said, 'Say, "Hi!" Say, "Hi!"' to Jim Toad, like one of those insufferable pet owners who use their dog as a way to avoid actual communication, which was probably worse.

"But I figured maybe he'd get more chatty once the braces finally came off, like that kid in the movie who can throw a 90-mile-an-hour fast ball once he loses his cast. I used to swear to Peg, or anyone else listening to us through the floor of our deck, that one day I'd get him talking fast enough through that deep, pillow-talkin' metal mouth of his that I'd see those sparks flying for myself."

"Can that happen? Are you a scientist, dude?"

"So I feel like shit after what happened. One night, way late, I'm sitting on my deck, watching the end of my cigarette flicker, watching for Slow Doris to come sniffing around to steal one, and I hear glass shattering somewhere in one of the apartments. So I creep down, and after seeing a giant hole in the door below us, I call 911. I wait out there until I see the cops come, flashlights bobbing around near the gas meters for awhile like the super sleuths they are, then I hear them finally rouse Hendrix, who is hammered from a night at the bar, probably breaking up with somebody of course, and I hear Hendrix say he was locked out and had to break his own door to get back in. It's the most I've ever heard him talk to a man, but the crime is solved, right? So I start to doze off in my camping chair, and fifteen minutes later Hendrix is running up and down the alley and the McDonald's parking lot screaming, 'Tom Joooooad! Tom Joooooad!' because either him or the police accidentally let the dog out during all the ruckus. So feeling guilty as hell and knowing it's a full moon, and realizing this is the widest I might ever see this mouth in the moonlight, I run down hoping for a laser-light show off those miraculous incisors. 'Jim Tooooooad!' I yell. 'Tom Joooooad!!!' he's screaming. He's screaming this so loud that I'd put three exclamation points on it right now if that was even allowed. So I know there's *got* to be sparks coming off those teeth by now. But as I switch my boots to the correct feet, I start to wonder: Is that the danger of metal in your mouth? All that hardware has got to be worse than a megaphone, almost battery powered. They say people can pick up radio stations on their fillings. How about broadcast from their braces? '57 Channels and nothing on' but poor Hendrix. Turned out it wasn't sparks I got to see after all, though, just the street light reflecting off them, but it was still an impressive display of fireworks."

"Fourth of Jooooo-lie!"

"But I do try to help him, fully accepting my punishment of wandering the streets with this drunk fuck, shaking bushes, looking for his green Chihuahua with the goofy name, and this is what we're doing for three goddamn hours. I have no idea if he knows it was me who called the cops, but I figure he must at least suspect it. But I'm not gonna bring it up with him half-crying over his toad. So I keep kicking around, and we jump every time a walnut drops from the tree next door, thinking it's Jim. Or Tom. Jimi, Bruce, whoever. At one point, I wreck another neighbor's bush, uprooting it to look for something that was scratching around in there like Cool Hand Luke signaling for a piss. I point out my amateur landscaping to Hendrix and say, 'Is that him in here? I think that's him!' But he won't even look over. He's on his cellphone with some ex, and he shrugs me off with a 'No, not him yo.' So I gut the whole stretch of Callery trees anyway, shaking those white flowers everywhere, which is doing everyone a favor since they smell like jizz, an anomaly the landlord used to blame on Hendrix, but I find nothin'. No cat, no rabbit, no clue, *nada*. Something had to be in there along that house making that noise, but now Hendrix is too busy calling everyone he knows for some reason, crying into his phone for sympathy and refusing to make eye contact with me. I start thinking, 'Yeah, he knows it was me who called the cops,' and figure my work here is done and head for our steps. 'You're welcome!' And when birds start chirping and the morning is threatening, I notice that both the front and back door of his apartment are wide open. And I officially declare the rescue effort too flawed to be a part of. I go back up and climb into bed, trying to wake up Peg and tell her the story, hoping she'll tell me it's not my fault, but not really, and she's like, 'Yeah, no, you fucked up.'"

"Yeah, man, you fucked up."

"Just listen. So then it's a week later, and still no Jim Toad. Then it's a month. Then we run into Hendrix at the art fair. He's with another girl, of course, and I get him talking about that night, you know, wondering who called the cops. It's weird, but he doesn't even talk about Jim Toad, that dog he was crying over right in front of me. Instead, he's just trying to figure out who was to blame. I lie and play along and avoid eye contact, but there's something about him that's off, and it doesn't hit me until later that his braces are gone. This bothers me for some reason, and I start looking in the alley again for the dog, even splashing around in the little babbling brook next to the McDonald's drive-thru, figuring if a stray could survive anywhere for a month, it's next to a fast-food joint. I'm all over their lot every free chance I get, only stopping when a voice comes out of the speaker telling me I need a car to be served at the drive-thru. I want to say something about McDonald's being the biggest eavesdropping disappointment in my life, how maybe all my trips through the drive-thru were action-packed before I moved there or something because all these motherfuckers ever do these days is order food or cry over their boyfriends. But instead I yell something about what kind of idiot puts a running stream next to a microphone?! But every time I thought I'd finally start forgetting about Jim Toad, I'd run into Garbage Dog, April's timorous monster, and I'd start thinking like the dad in *Stand by Me*, 'It should have been you, Gordie.' And it's true, it should have been you, Garbage Dog. Sooo many nights I'd stare at Garbage Dog and his tumors and yelping and his happy, slobbering face pushing the corners loose on our screen door, and I'd imagine sending him to a quiet place far away. Nothing violent like with my new hammer or anything, but maybe getting him in a headlock and sending him straight to Garbage Heaven, whispering in his torn ear the entire time, 'Shhhh, shhhh. Tell Jim I'm sorry.' Or maybe just, 'Say "Hi!" Say, "Hi!"' Seriously, if it had been Garbage Dog that ran away, I would have slept like a baby after letting it loose, instead of being responsible for the loss of the canine equivalent of a green, shivering, naked old man. Not that it *could* run away, having never been restrained from shitting everywhere and anywhere anyway. Peg called Garbage Dog my spirit animal once, and it's the closest I ever came to leaving her. Or adopting a dog. Speaking of everywhere and anywhere! I know we had a walnut tree next door that was kind of noisy, and we lived in an old creaky house with hardwood floors, but I know Jim Toad was still living on that block. There's just no way he wasn't around. How far could that little Benjamin Button fuck run without assistance? You never read that story? Seriously, I never even saw him *walk* on one of their famous walks. Hendrix could have been struggling to get his backpack to say, 'Hi!' to me instead of that dog for all I know. And, you know, I never really cared for Steinbeck, but this experience has definitely affected my enjoyment of any Springsteen with a mournful harmonica in it, which covers about six thousand and seventy-three of his songs."

"He has more songs than that."

"So I see Hendrix about five more times, hear the dog rustling around about twice as many times, and I try to bring up Jim, get some indication that he's still looking for him, that he even gives a shit. I even make sure I'm at that same art fair a year later, milling around in front of the booth where some hippie asshole spends her spare time covering dragonflies in scalding plastic to pretend they're amber paperweights and that she's not killing shit. Hendrix loves those kinds of trinkets, I guess, or maybe just the hippie selling them, but not enough to drop forty bucks. He just hangs around her booth to fondle some big, plastic balls, and when I see him again, I imagine Jim Toad frozen in one of those paperweights like Hendrix has stumbled onto a fortune teller. And maybe there's a little movie projected on the dragonfly wings, a flickering image of Jim sizzling at the bottom of the McDonald's grease trap in the back of our alley. I pretty much confess the last time I run into him, though, saying, 'Whoever called the cops, they may have been pretending to do a good thing, but it was really a bad thing, don't you think? And they should feel bad.' He says nothing. 'I mean you should feel bad, too, right?' I say. Still nothing. He just keeps changing the subject, but not in that 'It's too painful to talk about' kind of way. It's the 'I don't give a shit' kind of way. And his teeth are so straight I can't even hear him really. His voice is probably normal now. '57 channels and nothing on' for real this time."

"Good song. Terrible album."

"Anyhow, some time later, I can't remember when, I crawl into his apartment when he's sleeping, which is real easy since he's never fixed that hole he made when he broke in. And I take my new hammer, and I give him two shots with it while he sleeps. Just two for some reason. One to make sure he stays sleeping, and the other one to see if I can bring back the sparks. He wakes up between the hammer strikes, if you can believe it, and even though he's conscious for only about a second and a half between those shots, for about the time it takes Bruce to suck in that harmonica between notes, I still have time to talk to him. I tell him, 'I'm sorry I lost your dog, but can't you see that we're bad people?' Then the hammer hits his teeth, and I can see why the ladies always loved him."

"Why?"

"His smile lights up the room."

"Good work, Mike," Larry says, slapping his thighs. "You, too, Mike. You're the best cops I could have asked for. You guys were born to do it. You look like just the kind of assholes who would love Springsteen that much."

"Hey, they might call him the poor man's Bob Dylan, but at least he's not jockeying for the honor of being a poor man's Bruce like Bon Jovi or John Cougar! Like you, the poor man's doctor."

"Ignore him. It was fun. Let us know when the movie comes out."

"Sure."

"What was the point of that story again?"

"Didn't you ask why I rescued animals?"

"Nope."

Little Mike starts singing "Neighbours" by the Rolling Stones, accent and all, to remind Larry of jolly old England.

"You know that neighbours steal off my table, steal off my table… ain't doing all right."

Larry is learning not to look so confused when people talk about his movies. He used to get them mixed up, the ones he saw with the ones he made.

"What about that other movie we made? *Boys in Blue.*"

"You mean *Balls in Blue?*"

"Whatever."

"I used some of it. Couple scenes here, couple scenes there. Mixed it all together like a stew. But, you know, with balls."

"Is this a fucking joke?!"

"What's the matter?"

"You ditched me!"

"You weren't fast enough."

"You left me there on purpose."

"Why would I do that?"

"You tell me!"

She didn't tell him, but she moved a little closer and laid a head on his shoulder. He was driving again, but it didn't feel like his car anymore, not that it ever should. She'd been parked outside the drive-in, of course, and the only reason he was giving her another chance is the way he found her, sitting in the passenger's seat. Like she was waiting for somebody. He hoped it was him.

"I'll make it up to you," Bully said, her voice as sweet as he'd ever heard. He hated it. "You'll see. Three more turns and you'll forget you were mad."

But before they took three more turns, she had him slow the car to a crawl so that she could leave a cassette balanced on an orange traffic cone. As he watched her turn the spool with her thumb so that the tape was tight, he smelled the rot of a deer carcass somewhere nearby.

"They're like flowers, you know," Billy said to no one. "We don't even notice them anymore unless we smell them."

"Smell what?"

"Dead deer."

"Maybe. We notice the dogs though. A dead dog still horrifies people. Sort of like a toddler on the road. Well, not exactly like a toddler."

"Yeah, they're worse," Billy muttered, tipping his rear-view mirror. "What was on that 'Luck Bomb' anyway?" he asked.

"Everything," she laughed.

"When do I get one?"

She ignored the question.

Billy said, "Hey, remember when you said our story needed one good cop to make the other one seem bad? To balance everything out? That's what the dog is, I think!"

She turned around to pet the grateful beast, who jumped up panting, slobber increasing exponentially with any eye contact. Billy almost shit himself in shock. He hadn't realized it was out of the trunk. He had forgotten about it completely, as well as most of their plans. He adjusted the rear-view mirror again to hide from its eyes. Even though the dog's "official" collar had also been removed (which included a fun, tiny approximation of a police badge), Billy still felt like there was an authority figure in the car.

"So you're done, or what?" he asked, eyes shifty. "That's why you ditched me, right?"

"I never said that."

"I feel you're not as excited about blowing off ol' Bigcheat's head anymore."

"Well, I feel you're too excited."

"Fair enough."

"Why is that?"

"Because if a police officer's head comes clean off and flies through the air, that's a decisive win."

"For who?"

"Humanity."

The dog whimpered.

"You know why your dog is so stressed out?" she asked.

"Why?"

"Because of the horn blasting on this car! I'll bet you forgot about that, didn't you?"

"I think everybody did."

"Well, we're shouting at the top of our lungs. Have been for days."

They frowned at each other.

"Doesn't seem like it, does it?"

Then they both frowned, realizing that the horn had stopped again, and they had no idea when.

"When did-"

"Probably about the same time your nose started bleeding."

He took the bait and wiped at it with a shaking hand. Nothing. She laughed. He would later wrongly remember this as the beginning of the end. In her brain, she had filed away about five "beginnings of the end" by now.

"This better be good."

"Turn here," she said.

"This better be good," he repeated.

"Turn here!"

"I'm turning!"

"You're gonna lose Bigwheat."

Officer Dwight C. Bigbee's roller pulled over into some stones, near a patch of trees at the edge of Pierce Park, and he stepped out. A large German Shepherd followed.

"He's already got another dog!" Billy almost yelled, and Bully shushed him.

They drove past slow, craning their necks for a look. They saw a strange collar on the new dog, a thick cumbersome loop of plastic with a box near its throat. They didn't realize what it was until, just as they rolled by, the dog began to bark, then flinched and rubbed its snout in the stones as if a hornet stung it in the face. Then they saw the other squad cars and other officers leading German Shepherds from their back seats. Collars bulged on muscular necks, thick pink-and-purple buckles with something like disposable cameras bouncing under every slobbering chin.

"What the hell was that?!" Bully wanted to know, climbing over her seat to get a better look. "What kind of cruel bullshit do they use on them these days?"

"I don't know."

"Hold up, is that what an electric fence collar looks like?"

"No, no, that's one of those citrus collars. Sound activated. Spray a little mist when the dog barks to discourage it, like negative reinforcement."

"I thought police dogs were *supposed* to bark," she said. Then laughed, "So that's why our boy smelled like rotten fruit the day he pulled us over."

"Ha. I don't remember that," he said, then suddenly concerned, "Won't all those dogs smell the dog in our-"

"Do they sell that shit in the stores?" Bully interrupted.

"Why? Do you want one for *your* dogs? When's your birthday?" Suddenly Billy was convinced she'd stolen her dogs, too. "Do you know what they call those kinds of collars in the pet stores? No joke."

"What?"

"Neck Bombs."

"No fucking way."

"Yep. That's the brand name."

"What does that mean?"

"I haven't decided yet."

"I wonder if that dog hates him," Bully mused, watching the dog huffing its nose in the dust. "That dog must hate him."

"Why do you say that?"

"I read the other day that they were going to discontinue the K-9 program in Erie because the dogs were so poorly trained that they supposedly kept attacking the handlers. Maybe the citrus collars are the final solution."

"Crazy."

"I'll bet he never even bothered to name it," she hissed.

"The police academy in this town is truly clown college, ain't it?"

"Those dogs hate them," she decided as they parked around the bike trail and out of sight. They went tree to tree until they were close enough to hear the police radios crackling on their shoulders.

"Why do people always brag about how they could kill someone with their bare hands? That's just poor planning."

"Shhh!" It was Billy's turn to shush her.

Billy and Bully crunched through the woods, as close to the cops and the dogs as they dared. The dogs looked back occasionally, but Bigbee never did. This may have been one of Bully's worst ideas yet, but it *was* relatively easy to stay out of sight and orbit the cloud of rotten oranges.

"Can't say I hate it," Bully said, inhaling deep. "Smells like fruit. And dog."

"Do you think he knows we're following him?" Billy whispered.

"The dog sure does."

"I keep thinking it's gonna bolt, but it never does."

"I know."

"Why are we doing this again?"

"Because it's fun."

Billy wasn't so sure.

"Imagine putting one of those collars around that asshole's neck."

"I think we've got his collar covered, you know?"

"I'll bet it would stop him from barking," she giggled.

"You know what I like about dogs and cops?" he offered. "When they see a squirrel out your window and you put their nose up to the glass. It's like putting a baby on a nipple."

They weren't surprised by the sudden clearing near a sign that read: "Pierce Park Cemetery."

Recognizing this as the site of a renegade brushfire she had started a week earlier, Bully hauled Billy down, and they both quickly collapsed on all fours, heads low like felids. Excited, they pushed aside the ironweed, bloodshot eyes big as pizzas.

It was a search party of about fifty officers and a dozen dogs, heads down, kicking leaves, upending deadfall. Every thirty feet or so, cops would pull out lighters, thumb them on, then stretch tiny flames high above their heads.

"It's a search party."

"It's like the worst concert of all time," Bully giggled.

"They're checking the wind," Billy explained. "Isolating the fear scent. Which means I'm fucked."

"Get down."

"Haven't you been listening to the radio? They're supposed to be looking for-"

"Down!"

"They're looking for a dead body."

"It probably smells the same as your fear scent."

"Then I'm double fucked," Billy sighed. "I heard that a dog's senses are 10,000 times stronger than ours. When you smell a pot of stew, they smell the ingredients."

"10,000 times, huh? That means that dog probably hates our boy 10,000 times more than we do," Bully muttered. Then, "Lay the fuck down, dummy!"

She pulled him into the brushwood, and as he fell, he breathed in the sweet sweat on her scalp, tumbling, tumbling. She made a dirt angel after they rolled, not feeling the ant bites. Only once they popped up to watch an officer yawn, passing a silent scream down the line like a lazy baton between losing teammates. Occasionally, Billy would lean over to smack an ant on her thigh to steal a kiss. They laid there holding hands on an anthill for a half hour, listening to the search party's conspiracy theories and the hiss of the wheat. Billy stole all the kisses he could, waiting patiently for their bodies to be discovered. He had his story ready. Just a couple kids messing around in the woods. Must have fallen asleep, Sheriff…

Voices got close, closer, then faded completely. They stood up to see submissive tails curling into J's in the distance and sun-burned necks scratched in frustration. The search party had missed them completely.

"Unbelievable. What does that tell you?"

"That this field might have a marching band in it and they'd never know it."

"Maybe those fruit bombs are screwing up their noses."

A big dog whimpered, and the biggest cop leaned down to tap its collar. The man's sleeve slid up to reveal a tattoo in Blackletter script across a bulging forearm reading:

Some Are Born Brothers…

"Sexist," she scoffed. "Not born sisters? You *sure* that isn't an electric fence?"

"*Invisible* fence. No way. Those have prongs that hit you in the two big neck veins."

"How would you know?"

"Me and my buddy tried one on at a party."

"Did it work?"

"Well, after getting zapped just once, I really didn't want to leave the party."

"Figures," she said, then mumbled in disgust, "Wonder what his other arm says."

Billy saw he was losing her again. This was where his worst ideas always came from.

"Follow me."

Billy ran at a crouch, with Bully following. And when they were between two officers, they stood up tall. Downwind, with hundreds of twigs popping under boots, no one noticed at first. Without looking up, the men let them join their ranks, taking their hands like they were saying Grace.

"I knew I wore this Steelers jersey for a reason," Bully whispered. Billy looked around and saw that everyone, even the few civilians, were indeed in kind of a uniform, if not a badge then a sports logo on their chests.

"What's the name of the missing girl?" someone asked.

"I hope it's 'Amber!'" someone else laughed.

"That's not funny. Her name *was* Amber," someone else said, somber tone indicating she may have just been found.

They made it ten more steps before Billy glanced over to see that big cop's glare locked and loaded. The big dog's, too. Both were moving towards him, jaws working. Then all the dogs were barking, collars popping steam like manhole covers. They ran.

Billy lost his grip with Bully. There was some excitement in a denser patch of woods, and anyone not running for them was running to see what it was. Except the dogs.

The dogs bridged the distance in a less than a minute. A minute after that, they were passing Billy completely. They targeted Bully instead, which made sense, it being her crime scene and all. As he weaved through the tombstones, he caught flashes of famous names marking the graves of regular people. "Hitchcock," "Stark," "Lynch"…

Then the real one surprised him, and he almost clipped his knee.

"James B. Dean, 1931-1955."

He ran hard. Teasles peppered Billy's torso like bullets, goosegrass burrs filling up the exposed rings of his socks to weigh him down even more.

He couldn't keep up. She was always faster than he was. They were all faster than he was.

Billy slowed in disbelief at what he saw next. At first, dogs were snapping, ready to bring her down like a gazelle, then they were calm, running alongside her instead.

Then they were gone.

Billy looked down to see a collar at his feet, watching it spit citrus venom with the cadence of his coughs, when a voice bellowed behind him, and adrenaline fueled his legs with one final burst of speed. She was wrong. At least one dog had a name. The new dog.

"Fat Elvis! Meat!"

The last dog was on him, eerily silent, afraid to bark. Fat Elvis bore down on him like traffic, forcing Billy to turn and face the music.

Billy knew from the movies you were supposed to offer your forearm. But he figured stuntmen did this because they wore a padded cuff. So Billy went for an eye. He got a thumb in before someone stood him up off his feet.

It turned out cops offered their forearms, too, and a big one bloodied his nose to find his throat with brutal efficiency.

Billy recognized the VNR, or vascular neck restraint, from the newspapers. Sometimes fatal, it squeezed off carotid arteries and jugular veins as easily as garden hoses under a tire. Billy couldn't see the man behind him, but he could read his other arm:

"**...But All Others Must Earn It.**"

He didn't have the wind to scoff. The last thing he saw were Bully's tiny fingers smoothing down electric fur as she ran, reaching into hackles to unbuckle and release those hissing snakes along the road.

The veins powering the tattoo swelled with effort just

as Billy understood why chokeholds were usually fatal. You died because you really wanted to run.

You died because restraint without knowing who held you made your heart detonate like a rotten orange against a garbage can.

IV.

Shirts Vs. Skins – Unstoppable Revenge Machine – Billy Celebrates Veteran's Day in Jail – Leaving a Baby Luck Bomb on the Rocks (or Easter Egg Island) – Sucker! – Important Shit Revealed – Bad Hand Acting – Man Bites Shark – Larry Gets Confused about Octopus Ink

"And now I'm ready to feel your hand, and lose my heart on the burning sands"
—The Stooges "I Wanna Be Your Dog"

…tap, tap, tap… tap, tap, tap.

"You feel that? You feel that?"

Larry felt it all right.

Then, even more inexplicably than usual, Joe Fuck asked the girl under him, in his broken English, "Are you coming? You coming again are you? Are you coming again already?"

Then the smack.

"Choke yourself," he whispered. And she did. They always did.

"Choke marks are the new hickeys!" one of the girls said back when they were filming *The Meaty Urologist: The Last Word on Global Warming*. Then she added, "Purple is the new black."

Smack.

Smack.

"Cut!" Larry shouted. "Listen, I think we should-"

"Quit calling me that!" Suzie yelled, still drooling.

"No! Keep filming!" Stevey screamed from behind them. "Larry, get your head in the game. Look at the sky. We're at sudden death here. Damon wants this in the can."

In the 'can?' Always too many jokes. Larry sighed and laughed at the same time. *And two sports metaphors at once?*

Stevey loved his sports talk. Neither of those motherfuckers, him or Damon, ever played a sport in their lives. Unless maybe it was in a pool. But Larry had found himself in a tournament bracket with Stevey every year. See, even though Larry blamed the director's beard he first grew as a tribute to Kubrick, Spielberg, Scorcese, and Coppola, and maybe Brian De Palma ("Thought I was gonna say George Lucas, didn't you?" he told the grip with the "I'd rather kiss a Wiccan" T-shirt the last time he ran through that list of idols), Stevey always mistook it for a playoff beard instead. So he signed him up. Larry did win the tournament one year, when some kid lost his temper and flipped out, getting a technical and landing himself on the bench for three games during the Final Four. But all his life, Larry could never watch an entire basketball game.

Too many stupid tattoos in a basketball game. Too many dinosaurs doing reverse slam dunks and burning basketballs speckling their shoulders like a disease. Although filmmaking had taught him that tattoos looked a little better on black men, maybe, less like someone with Magic Markers caught them passed out at a party, and more like the noble shading around the arms and shoulders you'd get from working hard under a car all day. Sort of what they were doing on the court, actually. Nah…

Not like *a disease. It* is *a disease. Fuckin' idiots, the lot of them.*

But his idiots kept fuckin'. No matter what. It's what they did best. And it was what Joe Fuck did the worst. People were saying he was getting violent and trying too hard these days because of some new guy in the business, Boris something. No, it was "Aura Boris," not to be confused with Aura Borealis, the porn star with the glow-in-the-dark condoms, an idea he'd stolen from John Ritter's *Skin Deep*. No, Boris was named after "ouroboros," the snake eating its tail, a very popular porn tattoo for obvious reasons.

And guess what his talent was.

Larry worked through it all best he could, getting all the reaction shots, remembering that Clint Eastwood movie about the book about the movie *The African Queen*, where Clint played John Wilson playing John Huston, explaining to anyone who would listen that Hollywood was simply a factory town, just like Detroit. So, so true. The intersection of North Hollywood Boulevard Road and South Florida Street was, too, which was where Larry was shooting today.

Not as diseased as Detroit though. Larry remembered when that one asshole showed up talking about his Hepatitis C (and this was his actual asshole he was talking about), and there was a flurry of condoms at the shoots for about a month. Until the men started losing them in the women. This actually got to be a point of pride with the females, touting elasticity, muscle control and what not. Who could pull off the most rubbers by Friday. Larry thought it was a dubious honor really, but Suzie bragged for weeks how one time her partner started his scene bareback, but by the end he was standing there balls deep in a shriveled Trojan, dangling like the last scarf from a magician's hat.

"Can I stop a second, pleasepleasepleasepleaseplease?" Head Breakfast whined from another room, wiping the sweaty egg whites on his temple. He was on double duty moving furniture around. Tricky when you're naked. "I'm hungry!"

"Of course you are," at least three people laughed.

"Fuck the shit out of that pussy," Suzie grunted, those overplucked snaky sperm brows on her forehead all furrowed.

What did she just say? Larry thought. *Nasty.* He looked for the boom mic, hoped it hadn't picked up that line. No one would want to hear something like that, let alone see it.

It was getting done. Until he started to obsess over the "Sammy" tattoo again, starting to wonder if there was a way they could cover it up. With a beach towel? Maybe a houseplant? Maybe a fire.

One time, Larry had to deal with a tattoo of a Dashboard Mary on one of his actresses. Her trick was bobbing her bobble head just like it. And he'd seen a four-armed Mary on another girl. "Mary Fishnu," she called the creature. Sometimes he imagined his own Stone Mary coming off the lawn-ornament factory line with her teeth bared like a chimp and all four hands smashing cymbals, and those moments almost always led to silent screams. Sometimes he laughed.

Now the vein was back in his head. He thought he could cover it with blood if he had to.

But then he noticed the "Sammy" beginning to smear with the sweat and the friction. He couldn't believe it. Tattoos were so popular now, people were apparently faking them with ballpoint pen. "Sammy" turned into "Hammy," then turned into "Amy."

There was no "Amy" in the movie either. It was more than he could take.

Right then, Joe started to lose his erection and jammed it back in Suzie's mouth, pushing out her cheek again. Tap, tap, tap. "You feel that?" Tap, tap, tap. Deafening. And bad timing really.

Snap, snap, snap.

And before he knew what he was doing, Larry had a forearm under Joe's throat and was throwing him back over a crackling, plastic-covered sofa.

"Hey!" Suzie yelled.

"Shut up, cunt!" Larry screamed at her. "And who's this Sammy? Where the fuck is Sammy anyway? What does he think about all this?!"

It was amazing Suzie answered as calm as she did.

"*My* name is Sammy, Larry," she said. "My real name. What's yours again?"

Larry stopped a second, then turned all his attention to Joe.

"Hi, Joe. Hold this…"

He delivered a hard shot to Joe's nose, the locomotive punch he'd learned from the fist of the Virgin Mary's strapping lumberjack of a grandson earlier that morning, sending a starfish of black blood across his cheeks.

"But how did you know that?" Suzie was still asking, used to fighting all around her, apparently. "My real name, I mean…"

Joe soaked up the blow, then hit Larry back about fifteen times while Larry was thinking about Suzie's question.

And Joe could fight. The fucker was scrappy, always in good shape, every appendage red and well muscled. And as Joe beat him into a defensive curl, he found himself eye to eye with the angriest end of his actor. Back when Larry first started doing commercials, they warned him that the camera always added ten pounds. But in porn, it turned out the camera took off three inches. And Joe *still* looked good.

Larry covered his head, deeper and deeper underwater. Porn kids were tougher than they looked. He'd heard they were about a year from fucking modified holes in their faces. Glengarry swore he'd seen this, in spite of it making no sense biologically. And this was Glen talking, one of the business's foremost anal pioneers. They wrote it off as something they'd never understand, saying, "Every generation adds a new hole."

But they still had the same weaknesses.

Desperate under the barrage of body blows, Larry finally fell back on what he knew.

"Skins always win," his gym teacher told him once. Not today.

He grabbed Joe by his erection, catching it before it could turtle all the way back into his body for safety. No one believed it later, but Larry actually picked him up with it, held him off the ground like one of those retractable tape measures you would unspool just to see how long it could hover in midair before it collapsed. There was enough blood to bend it, bend it, bend it. Until...

Snap.

It turned out an erection broke like any limb, only it turned three colors first, even more colors after. Joe passed out from shock, but not before Larry straddled him to rap the top of his head just like the hollow coconut it was with a "tap tap tap, tap tap tap, tap tap tap..."

"You feel that? You feel that?" Then Larry tried that stupid Eurotrash accent, "Are you coming again already?"

Just as everyone was tackling him, Larry dealt a dozen-some savage elbows. They landed easily, almost like he was dealing cards. And when he slipped the KY grip of his sound guy, and smelled the dank, wet-earth exhale of someone else lining up over his shoulder for a perfect shot, he delivered his last elbow so dead-on that the satisfaction rang through his bones like the sweet spot of an aluminum bat.

But it was poor, poor Head Breakfast who caught it, the only one on the set who didn't deserve such a betrayal. H.B. stood up slow to stare at Larry in shock as tiny trickles of red yolk covered his Eggs Over Easy, now transformed into Eggs Benedict Arnold, pinballing through the stubble on his skull like Pachinko, finally filling the corners of his eyes until he blinked.

Larry escaped to his car eventually, shrugging off all the howls and threats, to drive around and steady his breathing again. He was desperate to find at least one station on his A.M. dial, but there was nothing but fucking "Seasons In The Sun" as always. So he settled on a dead stretch between the static where he thought he heard a voice. A voice that sounded an awful lot like a countdown. He'd heard the voices there before, usually on that stretch of highway where he sometimes saw shadows of giants moving in the woods. He had no idea this was the night the drive-in debuted their new technology: piping the soundtrack through the dead air on your radio so they could save money on those speakers that hung on your car window like cold food at the car hop.

If he had known this, it may have saved about eighty lives.

He turned up the volume so he could have a conversation.

When Billy woke up still alive, he was disappointed he didn't get to hold up the toy "Space Shuttle" in his mugshot. Then, about an hour into imprisonment, something finally started to dawn on him. He was suddenly sure that, with her skill cultivated from years of watching monstrous movie lips out her bedroom window, the girl he loved must have known that Radio Shack clerk was talking to the cops.

She'd ditched him on purpose, almost got him arrested that time. And this time she did.

He paced his cell awhile, humming the only Cult song he knew.

"...talk about fun... talk about fun... talk about fun..."

Then, just like his dog, he put his nose on the bars and waited for no one to come and bail him out.

Billy was only in jail for three days, but he scratched himself to pretend it was three years. His uncle Lee had been in way longer than that, and when he came out, he had tattoos of hash marks across his ribs, one line for every day, the usual fag bundle of four sticks with a fifth slashed through the middle. The gashes ran the length of his body, and when he first showed the family at the neighborhood pool, everyone thought they were stitches. His uncle went along with this misconception, swearing he'd had his heart removed.

When he was in there, Uncle Lee had also been pressured by the Aryan nation to get swastikas on his arms. But to cope with this decision, he got tattoos of arms on his arms, with swastikas that never *quite* crossed the border onto his own body. Technically. The difference might seem minor, but it was enough of a rationalization to allow Lee to work out sleeveless. Until his release.

Inside, Billy lifted his shirt and cut days into his body that he hadn't served. It made him feel good, like a martyr. Sometimes he did this with one foot not quite nine inches off the ground.

Billy used to dream about Bully at least every other night before they started plotting together. Once the plan was locked down, it switched to every night. And even though he understood that dreams were by far the strangest things human beings experienced on a daily basis, just as they had no business in good fiction, they has no business in conversations with her. He'd made that mistake before, and Billy found this impossibly unfair. It was like a trip to outer space or stumbling onto your third-grade teacher killing himself with a banana (another frequent dream for Billy) and not being able to report what you'd seen to anyone. Well, you *could*, but nobody would care because everyone takes this trip to outer space every night, touching down in a crater on the supermoon, or watching botched suicide attempts with a vast variety of fruits and vegetables.

But there was that one dream that deserved special consideration, one that occasionally squeezed out the others, even her. Nothing too tangible after he woke up. Just the memory flash of a child's skeleton, no, just the rib cage, lying in a shallow grave. Billy would remember climbing in the grave to get a better look and seeing a red rubber ball bouncing around inside, ricocheting off the curve of the bones. In jail, this dream took over after a cop hollered "lights out."

On the second day of his incarceration, Billy started to study his tormentors. No sign of Bigbee, his White Whale, as he was that breed of exotic Highway Patrolman and wouldn't be hanging out in the local precinct house. But one of the cops had a hint of a feather tattoo on his bicep, maybe hooked to a dreamcatcher ring under his sleeve, so Billy thought he might do.

The other officers called him "Bucky Balls" because of the "magnetic way he drew new collars in close to talk," hopefully to confide, to "give up the goods," as they say. And there must have been something to this nickname because Billy did start talking to him, telling him all about his crazy dreams. And Bucky Balls must have been starving for a sense of community because, after only a couple hours of chatter, he gave up everything. They apparently had video of Bully leaving the scene… of somewhere, or at least some hazy video from one of the new police "dash cams." Recorded on tape was this small, blonde-haired girl leaving a parking lot near a crime scene at high speed. B.B. said they were trying to tie her in with another video, of a small dark-haired girl running along a concrete divider with a gym bag over her shoulder, just blocks away from another crime scene. One on Eerie Drive, Erie, Pennsylvania, which ended with a circle of dead police officers minutes after the detonation of a bomb.

"When was that?" Billy asked, terrified.

"1953."

He rolled his eyes at the joke, but was secretly relieved. He was ready to believe that shit, and Bucky Balls knew it.

"Whereabouts currently unknown. Anything can happen on Eeeeeeerie…" B.B. laughed.

"Have you ever seen that movie they based on the 'pizza bomber' case?" one of the other cops asked.

"No. Why?"

"It was called *Delivered Relatively Fast and Hot or Your Next Five Pizzas Are Free.* I always thought they could have come up with something catchier, some other pizza-delivery saying. You know, like… I can't remember. It's on the tip of my dick…"

Billy still thought of him as a friend, probably suffering from what the newscaster in *Die Hard* wrongly referred to as "Helsinki Syndrome." But it gave him something to believe in while he sulked in his cell. He even told Bucky Balls about their illegal funeral for her cat. And he probably would have told them even more, until his interview on Day Two, when about six more cops stood around him as they played Billy a series of cassette tapes featuring his own voice, detailing approximately six hours of bomb-making details, as well as the eerie blow-by-blow planning of the attempted kidnapping and murder of an Erie, Pennsylvania, K-9 officer.

When they flipped one of the cassettes over, Billy caught a glimpse of the labels.

"Bad Luck Bomb," and "Billy's Kick-Ass Mix."

He closed his eyes, realizing that this was what she'd been putting into mailboxes on that officer's regular beat. That these tapes were what Billy, amazingly, had raised the red flag for, to incriminate himself even more.

Luck bomb indeed, he thought.

There was also a witness who claimed to have seen Billy in the woods, right before he'd been choked out and arrested. Billy probably could have confused the witness at a line-up, as he'd purposely worn a Pittsburgh Steelers jersey to blend it with the other 50 volunteers. But he lost his temper at the mere mention of this witness, refusing to repeat the phrase, "Do we win anything for finding her first?" as any person would have fingered the asshole who said something so obnoxious during a missing-persons search.

Later that night when the grilling was over, Bucky Balls sat at a desk near Billy's holding cell, watching a small black-and-white TV, listening in on the CB as two rookie officers declared their love for a certain dispatcher.

"I heard she just got engaged," one of them muttered as the other deflated.

The television screen was tiny, but Billy could still make out the title card for Evel Knievel's *The Last of the Gladiators* documentary. B.B. took mercy when he saw Billy's nose rabbiting the bars, and turned the television and the volume up so they could watch it together. They even talked a bit about Evel breaking his arms, and that poor cameraman who lost an eye. B.B. brought up *Happy Days,* laughing about Fonzie always jumping sharks and fried chicken. Eventually, they decided Evel should have been a little more evil with a name like that.

In the middle of the night, a voice tried to scare him straight with talks of "graduating to the big house." It whispered something about how huge everyone can shit in a toilet, then something about how that'll tell you exactly the size you can "take up the ass." Billy reminded the voice that his holding cell had no toilet, and that when he shit, it was typically nervous little rabbit pellets from lovesickness and lack of proper digestion, and the voice mercifully moved on to another cell.

When he woke, Billy asked for some water, and an officer whose name tag read "Mahoney" started to sing.

"Gimme some water... 'cause I shot a man on the Mexican border..."

Ironically, this exchange would trigger an alternate future for Officer Edward Joseph "Money" Mahoney, who would now maintain his position on the police department for his entire life, never pursuing his dreams of music. Everything else in this timeline would remain exactly the same.

The morning of Billy's release was also his last interview.

Impossibly, even more cops squeezed into that room, including the public defender. They came at him hard, ignoring the lawyer completely, but there was something else in their voice that gave him pause, even hope. They'd lost a bit of their swagger. Maybe their case.

"Let me get this straight, a vet put your cat to sleep?"

"No. Hers."

"I thought you said-"

"It was my dog. She had a cat."

"But I thought you said-"

"No, she was mad about her cat."

"A cat named 'Shaft.' Impossible."

"No. Well, sorta. More *Shaft in Africa* than *Shaft,* she would say. I told you…"

This made their eyes glow, and they left the room to huddle awhile. He wasn't sure why he lied about that, but told the truth about so many more incriminating things.

"Here's the thing, Billy Boy," Bucky Balls said when they got back. "We actually found this strange cat mummy you described, washed up along Elbow Creek. It goes a long way towards backing up *some* parts of your story, but…"

Holding on to that glimmer of hope, Billy stepped it up. He was suddenly convinced they were just having fun, pretending there was a real crime in their insignificant corner of the woods. Like all small-town cops, they didn't have shit to do except imitate television versions of themselves.

So Billy gave them the satisfaction. He begged. He pleaded. He cajoled. He negotiated. He bargained. He lied. And finally he just admitted he was trying to impress a girl.

And what the hell, the cop believed him. They let his ass out.

The night before Billy hit the street again, Bully broke into Bigbeep's house to leave a dreamcatcher behind, just for kicks. After a cursory search, though, she realized it wasn't necessary, that every cop was issued boxes upon boxes of Tactical Footwear, and the crusty pile of law-enforcing tube socks under his mattress meant that he'd been using them as personal dreamcatchers for years, wetdreamcatchers anyway, soaking up the ammo when he finished twirling his baton and walking his slumberland beat.

She took a bag of dog treats as a distraction, just in case he had a new partner, then left them all over the house like Easter eggs. She decided his next partner should be healthy if he wasn't happy.

While she looked around the officer's one-bedroom shitbox, she thought about the movie *The Thing,* as she often did, how the remake got rid of pesky females altogether, unlike the Howard Hawks original where Margaret Sheridan shrieked and flirted her way around First Contact. Her mother joked that the famous working title of the film, *Watch the Skies,* should have been *Watch the Guys.* She imagined herself more as Kurt Russell's R.J. MacReady, forever strolling through the world with a roll of dynamite, daring anyone to get too close.

She kicked around the shitbox, and she was immediately convinced that the cop was building something, too. Maybe not a bomb, but he did have three bizarre, custom-made weapons laid out on his kitchen table, constructed out of various household items: an umbrella, a gigantic cellular phone, a very realistic toy pistol, a plastic sword. The last one was an object that, years later when the smoke cleared, would be given more lab tests than the rest of the weapons combined (lab rats would only discover he'd used it to scrape ice off of his windshield).

Sniffing around, still unable to shake the voice they'd imagined for Bigby, she fantasized about him desperately trying to convince skeptics of the genius behind such an unassuming arsenal. She wondered if maybe they had more in common with their target than they previously assumed.

She stopped in front of a clipping on the 'fridge of him accepting an award from the local mayor, a man who looked like an alarming combination of every Marx Brother. The headline named a "Supercop Bigbee"

Wait a minute, who is this, Dwight or Dwayne? she thought. *Is it Big-bee or Big-bye? Fuck it. Same difference.*

There was also evidence of substantial gambling debt. Dollar amounts scrawled on Taco Bell receipts pinned with shiny toy-gun magnets, counting up instead of down, written in that distinct script relegated to panic. Also on the refrigerator were tournament brackets for March Madness wagering. On his broken bathroom mirror, a shrine of sports scores and newspaper strips that would have made a serial killer proud.

"Is this Bigtreat's motive for being a fuck? Gambling?" she asked herself in his mirror. "What a letdown."

Shit just got real, she thought. *Real silly.*

Then she turned a corner.

Ooh, this is a little better…

Thumb-tacked to his bedroom walls were the carry-out menus for every pizza place in a 25-mile radius.

Was that first pizza delivery a trial run? she thought, excited. *Force some poor bastard to rob a bank with a fake bomb around his neck? Or had it just given him the idea to do it for real?*

She opened his freezer, hoping for human heads, but only found moldy peas. She dipped her finger in an ice-cube tray. Water. She put her hand against the fan box. It was running, but the cubes hadn't frozen yet. This told her he had just been here. Next to a peeled sardine tin, she found an ominous-looking manila envelope that contained internal memorandum that detailed the entire neck-bomb case she and Billy had rolled up on. Red Magic Marker bled through one side of the envelope so the letters "I.A." read "A.I." on the other.

"Robots!" she squealed, rolling it up to tuck it into her back pocket. Then she went back to the take-out menus on his wall. Pizzas were circled.

The old ordering-a-pizza-for-somebody-else gag? The third-oldest trick in the book.

She stood over the kitchen table awhile, playing with his toys. Until she decided "fuck the toys," and started looking for the real ones. They were everywhere, too. She took the .38 out from under his pillow but left the baby teeth. She left the dreamcatcher in the toilet, hoping it had some affect on his dreams. She wondered if Billy's had changed since he pulled it off his mirror.

She thought of her favorite undergraduate creative-writing workshop experience, the last class she took before she dropped out for good. She'd written a violent, terrible story that everyone hated, and when it came time for her to workshop again, she was still pouting, so she attempted to write one that was even worse. In the days leading up to the class, there were some rumblings about how much everyone was really *really* hating her new story, about a Toilet That Predicted the Future, and they were probably going to skip that day. Then the day of class arrived, and there were only three of them due to this boycott. Which meant they missed the best line of all time when Jason the mystery kid that everyone wanted to get with took off his headphones long enough to mutter, "Why does the toilet tell the future? Whenever I look into a toilet, all I see is the past." They dated for a year, but he peaked with that line. He called her writing "Technicolor Noir," but still swore he knew what "noir" meant.

She made one last stop at the freezer and left the tiniest of cassette tapes in one of the cells of the ice-cube tray, one of those new tapes mostly for answering machines, sometimes for little pocket recorders.

Let him ponder that. Let all of them.

Her baby tape bomb contained her best baby-like voice, calmly reading the license plate numbers of every car that cut her off, flipped her off, or just laid on the horn. Just in case. Billy's was one of them. It was back before they met. She hoped that one day they all got a weird knock on the door.

Oh, yeah, she took all his plastic explosives with her, too.

Bucky Balls was standing at the release window when they let Billy go. Billy was getting back the change they'd emptied from his pockets, and everything else he'd forgotten he had on him when he regained consciousness, and B.B. was going through that whole, "Don't let us see you again, fly right, etc. etc…" speech. But Billy didn't really hear any of it. His nose just fogged up the bars until they opened as he studied the scabs on B.B.'s dreamcatcher tattoo.

Just shut the fuck up! Billy thought. Then he realized it wasn't a dreamcatcher tattooed on B.B.'s arm after all. He'd mistaken a feather for the action lines around a baseball bat. He had the goddamn *Bad News Bears* on there. All of them. Including the coaches. Including the sequels and the permanent memory of their diminishing returns.

He had one person on his mind.

When he got home, no one asked where he'd been. He went into the garage and polished the red eyes of his reflectors, stuffed his boombox full of fresh batteries, then made sure it was taped tight to the handlebars of his dirt bike. He ejected Billy Squier and searched the radio for voices, settling for Steve Earle's "Copperhead Road" instead.

"I went home with a brand-new plan…"

A good lyric, but he no longer needed a plan.

He sat on his garage floor and made some flyers of his own, head soaking up Magic Marker fumes to marinate his bad thoughts. He wrote:

"Free Movies For Everybody! Come One! Come all! Free Popcorn! Free Halftime Show! Free Everything!"

He put a lot of red, white, and blue on the posters, just like circus daredevils did. He made them all night, getting so into it he probably would have kept making them into the next night, too. It was lucky he'd scratched into his chest a way of keeping track of time.

He went out and put his advertisements under every windshield wiper he could find. Then he made sure he hit every tow truck in town, too. But only the new trucks.

The ones with the ramps.

"It's six years later, okay? A child's bedroom. Jacki Ramirez is trying in vain to wake up her daughter."

"'Please, honey, mommy has to go. Please, baby, I had to be there an hour ago.' Is that what you want? Something like that?"

"But she shakes the girl harder."

"'Pleeeeeeeeeeeeeeease, Toni, this is important. I know you can hear me!'"

185

"Perfect," Larry said, clapping his hands. "Okay, then Jacki stares at her sleeping child. See, she's had trouble getting Toni out of bed since what they called The Great Cat Integration of 2011. It ended with the willful destruction of all their clocks. Long story short, Anthony had finally moved in with them, and he'd brought two of his cats with him. Jacki already had a calico she called 'Nell Gato,' an undersized farm cat her cousin had rescued. From her first three years outdoors, Nell Gato had developed what Jacki was informed were 'overactive anal glands,' meaning she gassed you like a Bombardier Beetle if disturbed. She used to take Nell Gato to get 'expressed' at the vet, but she had more distaste for the word than the procedure and had stopped going. So Nell Gato's ass was this time bomb when Anthony finally moved in with his animals…"

"Why do I need to know all this? I can't remember all this."

"Trust me, you need to get into this character's head. Okay, so Anthony spent most of those early days resembling something like an idiot Spartacus, right? And you think about this image often. Broom in one hand, towel draped over his shoulder, ready to intervene when his two cats, Waffles and Sir Pizza, two short-hairs, flanked this hissing, spitting creature like raptors and got, first, a face full of anal secretions, then finally twenty right furry hands. And twenty right hands from N.G., or The O.G. as your daughter, Toni, always called her, was more like fifty, considering the fact that she was a polydactyl cat, two extra thumbs like those Hemingways, but also seven claws per hand. You liked to joke that Nell Gato was about one generation from making a phone call…"

"It's too much backstory for just some dialogue."

"…but that would be the worst phone call ever!" Larry laughed, ignoring his actress. "So, yeah, the battles had been contained for awhile, you see. At least until Anthony busted out the Furbys. Not even a Furby! We couldn't afford one, so we had a Blurby, the cheap-ass knockoff…"

"I fucking hate those things! Terrifying. I'll put a dick in my ass, but I will *not* feed a Furby with my finger."

"You ever hear them talk? The name 'Blurby' makes more sense, since its verbal ejaculations are exactly what you see splashed all over shitty movie posters."

"…and when Jacki asked why a grown man owned two mechanical gremlins that warbled and spit out baby talk and routinely demanded to be 'fed' with a fingertip on their grotesque pulsing beaks, Eric explained this away by insisting they were deterrents to keep the cats from scratching his TV…"

"Wait, who the fuck is Eric? Isn't he dead? I thought his name was Anthony? Who am I again?"

"Right, Anthony, whoever. Anyway, Jacki knew it was really because the Blurbies were both yellow and black, Pittsburgh Steelers colors. But his cats were so afraid of the Blurbies, that just by placing them near anything he wanted protected, the cats would poof out into pinecones and never think of approaching. But something went terribly wrong when Blurbies were combined with anal secretions and mutant paws. Jacki called this final stage 'Catageddon…'"

"Great. Lots to think about. So, you want me to say-"

"But something snapped in all of them! And at the time, any mechanical sound, any whirring of gears or voice from a speaker at all, even a transistor clock radio, became reason for the cats to jump on the nearest bare calf and play it like a harp. Waffles, the smaller cat of the two, would actually punch your shin, as if he was tenderizing the meat, or like a construction worker tapping on a wall looking for a stud to put in the nail. Waffles would work his way around the leg until he was away from the bone, so I guess that's the opposite of a construction worker actually, but then he would lock on! Putting enough punctures in your skin that you'd think he was trying to deflate you like a balloon…"

His actress sat down and blinked slow.

"…and another problem was Toni's alarm clock, this special clock. Shaped like a cat, it made a different cat noise on the hour, *all* twelve cats serenading you every morning, ringing the dinner bell for your juicy calves. 'Cause what Jacki and Toni initially thought was some sort of soothing cat lullaby in the store turned out to be some sort of war cry to felines. The first time it went off, even sweet, little Nell Gato went for any bare skin on Toni's body, and Eric ended up…"

"Anthony."

"…Anthony ended up smashing the clock with his favorite hammer. He kept it under the bed for self-defense and got mad when anyone used it for anything at all. There were hammers and brooms and towels in every room these days, but no more clocks."

"So what am I supposed to be doing?"

"You're Jacki! And you know that hammer is under there. And you, Jacki, look around nervously for any cats skulking near the door, then turn to the small TV resting on the floor by the foot of Toni's bed. You click it on and change channels until you find a loud talk show where the crowd is screaming at someone on a stage. The profanity 'bleeped' from the broadcast causes the little girl to finally open her eyes. Lately, it's all she can count on for an alarm without getting cut up by fucking cats. Got it? Good. So… action!"

His actress, Bubble, stepped into the room where her daughter, Toni, actually her real daughter, Bunny, was watching TV. Her daughter didn't know it was a movie, but that was okay. She wouldn't have been doing things any different.

"I don't know whether to laugh or cry," Bubble-as-Jacki said. "How is this show the only thing that wakes you up anymore?"

"What's up mommy?" Bunny-as-Toni asked, yawning.

"*You're* up. Finally. Come on, get dressed, gotta go."

"Awww, I want to watch the show. Fill in the 'bleeps' like you used to!"

"Jacki smiles," Larry said. "She used to play a game sort of like Mad Libs, replacing the glut of censored profanity with her own nonsense words. It made the morning talk shows almost bearable…"

"Not right now. Later. Let's go."

Toni had one last-ditch attempt to stall, so she burst into song. Peter Hannan's strangely ominous theme song to the cartoon *CatDog*.

"*One fine day with a woof and a purr, a baby was born, and it caused quite a stir. No blue buzzard, no blue-eyed frog. Just a canine feline little cat dog.*"

Jacki waited out this storm. Until finally, her daughter playing her daughter said:

"Momma?"

And everyone in the room believed it. Larry's heart soared.

Toni pointed at the TV.

"What?" Jacki smiled.

"Why did she just call him 'uncle dad?'"

"Did she say that?" Jacki frowned. "No, what did she say, really?"

"Bleep!"

"Bleep right back atcha!"

"Deep in a drawer somewhere," Larry said. "A Blurby answers, 'Bloop!'"

"I hope not." Jacki sighed, out of character again.

* * *

Hospital, later that day. Jack walks into the emergency room, looking for his partner, navigating through the crowded halls and around the bottle of the power drink he's guzzling. He finds two other paramedics leaning against a vending machine, drinking something a little stronger. They're the veterans. The Mikes. One bigger than the other, of course, just like everything else in the world. They used to be sort of rivals around the E.R., as they were both EMTs when Jack and Rick were still EMS.

Jack looks at them now and thinks, "Oh, how the mighty have fallen."

They've been around lately for lifeguard certificates. Most people would shake their heads at the idea of two drunken 50-year-old lifeguards, but a CFR certification would certainly be a leg up from the jobs they now held.

"Hey, they still get to drive an ambulance," Rick laughed once. Until they got in his way at a scene.

The Mikes bounce around the lobby like it's a ball pit. They're happily ignoring the mounting afternoon chaos around them, hiding beers in their sleeves. Jack catches the tail end of their conversation.

"...so, I say to this guy," Little Mike is explaining, even trying a deeper voice. "'If you're not supposed to stick your thumb up an asshole, then why does it fit so perfect?'"

"Good point," Big Mike can't help but agree.

"You mean 'cause it comes to a point?" Jack scoffs as he walks past and through the double doors, one eye squinted for the cacophony of pain and medicine that never comes. *He ducks in on sleeping patients and smiling nurses, until he finally finds his partner Rick behind a curtain, on an empty cot, eating a sloppy joe with one hand while trying in vain to catch the pieces of burger falling from his face with his other. Jack was hoping for the promise of a Big Mike/Big Rick duel, but he catches sight of the Mikes heading out the door in a hurry. He's pretty sure they stole something again. Big Mike is bellowing some existential rant, like he does whenever weekends are busy or slow.*

"Listen, I just know that it takes a pretty gnarly pair of nads to yank some poor soul from limbo and toss it into the ocean to ride the tail of that big ol' thresher... shark. Of life."

Then the Mikes are gone, and Jack looks at Rick and shrugs.

"What up," *Rick says around the burger.*

"What up. Ready to head out and wrestle some sharks?"

"Just let me finish this," *Rick says, taking a last bite.* "I know we won't be hungry later."

Jack leans against the wall and drains the rest of his nuclear green electrolytes as an old and disheveled orderly walks up in blood and dirt-stained scrubs. He jams a finger in Rick's face, grinning.

"Uh, can I help you, Derek?" *Rick asks him, muffled with meat.*

"You finally decided to eat a shit sandwich for real, huh?" *Derek laughs.* "Got tired of wondering what they taste like?"

"What?"

"You know, a shit sammich!" *The orderly is still laughing at his own joke.*

"Yes, Derek. You are correct. That's exactly what I'm doing. Eating a genuine shit sandwich. And it's everything I dreamed it would be."

"Thought so. Hey, hold on. That ain't from my lunch is it?"

"You know what?" *Rick goes on.* "I don't care what anyone says, you can never get enough jokes about eating shit sandwiches..."

"Did you know that they're making little tape recorders that look just like hamburgers? The pickle slice is the tape. Or the volume. One of 'em. You'd be lucky to get a shit sammich these days. At least it ain't listening to you. We gotta be careful out there, right? Right..."

"I think I'd notice that."

"No, they make them small, like the size of an apple. So you can hide them."

"Then why the fuck wouldn't they make it look like an apple?" Rick says, laughing. "No, wait, if you're gonna hide it, why the fuck make them look like anything at all?"

Derek stops laughing, realizing he's being mocked, and swipes the Louisville Cardinals baseball cap off Rick's head before he can react.

"You ever look at this fucking bird?" he asks them.

"I don't, but he does," Rick says, nodding at Jack and reaching, trying to grab it back. "It doesn't usually face me."

"No, I mean look at this fucking bird." He holds it up high.

They all look.

"First off, the mouth? Why does the bird have teeth? I mean, it's already got a beak."

"It's not real, asshole," Rick says, finally snagging it and screwing it back on his head.

"I know it's not real. But why would it have teeth and a beak?" Derek asks them.

"He's got a point," Jack shrugs. Everyone had a point today. Rick glares at him.

"Anyway..."

"I mean, if you have teeth inside a beak, what's under each wing? Fingers?" Jack and Rick are suddenly as unsure as the orderly.

"Think about it," Derek says. "Where does it end? Under each wing a spread of fleshy, human fingers."

He stares for a second too long, then pops a handful of sunflower seeds in his mouth, spitting a couple masticated shells at their feet before he stomps off.

Jack turns to leave, too. Then, over his shoulder:

"Stick around, Rick. I'll be back and we can get rolling."

A couple more turns and Jack finds a relatively quiet wall to lean against. He rubs his temples to soothe his brain, thinking about the last girl from his last car wreck more than he should. But it's like someone unseen keeps insisting.

There is a poster high on this wall of the huge, smiling face of a cartoon dog. It seems to be watching everyone. A comic balloon over the dog's head reads:

"Be Careful, Kids! I May Look Friendly But Not All Dogs Are Friendly Like Me!"

He thinks about the other girl, too, sometimes, the one from six years ago, but never about what he did to cover up that crime.

"Cut!" Larry yells, causing Jack to hit the deck.

"Fuck, man. Yelling that in a hospital is like yelling 'bomb' in an airport."

"Sorry."

"Tell you what, Larry. We don't need anybody to play Derek the asshole orderly. You got that part down."

Hospital examination room, same day. Jacki and her daughter, Toni, are sitting on the same side of a metal table. A doctor and Larry are leaning against the wall, going over their lines. Larry claps his hands, and the doctor starts tiptoeing closer to the little girl, a sucker in his outstretched hand. He's a real doctor, and Jacki clutches Toni's hand, nervous, then rubs a bite on her own wrist. Back at the school where she taught, she thought it was a brown recluse spider at first. They were common enough in her building, so common that one of the other instructors actually collected the dead ones, and she did, too, for awhile. Until some kid caught her counting the tiny carcasses in the dark during final exam week, hiding in her office from the parade of excuses from her worst students.

"What's that?" the kid had asked.

"A brown recluse," Jacki had answered.

"Like you!" the little fucker had laughed.

It had taken her a few minutes of blinking to realize this was a racial slur. Sometimes she forgot she worked in a red state.

"A red state! Like you!" she would laugh to herself after that, whenever she felt the blood rushing to her face.

The doctor is so close they can both smell the nervous sweat and aftershave, and his hand is swimming closer and closer to Toni with his sucker. Jacki doesn't know why, but his exaggerated hand movements infuriate her, the dishonesty of the motions making her want to swat the sucker to the ground. She resists the urge to smack the doctor open-handed across the face for overdoing it, making the whole act even more threatening because of his shitty performance.

Toni opens her mouth and reaches out. But at the last second, the doctor turns the sucker over and pushes the stick into her mouth. He rubs the stick against the inside of the little girl's cheek while she struggles against her mother. He removes the stick and she starts crying.

"I'm sorry, sweetie."

The doctor puts the sucker in a jar, then pulls another object from the pocket of his lab coat. He holds it behind his back.

"That was my fault," he says. "I got confused. Try this one instead, baby. It's strawberry..."

Jacki continues holding Toni's hand while the doctor approaches the child with a needle behind his back. The doctor holds out his other hand clenched in a fist, as if he is hiding something a child would want to see. Toni looks at the hand and smiles, reaching to find more candy. Then the doctor suddenly jerks his fist away, and Toni screams as she realizes that she's been stuck with the needle instead.

Larry lays low in his corner, afraid to remind them it isn't real. The scene is going too well.

"Sorry, honey," the doctor says. Then, whispering to Jacki as if the whole thing is hilarious, "She'll never trust a man again."

This joke makes Jacki livid. Toni is crying loudly now, and Jacki imagines the deep pain from a needle into an arm that small.

"Was all that creepy shit really necessary?" she asks the doctor.

"It depends," the doctor says, now defensive. "Most kids are scared of needles."

"Well, now she'll be afraid of getting stabbed with suckers, too, asshole."

Hospital hall, same day. Jack stood under the "Beware Of Dog" sign and rubbed his eyes like a toddler. He watched a young Hispanic woman come out of a nearby room and quickly walk towards him, Larry trailing her with a handheld camera. Through his watering eyes, he let his mouth drop, to indicate to an audience that he remembered her from the crash six years ago. She didn't notice him at all, and continued past, towing her little girl aggressively behind her by the hand.

"Jack is so shocked to see her again after three years that he bangs a knee on a cart marked 'biohazard' being wheeled past by Derek the orderly," Larry yelled from behind his camera.

"Who the fuck is Derek? Three years? Three years isn't long enough for how you have the kid acting."

"I meant six years. But, yeah, Derek, he's just me for now. I haven't cast him yet. Hopefully, there's an orderly here named Derek already, but if I really was Derek, the cart would tip, and Derek would grunt and catch a falling bag of blood in his hands. He'll squeeze it too hard with his ragged nails, and the bag will burst between his fingers! Jack, jump back to avoid getting splashed."

"Who's gonna play Jack?"

"For now I'll do Jack, too. Until Jack gets back. Anyway, 'What the *fuck?*' Derek will snort, trying not to touch anything."

"Sorry, sorry," Larry as Jack, rubbing his knee.

"Ewwwwww!" Toni squealed from behind her mom's leg.

"I should rub this shit in your fucking face," Larry-as-Derek hissed.

"C'mon dude," Jack pleaded. "It would have been funny if it was a cart full of fruit. Like in the movies? Or basketballs!"

Larry-as-Derek stared at his red hands as Jack turned away, still rubbing his knee, then quickly held out an arm to stop Jacki from walking past.

"'Wait. Hey, do I know you?' you'll say, Jack. Then Jacki will stare into his eyes for a second, not liking what she sees. Derek will bang the cart into the wall as he turns it around and rolls through some doors. Then she'll stare at this thick, hairy arm that's blocking her path until he slooooowly lowers it. She'll instinctively move a protective hand in front of her child, then start to move past him... try it..."

"I remember you. You fixed my cable, right?"

"No, it was years ago. I saw you at, I mean, I, uh, I brought you in after-"

Jacki interrupted him as Toni started to cry from the idea of the blood Larry had conjured up in her mind. Jacki leaned down to sooth her, still hiding between her legs.

"Years ago, huh? You hear that, baby? That was before you got hatched!"

The little girl peered out, and Jack reached down to shake her hand. Toni shook her head and pushed her face into the back of Jacki's knee. Jack pointed to the bandage on Toni's arm when she peeked out again. Toni saw him looking and suddenly spit angrily on the floor.

"Is she okay?"

Jacki hesitated, looking embarrassed and impatient. Larry motioned for her to keep going.

"She's fine. She had to get a shot. For real."

"Where? In the mouth?"

The little girl spit again, and Jack jumped back.

"No, in the arm. I'm sorry, it's not you she's spitting at. She ate a bad sucker."

"Well, that's why they call 'em suckers! Hey, can I ask you if-"

"We have to go, I'm sorry."

She walked off, and her child stared until they disappeared around a corner. Jack stared off into space, trying to seem deep in thought until a nurse came bursting through a nearby door and almost knocked the camera from Jack-as-Larry's hand.

"That could work," Larry said. "You stop a nurse as she walks past and lean in close to whisper a question in her ear. She thinks for a moment, then will answer him a little too loud, 'Paternity suit?' Get it? Then you'll run after them, crash through several doors until you're standing in the garage, looking up, down, left and right, catching your breath! You'll finally spot Jacki and her child looking for their car and run some more!"

"Then what?"

"Then you'll say, 'Hey, I know I don't know you but can we go get a beer'…"

"What is this movie about, Larry?"

"And the music on the jukebox stopped."

"There's no jukebox in a hospital, dude."

"So, you'll glance down at the child who's back between Jacki's legs, 'cause that's the answer to everything, right? And you'll say to the kid, 'Or an ice-cream cone or something?' And the brat will stick out her tongue and go, 'A beer and ice cream! Gross!' And the kid will be smiling for the first time after the shot and won't be hiding behind her leg anymore, so you'll get brave enough to finally tell her my name."

"Your name? Don't you mean my name?"

"Yeah, your name. 'Jack Grinstead.'"

"But that's your name, isn't it, Larry?"

"Not anymore."

"Why? What's wrong with it?"

"Nothing. It might be Jack again some day, depending on what kind of movies I can make."

"I like it a lot better than 'Larry.'"

"Only in an airport."

"What?"

"It's the only place I can still hear, 'Hi, Jack!' without hitting the deck."

"Cut!"

They all laughed.

Over lunch, they talked about names some more, and everyone assumed that Larry had changed his name because of the new jobs he was taking. But in fact, it was his old job he was running from instead, he told them. It was inversely as mysterious as he tried to make it sound.

Then an orderly rolled past them with a mop bucket, and they traded a look. Larry decided to film the garage scene later. This sorry son of a bitch was exactly who they'd been looking for.

Weaving through traffic down the hospital hallway, Derek stops rolling his mop bucket to linger next to a circle jerk of police officers infesting a doorway. Inside this room is Ron Flowers, soon to be "39-year-old Mr. Ronald J. Flowers from Fort Knox, Kentucky," and all over the news for soaking up about 35 Taser barbs, a half-gallon of pepper-spray, and a dozen forearms sunk deep into his throat. The cherry on top was the butt of a sergeant's shotgun to the back of his head, right where he stored his memories of an almost reciprocated crush he'd had on a fifth-grade teacher. The pressure of all these arms on his unconscious brain had caused Mr. Flowers to stroke out. Which is a lot like striking out, except you don't get a chance to spike your helmet for the cameras.

Instead, the cameras, cellphones and dash cams alike, had caught every twitch of Mr. Flowers' nervous system as the impotent rage of so many boys in blue crackled and pulsed through his body. Derek had already seen this apocalyptic beating on the internet today, and couldn't help but marvel at the way the winds of public opinion were already blowing. In fifteen minutes, 30,000 hits by calm, cool-headed, armchair lawyers were pretty sure Mr. Flowers deserved it. A trial would be unnecessary. About 50 or so amateur scientists wondered if Mr. Flowers was immune to electricity. Maybe he'd been Tasered too many times? And the other 60,000 hits sidestepped any procedural debate and jumped straight to this certainty:

Fuck him. This was the Bardstown Rapist.

Why else would he resist like that? Only a guilty man soaks up enough electricity to power a city block, pulling fishhook after fishhook of Taser wire from his torso, all while cuffing any cop that got too close with fists the size of Thanksgiving turkeys. A man only does this when he knows justice has caught up with him.

"Immune to compassion, too," those amateur scientists decided, "likely due to his upbringing." How else could anyone explain such an endless trail of victims left broken and bleeding at rest stops along the famous Kentucky Bourbon Trail?

But even though it seemed unnecessary in the eyes and fingertips of the online public, the police wanted a confession. They knew how they were going to look when those cellphones and dash cams hit the 11:00 o'clock news, and they were equally worried Mr. Flowers, a huge, raggedy man who had sort of resembled a black Meat Loaf before his beating (now *looking more like actual meatloaf) would either survive or be forever martyred by their assault.*

Either way, a hospital-bed confession was crucial.

Derek surveys the sea of blue suits and Batman utility belts surging in closer to the broken pile of tubes, blood, and bandages with every stuttering beep of the machines. He isn't sure how many cops are gathered, but it's too many, and they all seemed worried and furious, watering eyes and trickles of blood glistening toilet brush mustaches, random bleats and sputtered profanity about how someone should pull the goddamn plug on a piece of shit like 39-year-old Mr. Flowers, born and raised in Fort Knox, Kentucky, how he was a waste of hospital resources.

Electricity especially, *Derek thinks as he notices the spaces in the belts where the Tasers used to be.*

But as Derek attempts to mop around the rivers of black, spit-shined shoes, he notices there are two cops a little different than the rest. One big, one small.

This is not uncommon, and Derek knows immediately, just from being alive on this planet past the age of 18, any clear physical distinctions means they will be the worst cops ever.

And, sure enough, they're the only two faces anywhere near an after-hours emergency room that are smiling.

"Is it the guy?" *Big Cop asks.*

"Gotta be the guy," *someone scoffs.*

"Where's the girl he was with?"

"We just booked her," *Small Cop says.*

"Did he rape her, too?"

"Naw, she was in on it. She's always been in on it. White girl like that? How else is someone like this gonna get that close to so many females?"

"Why were they dressed like that?"

"Fuck if we know," *Big Cop says.* "She claims they were on their way to a costume party. But she's lying."

"Why do you say that?"

"You didn't see her smile when we took her picture? That's all she wanted. To get one of them sweet old-time mugshots. Like you get at Frontierland. Wannabe actors. All of them."

"I don't know. What if this isn't the guy?"

"She'll talk," Big Cop says. "And if she don't talk, he'll talk."

"Why?" Small Cop asks.

"Because he reported finding the last victim."

"And?"

"And she found the victim before that, too."

"And?"

"And nothing. That's a pretty big fucking coincidence."

"Really?" Small Cop shrugs. "Seems like once the number of rapes gets this high, it gets more likely someone would stumble across two victims in their lifetime, hell, maybe even three. Shit, one time this little kid found two ears on the same day!"

"He's the guy. DNA will prove it."

A nurse orbits the mob of police, not able to muster the courage to tell them to leave. She is able to push through and squeeze the bag of plasma feeding Mr. Flowers' massive forearm. Suddenly awakened by the tug of the needle, the baseball-glove-sized hand connected to this arm begins scratching at the handcuff locking it to the railing.

"Look out!"

"Don't worry. They said something in his head popped. That's all he can move. That one hand."

"That's one hand too many after what he did to you assholes," Small Cop laughs.

"Well, he ain't gonna move anything ever again."

"How do you know it's the guy?" Big Cop asks again.

"I said, forensics are gonna prove everything. You know, the blood."

"The blood, huh?" Big Cop looks at Small Cop, who finally laughs loud enough for them all to start glaring. Big Cop says to no one and everyone:

"Man, don't you hate those movies where someone says something like, 'Well, Joe, we checked the perpetrator's vehicle and found DNA and possible latent fingerprints,' then someone else goes, 'Whoa! Speak English, Copernicus!' 'Sorry, Joe. I mean we got the guy.' Gotta love when movies assume the audience is jam-packed with idiots."

"Who are you calling idiots?" a cop in the back asks, popping a wad of red tissue out of his nostril in anger.

"Exactly," Small Cop laughs.

Derek mops a little slower, but he knows better than to believe these cops are actually considering the innocence of the brain-damaged man locked to the bed. He leans against the wall and watches Mr. Flowers' finger stop scratching the rail and strain toward one of the officers near the door instead. The finger raises higher, higher, until it's pointing straight at the cop's chest. The officer looks down to his shirt pocket to see a stack of parking tickets and the pen holding them together.

"Did you write him a ticket?" someone asks.

"Yeah, started to, until he went ape shit."

"Hey, watch the slurs," someone says, quite serious. "We might be recorded."

"I think he wants your pen," Derek offers, head down as he slides a snail train of soapy water to the bathroom.

"DNA is overrated," Big Cop goes on. "Juries love it, but all those numbers? It's sort of like astronomy class. Doesn't mean shit."

"What does that even mean?" Small Cop asks.

"You know when they say there's 'six million stars' or whatever? I mean, that's a lot, but they could have said any big-ass number and it would have meant the same thing."

"Don't you mean 'six million Jews'?"

"Watch the slurs, Sergeant. Everyone's got a camera these days."

Derek snickers despite himself, and a couple heads turn. He mops faster.

"Do you have to do that right now?" someone asks him with a nudge.

Then the beeping of the EKG stutters, and they turn back to the broken man on the bed. He's still pointing to the officer's chest, fingers now twitching in desperation.

"He wants your pen. Give him your pen, man."

"Maybe he wants to write something down!"

"Bullshit. He's lying," Small Cop laughs.

"How can he be lying with his hand?"

"It's his bad hand."

"Which hand is his bad hand?"

"Depends on which hand someone uses for lying."

One of the officers wiggles a broken jaw that rustles like a bag of gravel, wincing as a busted incisor folds back onto his tongue, right where the taste buds used to register "sweet."

"Yeah, that's his bad one," he grumbles, afraid to touch the tooth.

"He just wants your pen."

"Yeah, maybe to stick a nurse with it."

Fingers thick as sausages flutter and grasp, the first two digits walking on air, trying to reduce the space between them, the index finger finally tracing letters in the air between them in frustration.

"He wants to write something down."

"Don't do it," Small Cop says, suddenly almost serious.

"Why not?"

"Did you hear what I said? He's lying."

"Lying how? That's not sign language. That's a fuckin' hand saying, 'Gimme your pen.'"

"Nope, don't buy it. He's full of shit. This man is the worst hand actor of all time."

"What?"

"Haven't you ever heard of hand acting?" Small Cop sighs.

"Like puppets?"

"No. Hand acting. You ever see a movie where they zoom in on somebody's hand going through a drawer? And all of a sudden the hand starts spending way too much time in that drawer? You know, picking up every battery and screw and paperclip, moving around just a little too much? Then it puts shit back down and floats out of the scene?"

"Uh… no."

"Floats?"

"Yes, floats."

"You watch too many movies."

"Well, I'm telling you, this cocksucker is lying. His hand can't act for shit."

"Wait, are you saying hand acting?"

"That's just one kind. There's hand acting, foot acting. You'll usually get foot acting when a chick steps out of a car. In some movies, it takes a high-heeled shoe an hour to touch the fucking asphalt."

"I saw fly acting once!" a cop yells from the back.

"Where was this?"

"Once Upon a Time in the West."

"He's right," another cop agrees, even taking off his hat in respect. "That fly the cowboy finally catches in his gun barrel should have got an Academy Award."

The fingers on Mr. Flowers' hand are now moving so fast they've disappeared.

"Yeah, so should this guy."

"Just give him your pen. And give him a ticket to write on. He knows he's caught. He's gonna confess."

"Yeah, he's gonna confess!"

"Bullshit," Small Cop snaps, and then they all reach up instinctively to protect their parking tickets. If there was one thing consistent about police officers, it was that, without fail, they all believed beyond a shadow of a doubt they were being lied to at all times.

"You know who's a good hand actor?" Big Cop says. "Sigourney Weaver. She is the greatest, and by that I mean the worst, hand actor of all time."

"In what?"

204

"*All three* Alien *movies.*"

"*How do you figure?*"

"*Okay, in the first one? When she's turning on and turning off the most complicated self-destruct mechanism of all time? All those buttons and switches she's lovingly flickin' and pushin'? Then in the second movie? When she's gearing up to go get the little girl and taping all those grenades to her gun, plucking them out of the box as pretty as a little girl picking posies?*"

"*I remember that shit!*"

"*What about the third flick?*"

"*I don't remember. I* do *remember that she throws the most believable punch I've ever seen a woman throw, inside or outside of a movie.*"

"*You know what other movie her hand is in?* The Ice Storm. *There's a shot of it plucking some car keys out of a salad bowl, the keys of the man she's having an affair with, and her fingers do this twirl with them that is just ridiculous. It's hot though.*"

"*You know what that twirl meant, right?*" Small Cop asks. "*Betrayal. Deception. Try to get that across with one finger.*"

"*Who does she hit? An alien?*"

"*Huh?*" Big Cop looks down.

"*Who does she hit with the most believable punch you've ever seen? An alien?*"

"*Nope, a fucking rapist.*"

At that, all eyes are back on Mr. Flowers. And his bad hand.

Suddenly, the sheet begins to bunch up around his midsection, and a cop slaps it back down.

"*He really wants that pen.*"

"*Don't confuse an erection for desire.*"

"*Fuck it. Here. Admit what you did, scumbag.*"

The officer lays a parking ticket across Mr. Flowers' chest and then works a ballpoint pen around the tangle of tubes and wires and into his broken fingers.

The officers tap the butts of their guns nervously.

Because of the diagonal line with which a stroke divides the human body, it's Mr. Flowers' right hand that still works. So it's the left half of Mr. Flowers' mouth that smiles.

He snaps a handcuff and plunges the pen into his own throat.

Derek watches it all in slow motion, suddenly feeling like he's swaying on the deck of a boat. He has to grab the doorway with both hands for stability.

Impossibly, the pen goes all the way in, vanishing into the meat of Mr. Flowers' massive neck. The tip of the ballpoint finds his carotid artery and unleashes a torrent of blood that washes over the first row of faces, grown men who now whimper like children, holding up smooth white hands in desperation as if in the path of an oncoming train. The blood pumps harder as one of the officers attempts to retrieve the pen, digging into the widening hole up to his knuckles.

Derek imagines the pen lost in the highways of those big veins forever, on its way to a weary heart the size of a cop's head.

Then it's over. The huge hand slumps. The EKG flatlines. And the cops finally let the doctors and nurses push through into the abattoir of blue uniforms now turned purple and their shocked, freckled faces.

Small Cop looks over at Big Cop. They're still smiling. They were in the front row, and not a drop hit them, of course. Derek, who will be cleaning the floor that evening, all evening, is suddenly convinced he'll find red outlines of every officer on the walls and tile floor, like the shadows of blast victims at Hiroshima. Every officer but two, one big, one little.

"That nigger was the best hand actor I ever seen," a voice whispers in awe.

Everyone nods. Nobody flinches.

"Case closed?" Small Cop claps his dry hands like a gunshot.

"Never leave it up to a jury," Big Cop reminds them. And they're gone.

Then everyone begins to file out the door, no longer interested.

Derek stands, keeping his mop arm's length away as always so he doesn't have to smell it. Most people approximate hospital populations like prison populations, that is by the number of beds. Janitors and orderlies, however, calculate the number of toilets. So that's 35 toilets per 10,000 human beings, Derek figures. And just like he knows three feet away is optimum for breathing in the lingering shit of all those patients, he knows those two cops are somehow responsible for everything that just went down.

Then Derek stops scrubbing, frozen by a dilemma. If he was the rapist, Derek decides, he would have to do it again. Tonight. Just to prove these motherfuckers wrong. If he was the rapist, even if he knew that by stopping today his crimes would be forever pinned on a dead man, he would have to do it again. Just because these cops and their split lips and faces as red as a baboon's ass couldn't be right ever.

He'd do it again tonight.

Derek bends over to finish cleaning the yellow stains around the screws on the toilet lid, then flushes to get everyone's attention. Then he does a twirl of his key ring with the same flourish he used to spin his lifeguard whistle when he was boy, back when he first started to notice the glut of lovely creatures populating his world. All that skin.

On the way out, as the bottleneck of bruises loosens to let him and his bucket roll through, he turns and silently motions to the cops with his hand.

No one doubts the sincerity of his gesture.

At the end of the hall, he turns the corner and sees another huddle of uniforms surrounding a doorway. He lowers his

*head and begins to work his way through them towards the
hiss and sputter of another machine.*

Larry was on his way to see his producer, *The* Damon
Gold. Summoned to the mountain. The Fortress of
Solitaire. Supposedly, this was to be a pep talk. Damon
had mentioned something about a "team-building
exercise" on the phone, but not a hint of concern for the
cock-snapping brawl on the set.

Team-building, my ass, Larry thought.

When he pulled in, Damon was on his porch, between
two white porch pillars like he was Supreme Commander
In Chief, drinking something alien, something that was
no color found in nature.

"You wanted to see me?" Larry asked, eyes as twitchy
as a couple of honey-pot flies.

"Come on out back, Larry. I think we should talk."

Larry knew they were headed for the pool. He
watched Damon take the corner with an extra swirl of
his robe, revealing a tanned, well-muscled torso. He was
disappointed this flourish didn't reveal a giant red "S" on
his chest.

"A long time ago…" he started when they got to the
aquarium shimmer of his backyard, "…when I was in a
job I hated, just like yourself, they decided to have us do
this task as one, to let us bond, so we'd feel like we were…
in it together. Now, we were all disgruntled as heck after a
half a decade of wage freezes, so we were in no mood for
this, I can assure you. So imagine our surprise when they
brought us into this conference room and opened the lid
on a jigsaw puzzle."

"And that was your Christmas bonus," Larry joked,
not really listening.

"Ha ha. Good one, Larry. No, it was even worse than
that. We were just borrowing the puzzle from them.

No one got to keep it. And it was 'Bollywood' themed, jeweled elephants, and a black sky with way too many stars. They stood there and told us we were going to work on this puzzle together, one piece at a time every time we walked by that room. So if we went for a drink of water, restroom break, whatever, grab a piece and put it in. And when it went together too slowly for their liking, thought we were using it to milk the clock, they moved it into one of the empty cubicles the last layoff had vacated. It was right by the door, so you really did have to walk by it in plain sight of the bosses every time you wanted to piss or buy some pork rinds from the vending machine. And we worked on that puzzle, too, Larry. Hard. Because we wanted to believe what they said, that it would really make us feel like a team..."

"Ha. 'Burn Bollywood Burn!' Did you participate?"

"Me? Heck, no. I never put a single piece into the darn thing. But there was this girl who did even worse than that. She took a piece home with her so no one could finish it."

"Nice. Kind of a dick move, but nice."

Damon took a long drink, staring at him over the edge of his glass, then he went on.

"So the puzzle was finished one day, except for this piece in the upper left corner in what would be that black, black nighttime sky. So you could see the white desk of the cubicle underneath. I never liked that job, but suddenly I felt like I had to figure out who took that puzzle piece. So I got as close as I could to everyone there, worked years longer than I would have, and when I finally got this particular girl to brag about the black puzzle piece of starry sky she'd tucked into the sun visor in her car, I pulled my pants back up and slapped that bitch open-handed across the mouth."

"Wow. What's your point?"

"Larry, you're out."

"What?"

"You never fit, that's no surprise. But now you're fucking everyone up, too. I'm gonna let Stevey direct. I know I owe you, so you're not gonna be unemployed, I promise."

He turned from Larry and dropped his robe, easing himself into the glow of the shallow end.

"I'm fixing up The Kid."

"The what?"

"The drive-in? I bought it when the Butch Cassidy went facedown. And I'm gonna be switching it to adult features from now on. Can you imagine that on the big screen?" he asked, excited, back still to Larry. "Sex projected on a surface that large? Out there in your car, it would be like God watching the New York Subway bust through the tunnels and into the sunlight."

"I don't understand what you think I-"

"Shut up. I need a projectionist. My last guy is moonlighting at the hospital. A janitor or a paramedic or some shit. So he keeps falling asleep at the wheel. And by wheel, I mean the projector. Sleep. I should be so lucky."

"You must be joking."

"It's a paycheck, Larry. Shucks, you'll be showing your own movies!"

For a second he believed things might work out. Larry had never been good at predicting trends. The most money Damon ever made was from an unremarkable videotape due to the bad translation his company left on the box. *Angie Rides Actively.* It was a cheeky hit due to the confusion, and the sequel, *Angie Rides Ardently,* was even bigger. That was the kind of success Larry could never duplicate, though his classmates back in film school kept trying, working to copy the hideous pre-fab cult films of Roger Corman's protégés, something Larry knew would someday be the end of B-movies as we know it. Still, he dared to dream.

Damon held up a finger.

"When I say 'your movies,' you know the movies I mean, right? No more talk about that 'real' movie of yours, you get me?"

"Fuck you."

"What were you calling that? Your life story? *Skunkwaters?*"

"Fuck. You."

At that, Damon turned around, and for the first time Larry saw the numbers all over his body, digits of every size, script, font, language. No dollar signs on them, but Damon didn't need dollar signs.

Larry stepped into the water after him. It was so warm, it was like stepping into a mouth. Damon's mouth. Damon did a little spin, graceful as the elephant Edison electrocuted

"What are you doing, Larry?" he smiled. "Do you want to play another game of Marco Polo?"

"Is that the one where you use bats?"

"No," Damon laughed. "That's just regular Polo."

Larry's arms suddenly felt all-powerful. He could almost hear the skin on his elbows creak as they split to let his muscles out to breathe deep. He scratched his arms so hard he thought they might ignite as he thought about how he'd fought Damon on his home planet last time. A planet where he'd forgotten his helmet in the confusion, surrounded by such a thin atmosphere. Larry squeezed a fist. He didn't need a helmet this time.

"Why did you change my script?" he asked Damon, but didn't wait for an answer. He was chest deep in the ocean of this strange world with his hands around an alien's neck. He crumpled it like a new dollar bill until George Washington's face was unrecognizable.

"Marco! Polio!" Larry laughed as he felt Damon losing strength and struggles turned to bubbles.

Larry did much better this time around. Later, he decided it must have had something to do with the clothes that had weighed him down with water at first.

Skins always win? Bullshit.

You fought against the extra weight on your arms and legs, just like Harrison Bergeron before the shotgun. No, more like a batter in the on-deck circle with every doughnut on your bat.

And when the doughnuts finally slid off your shaft and into the dust, before you struck out, for just that second, you were king.

Even with Larry's hands reducing his throat by half, Damon tried to swear the numbers he'd gotten his girls to smear all over his body in hypoallergenic watercolor body paint were just a joke. Gurgled something about it being Stevey's idea, maybe Glen's, maybe Joe's. Sputtered something about tattoos driving Larry "batty" lately. Larry processed none of this.

"I was kidding!" he bubbled around a crushed voice box, "They come off!"

Then he went under.

He put up a decent fight, but Larry felt thirty pounds lighter. A hundred pounds stronger. Wallet gone, engraved lighter gone, wedding ring gone, everything of value probably already bobbing in the filter, Larry didn't care. He walked back to the ladder like he was walking through smoke. He turned to watch Damon float away, saw the black paint stain a cloud around his body and smiled. Larry spit green sometimes. This shit all made perfect sense.

Is this what every animal does to try and distract a predator? Larry thought. *Maybe we don't see it unless we add water.*

He tried to imagine how many ridiculous tattoos an octopus would have with that many arms for a canvas.

The ink is probably expelled after death, he decided. *That's the key to getting tattoos off forever.*

V.

*Larry Draws His One Monster and Watches It Shout –
Introducing Evil Boll Weevil – Coconut Milk and Sea
Monkeys Is How You Can Tell – The First Story Ever – A
Blood Bubble under a Toenail Is Used to Signal Things
Are Happening Now Instead of Then – Everyone Missing
the Static between Stations after – Holding Hands over
Elbow Creek – Ghost Pianos, Idle Hands, and Road Rage
Rehearsals Teach Us – The Only Rule That Matters Is the
Stick – Spunkwater Is – Face Down in the Skunk Waters –
A Pocketful of Memories Won't Answer the Question – How
Did You Know My Name Was Jack? – A Mystery Man Jerks
Off into a Tree Stump – Larry Forgets His Helmet in the
Pool*

*"He said, 'Why don't you get a proper dog?'
And I said, 'Rover, ignore this copper'
And I pick up a stick"*
—John Hegley "Very Bad Dog"

Larry circled the strip mall, stopping his Grenada under a sign that read "Load Bearing Wall." He smiled with the memory of five previous signs he'd stolen. Their film budgets were microscopic, and the joke of having that particular construction sign above the bed in one of his projects was a gift that just kept on giving, albeit literally with diminishing returns. He saw they'd attached it with heavy-duty bolts this time, and he almost went to his trunk for his tools before he remembered he didn't have that job anymore, having murdered his boss just hours before.

His car spit out a muffled backfire in protest.

Is it pronounced gren-ah-dah or gren-aye-dah? he thought. *You say potato…*

Pulling out, he saw that King Ink, the tattoo shop on the corner, was closed and boarded up. Once, Larry went with a girl to this very same parlor to get a Japanese character buzzed into her neck. When she first said, "Japanese character," Larry worried it was going to be Godzilla. But worse than that, it was Japanese glyphs she'd selected just because they looked cool, with no clue whatsoever about the translation. He would have respected a tiny Godzilla stomping around on the back of her head a lot more than such a trendy roll of the dice. When it was over and the "artist" was rubbing the wax into the angry black slashes on her neck, that's about the time Larry noticed he had one, too. Right under his ear. Right where a sucker punch would have turned his lights out. A tiny Godzilla.

To be fair, Larry didn't have the same aversion to tattoos back then. In fact, he had offered his own monster for her to use. Everyone had one monster they learned to draw on their Trapper Keepers, ballpoint beastie noodling during phone calls, or personal freaks etched into desks, and he'd been drawing his for decades. It was a one-eyed creature with three more one-eyed creatures spewing from its mouth. A couple horns, some pointy wings to scare it up a bit. But mostly it was the head that Larry loved to draw, that cartoon eye like a boat with a sunrise in the middle. He always started there. Everyone got caught up in the extra eyeballs coming out of its mouth, but Larry didn't know how else you could put more eyes on a one-eyed monster without all the little monsters, too.

They didn't last more than a decade after that. And once she was gone, Godzilla disappeared beneath the waves. When Larry thought about it later, he couldn't believe anyone would immortalize a childish monster doodle on their bodies.

Then he realized that's really all tattoo artists ever did. All day, every day.

And that's what they had done to his wife.

Besides that random word on her arm that he couldn't decipher, she also had this little elfin thing on her ankle with a sprinkle of mushrooms around its feet. It disgusted him. Some nights he seriously considered an anesthesia-free removal. Especially around mushroom season.

"That's why you should never fuck around with a guy who does tattoos," he told her once when she was crying about her new boss at her grocery-bagging job who insisted she cover it up. "You paid for a variation of something some asshole first drew in kindergarten."

"I know this," she told him. "That means he's had a long time to get it right. And you should talk!"

But it wasn't the mysterious letters on her forearm, or even the forest creature that sickened him the most. It was really the mushrooms. See, one time during a real humid summer, she got this rash on her legs that was diagnosed as "fruiting bodies."

Fruiting? What the what? You say po-tah-toe, I say…

That horrific phrasing, mixed with the idea of actual mushrooms growing on her legs, snowballed in his brain, even made several guest appearances in his dreams. He would imagine her legs sprouting big, spongy fungus caps, concentrated patches that she would run her razor across, clipping them at the base with almost a knuckle-cracking sound and a puff of spores instead of blood. To this day, he would still gag just thinking about it. As a kid, he once had a dream that his fingertips were swollen with mucus and mice, and how he'd squeeze them in order to drain the weight and lift a pencil again. And that dream was pretty fucked up. But it was nothing compared to the mushroom dreams. Research turned up a magazine at the library with an article about a "Mushroom Man," but he was afraid to open it. But he got suckered into tuning in to a documentary which promised wonder and amazement as it followed the life of a noble "Tree Man," cousin to the Mushroom Man. He'd only recently gotten that abomination out of his head, especially the insects living between his horned fingers.

But those mushrooms. They distracted him from the word on her arm, a word that he'd seen before, that he usually mistook for Spanish.

Even though he hadn't seen her in years, Larry thought those mushrooms should probably be clipped, just in case they were poisonous. Just in case they *spread*.

He pulled into the driveway of their old house and watched her shape dance in front of the blue glow of someone else's movie. Nope, not one of his, he was certain. Never one of his.

A sign on the side of the highway said "Ramp," and his heart started hammering.

Not that kind of ramp, he told his heart, looking to the night sky. *Is tonight another supermoon? Watch her ask me to jump that, too. "You'll know when," she told me.*

He took the ramp anyway, turning so hard on his bike that he tapped a knee against the road. Someone had placed a memorial wreath with "Wild Tony Bee" written in flowers, and it angered him for no reason.

No way *someone died there,* he thought in disgust, pointing a toe forward like a jousting lance, and flipping the wreath into a ditch. He felt bad for a second, until he remembered his new name. He took the next corner even lower to the ground, imagining an announcer swallowing the microphone, "Introducing… Evil… Boll… Weevil!"

Evil Boll Weevil. That's me! Put it on a t-shirt…

He might have heard a novelty song use that name once, but he was 79% sure he thought of it first. That was plenty for copyright purposes.

Evil took the next turn so low that his elbow touched the road. The heat and dust of the asphalt smeared the words he'd written on his skin. It was an idea his brother had, when they were watching that NASCAR bullshit back before they knew better (hell, it was better than WWF). His brother said, "You know how the drivers have all those ads all over 'em? Let's do that to you!"

He wasn't sure at first, but then he remembered something his brother's hero, Evel Knievel, proclaimed once in an interview:

"Chicks dig cars."

So he stood in the mirror and let him cover him in imaginary sponsors. They decided to go with companies that would stand the test of time, those whose immortal products were the pinnacle of technology, never to be surpassed.

Coin-op arcade games.

They put *"Tempest"* on his tricep, *"Zaxxon"* on his bicep, *"BurgerTime"* on his belly, *"Asteroids"* on his ass (written backwards and upside down since he insisted on doing that one himself), a couple *"Froggers"* on his thighs, *"Joust"* on his forearms, a huge *"Defender"* across his back, *"Spyhunter"* on one shin, *"Spyhunter II"* on the other, *"Lunar Landers"* on the tops of his feet, and *"Excite Bike"* everywhere else there was room.

And right over his heart, *"Time Pilot."* Because that was their favorite. Even though it never made good on its promise, and playing it kept him right here in nineteen-eighty whatever no matter how many times the sun went down.

He recited something else his brother's hero had said, right before he tried to jump the moon and wiped out in front of thousands:

"I am the last gladiator in the new Rome. I go into the arena, and I compete against destruction."

On the next turn, he finally got too low, and the gas sloshed so hard in the tank that he stalled out the bike. Standing straight up, he finally noticed the present Bully had left behind. It was swinging from the handlebars, and for a second he thought it was another dreamcatcher to make up for the one she'd destroyed. No, this was even better.

It was the shark-tooth necklace. His own original neck bomb. The Sword of Damocles hanging over his bed. He gingerly laid it over his throat, locked it, then kick-started his dirt bike for the last time.

221

* * *

Larry was going to play "Jack," probably until the end, so he went over the scene in detail, but out loud this time, coaching himself as well as his crew, with the camera running nonstop, just in case they caught lightning in a bottle. Or at least lightning bugs.

"So, Jack and Jacki are sitting at a table with drinks between them, while Toni drops some quarters into a deer-hunting videogame. But it looks like a racing game that you sit in, because around here, you hunt deer with your car, right? And Captain Beefheart's song 'Electricity' is playing on the jukebox because Jack got there early. 'So this is the infamous L.A.P.D. Smokehouse, huh?' she says. 'You've never been here?' Jack asks. 'I always meant to, but I thought cops owned it or something with a name like that.' 'Naw, I think it stands for Louisville Area Beer Distributor, but then the "B" got messed up on the sign? Or maybe everybody kept remembering it wrong, so they went with it. "L.A.B.D." isn't nearly as catchy.' 'Sounds like some kind of mutt,' she says. 'So, do you like it?' 'It's cool,' Jacki says, looking around. 'Walking distance to a bunch of stuff, I guess.' 'Yeah,' Jack mutters, looking around, too. 'So, is the name "Jacki" short for something or what?' 'Yeah,' she laughs. 'It's kind of weird. "Jacki" is actually short for "Jacinto," after the Battle of San Jacinto? "Jacinto Ramirez." That's me. Sounds like war, doesn't it?' 'Isn't that a boy's name?' 'Guess not,' she says through her teeth, looking up at the ceiling. And right then, the jukebox seems to triple in volume!"

Larry started to sing in his best bluesy growl.

"'...*high voltage man kisses night to bring the light to those who need to hide their shadow deed... hide their shadow deed... seek electricity...*'" He couldn't keep it up and had to cough a second, then, "Yeah, that's the song belching out of it, and Jack asks, playing with his matchbook, 'Then how do you say it?' 'The town? It's pronounced "Hah-Sin-Tow."' 'So why isn't your named pronounced "Hacky"?' he asks her. 'Because… it's not,' she says. 'You'd have to sound like you're clearing your throat.' Got it?"

"No. Can you repeat everything after… everything."

Sherry, the new Jacki, and Larry's actress for the night, was chewing on the end of her thumbnail, not really getting it at all. She'd done a good job on a couple of the hospital scenes, but he feared she was losing the plot. Still, Larry hoped that her frustration would translate well for the final film.

Final film.

The little girl was a natural though. She was Sherry's niece, and Larry was going to make it work because the chances of finding a little brat who could memorize all her lines with a minimum of tantrums were gonna be slim.

"'Hack-ee,' Jack will say, Jack being me, and he'll be coughing at the same time. Jacki, being you, will have to smile and say, 'Yeah, something like that.' Get it? Got it? Good."

He ran to push a chair in front of the back door to let in more mosquitoes. Larry was so excited, he dropped the camera on his foot. The camera wasn't that heavy, but it caught his big toe just right through his ragged tennis shoe. He would have screamed if the little girl hadn't wanted so bad for it to happen.

"So, why are you named after a boy or a battle?"

"Jesus Christ. Okay, it's actually even stranger than you think," Jacki sighs. "We're sort of named after the cannons that were used in that battle."

"Wait, who's 'we'?"

"Me and my sister," she says, smile slipping.

Jack pulls a pen from his pocket, then opens a matchbook to write.

"And why again are you and your sister named after weapons and wars and all that? Did your dad want boys or something? Of course he did. He's Mexican, right?"

"No," she says, smile gone for good now. *"He named me and my sister, Anna, after the battle and General Santa Anna. And there were these two cannons that won the battle for America — hold on, you heard this before?"* she asks, picking up speed.

He doesn't answer, knowing it won't matter.

"Well, they called the cannons 'the two sisters,' and they were donated from somewhere in Kentucky, actually. No, wait, Kentucky Street, Ohio. Anyway, I think we were named after those cannons because they were delivered to General Houston on April 11th, our birthday and..."

"Just a sec. Your sister was named after the General that lost the battle?"

"Never mind. You're right. I guess he wanted boys," Jacki says.

They sit in silence a moment, both realizing she just unloaded a lot of personal information.

"Dad was complicated."

"...hide their shadow deed... hide their shadow deed... seek electricity..."

Jacki nods toward her daughter who's still hunting electronic deer with a car. Toni's studying the game's giant pink plastic steering wheel as she angles for everything on the screen that moves.

"What about her? What's the name 'Toni' short for? Anthony, right? Didn't you learn your lesson?"

"Sure didn't," she sighs, clearly annoyed. *"Toni was named by her father 'cause, yes, he always wants something else. Or at least he wanted something other than what he got."*

Jacki looks at her watch, and Jack understands she's talking about a family, not just a child.

"So, why did you ask me here again?" She shakes her head. *"Don't answer that. I'm sorry, that reminds me. We've got to*

go see her dad about her..." she lowers her voice to a whisper. "...birthday party."

"Okay, I don't know if you remember me, but a long time ago, I came to your hospital room after…"

Suddenly, she frowns and leans across the table. Jack freezes in fear.

"Don't move," she says. Then she reaches up, palm out, and smears a plump mosquito the length of his cheek, leaving a bloody streak of war paint to divide his face.

"Sorry," she says. "But that thing was getting fat. I don't know how you didn't feel it."

He taps his cheek and looks at his fingertips.

"Damn, that was kinda horrible," he marvels. "A nice hard smack would have been infinitely better than that."

They both laugh.

"I can't believe how disappointed I am right now that the night didn't end with you smacking me in the face," he goes on.

"Sorry," she says again.

He stares at her, so much to say on the tip of his tongue, but there's no way now, with his own blood and mosquito guts all over his face. He finally realizes who she reminds him of, besides the girl back in England, of course, the one who got him deported a lifetime ago.

She's the girl in the movies where the hero thinks he sees the love of his life, then she turns around, opens her eyes, and it's just someone who looks like her instead. Something like that. He wants to tell her this, too, but thinks better of it. Because, actually, whenever Jack watched a movie like that, he always thought the wrong girl would do just fine. He never understood why the hero never started conversations with everybody, doing all that heroic shit and all, he would tell everybody…

But now Jacki's gathering up her things, picking up her jacket, and Jack considers a funny story, maybe even a confession, to keep her there just a little longer. He suddenly *wants to tell her how he's always thought of himself slightly different from everyone else because the worst aspects of his personality were born from starting everything so late in life and worrying that he'd never catch up, that and the fact that he was born with two extra molars, and right as he gets the courage to pull down his bottom lip and lose her completely, mercifully, she takes the matchbook away from him and drops it into her pocket.*

"All my digits, house and phone, are on the-" *he starts.*

"I know. I'm sorry, but we gotta get going."

She shakes her head as she watches her daughter happily clicking the gun, pretending to shoot out every light bulb in the place. Jack imagines them popping one at a time, until he's left alone in the dark.

A gun *and* a steering wheel on that game? *he thinks.* Jesus Christ.

"So, what do you think her dad will buy her this year?" *he jokes, social skills now totally defunct.* "A football helmet, a bazooka, or a hunting license?"

Jacki stops and lights a match from the book she took from him. She lights it without tearing it free, then holds it up so he can see the flame burning through his numbers.

Later that night. A girl's voice echoes down the hallway of Jack's apartment building.

"That hurt, motherfucker! C'mon, Jack. Where you going now? What's in the bag..."

A door opens, and the sound of another party fills the hallway as Jack quickly exits, carrying a long camouflaged bag over his shoulder. He tries to slam the door behind him but a girl's bare foot kicks the door back open. Jack walks across the hall with his gear and stands staring at another apartment door. A stereo belts out a song that isn't even out yet. Or maybe Jack is singing it. Either way, it's impossible.

"You little fun remover... fun removal machine..."

Jack remembers once when he had to explain to a classmate how crucial it can be to rationalize the necessity for a blatant continuity error in his student film. This explanation would come five years before his film was made, but no one in the class would get the joke.

Fuck 'em, *he decides.* Most continuity errors were as important as this voiceover narration, meaning no one should hear it or even want to.

The sounds of the revelry behind him finally neutered, Jack pulls a single key from his pocket, unlocks the door, and steps inside.

It's still empty. Walls, webs, and brown carpet.

Jack blinks slowly. The hollowness of this place has a calming effect on him. He tugs the living room light-bulb chain and opens a window to let in the night sounds of crickets and locusts. Then he carefully rolls the green bag off his shoulder and lays it on the floor like a body.

Something metal rattles inside.

He checks every room, flipping every light switch he can find. The hallway, the back bedroom finally yanking the last chain in the closet.

A stone-washed jean jacket scares him, and he catches his breath, thinking how that's a relatively simple name for such a mystery fabric. For years, Jack would be unable to duplicate the pattern, even with the sharpest driveway stones and entire afternoons of snow angels. But his confidence that such a beautiful '80s creation would never go out of style will always give him comfort.

Then he sees them.

From the floor to the ceiling are photographs of attractive, dark-skinned girls, every snapshot revealing a girl asleep in a hospital bed.

Two-thirds of the pictures have black X's through their faces. Shadows pulse over them with the swing of the light bulb.

Jack steps into the closet all the way until the knot on the end of the chain taps him gently on the forehead. It's soothing at first, like the drumming of thoughtful fingertips on a table. Ten minutes later, still staring at the photographs, the tap of the chain feels like a wrecking ball rebounding off his crumbling home.

"Hospital garage. Next day. Jack and Rick are both taking turns foaming and scrubbing the chrome on their ambulance. Even though it was great to take advantage of the free vehicle for the movie, Damon is annoyed at Jack's attempts to make the back of an ambulance erotic. Thinks it's 'distasteful.' Tries to pawn off one of those pathetic Limey van versions you see around, the ambulances without the box in the back, but Jack talks him out of it…"

"Who? Is this part of the movie?"

"Jack was pretty sure he was just upset because the siren was fucked."

"What page are you on?"

"Oh, sorry. Okay, Derek shuffles over and lowers his sunglasses to survey their work with a sneer, 'Hey, I thought this was *my* job.' 'I don't mind,' Jack says. 'Hear that? We don't mind,' Rick echoes. 'Hey, did you guys hear what happened last night? With the cops watching that big guy in Room whatever it was?' 'Nope. But you don't have to tell us either.' And at this, Derek stops his story, glaring. 'No, seriously, you don't have to say anything at all,' Rick smiles. 'Like he said, we don't mind!' Then Rick will take a swig from a bottle as Derek squints and walks over to look at it closer. He'll seem angry and be like, 'What the fuck you drinking? That's not from my lunch bag is it?' But Jack and Rick don't look up, Rick just shaking his head and sighing as if he's had this conversation hundreds of times before. Then, 'Hey, you know what that shit looks like?' Derek giggles. Rick sighs again and holds it up in the light. He's drinking a white Piña Colada-type soft-drink with a lizard on the bottle. 'Why don't ya tell us, chief?' 'You have to ask?' Derek scoffs. 'It looks like a goddamn jizz sample, man!' Rick smiles at Jack and reaches behind his back to produce a sealed envelope with the name 'Derek' scrawled on it. Derek, he's still laughing at his own joke and barely fucking notices, right? 'How can you drink that shit?' he sputters in mock horror. 'What the fuck is wrong with-' Then Derek stops when he sees the envelope. He snatches it away, opens it and frowns as he reads it out loud, even though the joke's on him. It's the way he reads everything, out loud, but real loud:

"'Derek will comment on my sperm-looking drink exactly seven seconds after he sees it, thus proving that he is an expert on this subject, as well as a connoisseur of the shit sandwich.'

"Derek throws down the note in disgust, suddenly realizing those are my director's notes! Then he goes, 'What the fuck *is* he drinking, coconut milk and sea monkeys?' Derek still wants to know. 'Seriously. What else looks like that?' Then Rick suddenly leans forward and reaches out to touch the green plant bulbs he noticed sticking out of Derek's shirt pocket. Derek flinches and quickly walks off. 'Hey, wait. What was that?' Then he asks Jack. 'You see that shit? Fucker's been here so long he's actually got weeds growing out of his pockets!' 'I didn't see it,' Jack says, Jack being me, remember. 'You know what he is?' Rick will say. 'He's like the Birdman of Alcatraz, the guy with the mouse in his pocket? In the movies, the guy with the mouse or bird or bat in his pocket is supposed to mean he's the cellmate with the heart of gold, right? The problem is, you never hear about the prisoner with the *dead* mouse in his pocket.' 'Or the cactus!' 'See? Now *that's* our boy...' But Jack turns away, not really listening as he scrubs hard on a stain on the side of the ambulance.

His hand slows, distracted by his own eyes in the rear-view mirror. Spooky, right? 'Why do you keep picking on that sorry bastard?' he'll ask, blinking off the chill. 'Huh?' Then Rick takes a big drink! 'Fuck him. Every day it's the same jokes, the same shit. If I don't fuck with him, who's gonna make the effort?' 'I'm just saying,' Jack says, 'who sits down to write a note like that? You're telling me you didn't deliberately grab that nasty egg-drop-soup-looking fluid from the vending machine to get a reaction? I mean, what came first, the chicken or the egg? His jokes or your bizarre choice of refreshments? It's like the worst duel of all time up in this motherfucker.' At this, Rick stares hard, then they both start laughing as Rick finishes off the rest of the bottle and taps the end of it against his nose. 'Exactly,' he says. 'I'd watch your lunch. You're gonna give him ideas.' 'That cocksucker? Impossible! Best idea he ever had he stole from me.' And that's it."

"What's the point of that scene?" Glengarry asked him.

"I don't know. Maybe we just introduced the villain? Some red herrings."

"Some red snappers!"

"And what else are we going to do with this bottle of semen?"

"Good point."

"Most people just steal pencils from their jobs, boss."

"Another good point."

"Where's the script, boss? How do you remember all this without looking at a script?"

"I'm afraid to admit it, but now I'm hungry," Larry said, ignoring that last question. "Dry that thing off and let's get rolling."

Ambulance. Later that night. Jack and Rick are on their way to the scene of an accident. Jack is eating a burger as fast as he can and is relieved when traffic bunches up at a red light so he can work on it. Rick jiggles the siren to try to shake the cars out of his way, but gridlock is tight.

"Goddamn it. I hate when people only scoot a couple feet over, like that's enough to show they tried. Then they give you that stupid 'sorry!' look."

Jack puts the burger in his lap, looking around at the cars next to them, unwrapping a limp fruit roll-up from his shirt pocket.

"These things never cut it," he says, wadding it up and eating it in one bite. "They'd have to be the size of a parachute to satisfy." He slinks lower.

"What are you doing?" Rick asks him, elbow on the horn.

"Waiting to go."

"Eat your goddamn burger. You have about two minutes. You're not eating at the scene again."

"I can't eat with people watching."

"Nobody gives a shit about your hamburger."

"It'll look weird with the sirens on."

"What?" Rick laughs. "You're not joking are you?" He looks around them. "You're fine. No one has an angle to see you eating anyway."

"Yeah, but they could see my hands..." He holds up the hamburger quick, then tucks it away again. "...which means they'll see a burger go up then come back down. With half of it missing."

"Who cares?!"

"It's just weird."

"They'll think you're feeding our Dalmatian."

"That's firemen, asshole," Jack says as he ducks in the back to finish eating. Traffic starts loosening up, and the next time Rick turns around, Jack is frozen like he's been busted. He throws the rest of his hamburger out the window, and there's a scream and a car horn honks. Jack spits a metal spring out the window after it.

Suspicious, Rick turns on the light in the box to see Jack holding the defibrillator paddles up to the sides of his head.

"Dude, what are you doing?" Rick asks, alarmed. "What were you eating?"

"Nothing. Just locking this crap down so it doesn't slide on your turns."

"Well, I would keep those away from your head. Unless you want to lose your multiplication tables. Don't you read warning labels?"

Jack flips over a paddle and sees a childlike drawing of a stick figure holding what looks like huge cymbals to his ears and jagged lines of electric Z's coming off his head.

"Jesus Christ. Look at that drawing. You made that, didn't you?"

"Nope. Came with the equipment," Rick says. "It's for stupid fuckers like you who can't read."

"What the hell. You know, I saw that a while back and just thought it was a warning not to wear headphones while you drive."

"Funny. You about done back there?"

Jack ignores the question. He likes it in the back.

"Or maybe it's like those cartoons of babies going through windshields."

"What are you talking about now?" His elbow is back on the horn.

"Those cartoon things. You've never seen 'em? They show a baby crashing through a windshield. They're on the sun visors in most cars now. Like airbag warnings."

"No idea what the hell you're talking about."

"Do you not drive?" Jack finally climbs into the passenger's seat. "C'mon, you've seen them."

"I've seen a warning to correctly put the baby in the baby seat. Is that what you're talking about? Or a warning to turn the baby seat facing the back. But I've never in my life seen a cartoon of a baby's head cracking the windshield of a-"

"You're nuts. They're everywhere. They come standard on like every car now."

"I've seen the warning, in words. I've read it hundreds of times when I put my CDs up on the visor."

"That's not words you're seeing," Jack explains. "That's a cartoon. You're just so used to seeing cartoons everywhere that you think you're reading."

"Wait, you're telling me that on every new car, there's a cartoon of a bloody baby crashing headfirst through a fucking windshield?"

"Sort of. Not bloody. Just ready to hit the glass."

"Next you're going to tell me that every pop bottle comes with a drawing of the jagged end of it sticking in a baby's neck..."

"I can show you if you want," Jack says, exasperated.

"...or you're going to turn over your shoe and show me a sticker that shows a foot punting a baby through the uprights?" Rick goes on, taking a turn hard enough to sit Jack back down. "With a red circle and a line through it, of course, so there's no confusion."

"Dude. This sticker shows lightning bolts shooting out of this fuckers face and you—never mind."

Jack grabs one of the paddles again.

"Maybe they warn us not to put these next to our heads so that..."

"They're warning us not to put them on a patient's head!" Rick yells.

"...so that we don't try it just out of curiosity. Just to see what would happen."

"Who would try that?"

Jack moves toward Rick with a paddle.

"Maybe it's harmless. Maybe it just changes the color of your eyes or something."

"Stay the fuck away, Frankenstein," Rick says, low, serious.

Jack flips a switch, and the machine powers up with a whine, then he creeps closer, ready to attack.

"You know what drives me nuts?" Jack is saying. "When people think 'Frankenstein' is the asshole with the bolts in *his neck. That's Frankenstein's* Monster. *Frankenstein is the doctor."*

"That's what I meant," Rick says, squeezing the steering wheel so hard he almost turns it into a balloon animal. Jack backs off and laughs.

"But you got it right! And it just saved your life. Hey, what are you flinching for, dude? Maybe it just makes you smarter."

"Oh, in that case, give me a jolt."

Jack fakes a lunge and the ambulance swerves slightly as Rick swats at Jack with one of his catcher's mitt-sized hands. Jack laughs, flicks off the machine, then climbs back into the seat.

"So, you're pretty much the worst paramedic of all time, right?" Rick says. "How did that happen? I heard it wasn't always like that."

"I'll tell you later." Jack stares out the window.

Rick feels bad for bringing that up.

"Well, knock that shit off," he tells Jack, trying to stay angry. "We're almost there."

Roadside in a suburb. Minutes later. Jack and Rick walk up to see their rivals, Mike and Mike, stepping out of their debilitated former ambulance.

"What the fuck are they doing here?" Jack asks.

"Ten bucks says they're here to barbecue the meat," Rick says.

"Ten bucks says they're still talking about that tooth showing up in Mike's shit," Jack says.

Rick doesn't dare try to solve that riddle. As they get closer, the two Mikes' latest debate becomes clear. Jack's guess is in the ballpark.

"There's just something very unnatural about a turd smiling up at you from the toilet," Big Mike is saying. "You feel like you shouldn't flush it, you know? Maybe even name the goddamn thing."

"You owe me ten bucks," Jack says.

"Statistically, the most common bet is fifty," Rick says, reaching around to his back pocket and unsnapping it as Little Mike pushes past him to yell at a nearby fireman.

"Hey! We'll take care of that carcass! That meat is still good!"

"And… we're even," Rick mumbled, slapping two fives into Jack's hand and snapping his pocket closed. Big Mike and Little Mike walk towards the side of the road where a dead deer lies twisted in the ditch, its back legs crossed behind its head.

"My dog was walking down the street, minding his own business. Then this fucking car came and ran him over! Have you seen my dog playing round and round?"

"What the fuck are you talking about? And why do you suddenly have a British accent?" Rick asks.

"Saigon Kick, baby," Little Mike announces. "Part of the second British Invasion, coming soon! Their future is probably just another no-hit wonder actually. That country is fucked."

"You know, when I was in school," Big Mike says. "We all had to write us a story for English class, and this one girl showed up with a fable about a boy who looks into his toilet bowl to see the future."

"Ha!" Little Mike barks. "When I look into the toilet, all I see is the past!"

"That's what I said!"

Jack and Rick walk over to a hatchback Mustang where the firemen are working with crowbars to remove the door and get at the dog trapped inside. Rick shakes his head when he sees the animal's wet nose pressed against the back window.

"The hell? Was the dog driving? Where are all the people?!" Rick is furious.

"They'll be here soon enough," Jack says, nodding at some rubberneckers coming out of their houses.

"That's right!" Little Mike shouts, laughing. "You're on our turf now, motherfuckers!"

But then Rick walks around the car and sees the boy. He's in the front seat, nose against his own window and crying. His right arm is broken in dozens of places, wrapped around his own neck like a scarf. Sparks from a firemen's "jaws of life" fly around Jack as he pushes past the responders to get close.

"Stay off the vehicle until we're done!" a fireman shouts.

Jack ignores him and crouches down to talk to the child. The sparks stop.

"It's okay, buddy," he tells the boy.

"Is the horse dead?" the boy sniffles.

"Naw, horses are tough. It ran away. They don't die so easy, little man."

Rick frowns and turns to watch Big Mike and Little Mike struggling to cram the huge deer into their ambulance. The boy turns to watch and flinches in pain. Jack knocks on the glass to get his attention back.

"Hey! Look at me, kid. Everyone is fine. The horse is fine," he repeats over and over. The sparks start flying again.

From inside the car, the boy watches Jack's fevered, spark-covered face mouthing words at him, voice muffled from the fireman's buzz-saw. Over Jack's shoulder, the deer's head bounces off one of the real ambulances then falls loose to the ground. It bounces twice. The boy cries even harder.

"No! It's fine," Jack goes on. "That's just the special ambulance for horses."

The boy is hysterical, now starting to realize his limbs aren't working.

"Shhh! It's okay! They're just taking it to the woods so it can run away!"

Rick grabs Jack's arm and yanks him away from the vehicle.

"What are you doing?!" he asks him.

"What do you mean?"

"Do me a favor. Stop helping."

"I'm just trying to calm the kid down," Jack says.

"The kid was calm, until you started screaming."

Another fireman appears and starts hollering.

"What the fuck! If you don't hang back until my man cracks that door, I'm going to send you off the scene and use them two instead."

The second fireman cocks a thumb back at a Mike just in time to see them break the "needle bones" in the deer's legs to fold it up and slam the doors. Someone in the gathering crowd sees this and screams.

"Bullshit," says Jack. "They're not even on duty. You heard them. They're only here for the meat."

"Aren't we all?" *the Second Fireman says.*

He has a point.

"No, you don't get it," Jack says. "The only reason those fuck-ups are even here is because they're on a list to be called when there's roadkill to clean up. Hell, they'll probably mount the head. Hunters always pretend they eat antlers." *He points a finger at Rick.* "Now, we've *never* mounted a head in our lives."

The second fireman isn't interested. He's been noticing this animosity between paramedics for a couple of years now, ever since hospitals made the mistake of outsourcing their ambulance services to private first responders. Now whoever got there first won the honor of billing the patient. It turned the whole thing into a race. Not that it wasn't a race already. But now it was a game, too. And that was bad. Mother, Jugs & Speed *was now a reality show. Firefighters were finding ambulances flipped like turtles everywhere these days, wannabe* Ghostbusters *running into walls when they took a corner too fast (and they always took the corners too fast in those boxes). Firemen rescuing EMS guys rescuing firemen getting shot at by gangs from fire escapes.*

Bad timing really, but just thinking about such things, at this moment, is the last straw for the second fireman on the scene, and suddenly he's angry enough to punch a paramedic, any paramedic. At least in the stomach. He's been wanting to do this for about a year. So he does.

The fireman is short, so he hits Jack mostly in the belt. But the fireman is strong, so the punch is enough to knock the wind out of Jack and bounce him off the bumper of the wrecked car like ropes in a wrestling ring. Jack curls up in pain and doesn't see Rick turning the second fireman around with a handful of shirt. But Jack hears the smack, and from his angle, he sees several people on the sidewalk recoil from something horrible.

"Just stay the hell back," the second fireman is saying from somewhere else when Jack stands back up. Jack looks around and finds the second fireman sitting ten feet away, holding his head in his hands like he's trying to keep it on, cross-legged on the street like a preschooler on a carpet square.

The first fireman on the scene stands with the buzz saw like he's ready to use it on Rick. The boy inside the car is screaming.

The dog is pawing at the windshield like he's trying to bury it.

"I won't tell you again," the First Fireman adds, less convincing than a guy with a saw should be.

"Listen to the man, Jack," Rick says, fist still white.

"What's happening?" Jack asks everybody, even more confused than before the punch. "Where's the girl and the horse?"

Rick stares at his partner like he's never met him before.

Ambulance. Minutes later. Jack and Rick are heading to the hospital and something is wrong with the siren again. It emits a strained, choked warble like a bird under a bicycle tire, and Rick is turning it off and on to try to fix it. But his actions only make the sound of the siren ever more distressing.

"Just leave it!" Jack says from the back. The boy is on the gurney under him, calm from a vein full of pain medication. His arm is less like a scarf knotted around his neck now, more like a gutter a storm ripped off a house. "It's better to just get used to it."

"How is he?" Rick asks.

238

"Stable. Where do you think this kid was going in that car?" Jack leans down to the boy. "Where do you think you were going in that car?"

"Dude. I've been doing some thinking…" Rick starts.

"You couldn't even see over the steering wheel, kid," Jack goes on. "You'd have done better with that dog driving."

"…I don't want to sound like one of those buddy cop movies but, I've been thinking about… requesting another partner."

"You know," Jack says, still working on the boy, oblivious to what Rick said. "My girl and I hit a dog once…"

"Are you listening to me?"

"We were on our way to see a concert at The Troubadour in Hollywood, late '70s so it was Elton John at his best and ugliest, right before his fake retirement," Jack tells him. "But I'm lost as usual. We were driving in from fuck knows where. And my girl was unfolding a road map, and it was getting in my way when all the sudden BAM! a fucking dog goes legs up, over the hood and then SMACK! crazy dog face hits the windshield, then it's high up in the air again and then THUD! dog body bounces off the trunk and hits the road. I slam on the brakes. My girl's almost hysterical, so I tell her to relax, and I grab the map. I mess with this map more than I need to so that while I'm climbing out of the car it'll block her view of the dog. Then I hand it back to her, hoping that she'll try folding it up the right way and stall her a little more. And then I get out and run behind the car. And the dog is dead as dog shit, bent all wrong, head facing backwards. I look back and I can see her getting out of the car, and I start thinking fast. I think that our Elton John concert will be ruined if she sees this dog - I mean, this is back when the motherfucker was dressing like Donald Duck, right? - and I think she's gonna feel responsible because of the map and everything, and we still got like three hours in the car before we even get there. So I kicked the dog under the car. Punted it like a football. She steps out of the car and onto the road, and I think fast and run over to the ditch and act like I'm watching the dog run away. I'm like, 'Damn! Can't believe that tough little bastard lived through it! Not even a limp!' And she's squinting out into the dark and actually believing me. Doesn't even know that the dog is right under her feet, right under the car. Then she's finally breathing normal, so I climb back in and start driving away, the whole time thinking, 'If I pull this off, I swear I'll tell her the truth some day,' and right about then is when the back tire bounced over the dog's head."

Rick stares at him a moment, then switches the siren off and on again. The strangled sound gets worse. He punches the dashboard in frustration and leaves it screaming.

"Then what?" he asks, impatient.

"Huh?" Jack says, distant. "I don't know. We didn't last too long after I ran over that deer's head. Maybe if I'd just run over it once. Not twice."

"Deer? I thought you said it was a dog."

"That's what I meant."

"So you broke up because of the dog?"

"No, I thought you asked me why I became a paramedic?"

"Uh, nope. Never asked that question. Nobody asked you anything."

"Oh. Well, I wish that had been why we broke up. It would have been a better reason," Jack says, crawling up to the front to play with the siren, too. "What the fuck is up with this thing, seriously…"

The siren's wail is louder now and impossibly even more annoying.

"Sounds the same as it always did," Jack shrugs.

Jack climbs into the passenger's seat and pulls down the sun visor. A piece of paper flutters into his lap. Scrawled on the scrap in childlike script is a bloody picture of a stick-figure baby crashing head-first through a windshield. Jack looks at Rick, suspicious. Rick frowns.

"Think you're funny, don't you?" Jack says.

"It used to be funny. Now I'm not so sure."

"What does that mean?"

"You should have told her about the dog," Rick says instead of answering the question. "You should have shared that moment with her. The hell with the concert."

"I was gonna write a story about it, get it off my chest," Jack says. "But it would be my first story ever, and she'd know something was up."

Stevey called Larry's cell before he even made it a mile down the road, chewing his ass out. He said he'd never work for him again. He said they were trying to salvage the shoot without him, but Head Breakfast lost his erection staring at the tattoo on her back.

"Your fault!" Stevey barked. "He's thinking like you now!"

Larry remembered one of those idiots getting a tattoo on his dick, worse than that fucking fly tattoo. The guy said he was trying to give life to that old joke, the way magic gave Geppetto the bouncing baby boy he always wanted. The dick tattoo would read, "Hey!" when flaccid, then "Hello Jamaica Is Ranked 98th out of 100 on the Global Competitiveness Index In Everything Except Penis Size So Please Sponsor A Child Today!" when erect. But all the tattoo needle managed to do was damage the deep tissue so that it never drained properly, giving him half a useless erection the rest of his life. Looked good naked but couldn't do shit with it except tell stories. Larry also heard that story was bullshit, that it was just some S.T.D. gone bad that ravaged the thing.

Larry stared at his big toe, now popping clear through the hole in his decomposing tennis shoes. The blood blister from when he'd dropped the camera months ago was halfway to the end of the nail now. He imagined that bloodstain almost imperceptivity stretching to move under the keratin, like someone slowly tilting the bubble in a level, or that steak on the counter in *Poltergeist*.

Stevey went on to tell Larry that not even the little blue pills could bring H.B.'s cock back from the grave. He said they faked it as long as they could, and Larry imagined one of those horribly limp all-nighters he'd dealt with before, right up until they'd all given up and the man's embarrassed teardrop splashed the L5-S1 rupture scar that marked her spine. It was a common injury in this business. At least workers' comp covered it every third time.

"Was he crying, Stevey?"

"He *was* crying, Larry." Pause. "There's no crying in fuck films!"

"There's quite a bit, actually," Larry corrected.

"You had Head Breakfast crying," Stevey calmly explained. "Joe's in the hospital. We're losing use of the house. And this is all your fault. I'm sorry, but you're fuckin' done, man. You're taking a break. I'm calling Damon."

"Good luck with that." Larry let the giant phone sag in his hand, uninterested. He could still hear the voice loud as ever.

"You're taking a break, Larry."

"What? Three-game suspension?" he laughed down at a receiver the size of a drive-in speaker.

"You know what I mean."

"I quit already. Ask Gold. If you can."

"You better get the fuck out of town, Larry."

The song "New Girl Now" came on the radio, and he turned it up as high as it could go to drown out Stevey, a distant car horn that sounded stuck, and birds that had no business screeching in the trees. They should be sleeping, flying south, engulfing their babies' heads. Then the voices came through, right on cue, and he shook them off.

"Why would I leave town?" Larry asked the phone in the seat next to him. "This is my town." He figured they must have found the body in the pool by now. If not, soon, and it would tell them everything, narrate the whole story, all *Sunset Boulevard* 'n' shit.

"Joe called the cops!" the speaker was shouting.

"What?! Bullshit," Larry coughed. "That numbnuts barely speaks English. He probably called a locksmith by mistake."

"You're done!"

"Hey, do you have a tattoo, Stevey? Where's yours? Let me guess, 'Mom.'"

"Are you still going on about... I ain't got one. You know this. My body is a temple. There's something wrong with you, man..."

"Right. What temple? Machu Picchu?"

"I don't get it."

"'Cause, like, it's old. And it's all fucked up? Forget it. Goodbye."

Larry hit the button. Stevey tried calling back, but he let it squawk. Then somebody must have gone to see Gold, because everybody was suddenly trying to call him. His giant phone lit up like a Christmas tree at a drag strip as he drove on. He tapped his pocket that used to bulge with his engraved lighter, a birthday gift from Glen. Thought about the crime. Oops. He didn't know how much evidence he'd left in that swimming pool, but it was probably just everything with his name on it. No big deal.

But he didn't care. He had a mission. He remembered a hole in a fence that he used to crawl through as a child. It would let him get closer to the voices than he'd ever been before. He knew the hole would still be there. He scratched his elbow hard.

Holes everywhere.

"Did you know that in England, in the back of an ambulance, the patient faces the other way?"

"That doesn't seem right."

"Downright obscene."

"It's like a 69."

"Cut! Cut!"

"What's the problem?"

"Don't talk about a 69. It's a sore spot."

"If it's sore, you're doing it wrong!"

"Why's it a sore spot, boss?"

"Because of the difference between porn and real life, with regards to a 69, I mean."

"Which is?"

"Which is that both ends aren't working equally hard. The Ultimate Paradox of the 69 is that when one end works harder, the other end can't help but be distracted. Unlike Shakespeare's 'beast with two backs,' if the couple is doing it right, the two ends of this beast swing up and down as unevenly as the scales of justice."

"Hey, can someone adjust that radio dial? Tired of all the voices."

"What's wrong with 69 again?"

"Pick another number."

"How about 86."

"Perfect. And... action!"

In the distance, Evil could see the glow in the trees, and he turned down the music on his handlebars to remember the night, back when he was still Billy, when he and Bully dumped her dead cat over the bridge, a cat she'd saved for years in a freezer for the perfect ceremony with the perfect boy. The freezer eventually needed defrosting, so Billy would have to do.

They were in her car, and it was just starting to get dark. They heard a strange jingle advertising the drive-in that same night. Or at least they thought it was for the drive-in. Then they quickly realized it was dialogue from a movie. Two characters arguing about something they'd heard before. Always easily influenced, Evil started an argument with her, too, about which movie was better, *The Thing* or *E.T.*, those famously vicious debut-weekend rivals. There were people who swore by *E.T.* and people who swore by *The Thing*. It was like that Elvis/Beatles thing. Or was it the Elvis/Jesus thing? All he knew was he fucking hated *E.T.: The Extra Testicle* and loved, loved, loved *The Thing*. She'd liked neither. He decided to give her more time on that one.

When they got to the river, they popped her trunk. They pulled out her cat, a black baby bundle of garbage bag and duct tape, and they ran up to the bridge over Elbow Creek. They looked for the perfect place to drop poor little Wyatt Urp, finally stopping next to some elaborate graffiti monsters and the even more elaborate graffiti monsters that were devouring the first drawings. They decided this would be the best place to hide since it had obviously already worked as cover for at least two amateur artists.

The water was flowing in the wrong direction, and they were disappointed because they had to dump the cat over the wrong side and run across traffic, as if they weren't already looking suspicious enough, this teenage couple with their baby-sized bundle in the soggy paper bag. At first, they were going to fill a cat carrier with some stones and sink it. But she liked the little garbage-bag mummy she'd constructed. Honestly, she was hoping for traffic cameras or a suspicious motorist or two, actually praying to at least get questioned. Then maybe she'd stop feeling so bad about her cat.

While they stood there, Bully tried to get Evil to imagine they were a little higher up, maybe on a real bridge, so the tiny black bundle could be a full-size person bobbing along. Bully assured Evil that her cat would take on water and sink any second now... any second now. But he knew she was crossing her fingers that it would never go down.

They both talked about what children might do if they found the bundle. And they held hands, actually held hands, and talked more than they ever had. A connection turned to excitement, then turned to disappointment and disgust. She let his hand drop like it was dead, too. All the emotions of a six-year relationship while they stood there, the same length of time Wyatt Urp was alive actually. Back in her car, they listened to the theme song by Isaac Hayes for old-time's sake, as many times as they could stand it.

It was the closest they'd ever been. The most vulnerable she'd ever seemed. She even let Evil hijack her ceremony with a memorial present that celebrated his dog. And that's probably why she made her mistake, leaving the toddler-sized *Shaft in Africa* T-shirt on the cat for the police to find.

But Evil saw she could cry, and his heart swelled in excitement in that moment. But what he didn't realize was that it was Bully's anger making her cry. Not sadness, an entirely different animal. And he didn't know it, but this was also the day she realized she had the courage to betray him.

They'd stood there holding hands and watching the tiny body go down the river, both of them realizing that they had the courage to perform if it had been a real crime, even dispose of something bigger than a cat. Sadly, she was thinking maybe a cop, but he was thinking maybe a dog, tops. Maybe a dog.

A man, a woman, and her child, all walking too fast through a carnival. Jacki has that sweatshirt and black no-pants pants thing going on and is dragging Toni by the arm. She's dressed just like her mom. Jacki's boyfriend, Anthony, sweaty, red-faced and miserable, stomps along behind them both, a bundle of helium "Happy Birthday" balloons in his fist. Jacki didn't believe it when her friends used to claim Anthony was exactly the kind of asshole who wanted a boy so bad he named his daughter after him instead. But after three years together, Jacki no longer argues the point.

Today is the day the truth came out.

The "Happy Birthday"s bounce lower and lower as they rebound through the crowd, the excitement hissing out of them every few feet or so. The balloons, too.

One particular balloon, just a crumpled bag of deflated silver scraping the gravel behind them, catches every sharp corner and ankle it can, as reluctant as a kid hanging onto a doorjamb. Surrounded by bright colors, happy families and voices, this group stands out in their manic desperation to get on a ride, any ride.

Toni tugs, tugs, tugs on her mom when a shorter line of bodies suddenly catches her eye. She breaks free to run ahead, and Jacki watches her scamper up to the tail end of calmer family units waiting for some short kid with the audacity to check the height of others. Anthony takes advantage of the distraction to kick the rest of the sagging balloons away in disgust, and Jacki finally turns her full attention to him, eyes blazing in anger.

"What?"

"You know what."

The kid tries to measure Anthony to get a laugh from the crowd because Anthony is, of course, short as hell. But he knocks the stick out of the kid's hand and steps up to wait for a carny valet to bring around his car, arms crossed tight.

Ten minutes later, the three of them sit silent in a slow-moving Model-T, riding a rail around a track with no corner sharper than the curvature of the Earth. Toni hangs out the back window to stare at the other creeping cars, and Anthony sits brooding, his arms still locked and pale from loss of circulation. He watches the steering wheel turning on its

247

own. He knew the ride with the shortest line was gonna be the worst.

"Bothers you, not driving, doesn't it?" Jacki finally says without looking over.

No answer.

"Thought so," she sighs.

"What was that supposed to mean?"

Jacki thinks she hears the squeak of his brain working, then realizes it's just the wheel brushing his belly.

"This ride sucks!" Toni squawks. "Where's all the twists and turns?"

"It's not that kind of ride," her mother says.

"What was that supposed to mean?" Squeak.

"Where's the water?" Toni squeaks.

"It's not that kind of ride," Jacki repeats wearily, on autopilot, sort of like the car, more like those ghost pianos in the westerns that play tired, tuneless carnival music.

"Does it go any faster?"

"Not that kinda ride."

"Oh, yeah?" Anthony says sarcastically. "Then what kind of ride was it?"

He's asking about something else, so Jacki answers like something else.

"A calmer, comforting, more realistic one."

"What are you talking about?" he suddenly wants to know.

"What are you talking about," she says without the question mark.

"Talking about this," Anthony hisses, suddenly headbutting the steering wheel. "Is this how it happened? Show me how it happened."

"Jesus Christ, calm down, asshole."

Jacki frowns and looks away out the window. She's had this conversation way too many times while driving and doesn't want to encourage him with too much attention. And the idea of this argument in a car that doesn't occupy his hands suddenly terrifies her.

But he says it again, and now she's feeling spiteful.

"Show me how it happened, Jacki."

"How what happened." *Again, not really asking.*

"You know what."

"Anthony, please, not now…"

"Is that how it happened? Him behind the wheel? You on top? Just tell me. Is that how you two crashed that fucking car? Someone forgot to keep both hands on the wheel, didn't they? Then where the fuck were the hands? That's why he ended up dead, swinging naked like a chimp from a fucking tree?" *Pause.* "You're lucky to be alive, huh?"

Jacki knows he's not talking about the crash. What he's saying is more like a threat. A lot more.

"Just shut up," *she says, throwing a thumb back at Toni.* "I'm not talking about this again. Not here. Not again. Not ever."

"Not ever, huh? You know…" *Anthony starts, eyes on the fake road, hands floating over the fake wheel out of habit.* "…if you two would have been on this bullshit ride instead, that accident would never have happened. He'd still be alive, you two would still be fuckin', and I probably woulda never known shit. Would I?"

She says nothing, looking around to the families in the other cars. No one is smiling. And at least two couples have started arguing now, too.

No wonder this line was so short, *she thinks.*

"That couldn't have been the first time. No fuckin' way, no fuckin' way. No. Fuckin'. Way," *he goes on.* "That's what it took, huh? Him to get fucking killed before I found out?"

"Is that why I have to hear about this shit every couple of months? Because you feel you were robbed of your chance to kick our ass?"

"I just want you to admit it."

"*You don't want me to admit shit,*" Jacki turns full on him, furious. "*You know how pathetic you sound? You're not angry because I cheated. You're angry because he's dead.*"

He considers this a second, eyes lingering on the line where her crotch was devouring her tights. Her clothes always seemed to get tighter when she was mad, even tighter when they were at an amusement park.

"*Nah, I'm pretty happy he's dead, actually.*"

"*Anthony, you know what it is? You're just angry because you had to fake compassion by my hospital bed, right there in front of Mom and everyone. You don't think about how I was affected, or why any of it happened, or how someone actually died that day. And you don't care. You just feel like you were cheated out of a chance to hit somebody. Well, quit fucking whining about it and do something.*"

He considers this, hands greasing the fake steering wheel with a squeaky snakebite.

"*You can't stand the fact that what happened to him and what happened to me…*" she pauses to make sure she gets the mouthful just right, "*…was worse than what you think happened to you.*"

Proud of herself, she stops to watch his hands wring his sweat out of the plastic, laughing when he turns it hard left and the car doesn't do what he wants.

"*Actually, you know what?*" she says. "*The more I think about you, the funnier you get…*"

"*Where's the big twists!*" Toni suddenly shouts from behind them. "*I thought this was a ride!*"

"*It's not that kind of ride.*"

Jacki looks to the other rides on the horizon, wishes she would have picked any ride but this one. But it's been "Slim Pickens," ever since they walked in. And by that, she means every one of these mutts manning controls reminded her of that hayseed asshole in Blazing Saddles.

She never feels she's in good hands at a fair so cheap and ugly.

250

Fair? Or was it an amusement park? *she wonders.* Carnival? Anything but "theme park," always hated that name.

"*So, who was driving?*" *Anthony says, a bit quieter.* "*Just tell me that. Please. Then I'll drop it. Who was driving? You or him?*"

"*I don't want her to hear this, Anthony.*"

"*Twists!*" *Toni stomps a foot.*

"*Not that kinda ride,*" *she says.* "*This one's more like real life.*"

As if to prove this, Anthony actually reaches for a radio dial on the fake dashboard to drown out the child before he catches himself. In the distance someone is listening to Modest Mouse "Wild Pack of Family Dogs," but they can't really hear it because the car radios are as fake as the license plates, and because the antennas that pick up songs from the past and the future are still a couple years away from being affordable for everyone, especially on counterfeit vehicles with lawnmower engines.

"My dad he quit his job today, well, I guess he was fired but that's okay. And I'm sittin' outside my mud lake, waiting for the pack to take me away..."

"*Are you that fucking stupid?*" *Jacki laughs, then notices another couple off in the grass with their plastic hood up. The husband is hunched over the space where the engine would be, looking all concerned, wife pouting.*

"*He was driving, wasn't he? So you fucked him while he was driving?*" *Anthony says, punching the speedometer sticker once, twice. The car shakes.*

"*Enough. Six years I've been listening to this. I'm not talking about it anymore.*"

"*Six years and you've never given me any answers. I just want to know why you would even think about doing something like that, especially in a car.*"

Silence.

"*Fucking answer me!*"

251

Impossibly, oncoming traffic seems in danger of drifting into their lane, and the helpless drivers glance over at them nervously. The rest of the drivers are arguing, a flurry of loose hands, profanity, and exasperation. One man leans out to eyeball Anthony. Forgetting it's a ride, Anthony reacts like he would on any road.

"What the fuck you lookin' at?"

The woman in the other car reluctantly restrains her man.

"Keep driving, asshole," Anthony mutters. Then, "Hey, did that motherfucker just cut me off?"

Anthony reaches for a rear-view mirror to try and see any traffic behind him. He laughs when he sees there's no mirror, of course, but he's not very convincing.

Jacki tugs her leggings loose again and leans over.

"Are you losing your goddamn mind?"

"Could be."

He pulls hard on the fake steering wheel, and it turns out it isn't completely fake after all. The car bumps against the guide rail, and Toni giggles, finally excited.

"Do that again and we're getting out," Jacki warns him.

"No, do it again!" Toni squeals, clapping. He bumps the rail again.

"I'm pulling over so we can talk about this."

"You can't pull over, dumbass." Jacki says. "This isn't real. None of it."

Jacki slumps forward, her head in her hands in frustration. The sensation of a dashboard sinking into her chest is strange, but not unfamiliar. Not entirely unpleasant. She wishes it was dark enough to pull up her sweatshirt and feel the cold plastic on her skin again.

Staring at her, Anthony pulls on the wheel again and the car lurches harder against the rail, almost clearing it. Toni is actually clapping her feet now.

"You realize we aren't in a car, right?" she says softly. "You realize we're not pulling over on the side of the road to talk, right? You realize this is a fucking ride, right?"

252

Anthony ignores her and, with two more quick turns of the steering wheel, he finally jumps the rails. Other fake drivers stop punching their dashboards to voice their concern with threats, and their kids are crying as the renegade Model-T crushes its way through some ratty flower beds, cuts off the line of sputtering gridlock, and heads for the nearest fence. Jacki opens the door and jumps out, pulling her daughter with her.

"Where are you going?" Anthony pleads as they start running. "Please, just show me what you did. Show me on this ride and no one will get hurt, I promise. Show me. It's safer here. Think about it, this is the perfect place for it..."

Heads crane out of the other cars to watch Jacki with Toni in tow, and Anthony's car belches and bumps its way along the rope fence surrounding the track.

"Show me what you did!" he yells.

She says nothing, almost running now.

"Stop."

She still says nothing and gets ready to gather Toni up to run.

"How do I even know she's mine?"

Jacki is now holding her breath, the only way she can say less than nothing.

Then she stops and turns.

"Did you hear me?" he says, punching plastic over and over and over, fist running red.

"I heard you. Nobody's yours."

"I know what happened," he says. "So do you. You're not mine and neither is she. Tell me I'm wrong. You lied all these years."

"You're right. You know what? You're so good at predicting human nature, you should be named an honorary human being."

Jacki knows she's heard that somewhere before, and she searches her memory banks as Anthony takes a moment to imagine himself at this ceremony and what his "honorary *human being" trophy would look like. Then he jumps out of the fake car, too, deciding the trophy would be waist-high and topped with a little gold man flexing a bicep.*

Jacki and her daughter walk out the entrance, brushing past a man who's trying to talk the slouching teenager with the measuring stick into letting him on the ride with his dog. The dog is almost tall enough.

That's when Anthony is in front of everyone at the gate, blocking the way out with a small revolver he's pulled from his skin-tight jeans like a magic trick. He doesn't have to look at the teenager for his weapon to find his forehead like a magnet.

The kid drops his stick. Then, suddenly unarmed and helpless, the kid decides to run. Anthony turns the barrel on Jacki, Toni bites her lip in excitement, and there is an audible cheer from the back seats of the other Model-T's as the children mistake the action for part of the ride. Theme park indeed, Jacki thinks.

"Get back in there. Move!" he tells her, obviously trying to sound like the movies. She wonders why he didn't just shout "movies!" instead.

But past the measuring stick, real screams are starting now. She looks up to see soap-white fists wrestling control from steering wheels and taking every car off the rails. She imagines weapons flashing everywhere, snapping free of conceal-and-carry holsters or coming around from behind every back like that bouquet nobody wants. Pistols, rifles, even a buck knife, some jutting through the thin canvas roofs of the fake antique cars as workboots skid alongside in the dirt, sandals flipping off and toes digging in like the fucking Flintstones. One vehicle gets stuck on the rope fence, fighting it like a bug strip until another car rear-ends it and flips it free and over.

Someone turns up a radio. Jacki can't believe that's the one thing on the dashboard that's real. It's impossible. It's literally a drawing of a radio. But someone else is singing, too, just like Buddy Holly:

"Every day, it's a-getting closer, going faster than a roller coaster... every day, it's a-getting faster, everyone says go ahead and ask her..."

Jacki squeezes her face in her hands in disbelief as two men slide over the nearest hood, rabbit punching each other in the face until one of their boots hooks the grill and they wrench their sputtering ride completely sideways with them and disappear into a mushroom of dust.

What do they call this goddamn ride? Road Rage Rehearsals?

Then it's just Anthony, his five-foot nothing blocking out the scene as he walks slowly up to Jacki, then behind her, pressing something like a gun to the small of her back, and she thinks about how the carneys should use metal detectors instead of rulers.

He pulls up Jacki's sweatshirt with what must be the sharp egg tooth on a barrel, and as the cold metal sinks into her skin, she inhales sharp and starts to walk.

A gun stashed in anybody else's shorts would have warmed up by now, *she thinks.*

Toni's eyes are positively glowing in excitement. Jacki's too.

"Do those come with the cars?" *Toni whispers.*

Her mother says nothing as they march forward. Back to the ride.

"Mommy?" *Toni sighs, tugging on the leg of her mother's tights and popping them out of the crack of her ass one last time. She's trying to make sense of everything she heard earlier from the back seat, the talk about her conception.* "Was I born on these rides?"

"Maybe," *Jacki says, still not afraid. She's never been afraid of anybody that short and wouldn't start today.*

It's a hot afternoon, triple digits, and the cool kiss of the metal feels too good on her back.

255

The problem is the steering wheel, *she realizes*. Ghost pianos and idle hands.

Anthony pushes Jacki to move faster back onto the ride. She drags her feet like that silver birthday balloon, and he's pulling her like she's pulling Toni when backfires from the tiny cars and their lawnmower engines start popping like bullets, but more like cheap fireworks. She wishes he really carried a gun everywhere instead of this stupid hammer. He'd be a lot scarier. He says a line from a movie again, but he fucks it up.

"Show me on this ride or no one gets hurt."

"When it gets dark, they're on their way out. Anthony's long, long gone before the cops arrive, and Jacki and Toni walk past a man who's trying to talk the slouching teenager with the measuring stick into letting him onto one last ride with his dog. But, obviously, there's just been a pile up on the Model-T's, the park is closing down, the cops are running around. The dog is a huge hairless Doberman that turns and almost smiles as they pass by. Toni reaches for the dog, but her mother yanks her along. The man with the dog spins his baseball cap to face them, and Toni smiles at the dog's face stitched into it."

"Lotta dogs, dude."

"Then he says something about being blind, right?"

"No, you say, 'What if I *was* blind?' to the teenager, because you're still pleading your case. And he says, 'You're not, though. Please, sir, we're closing down anyway!' And then you go, 'But that's not the real reason…'"

"Right, right, right. And then I say, 'That's the only rule that matters. The stick.'"

"That's not the reason."

"It's not?"

"No, it is. That's what he says, 'It's not the reason.'"

"Then what?"

"Then we'll film in your car, 'later that night' and all

that. So please stick around. Shit's about to get crazier, I promise."

Car, later that night. Jacki and her daughter are on their way home. It's too quiet, and Toni unbuckles her seat belt to lean forward and turn on the radio. Jacki quickly pushes her back into her seat and locks her in.

"Sit back. Don't mess with that."

"But I want to listen to-"

"I don't care. You shouldn't play with the radio when you drive. You'll cause a wreck."

"But you're driving," *Toni whines.* "You *can't play with the radio, or you'll crash. I can do anything."*

Jacki glares at her daughter, and she slumps back in her seat with her arms crossed, pulling on the seatbelt like it's strangling her. Eventually she stops, defeated.

"Mommy, is daddy in trouble?"

Jacki doesn't trust herself to answer.

"Mommy? Was I born on that ride?"

"What?" *Jacki snaps, shocked.*

"Back at the park. Is that where I came from? On one of those rides?

"What are you talking about?"

"I heard. You said that's where I came from. And it was today, right? My birthday?"

"Well, we meant where you were conceived. Not born. It's not the same thing." *Pause.* "And it wasn't on that ride."

"What's 'conceived'?"

"Made."

"Where was I made then?"

Jacki looks at her, then back at the road. There's a crazy moment when she almost tells her daughter everything. Then suddenly Jacki turns on the radio, and the car speeds up. The song "Black Betty" is about halfway through.

"Black Betty had a baby bam-a-lam, damn thing was crazy bam-a-lam..."

"Mommy, can you conceive a sister?"

"No, I cannot," she laughs.

"But I heard babies can recognize other baby's faces. It calms us down!"

"You're not a baby. And you're talking about Furbies."

"Am not!"

"Yes, little one. You are talking Furby technology right now. Amazing toys, more electronics than the entire Sputnik space program, I hear. Face recognition software. But that doesn't work with peeeeeople. We don't know who the hell we are."

Toni pouts. Jacki looks at her a couple times, then the song repeats the chorus with more "bam-a-lams," and she turns the car around so hard that her graduation tassel on the rear-view mirror flips up and over to the right. Jacki laughs, thinking this must mean she's still got a lot to learn before she can stop herself.

"You didn't even get me a Furby," Toni says. *"You got me a Blurby."*

"Okay. You wanna know? You wanna get to the bottom of this? Me, too. Let's go."

"Yay!"

Their car passes a pick-up truck with tinted windows that slows as they pass. It pulls a quick U-turn in the stones to follow them, but Jacki doesn't notice.

The truck turns off its headlights. Jacki doesn't notice this either.

Crash site.

Jacki and Toni stand hand-in-hand on a stretch of road. Jacki points to the ground at their feet.

"Somewhere right about here I think," Jacki says, thoughtfully, kicking around.

"What's 'right about here?'"

"This is where you came from. Right about... here. Right before the car left the road."

"But how could I..."

Jacki ignores her as she walks toward the trees. She's lost in thought, remembering something buried in her brain. She walks to the stumps of several broken trunks, hearing a familiar voice whispering in her head.

"Three more minutes and it never happened..."

"This is where he died," Jacki finally says.

"Who?"

"Your daddy. Your real daddy. This is the tree that killed him."

She reaches down with a finger and splashes the rainwater that's collected in the stump.

"Gross!" Toni yells, hand over her mouth. "Don't do that! There's mosquito eggs and poop in there. Uck."

"That won't hurt you, there's mosquito eggs and poop in everything we eat, baby."

Toni's eyebrows arch as she soaks in this offhand comment. Jacki realizes she'll probably never forget it.

"Come over here, baby. You never heard of 'spunkwater' before?"

"You mean 'stumpwater?'"

"No, honey. It's called 'spunkwater.' Haven't you read Tom Sawyer yet?"

"No, we were gonna, but they said it had too many swear words, so the teacher changed her mind."

"There's no way you're old enough to read Tom Sawyer. We'll start you with Huck Finn. Well, if they woulda let you read it, you'd know that spunkwater can cure all sorts of things. Gets rid of warts on your hands, hiccups, toothaches, bad daddies..."

Jacki trails off, thinking hard.

"...or maybe Tom had to drag a dead dog on a string for the hiccups. I can't remember."

Toni looks down into the stump then backs up holding her nose.

"Why is it all white? Looks like Egg Drop soup. It's soooo gross. Please, can we go home now?"

Some twigs crack behind them, and Jacki jerks her hand out of the water as if something bit her.

"Yeah, okay, let's go-"

Suddenly a man steps from the shadows. It's Anthony, furious as always. He bridges the distance in three seconds and shoves Jacki back, tripping over the stump.

"I can't believe you brought her here," he snarls. "I can't believe you keep coming back here to rub this shit in my fucking face…"

She jumps up, grabs her daughter and turns to run. She stops. She looks to the ditch along the road, remembering something else now. Her eyes are distant, and the only sound is their three heartbeats hammering. Even Anthony feels the weight of this moment, and he stops coming toward her, looking around nervously.

Then the low growling of an animal makes him flinch. Almost in a trance, Jacki walks toward the drainage ditch, still dragging her daughter by the arm. As he tries reaching for them, Anthony leans out awkwardly, afraid to move his legs because of the growling, which is getting closer and closer. Jacki ducks out of his reach easily.

"Where are you going? You're showing her! Why not me? Show me where he died. Show me the tree he was hanging from."

Lost in thought, she continues to march toward the ditch. Anthony is screaming now, and the sound of the growling is louder. He slaps a nearby tree and tries not to wince.

"Is this the one?! Did he die here? Where did that motherfucker die?"

He punches another tree, aiming for the yawn of a black knot on the trunk.

"Is this the tree? Fucking tell me…"

He punches another trunk and blood splashes across the bark.

"Is this where he died after you fucked him?! This one? C'mon. I want to carve our initials in it. Maybe build us a birdhouse. One question? Why the fuck didn't you tell me? Six years of this shit…"

Toni is crying now, tugging on Jacki's arm as she keeps walking, oblivious to both of them. Then Jacki snaps out of the trance and turns on him as she moves her child toward the car.

"What good would it have done to tell you anything?" Jacki asks him. Her calm is infectious and he stops punching trees. They stare at each other for another moment, then she pulls Toni into the car, starts it up, and peels out. Watching her drive off, Anthony punches one last tree with his bloody knuckles, showing off to nobody now.

"Fuck you. Just fucking tell me where-"

He's throwing another fist in case she's watching in her rear-view mirror, when a shadowy figure drops down from the tree he's under. Before Anthony can react, he's knocked down so hard and fast that his face and shoulders are almost underground. Then he's underwater instead, struggling as large hands drag him over the lip of the stump to push his face deep into the murky stew. Anthony splashes and bubbles as he flails around and digs into the arms of his assailant. But the hands hold him easily until his struggles wane. The last thing Anthony hears through the burbling of stagnant water is a dog barking, seemingly a hundred miles in the sky.

Then the dark figure is quickly up and stomping away through the brush, and an animal's shadow runs to follow. Anthony's body spasms one last time, that final jolt of electric protest through his nervous system, not nearly strong enough to discourage the insects already finding his mouth.

* * *

Even after the sliding glass door hissed closed behind him, he could still hear the song "Tropical Hot Dog Night," playing on his car stereo. Larry loved that song. His stereo was shot now, so sometimes it played too slow or too fast. But luckily with Don Van Vliet, born Don Glengarry Vliet, a.k.a. Captain Beefheart, this rarely mattered. He loved this song in particular, a song his ex-wife was convinced chronicled his chosen profession.

"Two flamingos in a fruit fight! This is your captain speaking!" he cackled along with a song no one else could understand. "You were right! What else could we be?"

Impossibly, Captain Beefheart started skipping, too, just like it was an old vinyl LP.

And the sky turned white in the middle of the night... sky turned white in the middle of the night... sky turned white in the middle of the night..."

His stereo had eaten a Thanksgiving feast worth of his tapes, especially when it rained, but it had never skipped like this. Sometimes eating tapes was a blessing. It made him work harder to hear a song, pay more attention to the meaning behind lyrics. If getting through an entire song wasn't so rare, he never would have discovered that Queen's "Another One Bites The Dust" started off by saying his name, his real name, in the first verse. Even African Queen's version of the song, that reggae cover band, they did it, too.

How crazy was that shit?

"What are you doing here, Larry?"

Who?

She was standing at the top of the stairs, pulling the belt on her robe tight, just like they always did after his movies wrapped up. He'd forgotten her accent. She was Welsh, or pretended to be last time he talked to her, some lingering method acting from her last movie. But his

them enough not to wipe them off, but instead stuffed them into his pockets to keep them safe.

Campus. Jacki walks down the hall of the "Science Building" at what's supposed to be "Emmanuellatown Community College," according to hasty, hand-made signage. Jacki is carrying Toni in her arms. It's an hour drive to work, and she falls asleep most days while doing it. Jacki has already put in her vacation days for the summer, but she needs to give her students their final grades. The school is a ghost town, so she's a bit alarmed when she turns the corner of her hallway and sees the crisscross of police tape across her doorway. Her heart hammering, she tiptoes up to it, only now noticing the "Happy Birthday" balloons nearby that have broken loose. She hasn't been around in weeks, and she decides her colleagues must have decorated her door as a joke. She rips down the yellow crêpe paper with "Crime Scene!" and smiley faces she hadn't seen before. She steps inside her office.

She turns on the light Anthony had given her when she first got promoted to full-time. He'd painted the lampshade himself with an oil-based paint, which meant that only lower-watt bulbs could be used to keep the shade from igniting, or at the very least filling the halls with smoke. He claimed this was on purpose, that he'd painted it red and black to complete the illusion of a volcano erupting. She asked why he couldn't have simply framed her diploma like she'd asked him to.

She puts an ear to the wall that connects to the labs where the scientists never feed the turtles. Someone is rocking out to Steely Dan, and she imagines this happening in a room of white coats and clipboards:

"So rip off your mask or the best you can ask for is a mattress in the city pound..."

Jacki lays Toni down on the yoga mat in the corner where she catches Zs during long office hours, then slumps in her chair, breathing slow, blinking slow. If any students had intended on picking up their final papers, the police tape keeps them away all day, and they both achieve the deepest sleep they have in weeks.

When she wakes, Jacki picks a yellow stream up off her foot, and that's when she reads the tail end of the crêpe paper, where Anthony had torn it off the roll after he'd finished decorating.

"I love you, Jacki. We're gonna have a great summer, baby. Love, Anthony."

She wraps it around her shoulder like Miss America and curls up with Toni on the yoga mat to stroke her hair.

She doesn't know why, but as Jacki slips into sleep again, she actually believes him.

Roadside. Same day. Jack and Rick are running up on a car wreck, tackle boxes swinging, and they're surprised to find two bloody-nosed drivers engaged in a road-rage fistfight. A security guard from a nearby strip mall halts them with a palm, then trots over to where a pedestrian is trying to break it up. Neither man shows any signs of injury, and Jack turns to leave, even though it's against protocol. Rick wants to examine them, but also wants to watch the fight.

"C'mon," Jack says. "This is a waste of time. There's got to be a better accident somewhere."

"Who do you think you are, Batman?" Rick laughs. "You're all serious like, 'There's got to be a serious crime somewhere, citizen.' We can't just leave anyway."

"Let's go, man! We're on the border of three hospitals' jurisdiction. There's probably two more ice-cream trucks on the way and they don't even need one."

"It doesn't work like that and you know it. What's your friggin' hurry?"

"Now it does and you know it," Jack says. Rick ignores him.

Back at the fight, one man is yanking a Taser barb that caught his shirt sleeve but didn't penetrate his skin. The man makes a lunge and catches his opponent with a clumsy sock in the ear while the security guard goes for his flashlight as if it's a gun. Sirens grow in the distance, and Jack cocks a thumb at the bumbling circle of humanity.

"If we fuck around here long enough, someone will need to go to the hospital. Let's go while we can still look for clues."

"What?"

"Seriously, I'll owe you one, okay? Hear the siren? Those guards have this under control."

"What the fuck are you talking about? Where do you want to go so bad?"

"There was something else on the scanner. I'll tell you on the way."

Rick stares, unconvinced.

"Please, let's just fucking go."

Overgrown field. Same day. Jack and Rick are at the scene of another dog mauling. They crunch through the high weeds to where a father and his daughter are crouched in the distance. The shadow of a run-down house looms over them on a hump of landfill. Suddenly, Jack starts running full-speed toward them, the first urgency he's shown all day, and Rick is suspicious. He jogs to catch up with his partner, asking:

"Do you know her?"

"What are you talking about?" *Jack says, stopping at the girl's side.* "Keep your mind on the job."

Rick shakes his head in disgust. "Whatever, Jack."

"Hey, how'd you know my name was Jack?"

Rick can't help but smile at the old joke. Jack starts tending to the girl's wounds in a reasonably efficient manner, so Rick goes to ask the girl's father some questions. At first, Jack is all business, but eventually he begins to slow to study an arm here, a leg there, until he's stopped working on the injuries entirely and is carefully examining her fingernails as if he's standing over a corpse on an autopsy table. He reaches down and starts unbuckling the girl's belt, and Rick sees this just before the girl's father does and finally snaps. Before Jack even sees him take one giant step towards him, Rick has punched Jack square in the face. But by now, they're both almost used to this.

A roll of gauze flies from Jack's grip, landing on a nearby bush and unspooling like a high-school toilet-paper prank. Jack rolls over, holding his nose but quickly jumps to his feet.

"No, no, you don't understand..."

Rick takes another swing, but Jack ducks it. Then Jack comes back with a left hook that knocks Rick back over his box of emergency equipment. Rick gets off the ground fast and runs toward Jack, burying his head in his chest. Jack backpedals and they both stumble over the crying girl, someone's flailing boot catching her in the jaw, which finally brings the father into the fight. He's got more of a righteous cause than either of them, and he punches Jack in the stomach, doubling him over and knocking the wind out of him for good. Then the man turns on Rick, and a solid uppercut takes Rick off his feet and drops him on his back in the weeds. The father wipes his hand on his pants and calmly picks up his daughter to walk toward the ambulance while Jack and Rick sit dazed on the ground, staring at each other.

"Get the fuck up and take us to the hospital," *the father says.* "Hurry the hell up. Unless both you motherfuckers want to be riding in the back with the meat."

Ambulance. Later that night. Rick is driving and Jack is back in the passenger seat. They are bloody, bruised, and brooding. "San Jacinto" by Peter Gabriel is playing on Jack's portable cassette player. Finally Jack speaks and Rick blinks long and slow in frustration.

"*What if I'm right? What if that girl had been raped and it had gone bad?*"

"*Who? That girl? Raped by her dad?*"

"*No.*"

"*The dog?*"

Jack doesn't say "no" fast enough.

"*Shut the fuck up,*" *Rick says as Jack's mouth opens to unload more bullshit. Rick shakes his head and turns on the broken siren to drown out his partner's nonsense with its warble. Parts of Jack's paranoid ramblings can still be heard over the warbling siren and the song on the stereo...*

"I hold the line... I hold the line..."

"*...and if there is a rapist, maybe he freaked out, maybe he had to rub the dog's face in it... to punish himself... or punish the dog...*"

"...I hold the line... the line of strength that pulls me through the fear..."

"*...he pulled out one of the dog's teeth... dog's teeth are loose, every one of them... so he tried to cut her throat with it to cover up... bet the dog hates him now... bet it licks the mailman but growls at him every morning...*"

"*That's not how the song goes, is it?*"

"...I hold the light... I hold the light..."

Rick stabs some knobs to turn off the radio and the siren, finds some Cat Stevens loving his dog instead of Peter Gabriel singing all spooky, then he glares at Jack.

"*Asshole. Listen to me. You are looking for meaning where there is none.*" *Rick smiles sincerely.* "*And tonight is the last night I deal with your bullshit.*"

"All the pay I need comes shining through his eyes. I don't need no cold water to make me realize..."

"*How can you say it means nothing? Everything means something. I mean, I'll admit that I might be wrong about what something means but I know I'm right when I say it means something.*"

"*What the fuck do you mean* 'something'*?*" *Rick shouts as he slams the brakes to keep from back-ending a truck.* "*Did that old man rattle your brains when he knocked you out? Fuck!*"

"*Relax. Relax. And he didn't knock me out. He hit me in the breadbasket.*"

"*Where?*"

"*Never mind.*"

"*Did you even go to medical school?*" *he asks Jack angrily, tapping the windshield with his finger.* "*Hold on. You almost made us hit that...*" *Rick's voice fades as he notices his partner squinting at the back of the truck.* "*Are you fucking kidding me with this? Hey. Hey! Tell me what it is about that truck that you see right now. What are these new clues, Sam Spade?*"

"*Fuckin' racist,*" *Jack mumbles, leaning forward. In spite of himself, Rick finds he's studying this vehicle right along with him. It's a red pick-up truck with barbed wire around the license plate, a huge* "*No Fear*" *decal across the back window, and a bumper sticker that proudly states:*

"**My Kid Beat Up Your Honor Student**."

Oh, yeah, it's also adorned with those glowing aquarium lights under the exhaust, a bloody, fake, Halloween-prank hand hanging from the trunk, and, finally, a pair of swinging metal testicles where the trailer hitch should be.

"*See that truck?*" *Jack asks.* "*All that shit?*" *Rick actually waits in anticipation, and the urge to slap himself for being caught up in the suspense of Jack's next sentence is overwhelming.*

"*Doesn't mean shit,*" *Jack finally says.*

"*Wow,*" *Rick sighs.*

"*You know what really upsets me here?*" *Jack asks.* "*Why can't that be the villain of the story?*"

"*Oh, he is. Trust me. Just not ours. A story set in the '80's, I'm guessing.*"

"*Oh, yeah? Then who is it?*" *Jack laughs.*

"If you have to ask that, of course it's gotta be you, fucknuts. Have you ever even seen an '80's movie?"

"What time is it?"

"Why?" Rick sighs again.

"I have something to do."

"When?"

"Just get us back to the garage. I have to tell someone something."

"What?"

"The answer to a question that's six years old."

"Who?"

"Exactly!"

"Can't wait to drop you off for good, Costello."

Woods. Same night. The tall, shadowy figure is crouched over the broken tree trunk where Jacki crashed her car. A ring of green seedlings are growing around the rim of the stump, glowing in the bobbing beam of a tiny flashlight. The shadow pockets the flashlight, which illuminates his jeans from the inside. He unzips his glowing, orange pants, and leans over the rainwater gathered in the dead wooden bucket. He masturbates furiously. In seconds, splashes of milky-white liquid swirl around the water like larvae. He reaches into the stump to soak his hands.

The stump water swirls around them until the water is red again with blood.

A smaller shadow leans against a nearby tree, cracking some knuckles to keep busy.

Same night with no invite, Jack pulls into Jacki's driveway, jumps out, and practically sprints to her front door. He bangs on it like a woodpecker chasing grubs. A light bulb flutters behind a curtain, and she opens the door dressed for bed in a flannel shirt and no pants, confused and squinty, arms crossed and defensive.

"What the hell's going on, Jack?"

"Can I talk to you?"

"Well, that's what you're doing." *She looks up and down the street.* "What's happening?"

"Can I come in?"

"I guess," *Jacki says after a moment, feeling the heat waves of desperation coming off his skin like a bonfire.* "We have to get up early tomorrow though, so I need sleep."

Jack steps inside past her and slams the door.

"Take it easy. You'll wake up-"

"This won't take long."

"Listen, I'm not trying to kick you out, but we have to go back to the hospital tomorrow."

"Is Toni okay?" *he practically shouts.*

Jacki shakes her head "yes" and "no" at the same time.

"It's nothing serious. She's just allergic to something, and we can't figure out what."

"Probably me," *Jack laughs.* "That'll be $300 for the diagnosis, please!"

Jacki smiles a bit, relaxing her posture, but backing up to a bookshelf that hides one of Anthony's hammers.

"I wish it was that easy," *she says.* "Tell you what, I'm not ready for her to get any more shots. And I don't like the way that goddamn doctor keeps sneaking up on her to do it."

"You're right, it's kinda weird they do it that way. You'd think they'd have it down to a science by now. Especially since your situation is getting more and more common every day."

"What situation?" *she asks. He doesn't answer, so she lets it go.* "Anyway, now I'm thinking I should just wait for her to skin her knee and send a scab in an envelope. Know what I mean? Less traumatic. Sick of this shit."

"Let any kid play past dusk, and they'll always end up scratched."

"Play till morning, and I'll clip her wings."

"Scary! You're gonna give her nightmares. And by 'her,' I mean 'me.' You're gonna mail what again?"

Jacki sits down on the couch, and Jack sits down on the far end, almost falling off. He starts cracking his knuckles nervously, then picks up a small wooden-framed photograph off a splintered, wire-spool table.

"This isn't a very good picture of you."

"That's because it's not me," Jacki frowns. "That's my mother."

"I'm sorry," Jack says embarrassed. "I don't mean she's ugly or something, it's just - She looks just like you. Exactly like you. Toni, too... but worse?"

"So, what's up?" she asks impatiently.

"You know, there's probably a hundred ways you could give Toni a shot in the arm without her knowing it's coming," Jack starts babbling. "If we were to think about it long enough, we could figure this out. I mean, there's hundreds of species of stinging insects alone, and-"

"Is this why you came over here?" she interrupts, starting to stand.

"I'm sorry. No, no." He looks up, down, left, right, left, right, but doesn't feel any braver. So he spills his guts.

"I'm here because I was there six years ago when you crashed into that tree."

Jacki blinks to let this information, as well as the memory, sink in.

" You came to my hospital room. I was there, remember. Go on."

He slowly turns to face Jacki, a melodramatic move that infuriates her. Jack knows about this kind of scene from the movies. He knows it's supposed to be important. This is a big, important moment, goddamn it. He imagines grabbing her face.

"Here's the thing," he says. "I believe that you were raped. I believe this happened while you were lying unconscious after your car crash. I believe I found evidence of this rape when

I pulled you out and put you in the back of our ambulance. And because of this, I decided to cover up this evidence while I rode with you to the hospital. And I did this for you."

He's trying to be sincere, but it all seems so smug and self-satisfied that Jacki has to struggle to control her hands. She imagines grabbing his face.

"And you did this why?"

"I don't know. Because I thought I was given this opportunity, you know? I had this chance where I could erase this horrible thing. Where you didn't need to ever know what had happened. Where no one *would ever know what happened. And you had all these other injuries, too, and I thought, 'Fuck it, why not make this one less thing for her to deal with?'"*

She stands up, and he follows her around the room, still talking.

"I thought, 'Why not make the worst thing to ever happen to her go away?' I mean, I didn't have the power to save your human cannonball in the tree, even though I was doing all our driving back then and we got there sooooo fucking fast! And I didn't have the power to save the kid under the car the day before that, even though we were first on the scene by at least eight minutes. And I didn't have the power to save that fucking cat in the sewer the day before that, but with you..."

She goes for the door, and he grabs her arm to stop her. Right out of the fucking movies.

"I had the power, don't you get it? Finally, more power than just getting there first. I got there before it even happened! I had the power to go back in time and make it so you were never raped. You're welcome!" He has his hands out like he's accepting a standing ovation.

"What the hell are you talking about?!" she yells, jerking free. "Just because a kid can write 'Time Machine' on the side of something doesn't make it true, you child, you fucking idiot. You didn't stop anything. How do you even think that you..."

"I never wrote 'Time Machine' on anything," Jack whispers. "Not a bad idea…"

She turns away, done talking to him.

"But I did stop it," he pleads. "If you didn't know it happened, then it didn't happen. That's how it works. Your character wasn't given this information. This was the worst thing that ever happened to you, and I took it away. Any other wishes you want me to grant?"

"Are you fucking serious? You think rape is worse than death? You think a random cock is worse than murder? Don't fucking flatter yourself. I think you're giving that thing way too much credit. Rape is worse than a car wreck? Maybe, but please don't confuse me with a new generation of victims who wear rape trauma like a badge of honor. I will not be that."

Jack holds his hands up in surrender. He doesn't understand her resistance. He thought everyone loved big, important, Oscar-fellating moments like these.

"It's not that, I just…"

"You 'just' nothing. All you did was do something no one asked you to do. Worse, you probably helped that monster get away by destroying evidence."

"…just thought that…"

"Just stop. You were wrong then, and you're wrong now. You did nothing to help me. You have nothing to offer me."

Jacki walks to the window, catches her breath. After a moment she turns around to look at Jack, and another revelation twists the expression on her face three different ways.

"Unless it was you."

"What do you mean?"

"Unless you raped me. Maybe that's why you covered it up."

"What?! You're nuts. All I did was try to-"

Jacki is following him around the room now, talking through her teeth.

"Think about it, asshole. What's more likely? That you're a one-time, time-traveling vigilante, quite possibly the least-effective of all time? Or that you were fucking around with me on the side of the road like a freak. Or maybe you were just fucking around with me in the back of your ambulance, huh, Jack?"

Jack keeps backing up. He notices the hammer that's slipped smoothly from the sleeve of her flannel shirt and into her fist. He's loving the suspense.

"No, no," he says. "It wasn't just this random thing. When I saw you, I-"

"Wait a second. Are you now going to tell me how you fell in love with a bloody, unconscious car-crash victim? How are you not the rapist again?!"

"But it's not just about you anymore."

"You know what's really scary?" Jacki says, her voice picking up power and speed. "I believe you when you say that. I believe it's not just about me anymore. So, how many are there, Jack?"

The hammer is up.

"Listen," Jack begs, palms out. "Don't you get it? It was six years ago this week. The day Toni was conceived, and..."

The hammer hovers.

"...the rapist is your father. I mean her father."

The hammer drops.

The hammer drops? How perfect is that? *Jack wishes someone said those words out loud, like stage direction.*

"Shut the fuck up. Get the fuck out."

"But-"

"Get..." She shoves him by the face to divide her command in half. "...out."

"I'm sorry," he says, now in the open doorway. "I thought I could make it so you never knew. Then shit got weird. I thought maybe you'd thank me."

Jacki's voice gets low and scary, like it's made of hammers.

"Listen to me very carefully. I know I was raped. I knew

this before you told me. I knew it then, and I know it now. I wasn't unconscious in the back of that ambulance, and you didn't save me from anything at all. Goodbye."

She walks back inside.

On his way to the drive-in, Larry's stereo devoured his Captain Beefheart cassette, of course, and he almost went for Meat Loaf's *Bat Out of Hell* instead, at least to hear the intro. He'd always suspected Meat Loaf was Beefheart's practical joke persona anyway. "They're both meat based!" he'd tell anyone who listened. This was before Don Van Vliet's duplicity had been conclusively proven in court, of course. But the tape must have been equally delicious because the stereo ate it before the piano even slowed down.

He reached into his glove box, dug around for some more music, and came up with two airline tickets instead.

Daytona to Heathrow. Five hour difference. Just enough to make it the next day. Just enough to make it something like time travel.

Sometimes Larry forgot which job he was doing, or even which decade he was in. Clothes weren't a reliable clue as fashions recycled. Movies were slippery with the popularity of period pieces. Slang was even slipperier. One thing that used to reliably establish a specific time, mostly due to their truncated shelf life, was whatever song you could locate being broadcast at that moment.

So he turned on the radio. A.M. was all he had left, but that's where the voices from the movies, the real movies, came through his speakers the clearest.

He scratched at his elbow, pushing aside dead skin, purple fluids, and fading scars of his teenage dog bite to reveal more of the spider web underneath. And the spider in the center. A classic and popular piece of body art, those elbow spider webs, especially for ex-cons. Larry rolled down his window, feeling his muscle strain with the effort, and he pitied the new generation of kids with power windows who wouldn't gain the strength that years of this motion could give you. A little exercise was better than nothing with the scrawny kids these days.

He leaned his head and arm into the night air, feeling the strips of skin peel from his elbow like bacon, debuting the glistening, red-marbled meat beneath. Looking up, he saw what he thought was a layer of fog, then realized it was actually a thick haze of insects, swarming easily above every car on the highway, adapted to no longer fear windshields at all.

Halfway to his destination, he got a flat. And when he checked the tire, he found the tip of a broken bone. He realized that everything was changing, coming up with defense mechanisms. You could run over any creature you wanted, just like you used to do, but now a busted bone or stinger might take your car with it. He drove on the rim anyway, leaving a trail of sparks likely visible from space.

He blew threw a dozen red lights, but stopped at one intersection when he heard the echo of music. It was the kid on the dirt bike. The kid he'd accidently covered with mouthwash on Pennsylvania Avenue. He recognized the tiny, winking battery light coming from the radio strapped to his handlebars. They both turned off their electronic voices and stared at each other for the duration of the red light, the green light, the yellow light… then another red again. Larry gunned it before it could change again, and the dirt bike turned to follow him and the blazing fishtail of fireworks coming from his rim until they came to the edge of some woods and the curve of the monstrous crop circle that marked the borders of the drive-in.

There was a line of cars filing in past the ticket taker, more machine voices rumbling towards those movies than either of them had ever seen. Then Larry's rim got stuck in the mud and started to spin, and the kid on the dirt bike passed him up to join the line of vehicles. Larry eventually slunk out of his driver's seat to walk around the gate and study the old lifeguard booth where the teenagers were making up prices depending on your face. Larry knew there would be a hole in the fence. In the back. There was a hole in every fence. And he knew this hole would be the exact shape of his new body. His younger body. The body that had been waiting underneath.

Once through the hole, Larry stood in awe of the spectacle. He'd seen deserted drive-ins on occasion, and he pitied anyone too young to know that deep shudder of excitement that came with such a vision. But the only thing more haunting than a deserted drive-in was one that was not.

"Yeah, just a bunch of cars watching a fucking movie," he laughed sarcastically, not sounding crazy at all. "No big thing."

VI.

Assholes and Elbows – Big Cop Small Cop Good Cop All Cops – The True Origins of the Make-A-Wish Foundation – Seeing "Die" Dog Revealed – Three Blind Mice Arrive at the Eleventh Hour (or A Cop Unsnaps His Gun for the First Time in His Life) – Green Monkey Blues – Larry Asks Just One Question – If a Tree Falls in the Forest, Find Out Who Was Last to See It Alive – Fuck Turtles, Trophies Are for Rabbits – The Bastard Sons of Plagiarists and Their Lonesome Balloon Animals – Heartbleeps

*"I went to the movies, and I saw a dog 30 feet high
And this dog was made entirely out of light"*
-Laurie Anderson "Walk the Dog"

When Larry came to the clearing, he had to blink to make sure he was really seeing what he thought he was seeing. There were no speaker stands, no umbilicals connecting the vehicles, no speakers leaning on windows like the roller-skating waitress just dropped off a burger, fries and Cherry Coke. Everyone was locked inside their cars, sealed up, windows tight. They looked unnatural. More like a gathering of machines and less like rows of human beings.

He looked up to the screen and saw a giant husband and his pregnant wife beaming over their new crib. He thought he might scream if he saw the baby at that moment.

Larry knew this drive-in well. They used to have two around town. There was The Butch Cassidy Drive-In, closer to the city and much more popular, until it got hit by a tornado ("Why don't tornadoes ever go through cities?" his wife wondered about a week before the storm. "You never see anything on the news where a tornado is zigzagging around some skyscrapers!"). So with Butch Cassidy reduced to rubble, only The Sundance Kid remained. It was tucked away in the 'burbs, next to a baseball diamond, and when he was younger, Larry and his friends used to lay out a blanket on the top of the concrete bunker where the projector was buried and watch all the movies for free, barely catching a bit of dialogue here and there from the loudest speakers, but not caring if they couldn't follow the story.

But everyone called the Sundance Kid "The Spotlight Kid" these days. First it was just a mistake on the flyers, but Larry thought Damon did that on purpose. He was the one who pushed all those insane Captain Beefheart albums on him back when Larry first got hired, *Clear Spot* and *The Spotlight Kid* being Damon's favorites. Damon told him it was rumored Vliet had retired nearby on Everglades Street to be a painter. There were regular sightings in the area, both on the ground and in the sky actually. Damon once claimed he enrolled in flight school with him and about 15 Saudi Arabian teenagers. Damon bought one of his self-portraits for six-hundred grand. He also swore the name "Beefheart" was based on a nickname. Vliet's uncle had given a fistful of wrinkly balls and cock when he terrified his nephews. Then someone changed the story to claim it meant having "a beef in your heart against the world." Larry liked the sound of the second story better, but he never forgot the first.

"And if you're talking about a drive-in, a 'spotlight' makes a hell of a lot more sense than a 'sundance,'" Damon told him. "Hell, the sun is Kryptonite to a drive-in…"

That shit again? Kryptonite was everywhere these days, Larry thought. *Like these green-eyed monsters…*

He'd always hated the theaters' namesakes anyway, considering that particular movie the flashpoint of all the smug, self-satisfied Hollywood westerns to follow, the cult of personality intruding onto the screen, famous people playing dress-up instead of making you believe they were doing shit for real. Fiction shouldn't be a vacation. Fuck those rich fucks.

Larry followed the beam of the drive-in projector to the stone bomb shelter that housed the important equipment. He decided this would be his target. Under one arm, he carried his movie like a metal pizza, loving the weight of all his hard work. If Larry was going to be reduced to a career as a lowly projectionist, he figured he might as well take Damon's demotion tonight. And if they were switching to adult movies at this drive-in, he knew that the end was nigh. No drive-in stuck around long after it started showing porn, even if the movies were as good as his.

He looked back at the screen over his shoulder, squinting through the movie. It was an old one screen, the last of the concrete slabs they were replacing everywhere with thin steel ribs and siding, like the flimsy walls of an above-ground pool. No, this one was solid. Thick and white, eroded smooth around the corners, sort of like a piece of monstrous, crumbling Wonder Bread. Larry thought it looked vulnerable but beautiful. Dying but glorious, with the deathbed glow of a loved one.

He decided to go straight for the bunker, and jogged straight through the playground under the screen, happily swinging his 15-inch projector reel under his arm as if he worked there. He doubted anyone would try to stop him. Security was always lax at these artifacts. You were still expected to smuggle people in your trunk, like it was good sport, and no one was ever in the booth at the end of the movie to even notice that the heads in every back seat had suddenly multiplied on the way out.

But this would all change once they started showing X-rated films. Security would tighten up.

Larry walked up to the first car he could find with wires hanging out of its window.

Finally, a speaker, he thought, looking forward to holding the box to his head and hearing the voices more clearly, maybe even the ocean. But the shadow hanging out of the window wasn't a speaker. It was an elbow trailing tattered shreds of a flannel shirt sleeve, with a spider web on it, of course. He was disappointed it wasn't an anchor.

He grabbed it and pulled it up high until it cracked. Over the scream, he finally heard the voices from the movie, coming from their car stereo now like all the new drive-ins.

"Can you hear that?!" Larry yelled. "They're talking on the radio!"

"That's how a drive-in works, you dumb fuck," a kid from the back seat said, not as scared as he probably should be. Then another elbow caught Larry along the jaw and spun him into the stones. His movie rolled free and disappeared under another car where he could see the driver jumping up to pull on his pants.

Assholes and elbows! Larry thought crazily. He'd first heard this phrase when some Sergeant was screaming at the ROTC kids at his school. Later, he heard it meant something about working so hard that's all you could see. Fighting for something until you almost disappeared.

He always thought this applied perfectly to pornography, too.

Next day. Two cops, one big, one small, like every pair of everything in the world, are standing in Jacki's living room, questioning her about the murder of her boyfriend, Anthony. They're wearing police blues but talking more like detectives. Criminals pretending to be cops pretending to be detectives would be a more accurate description. They've been questioning her hard for a while now.

"You say you were showing your daughter the scene of your accident?" Officer Stansberries, the Small Cop, says. Jacki doesn't answer. She's watching her daughter out a window and lost in thought, having tuned them out nearly an hour ago.

"I said, 'You say you were showing your daughter the scene of your accident,' am I right? Why were you doing this?"

"It was her birthday. She wanted to see where-"

"Where what?" Officer Garcia, the Big Cop interrupts.

"Where we crashed. Where she was conceived."

"That's a very strange place to take your child," Big Cop shrugs.

"So?"

"Sounds like a lot has happened on that stretch of road," Small Cop says. "Someone born, someone dies-"

"Two 'someones' died," interjects Big Cop.

"That's right. Two someones," Small Cop agrees. "And what do all these people have in common?"

Jacki steps closer to the window to make sure her daughter is still in the yard.

"Hello?" Big Cop taps his chipped front tooth. It sounds like someone knocking on a door. "What were you arguing about?"

"Same thing as always," she sighs.

"So tell us."

"Jealousy." Jacki turns. "He is always jealous about something."

Small Cop reaches into his front pocket and pulls out a matchbook. Jacki frowns when she sees it.

"You mean 'was jealous.' You know those matches, don't you? Did these have something to do with the argument?"

"It was an old argument."

Small Cop reads off the matchbook.

"'Bob, Jerry, Steve, Randy, Mike...'"

"He wanted me to write them all down-"

"'...John, Dave, Rob...'"

"Wanted you to write what all down?" Big Cop laughs.

"The names of everyone I'd been with before him."

"What's this squiggly line here between 'Anthony' and the second-to-last name?"

"It's just a mark, to show when the line was. You know, between Anthony and everyone before."

"No, I don't know. Wait, who's 'Mark'? Did you say 'Mark'?" Big Cop asks, almost tripping over himself.

"What? No, I said it was *a* mark, to show-"

"I thought you said the squiggle meant 'Mark.'"

No one notices the cats creeping into the room, asses low, one stalking the other.

"Jesus Christ. That's not what I said."

"Do you know anyone named 'Mark'?" Small Cop asks.

"You guys are some kinda miracle, you know that?"

"I said, do you know anyone named 'Mark'?"

"No. I said-"

"Because this squiggly line looks like you started to make the letter 'M.' Then changed your mind."

"What the hell are you talking about?" Jacki snaps. "Why would I do that?"

A muffled electronic voice on the officer's shoulder crackles some sort of information, and he leans down to bark a quick, "10-4" into his CB. The noise causes both cats to go on Red Alert, now stalking the Small Cop's black shoes. He doesn't notice, adjusting his radio and sighing at Jacki.

"Maybe because he asked you for the list, and you started to write down the name 'Mark' and then realized that Anthony knew him, and you'd been with this 'Mark' while you and Anthony were still together," he says, then louder, "Or maybe this 'Mark' was someone you swore you never had sex with before, so you left a squiggly line instead. Squiggly means, what, almost?"

"You keep saying 'Mark.' It's not 'Mark.' It's *a* mark. And why the fuck would I just not write anything at all if I had something to hide?"

"Exactly!" Big Cop says, excited. "Maybe you already told him the number of men, and if you left off 'Mark' you'd get the wrong number-"

"Seventeen," mutters Small Cop.

"Bullshit. There aren't seventeen names on there," Jacki laughs. "How the hell could someone write seventeen names on a matchbook?"

"That was our next question," Small Cop says, smiling.

"That squiggly line was for the math, right?" Big Cop asks. "So that the number matched? Sure it was. But mostly it's for you, so you won't forget this mystery man, right?"

There's another crackling voice on Small Cop's shoulder, and now Jacki sees the cat about to strike. She almost warns him, then stares another minute, slowly starting to smirk. She shakes her head. The cops look at each other, and one shrugs while the other can't help but smile with her.

"What's so funny?" he says.

"You. Both of you. All of you. Loco for Cocoa Puffs."

"All of who?"

"Men. Monkeys. You and him. Every goddamn one of you plays the same game."

"What?" asks Big Cop, laughing, too.

"This is exactly the conversation I had with Anthony. I'd say you both remind me of him, but you know what? It's not just you. Listen to me right now… it's all of you."

Small Cop stops laughing.

"Also, you should turn down your CB. Electronic voices set off my cats. I have no idea why."

"Let's get back to this talk of how men all sound the same…"

"No, no, no," Jacki cuts him off. "You do! You sound exactly the same! How do you do that? What kind of effort must it take to always cover the same ground? How come it all comes back to 'Who the girl fucked'? Are you men so hopelessly insecure? Are you? Even when you're talking to a stranger like me, you find it necessary to stand in for the dead man 'cause God-fucking-help you if someone doesn't get some hateful jealous bullshit thrown in some woman's face before the end of the day…"

"Jesus, just calm down, please," says Small Cop. He seems sincere, until he grabs her upper arm and squeezes to half its size. She tries to keep the fear out of her eyes. The cats scatter.

"I think you misunderstand the situation," Small Cop says. "We're here because the last two men you fucked died

289

within five feet of each other. I don't see how you even pretend to be surprised that these circumstances would bring us to your door."

Big Cop holds out an arm to calm him down.

"This is for your safety, too," he adds, squeezing harder. Resisting the urge to shout, Jacki shows her teeth.

"If people around you are ending up dead, then... wait. Do you see what you're doing with your mouth? When a chimp does that in a movie, they think he's laughing. But that's because they've been whipped by their trainer. That's how they show fear. What are you afraid of?"

Satisfied, he pushes her into a chair and tosses the matchbook in her lap. Jacki throws it against a wall.

"There was a fucking car crash," she says. *"And his name was Eric. I didn't write it down because it was already over. If you check 'the file,' you'll see there's no mystery to who was hanging dead in the tree, you dumb fuck."*

Small Cop glares.

"Your math doesn't add up and you know it."

Their eyes lock for a solid minute.

"Then who's Mark?!" Big Cop laughs, not really laughing or asking.

Jacki glares at the men for another minute, thinking of one of her classes, how she tried to discourage exclamation points in their papers by allowing only one per semester. But she let them use unlimited interrobangs, that trendy punctuation from the '70s that added a question to peoples shouting and saved just a little more ink in their typewriters. She decides to rethink that policy. Then she stands as if she's remembered something important to do.

"I have to take my daughter to school soon."

"Here's the thing, Miss Ramirez. We're also investigating a series of assaults in the area. Have you heard of the Bardstown Rapist?"

"You mean that poor bastard the police killed for no reason?"

"No, like you said, that was the wrong guy. We're looking for a man who has raped several women, several Hispanic women."

"Latino," Small Cop corrects him. "Or Chicano."

"Not Indian?"

"Like 'scalps' Indians?"

"No, dumbass! Like from India?!"

"Indians confuse me. They look like white people in blackface."

"Christ," Jacki shakes her head.

"Listen, don't think we're like that, Miss Ramirez. Smallberries has a cousin who adopted a black baby."

"What does that have to do with anything?" she asks.

"That's what I told him! Really, my only concern for two white people adopting a black baby is if that baby is seen out in public with both parents. You start getting that infidelity vibe," Big Cop shudders. "But if the baby is seen with one adopted parent at a time, they'll just assume the other parent is black and the baby isn't a cuckoo egg. No harm, no foul."

"Amazing. Like I said, I have to take my daughter to school. Now."

"What did I say?"

"When you left the scene, what was Anthony doing?"

"I don't know. I was distracted."

"Distracted by what?"

Pause.

"I don't know. I think there was a dog loose in the woods."

At this, the two cops look at each other. They seem to decide something.

"We may have more questions," says Big Cop. "We'll let you know."

"Stay away from that road," orders Small Cop. "You want to show anyone else in your family where you wrecked your car, draw them a fucking map."

They walk out, but Big Cop leans back in for a last word.

"Keep those cats under control, ma'am. I've had to Taser one before. It caught on fire."

Then he slams the door. Jacki doesn't watch them go. She reaches into her pocket and pulls out an identical matchbook and studies a burn in the center. Written on the cover are numbers so scorched and tiny they're practically unreadable. She'll decode it all later, she decides, and grabs the phone after she locates her daughter again outside the window.

Then she notices Toni reach down to pick up something crawling across her shoe, and Jacki puts down the phone to watch. Toni looks down at her tiny hand, then smacks her palms together. Jacki blinks in surprise, then balances the phone between her chin and her shoulder as she opens the window to yell.

"It's time to come in! And what did you just kill?"

Toni runs toward the house.

"Don't worry, Mom! It was a ladybug. That's how you make a wish!"

Jacki nods her head in agreement. Why not.

That night, Jacki dreams of law enforcement, interrogations and interrobangs. She dreams of taking a police officer's face in her hands and gently removing his mirrored glasses from his nose. Then she squeezes his head, and insects boil up to the surface of his skin, covering him in wriggling, glistening black beads. When she stops squeezing, the bugs vanish back into his skin, now only visible behind his eyes, where there's never been anywhere to hide.

Jack's Apartment. Same day. Jack is washing a large brown Doberman with the attention usually reserved for European Indian funerals. The dog is in heaven, slowly chewing a squeeze bulb with the slow pulse of a horror movie soundtrack coming from the television. Jack checks the dog's ears for mites, its nails for debris, scrubs its feet with a sponge, dipping it into the soapy bucket and laying it gently on the dog's back, like everything could break at any moment. He brushes the dog's teeth with his own toothbrush.

A knock on his bedroom door breaks the spell. It's his roommate, mercifully with gum instead of ice filling her mouth this time. But she's chewing faster, inspiring the dog to do the same. This competition goes on between them for several moments.

"What?!" Jack finally yells, squirting suds out of his sponge.

"God!" she says, nose wrinkled. "They're here to pick up the dog. Fuck you for yelling at me."

"That was a quick week," Jack mumbles.

"You only watched him for a day," his roommate says.

Jack says nothing to this, and towels the dog's feet dry.

"You better not try to sneak a dog in here, like, permanent. I'll tell the landlord."

"Come on," he says to the animal that's no longer his.

"This is the last stray you bring home, too."

They both brush past her. The dog has no interest in her either.

"I'll tell. I mean it."

Evil paid his two bucks at the drive-in ticket booth, then hopped and angled the front wheel of his dirt bike for the playground. He figured this would be the best vantage point to see everyone who was in attendance. He was sure Bully would at least make a guest appearance. Either that, or she was all jungled-up in a car with someone else. She probably was. It was a supermoon after all.

He sputtered up near the monkey bars, then reached down and ripped a flyer from under his front wheel. It was one of Bully's posters on the ground, advertising a Triple Feature:

"She's Having a Baby, Baby Boom, and *Three Men and a Baby*! And Kids Under 5 Drink Free!"

It was a joke, of course. He'd seen the marquee when he drove in. Same theme, but three very different movies: **"*It's Alive, It's Alive II: It Lives Again* and *It's Alive III: Island of the Alive.* No Kids Under 5, We Mean It!"**

But Bully's gag must have fooled a ton of people, because the playground was packed to the gills with children. He looked up to see a woman on the screen being wheeled into an emergency room. The movie had just started, but it was only a matter of time before people would react. He'd seen the ads for *It's Alive* and knew what was coming, even though the teaser trailer was just a slow zoom on a crib with a claw hanging out of it. Combined with some inhuman crying, it was certainly creepy. Now that he thought about it, Bully was there when he first saw it.

"Does 'Rowdy' Roddy 'Pied' Piper play the baby?" she'd asked him, then laughed, "No, that would be *It's Alive V: They Live Again!*"

Then he saw the dog tied to the slide. It was "Hansel," the German Shepherd he'd stashed in her trunk. That was the name on its badge anyway. He'd been shocked that a police dog wouldn't have been sprung from the pound immediately. But it was fallout from everybody's German Shepherds impersonating officers these days. And Hansel stood frozen like a good German, maybe more like an American soldier behind enemy lines. Some of the children stopped to pet it, but mostly they gave the dog no notice. It was one of those crazy covered slides that drew their attention like the Pied Piper, an especially rowdy one.

Evil revved his engine to inch a little closer, and that's when he saw the collar around Hansel's neck. It was beautiful but hideous, alien yet familiar, a colorful menagerie of plastic, wires, and rat traps, the homemade neck bomb finally assembled in all its glory.

* * *

Bully crept her way around the cars, sticking close to the ones with the most steam on their windows. She figured they'd be the least likely to notice her, guessing there was a good chance several cars contained solitary masturbating men, like everywhere else in the world. But one steamy car did notice her. She was crouched down by a front tire when she heard a fingernail tap, tap, tap on the window above her. Then a forearm squeaked through the fog on the glass to reveal a leering face and finger pointing down below his steering wheel. Gross. She moved on faster.

She stepped on one of her own flyers and laughed. All the free advertising she'd provided this place, and not once had she asked for thanks. But she deserved The Spotlight Kid's attention. Just like she'd deserved The Butch Cassidy's attention a year earlier.

Last fall, right before it got too cold, Butch Cassidy had promised the "Perfect Apocalypse Triple Feature!" It was *Escape from New York*, *The Road Warrior*, and for anyone who was still awake in their cars that late, the little-known *Ultimate Warrior* with Max von Sydow and Yul Brynner as the titular badasses. And if you sat on the top of the tallest slide in nearby Sun Oil Park on one of those nights, mesmerized by the monstrous silent figures in the distance, you could weave all three storylines into one. Minimal dialogue, long, lazy pacing, and all of these factors revealing to Bully about a third of the way through the third film that *Ultimate Warrior* really was the father of the two most popular end-of-the-world action flicks in recent memory. She got more of a sense of accomplishment from this light bulb over her head than all five years of community college put together.

So when Butch Cassidy switched to porn, she may have been upset. She may have snapped a little. Just a bit. She'd spotted the marquee and wrongly assumed *E.T.:*

The Extra Testicle was a Cheech & Chong parody. And a quick glimpse at the second feature's title, *The Thang*, and anyone would have forgiven her if she mistook it for John Carpenter's seminal film. Then the first movie started. She didn't realize how in demand satirical titles had become in the porn industry. Shockingly, copyright law let parodies of a parody slip through, too, even if that kind of double-negative math should have caused you to end up right back where you started with the real thing. Straight-to-video knockoffs were even less regulated. But on the big big screen? She couldn't believe it. It would have been funny if Butch wasn't the second-to-last drive-in for miles, which pretty much made it the last drive-in ever as far as locals were concerned.

Fuck 'em. They should have taken real movies more seriously.

"Let me get this straight, you put the lime in the coconut, drank 'em both up…" she sang to herself.

In her hands was a huge remote control, the kind with the big batteries. The one you got with the most expensive toys. Or the most explosive.

The three police officers passed by the booth without buying tickets. Officer Dwayne B. Bigby, Officer Something "Bucky Balls" Something, and a third cop who was mere hours out of the academy. No one would ever learn that guy's nickname.

They all were being led by three bomb-sniffing German Shepherds, noses to the group and straining their harnesses. They were heading for the playground under the movie. Officer Bigby was on point, shaking his head in disgust at the cars with their windows shut, drive-in speakers forgotten on the ground. He hoped they were full of couples, sneaking alone time under the pretense of seeing a flick. But in his experience, he knew it was more likely there were nothing but men inside those cars,

How about wheels within wheels within wheels? Larry thought. *Why not?*

"I know an old man who swallowed a car," Larry sang. "He'll go far…"

Larry laughed and rubbed his eyes hard, but the old man's spiders never went away. His wrinkled cheeks and forehead were covered in them, faded green creepy-crawlies of every size and variation, hairy, spindly, bellies bloated with babies or poison, some cartoonish, most remarkably realistic. Larry was in awe. He couldn't imagine the kind of man who cared so little about assimilation with other human beings that he would get spiders tattooed on his fucking face. The old man spit at Larry to snap him out of it, spouting gibberish.

"You here to wash my cock? Come on, nurse. Use that oatmeal soap like I like. Exfoliate my shit. You gonna pay for that?"

In his lap, the man was clutching a stuffed animal, a key-lime-colored monkey. It looked like it had been a Curious George at one point, but now it was covered in sparkling spray paint. Larry thought of the AIDS monkey in the news recently, something that had been part of many high-level conversations in his accidental profession. Damon loved to spread that bullshit propaganda about an HIV "Patient Zero," and how someone supposedly fucked a monkey in Africa to start that whole epidemic. Larry would try to bring up the movie *And the Band Played On* and how Reagan dropped the ball, but everybody loved that cowboy cocksucker.

A new problem was also rearing its head, where increasingly conspiracy-minded masturbators had Sherlocked that AIDS and condoms were invading the porn industry at the same time for the opposite reason. Those clowns would one day be convinced vaccines caused autism.

The old man made a grab for Larry's throat, and Larry watched his sleeves come off at the cuffs to peel back more layers of the oily chicken skin that was sloughing off his body like a rotten onion. His itching had subsided a bit, though, like it was three people deep.

Larry decided maybe he should steal that green monkey just to be safe. Maybe get it back to the lab for some tests when this was all over. He imagined millions of green monkeys working in the mouthwash factory on some new-fangled AIDS repellant, every so often one monkey tumbling into the grinder and ten more pissing green on it for laughs until it all flowed out into the Maumee river and into Lake Erie with the algae to put out the garbage fires and start the cycle all over again.

So he grabbed it by the tail, and the old man howled, picking up the passenger's door one-handed to shield himself. Larry struggled with old arms like granite, and suddenly he knew why this man was covered in spider tattoos. This is what happened to comic book villains when they retired.

Then the old man finally got ahold of Larry's neck and held tight, dragging his yellow old-man nails across Larry's Adam's apple. Larry backpedaled, bringing most of the old bastard outside with him.

Damn, old man fights like a puma. A puma in a wheelchair anyway…

There was a rip as the old man and all his spiders and wheels tumbled onto the ground, and Larry was satisfied to stand up with about half of the stuffed monkey intact. He made a wish.

But that's when the rest of the crowd turned on him. Car doors started to slam, irate, sad-sack, moviegoer loners crashing his party with shock and anger pinching their red foreheads like toddlers before a tantrum. And right about then, the flyer for *Three Men and a Baby, Baby Boom*, and *She's Having a Baby* flipped over to reveal an opportunistic and earnest anti-abortion ad that Larry thought was far creepier than intended:

"Before I was born, I had hiccups. Before I was born, I had a dream. Before I was born, I had fingernails."

Ugh.

As he stood there making a paper airplane out of it, he couldn't help singing his wife's favorite song, the one with 984 "baby, baby, baby"s. He was singing a lot lately. He switched up the lyrics this time, making sure he stressed the right syllable so it sounded right.

"Tat-*too* removal machine…"

They were moving in so fast now, swarming to help up the old man but looking eager to punish Larry as soon as they were done. He retrieved his Goldberg reel again, now trailing a weary bit of tongue, and ran for the concession stand. The projection bunker was close. Directly behind the popcorn.

He turned the corner and froze. Standing in the doorway was a small boy with another toy, but this one wasn't fluffy like the monkey. Larry recognized it as the tie-in G.I. Joe-sized skeletal monster from the horror film *Alien*. He laughed, remembering its hard-R rating, another attempt to move science fiction into the adult arena, while at the same time courting children with a line of tie-ins. He even saw ViewMaster cartridges for *Alien*, too, another desperate move in what had to be the most misguided attempt at product placement ever. Then again, there were tons of kids at a horror triple feature right now with no signs of trauma yet. Things to come?

He couldn't believe toy manufacturers would waste money on a flick that clearly had zero chance of ever spawning a sequel. Not that Larry didn't already try his hand at making a "true" adult version, *Illegal Aliens*, a Hispanic tour-de-force where he upped the number of skeletal monsters and cast newcomer "Sigourney Beaver."

But even without a porn parody, Larry could never take the original seriously. If the fictional crew didn't want to have such a nightmarish encounter, maybe they should have named their spaceship something less haunting than the fucking *Nostromo*.

"Would they have run into all that trouble if they'd called it something jokey like *The Hull Truth* or *The Gone Fission*?" he'd asked his wife on their third date. She reminded him, as they curled up in its vast, faux leather backseat, that he was affectionately calling his Ford Grenada "The Rhinowagon" and look where *that* had gotten him...

Larry slapped the toy away, breaking its tail against the doorjamb, then shoved the kid into the glass box surrounding the rumbling popcorn cauldron, not caring who saw him do it. He figured it was too late to win over the crowd.

"Before you were born, *you* had a tail," Larry told the boy for consolation as the butter bubbling from the metal pot scalded his shoulder and he screamed and ran to hide under the row of gumball machines. The boy would remember those words until his death. Which was about fifteen minutes away.

"Does anyone know we're making this movie?"

"It's gonna be a surprise."

"Ain't that the truth."

"Do you know your lines? I think I'm just gonna be 'Jack' again to save time."

"Save money, you mean. Will we ever get paid, Jack? I mean, Larry."

"Patience."

"We can't afford *patients*."

"I never thought I'd say this, but can we please hurry up so I can go fuck someone I hate for a small amount of money?"

"Almost done."

"Can I be one of the cops this time? How come Joe and Freddy always get to be the cops? And they get to play those two other assholes. They get all the best lines."

"Listen to me. I need you to be who I need you to be. You see, men, because of our successful infiltration of the adult film community, we have an unprecedented opportunity to blur the line between reality and movies once and for all!"

"You just wanna make a real movie. That's what everyone in porn wants to do."

"Yeah, you're a dime a fuckin' dozen, Larry."

"Wrong. Everyone in porn doesn't want to do this."

"Where did you get this ambulance?"

"It was mine."

"Weird."

"No shit. They're even weirder in England."

Ambulance. Same day. Jack leans on the dashboard, his partner driving. They're arguing over the blare of the sirens. Jack has just asked him a question. More of a riddle really.

"I still don't understand the question," Rick says. "Never have. Of course it would make a sound!"

"How do you not understand the importance of this question? There's a reason people still ask this."

"The tree makes a sound. Case closed."

"Why are you pulling over?!"

"Sorry, the siren in that damn song gets me every time."

Suburban front yard. Same day. Jack and Rick hop out and trot up to an overgrown front lawn with their tackle boxes swinging. A young boy, about 8 or 9, is sitting in the grass with his mother. The woman is holding a bloody towel around the boy's hands, which are still clutching the tattered remains of a large kite. Rick gently removes the woman's hands, then some superficial plastic and wood kite fragments to clean the wound a bit, all the while talking to the boy, but really addressing his questions to his mother.

"What happened here, son?"

"His kite got stuck in a tree," the mother says. "So he was throwing firecrackers at it."

Jack smiles at the boy.

"Of course, that plan made sense at the time, didn't it?"

The boy coughs but says nothing. Not needed, Jack stands up and looks around the yard. Rick plucks another kite shard, then carefully tests the boy's fingers for mobility.

"You did this with some firecrackers?" Rick asks, frowning at the boy's injuries, keeping his voice even and soothing, the way he was trained.

"Well, he was playing with a can of spray paint and some gasoline, too," his mother says.

"With spray paint and gasoline, too?" Jack says from behind them, laughing. "What's that all about, Mom? You all out of sharks and chainsaws?"

Rick glares at Jack to shut up.

"Did the paint can explode?" he asks.

"Yes," his mother sighs. "I guess he wanted to see what was inside."

"What was inside?" Jack says, suddenly interested. "What was inside? I've always wanted to know this."

"We're going to need to take a little ride now..." Rick tells the boy, trying to ignore Jack.

Jack crouches down next to them.

"No, seriously, what was inside?"

Rick is gritting his teeth.

"Jack, will you please get..."

Jack turns to the mother.

"What was inside the paint can? Anyone get a good look?'

Suddenly Rick is standing up, fists clenched. He takes a deep breath to maintain control and speaks slowly.

"Why don't you just wait in the truck?" he finally manages, forcing a smile.

"I just want to know what's in there," Jack says, defensive. "I mean, it cost this little dumbass two fingers to find out and you're not even curious? What the hell is wrong with you? Didn't you ever ask yourself the same question when you were little? Look at you. Of course you did, big city kid like you." Jack slaps him on the shoulder. The woman looks to Rick, and Rick gives her a shrug and a weary head shake.

"You asked yourself how many balls were rattling around inside spray-paint cans when you were shaking 'em up and getting ready to vandalize something," Jack goes on. "They had to be balls, sure. That was obvious. But how big are the balls? And what are they made out of? Ask the fucking kid while we still got the chance..."

Rick starts walking the boy to the ambulance, calling out to his mother.

"Now, we can't let you ride in the back unless we tie you down, so I'm going to need you to follow us..."

"My car is out of gas," she says, embarrassed.

Jack steps in front of them.

"One last question. Which tree did the kite get stuck in?" he says, holding up his stethoscope, smiling. "I need to check something. Me and my partner are sort of in the middle of a debate."

The doors on the back of the ambulance slam, and Rick climbs in, pulling out of the driveway with their hideous broken siren blaring while Jack runs to get to the other door. He has to run to jump in.

Ambulance. Same day. Jack and Rick weave the ambulance through traffic. Jack is driving now, and Rick is flipping through his wallet counting the change as an old man crouches down between their seats. The broken siren is off. Tori Amos' "Space Dog" is on the radio. No real sense of urgency. Jack imagined a porn parody version of the singer who would call herself "Torn Anus."

"Someone somewhere must know the ending. Is she still pissing in the river…"

"I'm sorry about that," Jack says. "I was just trying to make the kid laugh. I think."

"When did you become motherfucking Patch Adams, dude?" Rick asks from between the two front seats where he's gripping the dashboard to steady himself against Jack's driving.

"I don't know. Just trying to make shit interesting. Ruin the betting pool on our burnout rate. But back to my question. So you still think it makes a sound?"

"I think you *make a sound," Rick says, then turning to the patient in the passenger's seat. "Sir, why don't you climb back onto the gurney, please," Rick says. "I'm trying to budget my lunch."*

"I'm fine," the old man insists, grabbing the handle over the passenger's window. "My arms are strong. I ride the subway every day without falling over. I just want to look out the window."

"No, the reason you're not on that gurney is because that's for people who are actually hurt," Jack laughs. "Not birdwatching."

"Please, sir," Rick says. "Let's get you back onto that gurney, right now."

The old man grips the handle tighter.

"I'm fine up here, boys. Don't you worry about me. There ain't no windows in the back of this thing. When you going to get around to fixin' that?"

"Yeah, we'll get right on that for you," Jack grumbles. "If it's one thing we need back there, it's windows so people like you can keep using us for a free taxi service."

The old man purses his lips, and Rick holds up a hand. "Come on, Jack…"

"We know this guy," Jack snaps. "Just like his wrinkled ass knows our routes, knows the insurance, knows which crew has seen too much of him this week. He's a Frequent-"

306

"'Scuse me?!" the old man snorts.

"Jack, you know we're not allowed to use that term anymore."

"You heard me," Jack says. "How many times have we driven you to the hospital so you can walk right past the fucking front door and get your lottery ticket on the corner?"

"Relax, Jack," Rick says. "Who gives a shit? He ain't hurting anyone."

"These Emergency Rooms are getting weirder and weirder. It's not right that I know all your middle names by now. You'd think they were in line for a rollercoaster instead of waiting to endure a thumb up their ass for a fix. Redeeming their fuckin' Frequent Flyer miles…"

"Just drive."

"Boy, I've never had a thumb up my…"

"Enough," Rick says.

"Not even close to enough," Jack says. "I know this guy. I watched him the last time he called us. He turned right around at the emergency room doors and went to the leather shop a block over."

"Huh?"

"He was getting the buckle fixed on his Civil War belt," Jack says. "He's wearing it right now. I seriously doubt his broken belt buckle had anything to do with his 'chest pains.'"

"How do you know that he was getting a belt fixed?"

"Because I went in there after him and acted like I was his grandson. I had to pay for the repair to get the information. So I walked out the door and snapped off the tooth, then took it back into the leather shop again so he wouldn't know."

"Jack, you're like the worst private eye of all time."

"Son, there's definitely something wrong with him," the old man agrees.

"And you did all this when you said you were taking a shit last Thursday?" Rick asks him.

"Probably," Jack says.

"Just drive, dude, still gotta get there, remember?"

"Fuck that," Jack says. "Maybe we have to get there, sure, but we could've been carrying some kid with his head caught in a lawnmower instead of this worthless piece of shit."

"You can't fit a lawnmower back there," the old man lights up. "Not with those fumes. Now if you had some windows-"

"Shut the fuck up," Rick says.

"Ambulance. Same day."

"I know where I am, Jack."

"The whole point of the question is, how do you know it would make a sound if no one was there?"

"Yeah, yeah. I'm so bored with that puzzle. Okay, maybe there's no people there, but there's other things there, too. Other things that can show evidence that it made a sound."

"That's not the point. I mean, imagine that there's nothing there. No way to prove it-"

"But there is something there. Just by saying there is a tree there to fall down, you're saying that there's something there. To have a tree, you need an environment that supports trees, that means that there would have to be animals. And animals have ears, asshole."

"Animals have assholes?" Jack says, acting confused. "Listen, the point of the whole fucking question is this, if nothing is effected by an action, did the action happen at all?"

"Of course. At least it did with your stupid tree quiz. Now, if you give me an example that ain't some Aristotle crap and has rules that make some sense, I'll give it some more thought."

"You ever hear of quantum physics? Yes? No? They say that, until an electron or a photon or a proton or whatever the fuck it is, is observed, it's in two places at once..."

"The only thing scarier than you talking philosophy is you talking physics."

308

"*...so, unless the tree is observed, then it's not doing shit, even if it's cut down, on fire or walking around.*"

"*You realize that, ever since I met you, I've hesitated to give you any reason to run with a little bit of knowledge because you always miss the point and take everything into a direction that suits you.*"

"*What? Okay, what if-*"

"*It's like you're saying, if a man punches a man in the face, if there's no face to punch, does he punch a man in the face. It makes no fucking sense-*"

"*But-*"

Rick leans over and punches Jack in the face. Not too hard. Just enough to make his teeth clack and make a point.

"*That's what I'm talking about.*"

"*Motherfucker,*" Jack mumbles, rubbing his mouth on his fist. The punch is effective, and Jack's quiet for at least 23 seconds.

"*Okay, what if you replaced your daughter's dead dog with one that looks exactly the same?*"

"*Aaaah!*"

"*Just listen-*"

"*Where the hell did that question come from? That shit's in* Pet Sematary*! A-ha! Spelled with an 'S,' by the way.*"

"*And?*"

"*I don't know. I guess it would depend on how old she was, how sensitive she was, but how many lies would you have to tell over the years to keep up the illusion? It's not worth it, to have to lie to your family for how long? I mean, if* Pet Seminary *taught us anything…*"

"*Okay, what if it was a stranger? What if the swap was timed perfectly?*"

"*Wait, so now you're saying, what if we went around replacing dead dogs with sneaky copies? Is that really a rational question? You going to find some kid and her dog then sneak into the house the moment it dies and swap it with-*"

309

"Obviously I'm talking hypothetically. And why did you say 'her' just now?"

Rick ignores that question and answers Jack's other one.

"Then I'd say no. A tree that falls in the forest makes a sound. Definitely. You know why? Because a dog makes a sound, dude. We all make sounds. And the only animal you can replace without any guilt when it dies, and this happens all the goddamn time, is a fucking goldfish. You know why? Because it doesn't make a sound. Forget Hitchhiker's Guide to the Galaxy. *A goldfish don't say shit. No matter what hole you stick it in."*

"Okay, think about this accident we're heading for right now…"

"Yes, please, do that. Start thinking about your job, man."

"…what if, when get there, we come across a car wreck and someone who's unconscious with a dead puppy under their arm. And the truck they hit was on its way to the pound and happened to be full of the exact same puppies? And we could go over to the truck and replace the dead puppy without the girl ever waking up and knowing…" he trails off.

"Knowing what?"

"Knowing about this bad thing that had happened to her."

"We're not talking about trees or dogs here anymore, are we, Jack?"

"Not sure that we ever were."

Rick stares at him hard. Jack tenses for another punch.

"In that case, Jack, it makes a sound."

"Fuck that. You're wrong."

They park just past the comet trails of blood on the pavement, just like they were trained to do, then they rush to the girl lying unconscious on the sidewalk. Rick has trauma dressings and tape. One look at the girl and he grabs the intubation kit, too, along with his bag of shots, the "Halloween bag of suckers" as Jack calls it; fentanyl, morphine, and Versed, depending on if they have to really plug her up. He's relieved to see her chest moving.

"Dog got her," a kid on the scene says around his ice cream bar, but Rick knows this just by looking.

He checks her injuries, deep, ragged bites on her forearms, massive tissue loss on both legs. He checks her eyes for a response, then her blood pressure. Jack gets the gurney off the back and compacts the legs and wheels to prepare to load her up.

"I don't like her eyes," Rick tells Jack. "She didn't flinch when I pinched her, nothing. Shock. Or worse. Be ready to move when I move."

"Where are we on the map?" Jack asks. Rick seems confused by the question, then understanding washes over his face.

"Let's get her out of here before they get here."

Too late.

Another ambulance arrives on the scenes. Their former rivals, the two Mikes, Big Mike and Little Mike, come flying in hot. There's no siren on their vehicle, as it's been converted into something a little different. The side of the box reads:

"Highway Wildlife Services."

Under that, a smaller, hand-written sign:

"Nuisance Wildlife Control Operator. Skunk Specialists!"

Then under that, even smaller:

"Not A Dog Catcher. Please Call ~~Daytona~~ Animal Control."

They jump out of their truck, still wrapped up in their own philosophical debate, a stark contrast to Rick and Jack's conversation.

"So I'm finishing the last ear of corn," Little Mike is saying, "And suddenly I'm tasting metal. And now I'm worried because you shouldn't be finding no buckshot in your corn, you know? Your turkey, sure, maybe your squirrel, but not your friggin' corn..."

"Uh huh," Big Mike mutters.

"...then I realized that my mouth feels weird, and I flick my tongue around and find this fang, and it ain't even Halloween yet. Turns out I swallowed half my tooth."

"So?"

"What do you mean, so? That's a terrible combination, teeth and corn? Now when I shit next it's gonna be smiling back at me!"

"Ha!" Big Mike suddenly frowns. "Wait. Why do you say smiling back? Why would you be smiling at your shit to begin with?"

"Relief? Pride? I don't know. It's a joke, stupid. You know what I mean? Hey, a dog smiles at his own shit, don't he?"

"Dogs always look like they're smiling."

They stop when Jack and Rick roll the victim past them.

"Oh, shit," Rick says to Jack. "It's Of Mice and Men to the rescue." He turns to the two Mikes and waves them away.

"Hey. I don't know what report you got, but there's no dogs here for you, dead or otherwise."

The two Mikes slump visibly in disappointment.

"Yeah," Jack adds. "Take Lenny to see the rabbits or something. Did you know you're about ten miles outside of your electric fence jurisdiction? Didn't you feel your collars buzzing?"

"No," Big Mike says, answering the second question.

"We heard the call on our scanner," Little Mike says. "We just wanted to see it."

"We know you did," Rick says.

Over the girl, Jack stops working when he notices her face. They're in the Hispanic side of town, and she looks a lot like Jacki. He shakes it off, telling himself that any pretty girl down here would look like her, too. Still rattled in spite of the casual racism, he turns to walk back to the ambulance and starts to pull out more equipment. Rick grabs his arm.

"What the fuck are you doing with that?"

Jack looks down to see that he was dragging the defibrillator unit. Confused, he quickly shoves it back into the ambulance, grabbing the gurney instead.

"Sorry," Jack says. "I thought I knew that girl, then I thought... never mind."

He collapses the metal legs and reaches for her again, then stops again, as if he's seeing something that really disturbs him. Rick quickly pulls him up by his arm and gets nose to nose.

"Dude, your hypothetical dead dog scenarios are weird enough for one day," he hisses. "Please get your head out your ass and get to work."

Jack looks past Rick to the girl.

"Sorry! It's just... I just think something strange is going on here. I mean, does that look like a dog bite on her calf? Or does it look like someone wanted it to look like a dog bite?"

Rick gets louder.

"What?" *He calms himself down, then says with his eyes closed.* "Jack, just clear her leg so we can close these doors. You're driving."

Jack leans in real close.

"Hold on, that's not a dog bite. It's a tattoo of a dog bite. Why would anyone get a tattoo like this? What if every time I thought I was seeing a dog bite, it was actually just a drawing instead. This is starting to make some sense..."

"Not at all."

"Listen, just switch with me on the way there. I could ask her some questions like-"

"Dude, you're scaring me. She's in shock. Get up front."

"No, it's worse. Was she really attacked by a dog?" *Jack asks, blocking Rick from climbing in the back.* "I mean, who saw a dog?"

"That kid saw a dog."

"How do we know that?"

"What the fuck are you... okay, tell me this. How do you fake a dog attack?"

"Well, first you'd still need a dog."

"Oh, my God."

"What?"

"I thought you said there was no dog!"

"You need a dog to fake a dog..."

"That kid saw a dog."

Jack runs over to a nearby car and starts kicking the bumper sticker. It reads:

"A Dog May Be A Man's Best Friend, But A Tree Is A Dog's Best Friend!"

"You see this shit? Come on, that can't be a coincidence. Maybe the kid saw this and got the idea. Wait... maybe the guy who owns that car has the dog we're looking for. I'll wait here-"

Rick finally snaps and walks over to grab a handful of Jack's neck. His hands are big, and his thumbs almost touch his fingertips, like any normal-sized man choking up on a baseball bat. A small crowd of children has gathered, and Jack searches their faces, finally seeming to come to his senses. Even the Mikes are confused. A little kid hands a small dead dog to Little Mike. Half its face is skeletonized.

"Thanks, buddy!" Little Mike says. "I think this one is innocent though. Been in Doggy Heaven for more than a little while."

"Goddammit," Rick whispers quiet but savage to Jack. "Do your fucking job."

Jack slowly untangles Rick's hand from his throat and climbs into the driver's seat.

The Mikes get into their truck, too, chattering like kids, Little Mike swinging the dead dog by its hind leg like a toy. He opens the back door of his truck and throws the dog against the wall. The kids scream.

Rick looks at them, then back at Jack. He doesn't need to say it. Usually, Rick and Jack hated the Mikes because it reminded them of what they could end up doing.

Today they remind them it's what they already do.

* * *

Once upon a time, Bully heard a story about a cop who unknowingly bore the load of a bomb on his shoulders for an entire eight-hour work day. Until it was allegedly detonated by a disgruntled former partner. Bully didn't believe this, figuring that unless you're Flavor Flav, there were only a few things someone would voluntarily put around their necks that could hide the weight of a bomb all day. The story was detailed in a memo marked "A.I." or "I.A." (Internal Affairs or Artificial Intelligence, it was all the same to her), but Bully guessed it eventually morphed into an urban legend chain letter by the time she got it. It read more like a gleefully fucked-up Aesop's Fable, though, specifically that one with the turtle and the bunny:

"The scene opens on the sun-cooked side of the highway. A police officer's decision to wear his bulletproof vest 24/7 combined with a chronic lack of exercise during the holiday season has slowed him considerably. His dashboard camera reveals a weary, sluggish man who's forgotten most of his training when it comes to approaching vehicles, and he's clearly unaware of what is about to happen next.

"One minute, he's hunched over the driver's side window, fumbling for a pen to write a reckless-op ticket, the tortoise-like hump of his vest bunching up between his shoulder blades. The next minute, both barrels of a shotgun are lifting his chin high, followed immediately by the silent flashbulbs of that figure-eight, a blast of infinity which propels his head up through the blue stop sign of his cap and out of the frame forever.

"What the cruiser's dash cam doesn't show, however, is the unlucky officer's head traveling in a lazy football spiral, rebounding off the Interstate-75 mile marker and tumbling up the yellow lines of the on-ramp. Back on the highway, it pinballs unnoticed between the wheels of rush-

315

hour traffic for fifteen minutes, until it finally becomes lodged in the maze of a lowrider's exhaust system. The cranium is then carried over fifty miles from the scene of the crime, pinned even tighter by some uneven railroad tracks, lower jaw still frozen in surprise, now a cow-catcher to scoop cigarette butts and gravel, even the occasional candy wrapper piled deep in its maw.

"The boy piloting the gleaming, two-toned machine is unaware of his gruesome cargo until his last stop of the night, the King of Kings Hydraulics competition. For the first time ever, he places third and is awarded a lucky rabbit's-foot keychain and a small trophy topped with a league bowler whose ball had been hastily removed with scissors. The first-place winner, however, encouraged by the frenzy of a crowd who has noticed first the blood, then the deceased officer's visage leering down from the jungle of undercarriage piping during the final Victory Bounce, surrenders his first-place title to the boy, which included the tallest trophy of them all, almost five feet from base to hood ornament, a chrome flying pig polished to perfection.

"At the ensuing press conference, the Chief of Police explains they have no leads at all, except for a strange necklace found draped around the remains of the officer's ragged neck, a tangled menagerie of turquoise, beads and string initially mistaken for a bomb, but which is later identified as an inexpensive dreamcatcher, sold by the hundreds at most gas stations in the area.

"'What's that?' a reporter asks.

"'Bunch of shit hanging off a hoop,' the Chief answers, impatiently looking around for a better breed of question, the kind a fallen hero deserves. 'Catches dreams,' he adds.

"'Sure does, motherfucker!' the boy shouts at his television, now a local celebrity who's been quickly cleared of any connection in the shooting. His trophy stands proudly on top of the TV, mere inches from the ceiling, vibrating to the beat of something called *Kraken XIII*, the only CD he owns.

"The next day, the boy's sister raises the hydraulics and checks every inch of the 1973 Impala's undercarriage, finding everything that, impossibly, the forensic team has missed or ignored: a garage sale sign, the rest of a turtle, a child's jumper covered in pink starfish that would have likely solved an unrelated kidnapping, one of the new ten-dollar bills, a dust cover to a typically sanitized version of children's fables, and exactly half a gigantic foam cowboy hat.

"'It's like when they cut open sharks,' she whispers, cradling as much of the treasure in her arms as she could.

"'Only if they kept on swimming,' her brother answers proudly, baffling her.

"'Is all of this stuff under every car?' she wonders.

"The question terrifies him, minimizing his little victory, and they never crawl under one again."

Bullshit, Bully thought, every time she finished it.

Variations included remnants of a bomb around the cop's ragged neck instead of a dreamcatcher, or even the "tangled menagerie of turquoise, beads, and string being initially mistaken for a bomb." However, the chain letter always ended with a happy "Send this to five of your friends for good luck!" or some solid fear-mongering like "Have you looked under *your* car lately?!"

Bully practically lived under her car, looking for treasure and bombs and dreaming of bullet-proof vests even before the chain letter.

Then, one day, she actually tried on a Kevlar vest that one of those over-eager, "Just Say No To Drugs" officers brought to her high school.

Then she let him give her an over-eager ride home.

Then she let him take her to Butch Cassidy drive-in by his house to play some over-eager grab ass over the gear shift and the shotgun lock. He'd had all sorts of props for his school demonstrations tucked away in his squad car, some more realistic than others, some trying to pretend they were fake, like the bricks of modeling clay with a couple token birthday candles jammed in the top.

Those birthday cakes turned out to be way more powerful than a ring of rat traps could ever hope to be...

Bully watched the three officers lead their dogs toward the playground and imagined explosive vests and dreamcatchers strapped to all their chests.

Dare to dream, she thought. *Oh, the Fourth of July fireworks I always wanted...*

She saw a little boy listening to some headphones and dug a cassette tape out of her pocket to give to him. The little boy ejected his song, and pushed play on hers. He listened as best he could, mostly because the girl's voice on the tape that was reading the otherwise official-sounding report sounded fun. Barely older than he was:

"On August 28th, at 1:30 p.m., a woman named Angela 'Stretch' Strongarm, a 10-year veteran dispatcher, went to a nearby gas station around Eerie Drive and Ohio Rue, Pennsylvania, called Mama-Mia's Pizza-Ria and ordered two sausage and pepperoni pies, one with pineapple. The gas station's surveillance cameras record them arriving at the station and later speeding away, knocking over a dumpster during their escape. Mike 'The Machine' Green, a local man whose number was logged as he ordered the pizza, was later revealed to be a vegetarian. He would also deny making the call. A jury of his peers would agree that this combination of ingredients was, at best, 'inedible.' Note manual correction as a court stenographer accidentally typed, 'impossible' instead. Soon after this getaway, at 2:00 p.m., 41-year-old Ryan 'Hells' Bells set out to deliver this suspicious order for two pizzas to an even more suspicious address, which turned out to be the location of a local radio tower on 371 Peach Street. The collar forcibly attached to Mr. Bells at this location was 'unique in its construction,' including a lock with five keyholes and a 9-digit combination dial. It was set by the perpetrators to detonate in precisely 75 minutes. Bureau officials also said it was a triple-banded metal collar that had been fastened and locked around the bomb victim's neck, and that the crude locking mechanism kept it in place. The attached bomb had several facades, including turquoise, beads, and string, as well as several copper wires that went nowhere, connected to nothing at all, only making it appear as if the device was much more complicated than it was. It was also determined, before detonation, that the collar had a faint, citrus odor. This was reported by the bomb squad as 'not entirely unpleasant in small doses…'"

"As soon as we got off the ride, he said he was done with me," Jacki is saying. *"With Toni and me."*

Night time. Jack and Jacki are sitting at a table in a bar, between a jukebox and a band. The band is noisily setting up their gear on the stage behind them, and Jacki snickers when she sees the drummer roll out his equipment. Written on the bass drum is the name, "Relationshit."

"What?"

"Nothing," she says.

"So, Anthony was Toni's father?"

"Yes," Jacki says, shaking her head 'no.' "I mean, he raised her. But he's not the biological father. That's one of the reasons he's gone, I guess."

"You mean one of the reasons he left."

"Yeah, that's what I said," Jacki says, unconvincingly.

"What did they say happened to him?" Jack watches the band, worried they're going to start playing and interrupt them at any moment.

"He took off," she says, tilting her head slightly. "I don't know. No one knows."

"So, when I saw you in the hospital the other day, when your daughter was spitting at me like I was on fire-"

"She wasn't spitting at you," she interrupts. "A doctor had just scraped the inside of her cheek. I guess he wanted to see if she was allergic to anything. Then he tricked her with a needle to take blood for the paternity test I wanted."

Jack smiles.

"Actually, you got the two things backwards. That needle was to check for allergies. And they scrape the inside of your mouth for the paternity test."

"Really? You'd think you guys would need blood to find out who the father was, instead of just some spit. Saliva doesn't seem nearly important enough."

"I don't know. Would you rather have someone spit on you or bleed on you?"

"What? What the hell kind of question is that?"

Jack has no explanation.

"Okay, now that I think about it. I love the fact that a paternity test is done with spit." Jacki slaps her palm on the table, rattling Jack's beer. "In fact, I downright adore it. It makes the issue seem perfectly irrelevant."

"Well, it's not the saliva they're after, but it's still an important test," he goes on, missing her point. "They're scraping the inside of her cheek to collect cells to test the DNA, and it's more complicated than people-"

"Anyway," Jacki cuts him off. "Anthony always suspected that Toni wasn't his. He made me take that test. Even though she always called him 'daddy,' knew him as 'daddy,' had no other 'daddy,' it apparently wasn't enough for him. Hell, he probably made me take it to test whether I was his, too," she laughs.

"Did you get the results back?"

"No," Jacki looks away. "It doesn't really matter now anyway."

"Why's that?"

She studies his face as if she's trying to decode something. The guitarist strums some catchy tune-up noodling, and Jacki mutters the lyrics to the Snow Patrol song along with it.

"Let's waste time, chasing cars around our head."

"What?" he asks.

She suddenly decides to tell him more than she intended.

"Let me tell you a story. I met Anthony the week my father died. We'd spent that first night talking in my car about our families and all that. And I said a lot about my father, none of it good. But I never got around to saying that he was sick or dying from throat cancer or anything, okay? Because he was, okay? I just didn't feel like talking about it. Then, the next weekend, the day before we went out again, they call and tell me my father is gone. Choked in his sleep. I had all sorts of crazy feelings about it, and I wasn't ready to tell Anthony because I didn't know him that well. Neither him or *my dad*, actually, if you want to know the truth of it. And I still don't know why I didn't call off the date. So, a week goes by and, for no good reason, I'm still avoiding the subject of my father's death. Then something happens where I finally have to tell him that my dad's dead - I forget what - and he gives me the craziest goddamn look. It's like first he doesn't believe me. Then he's wondering what kind of person doesn't mention the death of their father, right? Especially when it happened the night before we were in bed together. I think he was convinced I was lying about it, at least at the time, maybe to get sympathy or attention or something? Otherwise, it just wouldn't make sense to him that I would keep something like that to myself. Anyway, long story short, Anthony never trusted me from the start."

"But he found out it was true."

"Of course he found out it was true. But that was later. And that first impression of me as a liar always stuck in his head."

Jack waits a second, not sure if he should ask his next question, but does anyway.

321

"It's kind of weird you didn't tell him though, right?"

"What? Just because I didn't feel like telling him every fucking thing about me and my father, every pain and disappointment and argument and our entire lives summed up over that first beer? That's what I was supposed to do, huh?" She scoffs. "Whatever. So, yeah, he never trusted me after that, right up until..."

She fades off. Jack soaks in the information in silence as they drink and the drummer bangs around a bit.

"So, why did you waste so much time with the guy?"

"Okay, if I could sum him up, the way he must have summed me up, it would have been back when I first started teaching, when he anticipated that the little kiss-ass student who was giving me books to read after class – this kid would pass me all these books with dreamy passages marked with beefy bank receipts – was putting the moves on me. Anthony was convinced this kid would eventually try something on our weekly walk to our cars."

"Why did you let him walk you to your car?"

Jacki ignores this, but talks slower.

"So when Anthony's crazy throwback bullshit was proven right for the first time ever, and the kiss-ass student did ask me to 'go get coffee or something,' I made the mistake of letting him say, 'I told you so.' And he said this no less than nine times. It was the happiest I ever saw him actually."

"And?"

"And? That's it. That's the kind of person he was. He was never more miserable than when he was wrong, even if that meant I was not screwing around."

"So you went out with this kid?"

"Jesus fucking Christ," she laughs.

"Do you still teach?"

"What else you got?"

Jack changes the subject back to one she hates even more.

"Why do you think you kept your father's death to yourself?"

"I don't know. Maybe because of a lot of stuff. For one, Anthony always suspected that he wasn't my real father. He said-"

"Wait, did you just say 'Anthony' wasn't your real-"

"No, no, no. I meant my dad wasn't my dad. What did I say? No, my dad didn't think he was my real father. He said this in front of my mom on several occasions, mostly holidays. I wanted to scream at him, 'Is it so goddamn important?'"

"I don't know," Jack shakes his head. "Not to take Anthony's side, but it is weird how first impressions can stick with you forever. Even if you prove someone wasn't lying to you, you always remember that initial feeling of being lied to. And you associate that feeling with them forever. Even if they tell you the grass is green, you look twice."

Jacki looks at him for a long time, deciding something. She leans forward.

"Okay. I have to tell you something."

"What?"

"Anthony didn't just take off. He was killed last night."

Jack blinks once, twice, looks around and wishes he would have had a mouthful of beer to spray out in shock.

"What? Where? I thought you said – how?"

"I don't know. They're telling me drowned? Only there's nowhere he could have drowned. Two cops came to tell me about it today. More like interrogate me about it, to be honest. I laugh at those kinds of tactics, but to be honest, something weird happens to you afterwards. I seem to have this urge to tell you all sorts of personal shit, and it's not like me at all."

"This was today? And you're at a bar the same night? And you don't even mention this at all while we-"

"Wow!" Jacki sighs. "See, that's what I was talking about. And men wonder why women are reluctant to talk about personal shit. When they have to constantly worry about their responses being inappropriate to the situation."

"Yeah, but, come on, this is a little different. I mean, I'm sorry I was surprised, but it's not like all women have a day like yours."

They both take a drink, suddenly noticing the band has been playing David Bowie's "Diamond Dogs" for quite a while and they've just been shouting over it. The crowd is small, and the singer aims his microphone at their table.

"I'm sure you're not protected, for it's plain to see… the diamond dogs are poachers and they hide behind trees…"

"I'm sorry," she says. "Maybe I'm just ashamed I'm not that sorry."

"Drowned? Seriously? Did they tell you that?"

"Can you do me a favor?" she asks him.

"Um, okay."

"Can we pretend that I didn't tell you my husband was just murdered or my dad choked on throat cancer so we can have a conversation about all the shitty things they did without feeling guilty?"

"Sure," Jack says, not sure at all. "We don't need to talk about your husband being killed. Yesterday. I did all sorts of crap today we can talk about."

Jacki has to smile at the sarcasm.

"Like I said," she explains. "Anthony always thought Toni wasn't his. Even though he burdened a girl with a boy's name, even though she tried to love him - and he loved her back, I guess - he held it against us both that he wasn't her real father."

"Who was?"

"Eric. The boy who died that night in the crash."

"Derek?"

"No. 'Eric.'"

"The one hanging in the tree? Are you sure?"

"Yes. Well, no. But Anthony was sure. And it bothered him off and on for a long time. Only lately did he finally grow the balls to insist on a blood test. I only agreed because I wanted things to calm down. But now I think it was a mistake. It's a *waste of time. In fact, I think the split-second of pain in my daughter's arm from that needle was more attention than this subject deserved."*

The singer keeps demanding their attention, seemingly arching every line toward them.

"...the Halloween Jack is a real cool cat..."

"Well, some might disagree with you on that subject. Did you get the results back?"

"It's no one's business but my own. And I said 'no.' Didn't I say no?"

"I don't remember."

"Me neither. You know, I just hate talking about this stuff. It's probably not you. I just don't want to come across as a victim. I don't want it to seem like my dad and my boyfriend have been the only things that have affected my life. I'm defined by more than just the men who cross my path, you know?"

"I know what you mean."

"People should know that I've made choices that have done infinitely more damage than they ever could."

"That's not what I thought you meant."

They listen to the music for a bit. It starts terrible and never gets better. "Diamond Dogs" is a rough song to play anyway, and Relationshit's rendition is even rougher. Jack is especially annoyed when the singer forgets his favorite lyric. The one that's more like a question. Jack watches Jacki as she watches the band. Finally, she shoves away her beer and crosses her arms.

"You know, even when I tell myself that I'm unaffected by certain things, my body... it knows the difference." She sighs. "Sometimes my stomach hurts as if I've eaten a sandwich full of thorns and bullshit."

"Sweetly reminiscent, something mother used to bake... wrecked up and paralyzed..."

Jack turns back to her and sits up high to get between her and the band. He feels she's ready for a speech.

"I've been thinking about some things lately," she goes on. *"And it amazes me how some men don't understand what they are doing to someone that they supposedly love. I was thinking today that, what if, instead of causing a headache or a stomach ache with their anger, what if their jealousy caused their girl to get a nosebleed every time he accused her of cheating?"*

He considers this. She finishes her beer, then takes Jack's while she talks.

"Every time some asshole accuses their girl of smiling at someone else, every time he checks her email all sneaky, every time he suspiciously unfolds a scrap of paper from the jeans she left on the floor where she dropped them... she gets a nosebleed. Without anyone laying a hand on her. Think about it. What if, every time you screamed at your girl about how many guys she's fucked, a little drop of blood ran out the corner of her mouth? Would you think twice about what you were doing to her?"

"In the year of the scavenger, the season of the bitch... sashay on the boardwalk, scurry to the ditch..."

"Probably not," Jack admits. *"Now, maybe if I started bleeding..."*

She looks at him with an expression of amusement, horror, then understanding. Then she looks around the room, lets the band take over awhile. But the voice in her head drowns it out.

"Three more minutes and it never happened..."

Distracted by some noise behind them, Jack turns his chair toward one of the four televisions in the corners of the bar where they're showing a lumberjack contest. One of the barflies is turning up the volume on a TV to keep listening, and the frantic sawing of the wannabe lumberjacks sounds a lot like the band.

"Are you into that?" Jacki asks him. Then louder. *"I said, 'Are you into that?'"*

"*Sorry,*" *he says, turning back. "I was always one of those kids who was afraid he'd miss something on every channel.*"

"*Is that why you got here an hour early?*" *she asks.*

"*Huh? How did you know that?*" *He's shocked by her words at first, then calms down. "No, it just always pissed off my dad because I'd fall asleep with the TV on every night, or I'd refuse to leave a movie theater until the last of the credits was finished rolling. But right now I'm just wondering how the fuck do you win a lumberjack contest?*"

Jacki doesn't care. "So, you're a paramedic, huh? Tell me a story. Like how many you saved last night."

"*Hard to say,*" *he frowns.*

"*Uh-oh. Is this like that nonsense with veterans where you can't ask them if they killed anybody? But it's always for the opposite reason you'd think…*"

"*No, it's just that eighty percent of our trips are bullshit. People using the ambulance for a free taxi service to the hospital because their insurance covers it. But the real stuff? There's still plenty of that, too. Over the last couple years, I've given myself a couple limits. I will park it for the night and go home if I've hit six saves or three losses, depending on which comes first. That's where I draw the line. Sometimes I forget though.*"

"*So you have a limit, huh?*"

"…you'll catch your death in the fog. Young girl, they call them diamond dogs… young girl, they call them diamond dogs…"

"*Just with my job.*"

"*What's the most people you've-*"

"*Twenty six-*"

"*What?!*" *Jacki laughs, cutting him off. "You didn't hear the rest of the question! Are you telling me you saved twenty six people in one night?*"

"*Oh, no, sorry. I mean twenty six dead.*"

"*Yikes,*" *she says, looking away. "How can you even function after seeing that many stopped hearts in one shift?*"

David James Keaton

"I couldn't, to tell you the truth."

"Where was this? A car crash?"

"Worse. Lumberjack contests."

He waits for a laugh. He would have heard the crickets if it wasn't for the band.

"So, does everyone at your job keep track of the numbers like that?"

"Some of us do," Jack shrugs. *"Some keep track of their saves vs. losses. One asshole tries to up this average by fighting over calls he knows are easy. Stubbed toes and cat scratch fevers 'n' all that hypochondriac shit."*

"That's not really saving a life though," she says, but Jack ignores this.

"One time, just because there was some kind of betting pool between crews, three ambulances from three hospitals raced to a bee-sting only to find that, yeah, it had started with a sting, but after the man in the car called it in, he flew off the highway and crashed through a boatload of Boy Scouts happily bobbing down a river. Serves 'em right. The crews, I mean, not the Scouts. And don't get me started on the Wildlife Clean-up crews. That's where the worst of the EMTs go to die. EMS, I mean..."

"I don't believe any of that."

"I'm telling you. Numbers are very important to these guys."

"Is that what you're doing with me?"

"What?"

"Working on your batting average. If you are, sorry. Not only am I not allergic to bee stings, the stingers barely hurt me at all. I used to swat them with my bare hand when I was six. Even my dad would duck for cover, and I'd just grab them like they were soap bubbles. Something to do with my blood-type or something."

Jack looks at her like he's in love.

"No shit."

It's not a question.

Jack watches the bare-chested lead singer for a second, shaking his head at the shark jaw he has tattooed across his torso. He pulls out a twenty to pay for the beers, then starts to doodle on it with the waitress's pen.

"What are those?" Jacki asks.

"Bees. And spiders. I usually do 'em on dollars. But if you draw bugs on a dollar bill, they don't last a year."

"Why's that?"

"Because people get rid of them too fast. That means they get passed around way more. Makes them fall apart."

"Bees and spiders on my dollar bills wouldn't bother me. You should draw ladybugs instead and see if the money lasts forever."

He shrugs and draws a big ladybug over Andrew Jackson's face. Jacki snatches it up with a laugh to stuff it in her pocket.

"That seems kind of dangerous," he says. "Pushing your luck. Like wishing for more wishes."

The song ends, and they gear up for another.

"Thanks for coming out, guys!" *Jacki yells, standing up and pretending they're finished. The band ignores her heckling.*

"Did you know that original copies of that Bowie album go for like ten grand?" *Jack says, standing up, too.* "Bowie is like this dog dude on the cover, complete with little doggie dick. Now that's someone taking their *doggelgänger* to its logical conclusion!" *He frowns.* "They took the dick off later though. Or blacked it out…"

Blacked it out…

She shakes off the voice and moves around the table to get closer to him.

"Don't move," *she whispers. Then she smacks him hard across the face. He closes his eyes but doesn't flinch. He expected worse.*

"How many times am I gonna get smacked today?" *he asks her.*

"Aw, you must deserve it," she says, squeezing his mouth. "No, no joke, there was a ladybug on your face. And that's how I make a wish."

"That's not how you're supposed to do that," he mumbles, mouth squished around her hand.

"Think of all the wishes your face granted today!" Then she pulls her hand away and backs off. "Wait, I want another one. I'll wish for more ladybugs."

He rubs his face.

"You're like the goddamn Make-A-Wish-Foundation," she laughs, heading for the door. Then she comes back and decides to try smacking him one more time, loving the way it felt.

"Hold still…"

Jack catches her hand. Holds it awhile.

Jack's car, later that night. He's driving Jacki home. Finally outside the noise of the bar, they're both quiet and pensive. The ominous tune "Simonize" by an impossibly young Pete Yorn leaks from the speakers, in spite of the radio being off. Jack would be concerned but he's relieved it's not a drain on the battery:

"Lose your life today… and follow me into the alleyway…"

Jack turns it off too fast, making Jacki suspicious, and she stares at the dashboard numbers trying to anticipate the rest of the lyrics. Then she drums her fingers on his knee.

"You know what I remember?" she asks him, almost inaudible.

"Remember from when?" Jack asks.

"From the crash."

"What do you remember?"

"I remember someone's voice."

"Whose voice?"

"I don't know. Someone familiar. I hear it a lot lately."

"*Familiar then or familiar now?*"

Jacki had never considered that question, and he sees this in her reaction. So he quickly asks her another.

"*What's the voice saying?*"

"*The voice says, 'Three more minutes and it never happened.*'"

Silence in the car. Jack squints out at the road, catching a glimpse of a dead animal on the yellow line right before he swerves around it. Then he reflexively checks his rear-view mirror for the Mikes to pick it up.

"*Did you just try to run that over?*"

"*No, I was avoiding it.*"

"*Are you sure? It looked like you were trying to hit it.*"

"*No, I'd never do that.*"

"*Really. Wasn't it in the middle of the road anyway?*"

"*No!*"

"*Christ, relax.*"

"*Listen, I got in a fight with an ex-girlfriend for doing that once. I swerved to miss this smashed road critter, whatever it was, and she got all mad saying it was still moving and I should have put it out of its misery. But I don't believe in that shit.*"

"*Don't believe in what? Roadkill?*"

"*I think people just use that saying, 'out of its misery,' as an excuse to kill something.*"

"*My dad said something like that once. We were watching a horror movie, and there was this scene where they found this monster baby that kept screaming and screaming, and I said, 'Why don't they put it out of its misery?' and my dad got friggin' furious.*"

"*Why?*"

"*He was all like, 'That thing is fighting for every last breath it can get.' And I was like, 'But it's a mutant lizard thing, and it's suffering.' And he's like, 'It's fighting to live, not to die.' And I just kept saying, 'But it's a monster.' And dad finally goes, 'It doesn't know it's a monster.*'"

Jack ponders this hard. Then there's another shadow on the road, and he swerves again. More silence. Jack keeps looking at her like he wants to tell her something. Anything. He scratches at the window for a couple seconds, then nervously blurts out the most tiresome hypothetical question of all time.

"So, if a tree falls in the forest and there's no one there to hear it, does it make a sound?"

"You just think of that one?"

"Does it?"

"I don't know. Maybe," Jacki says quietly, mind wandering to another memory. "If there's a dog loose in the woods, does it make a sound…"

"Huh?"

Then Jack swerves again, almost taking them into a ditch.
"What the hell?!" she yells.

"Sorry. I thought I saw something."

"Why is there so much shit on the road? Are you taking a shortcut through a petting zoo?"

Jack grips the wheel with both hands. He wants to confess all over again, but instead just keeps them talking.

"Uh… have you noticed a lot of dogs around lately?"

"Well, you know what they say, if you think you're seeing a lot of dogs everywhere, then you'll look for them, and you really will *see dogs everywhere. Or something like that."*

"I think they say that about numbers."

They drive on. There's another shadow in the road, and Jack squints to see that it's still moving, or, at the least, the wind is fluttering a broken wing. He glances at Jacki and sees her yawning with her eyes shut. So this time, he doesn't swerve. She doesn't notice the tiny bump under the tire.

Jack has always thought passing a yawn back and forth was incredibly intimate. Or maybe he just always figured "I'll take it," when he traded them with pretty girls on trains. Then he shared one with a stray cat at one point, and the exchange lost its allure a bit.

Jack fights it for another mile, but finally he can't help but yawn, too. He wishes someone could harness that impulse, the infectious yawn. Harness all impulses…

When they pull into Jacki's driveway, they're both so tired they don't notice the car parked two houses down with the two shadows inside. One big. One small.

Idling in front of her house, Jacki yawns, but Jack ignores it.

"So you never answered me at the bar. You said you were a teacher, right?"

"Did I?"

"There was nothing in your garbage cans that suggested you were a teacher."

She smiles a bit at this, then inhales deep.

"I was until recently. I sort of lost it on a student and retired myself early. A meeting got outta hand."

"No shit."

"No shit."

"Okay, in a nutty fuckin' nutshell, I had this student who was plagiarizing like crazy, and I called him out on it when he used an old paper from another class, and got into this correspondence with him via email, only it was his mother pretending to be him, and…"

"So she plagiarized her emails, too! That's awesome."

"Not even the half of it. Just listen. Anyway, I'm emailing whoever it is. Even though it's coming from the kid's account, this James David Oswald – I know, I know, how am I not afraid of a kid with one of those three-name names tailor-made for assassinations. But if you'd seen him, he's fucking adorable. At first. Anyway, at the end of his emails, the dumb bitch keeps signing them 'Brit.'"

"She's British?"

"What? No, it was short for 'Britannica…'"

"She's black."

"No, she's white! Shut the fuck up. So J.D. or Brit or whoever starts insisting he/she should be able to use any

*paper he or she wants because — and he/she actually says this
— because we teachers use the same curriculum every year.
So we're plagiarizing, too, right? Also, the mother eventually
emails me from her own account, also signing it 'Brit,' and
she says she routinely helps her sons. 'Sons,' she says, so there's
probably fifty of them, hes, shes, hermaphrodites, he/shes,
whatever, and that shouldn't be considered plagiarism either,
because they all share the same blood. And looking back, they
are all definitely written by this woman."*

"I'm convinced. Did you give it an 'A'?"

*"I should have. That kid will be the editor of a major
publishing house one day. But no, J.D. and his mom wouldn't
let it drop, and eventually I'm forced to meet with him, Brit,
my Division Chair, and the Provost of our college…"*

*"Wait, back up, how did you know Britannica wrote all
her son's essays?"*

*"Because when you talk to this idiot, in person or via
email, she sprinkles the word 'certainly' into every sentence."*

"Like fairy dust."

*"More like rat poison. But J.D. has submitted a formal
appeal of his failing grade by this time, which was peppered
with about nine thousand 'certainly's, of course, meaning the
dumb ass plagiarized her plagiarism appeal! But we all meet
together anyway, because they're chickenshit at that school,
and this is when Fall Fest is going on all over campus, so
there's balloons and cut-out leaves and crêpe paper all over
the Provost's office. So J.D. starts playing with balloons,
because the kid's not all there, right? And Brit just lays into
me, saying I'm* certainly *the worst professor she's ever had,
and she's* certainly *not going to pay for this class, and even
though this is the third time J.D.'s failed the class, the common
denominator in this equation is* certainly *not her son. And
'certainly certainly certainly,' and on and on and on. And
while the 'certainly's are flying, at one point I'm pretty sure
I hear her quote* Rollerball, *without citing the source, of
course, and I'm just thinking about how J.D. and his mom*

seem dead set on plagiarizing in all possible forms and trying not to snap…"

"Oooh, please tell me you snapped."

"Well, we all snapped in our own way. But I had that pre-snap where I knew I would make somebody else snap with just one word, thus paving the way for my snap. You know what I mean?"

"Hell, yeah. What was the word?"

"What do you think? 'Certainly.' Turned out it was Kryptonite to this bitch. She actually got up over the table and went for my neck, even scratched me a little bit under my chin with her ghetto-ass nails. But I was married to Anthony long enough to learn how to fight back, and I caught that arm and turned it into a pretzel. But before I started breaking it, I could feel the bone in her elbow balancing on that fence - you know, this way it breaks, this way it's fine? So we both hold that pose a couple of seconds to think about what's next while my Division Chair and the Provost still worked their way through all the balloons to us. Do you know what I'm talking about? You know that moment when you know your knuckle is going to crack but you're not sure if it will hurt? Seems like forever, right. I just held her eyes long enough for her to know it was going to be on purpose. Then she looked scared and exhaled and we both felt her body sink onto that bad angle and snap!"

"Damn. You caught her epiphyseal, right over the synovial."

"Yeah, and the bitch bone connected to the cunt bone."

"Gave her an 'uppercunt!'"

"Whatever it was, it was like a gunshot. Then all the screaming and accusations were flying, this time coming from the colleagues who had been on my side all the way up to the snap. But through it all, J.D. said nothing. Which was crazy. Even when his own mother screamed, never a peep. He just rubbed some balloons together to make the static pull his hair up into a Mad Scientist 'do. It looked like he'd tried to *make a balloon animal of some kind, probably trying to copy the sculpture of Buffalo Bill on the Provost's desk, but he was fucking that up, as usual. Even worse, and I don't know if it was rubbing all those balloons on his jeans, but it wasn't there until that bone popped, but I swear it gave the kid an erection."*

"Hey, his body betrayed him," Jack says after a second. "Hard to blame a kid for that."

They both laugh at this.

"So, where do you work now?"

"For a paper mill."

"No shit!" Jack says, laughing, impressed all to hell. "No wonder you couldn't take your eyes off that lumberjack contest. That job is no joke. They say the lumber industry is the second most dangerous job on earth, after crab fishing..."

"No, a paper mill, like where freshmen buy papers."

"Are you serious?" Jack says, appalled.

"Yeah, it's good money. I get about fifty bucks a page, a hundred a page if the student needs it the next day. I've got good word-of-mouth, too, since I know exactly what professors are looking for."

"But after all that stuff about plagiarism?"

"What does one thing have to do with the other?"

Jack can't answer this, no matter how hard he tries. He looks her up and down, trying not to judge, but with her blatant hypocrisy, it's almost as if she's just admitted to shitting her pants. He shakes off the thought, and she yawns, big and dramatic. Jack catches the yawn, then waits for her to yawn again so he can lean over to steal a goodbye smooch. He's inches from getting his kiss when a strange electronic squawk makes Jacki jump back. She reaches down to tug on some extra electronic equipment under his radio.

"What is that? A CB?"

"Police scanner. Most of the staff has 'em."

"I saw it flashing. I just thought it was an equalizer. Those were big in the '80s"

"Ha, we were all big in the '80s."

"Really."

"Actually I was in England in the '80s."

"Did they have equalizers?"

"That's funny you called it that. Because that's exactly what I like to call it, too. An 'equalizer.'"

"Why?"

"Because if the cops know what the paramedics are up to, we figure we should know what the cops are up to. Firemen, cops, lifeguards. It's the same food chain. Scooping up the same nutrients from the ocean, you know?"

"Certainly," Jacki says, forcing a smile and climbing out.

"See ya."

"See ya."

Jack drives off, adjusting his rear-view to watch her go in, still not seeing the parked car and the headlights that pop on to follow.

Jacki walks in the door, and the babysitter, a grinning teenage moppet curled up on the couch with her knees against her chin, quickly springs up to greet her.

"Hey, Jacki," she says through braces and a yawn. "Toni's sleeping. Me, too, almost."

"How'd she do?" Jacki asks, looking around.

"She was fine. We played chess. Watched E.T. Well, she wanted to play chess, but we really just played checkers with the chess pieces."

"That movie isn't on video yet, is it? I thought it was still in theaters."

"No, it's old," the teen says. "We used to copy it, try to ride around with our dogs in our baskets and jump the moon. No way you can jump anything with any creature on your handlebars though."

"Why's that?"

"You ever try riding with a boombox in the basket? You'll tumble right over on your first curb."

"They still make boomboxes?" Jacki asks herself, walking over to the brass chess set on the coffee table and rattling around the horses. She picks up the knight, then balances it on its crown. "Yeah," she continues. "Toni used to want me to teach her, but she can't sit still long enough. She just plays with 'em like army men. Her grandpa taught her that."

"Isn't that what they are?" the babysitter laughs. "Army men?" Then she grabs her book bag to leave. "Okay, gotta go. She was sooo cute all night. See ya next time!"

Jacki hands the girl the twenty-dollar bill with the ladybug President. The girl doesn't notice the drawing, and Jacki closes the door behind her.

She side-arms her keys on the table, knocking over the bishop, then heads for her daughter's room. She finds Toni sitting in the glow of her tiny TV, still wide awake. Jacki gasps in mock surprise and reaches to turn off the TV, then stops.

"What the heck are you watching, girl? This again? Are you kidding me?"

On the screen, the studio audience of a low-brow talk show has erupted in a screaming match while the guests on the stage try to struggle loose from the security guards to attack each other. Every other word is bleeped as they unleash a flood of profanity. Jacki finally turns it off.

"C'mon, enough of this crap, I'd rather you try to sneak a beer into bed than watch this garbage."

"Mommy, noooooo," Toni whines. "Why do they make those noises? Is that what noise comes out when you get really angry?"

"What? No," she sighs. She's explained this before. "Those are just, uh, bleeps."

"Huh?"

"Bleeps, beeps, whatever. It's what they do when someone says a swear word on TV."

"*Why not just tell them they can't swear on TV?*"

"*Nobody listens. Actually, they probably tell those idiots to swear as much as possible.*"

"*Why?*"

"*I don't know! Because people like hearing bleeps. Then they get to fill in the blanks with the nastiest words they can think of.*"

"*Like what?*" Now Toni is utterly fascinated.

Jacki remembers her job training and recognizes the "teachable moment." She turns the TV back on and sits down on the edge of her bed.

"*Okay, let's listen, and you tell me. Every time the TV 'bleeps,' you try to fill in the word.*"

"*Okay!*" Toni is bouncing all around as her mother turns up the volume. Two people on the screen are nose to nose. The bleeps are flying. "*Sounds like my Blurby!*"

"*I will [bleep] on your [bleep],*" one of them hisses. Then the show cuts to a commercial. Toni looks to her mother for help.

"*Uhhh...*"

"*C'mon. You're supposed to fill in the blanks. I mean 'bleeps.'*"

"*I can't think fast enough,*" Toni says, frowning.

"*Exactly,*" Jacki says, smiling and turning the TV back off. "*Neither can they. And that's the whole goddamn problem.*"

Her daughter frowns as she contemplates this and climbs into bed. Her mother turns out the light and starts to leave, but Toni has one more question.

"*On that show, how come they were calling the mommy 'mother sister?' Can she be both?*"

"*Sounds horrible,*" Jacki says.

The door closes.

Same night. Jack locks his front door and turns to enter the apartment directly across the hall. He's carrying a long, *camouflaged bag rattling on his back. He steps into the empty apartment as he swings the bag off his shoulder, making no move for the lights as the door gently closes behind him and locks him safely in the darkness.*

Bully climbed to the top of the bunker to get the perfect view, her thumb tickling the button on her helicopter remote control.

Then she saw the tow truck. The one with the ramp.

She forgot about promises of fame and destruction and stopped tickling the remote control for a second so the world could catch its breath. The tow truck was leaving the drive-in, but it was still stuck at the back of the line, not quite lined up straight enough. Not yet. But it would be.

And if a truck with a ramp was here, she knew that meant he was here, too. Her eyes watered. She had more than a little bit of affection for someone trying so hard to court her, and she thought she might wait for him to try his stunt before she hit the button marked, "Ascend."

But it would be hard. She couldn't think of a more perfect word.

VII.

Flashbacks to the Crashbacks – That's Not How a Rorschach Test Works, Dude – Slap! "She's My Daughter and My Sister!" Slap! – Approaching the Ramp and Remembering Why He Should – Never Pick up Strange – Ten Dollar Private Eye – Only a Fool Wouldn't Wish for More Wishes – In the Bunker – The Voice in His Ear That Makes Him Do What He Do Just Because – That's Not What Her Shirt Says – I Know an Old Lady Who Swallowed a Fly – Perhaps She Lied – Sun Delay – You Can't Teach a Dead Dog New Tricks

"Will power made that old car go
A woman's mind told me that, so…"
—Lobo "Me and You and a Dog Named Boo"

Six years ago. The crash.

Jacki is wearing only a T-shirt, naked from the waist down, back arched against a steering wheel and riding Eric in the driver's seat. They're racing down a road flanked by trees. Both windows are down and the night air pulls hard on their hair.

It was six years ago tonight...

Don't you wish it was a year ago tonight? Doesn't that sound better?

Shut up and listen.

Jacki looks down at the driver. Some sort of "nü-metal" music fills the car while she grinds, but her face signals an approaching orgasm anyway. The new metal, too. The driver's eyes are closing.

He was distracted because he was coming, and I was distracted because I knew that meant I wasn't going to be able to...

Jacki frowns in disappointment as he finishes before her. Then she sees the driver's eyes dilate in horror, and he shoves her off the steering wheel and into the passenger's seat. The car is airborne, leaving the road for three glorious seconds before it tries and fails to sucker-punch the thickest tree around. Jacki is thrown forward and crushed down into the wreckage like a thumb packed her into a pipe. The crumbled car's seat engulfs her body and she's almost gone, part of the car now.

I felt the car collapse around me, like someone squeezing me in a metal fist. The last thing I saw was him taking flight...

Eric's naked body rockets past Jacki in slow motion, bursting through the blue diamonds of the windshield. Impossibly, he rockets straight up into space.

It sounds crazy, but I remember thinking, just for a second, "Did he have an ejector seat?" Then that metal fist was drumming my head, and things got fuzzy.

The hissing wreck rocks back and forth against the splintered but still-standing trunk, a small fire starting to burn near the back tires, one front wheel spinning. A dog howls in the distance.

Come on, no one really hears a dog howl in the distance.

I swear. I remember someone pulling me out while I'm thinking, "Why did the paramedics bring a dog?"

We didn't bring a dog. We didn't get there first. Someone else got there first.

I told you to shut the fuck up and listen. I thought you wanted to hear this.

An arm reaches into the twisted metal and upholstery, and Jacki squints through the smoke to see the shadow of a man pulling the crushed passenger seat off her torso.

At first I was grateful...

The figure carries her from the wreckage, Jacki hanging limp across a pair of shoulders. One eye opens, and she looks back to the growing fire cooking under the car. She raises her head high enough to glimpse bare legs dangling from the tree, a strip of denim trailing from a toe. She watches a large dog suddenly run up to growl and snap at the shred of blue jeans. The dog catches the fabric on a tooth, and the tree limbs stretch and stretch, then rebound like a diving board as the dog shakes its mouth loose. The naked body snaps into a final contortion, arms and legs now pointed toward the sky that was denied.

That's when I blacked out. But I wasn't out for very long. The car hadn't exploded yet. The cars always explode, right?

Jacki opens her eyes and through her blurred vision sees the dog back trying to grab Eric's foot, now way out of its reach. Then her body is being pulled away so hard and fast that her own jeans, previously bunched around her ankles, fly off into the dark. Blood stings her eyes, and she struggles to raise an arm to wipe it away.

Then she's on the ground, laid out like a grave.

She sees the shadow back up, then lean back in, now struggling to climb on top of her. She looks over the shadow's shoulder to watch the dog jumping higher than the tree now, snapping at the naked boy as he finally begins to fly. The shadow grows frustrated with her body, moving her limbs to satisfy, and she concentrates on the dog, now flying, too, snapping at the moon. Then the shadow is bending her legs the wrong way, and Jacki carefully puts the palms of her hands down on the ground for leverage. Then she slowly lifts her rear off the ground so the shadow man can easily remove the underwear that she had only pulled to the side for Eric, the dead boy in the sky. The lace tears and snaps over the shadow's other shoulder to catch and sway on the tops of some cattails in the drainage ditch. The shadow sways with them.

Then the car explodes.

I let him do it. I don't know why. Maybe I realized I owed him. For saving my life. If he hadn't come along, I would be dead. I know how that sounds, but it's the truth. I can admit that to you. Or to anyone who asks. It's just that simple. I won't be questioned about this. I was grateful enough for my life to give him what he wanted. One thing was less important than the other.

Finished with her, the shadow man stops to watch the car burn, and Jacki is sitting up now, too, up on her elbows, hypnotized by the same flames. She turns to find the shadow man in the smoke, but she can't see anything but the dog running hard toward her, trailing spit, nostrils flaring. They embrace.

Jacki's house. Night. She's standing silent at a window, her story finally told. Jack is looking at her in disbelief. She turns as if challenging him to judge her.

Then she decides it's time to drop the bomb.

"I was in and out of consciousness, but I know it was you. I remember you there, Jack. I know it was you who held me next to the fire."

"No," Jack says. "I…"

"I thought you said you always *get there first.*"

"Yeah, but not that time. The fire was out when I got there. When we got there. It couldn't have been me. There was someone else."

"You're lying. You held me."

"Yes, I was holding you. In the back of the ambulance! But someone else pulled you from the car."

Jacki turns her back on him again.

"I don't believe you. Maybe it wasn't you. Maybe there wasn't even a dog. Maybe I don't fucking care anymore."

Jack doesn't believe this, so he reaches for the picture of her mother again, hoping to distract her.

"What do you remember about your mother?"

"Not much." *Then, casually,* "She was raped."

"What?" *Jack asks, still staring at the picture.*

"That's how I was conceived actually," she says, still emotionless. "At least that's what my dad believed. She was attacked on Daytona Beach. Under a pier. The rapist was pretending he was blind, and she was helping him. She took him by the arm to show him the water. Or tell him the time. Something like that."

She walks toward the door, considers opening it.

"'Conceived!'" *she laughs.* "Isn't that a great word?"

"How is that a great word?"

"It fits. It almost tells you everything you need to know. Now..." she opens the door.

"Wait-"

"The thing is," Jacki says, cutting him off. "I can accept that that is how I was conceived. But I'll never accept that's how my daughter was conceived."

"So you're not going to tell her."

"You know what, Jack?" Jacki laughs. "I think you need to get the fuck out of my life."

"You not telling Toni is the same thing as-"

"I'll be honest with you. The only thing more disturbing than wondering if you might have raped me in a car wreck six years ago, is wondering if you saved me from one."

"I find that pretty hard to believe."

"Why? I don't want to owe anyone anything. Revenge, hate, guardian angels, I just have no time for any of that bullshit right now. I don't need any of that shit..."

She trails off, noticing that Jack isn't listening. He's found another photo on her wall, tapping the metal frame.

"Now this is a good picture of you."

"I told you," Jacki says, frustrated. "That's my mother." She points to the first picture he picked up. "And that's my mother," pointing down the hall. "And over there... that's my mother. And that's her, too. They're all my mother! Why are you having trouble with this?"

Jack is frozen, chewing on his tongue. Something horrible has just occurred to him.

"Your mother was raped?" he says slowly.

"I already told you she was. So what?"

Jack reaches out an arm to brace himself against another photograph. To Jacki, it looks like he's doing calculus in his head, and it's painful to watch.

"Listen," he says. "I came here tonight to tell you that I believed that the same man who raped you six years ago is here, now, still doing that kind of thing. I came here to tell you that I believe that he chooses his victims because they fit a *certain description. And I was going to tell you that, not only do you fit this description, it was you that he started with. You're the prototype. That's what I was going to say when I got here. Until I saw those pictures…"*

"Jack…"

"*…but now I think it goes back farther than that. I think he'd followed you for a long time. And I think it's because you remind him of someone else.*"

He stabs the hanging picture with his thumb.

"*You remind him of her.*"

Jacki's hand is back on the doorknob.

"*I think you should go.*"

Jack grabs her again, high on her bicep, like a cop.

"*No! Listen. This man raped your mother under that pier. Then she had you. And he raped you after the wreck. Then you had her…*"

Jacki struggles.

"*Let go.*"

"*I'm telling you that this man is your father. And I'm saying that this man is the father of your daughter. And I'm saying that he's going to stay in your life until Toni is old enough, wait for her to get stuck under a car crash or pinned under a 'fridge or trapped in a fucking revolving door and then-*"

Jacki breaks free.

"*Get out!*"

"*Think about this. What if he's been part of your family for longer than that? Wait, do you have any pictures of your grandma?*"

Jacki snaps and throws a half-punch, half-shove at Jack's face. He ducks around it, staring at her in disbelief.

"*Whoa. I'm trying to help here-*"

"*I told you to leave. I don't want to hear any more of your theories. Don't you realize that you're the suspect in every new idea that comes out of your fucking mouth?! You are the most* suspicious man I've ever met. You tell me you were there that night, you tell me you had your hands on me-"

Jack's back is up against the door.

"No, no," he pleads. "My hand was on you because his hand was on you. That night, you had a five-fingered hand print on your stomach and skin under your fingernails, and other evidence, too. And when I saw it I knew someone had to do something-"

"Go!"

"You never saw any of this because I made it all go away. I'll admit I put my hand over the hand print, and I squeezed your leg even harder. Maybe that's how I indict myself, but I took the chance. Maybe you felt me doing that, but me turning that bruise into nothing you would recognize was to erase his crime. I turned that bruise into a Rorschach Test, into something that only I could see, just another bruise on your stomach, or your leg, your arms, or just a hand on your hand, and I did this for you-"

"Go!"

Jacki shoves him aside and opens the door.

"Go or I'm calling the cops."

"You know, you don't make any sense to me, Jacki. You tell me to fuck off because you think I'm the man that raped you, yet you tell me that you owe your life to that monster?"

Jacki looks through his open mouth, right through the back of his head to the night sky beyond.

"That's my problem, not yours."

She closes the door on him while he's still talking.

Later that night. A phone is ringing on the kitchen wall, and Jacki stumbles out of her bedroom to answer it. Her head sinks in exhaustion when she realizes it's Jack. It's always Jack. It's his third call in an hour. She lays the phone on the floor, walking in circles in the dark, her bare feet squeaking on the *tile like basketball shoes, letting his voice fill the room instead of her head.*

"...think about it. He covers them up perfectly, maybe using the same methods I did in the back of the ambulance that night..."

Jacki stops in front of her refrigerator and touches the collage of magnets, family photos, recipes, stopping on her daughter's artwork. The largest of Toni's drawings is a purple crayon outline of herself, Jacki, and her grandmother. The portrait is titled "Meme, Mama & Mumu." She smiles and flicks dried chocolate off the corner, then stops smiling when she sees an old photo of her and her father.

"...maybe your dad was right, maybe this man was her father and your father and her father and..."

Her hand tickles some more pictures, lingering on another one of her mother. She's never realized how many eyes she's attached to this appliance. They're suddenly everywhere, following her like paintings.

"...maybe I was trying to rescue you from the truth back then, but now I'm just trying to stop him... if this guy has been in your life for two generations then what stops him from going for three..."

Her hand brushes her daughter's drawing of a snarling dog she's never noticed before.

"...what if he goes after her? Of course he goes after her..."

Jacki kicks the phone down the hall so she won't hear him anymore, then she flicks the edge of a construction-paper Thanksgiving turkey that her daughter created from the outline of her own hand. She puts her shaking palm over top of her daughter's. It isn't much bigger, never has been.

Same night. Jack's secret apartment. In his head, he's in the back of his ambulance. It's six years ago. Then nine years ago.

350

He's in the back of all his ambulances, something like a dozen total.

No, it couldn't have been that long ago. He remembers The Deftones' song "Passengers" coming from somewhere.

"Drive faster, roll the windows down. The cool night air is curious. Let the whole world look in. Who cares who sees anything?"

But his brain flashes to Jacki in the back of his ambulance, and his hand covering the black-and-blue handprint rising on her stomach. His hand fits perfectly inside the outline. Then he's squeezing her stomach hard, erasing that crime at least, and her skin turns white, then purple.

Back then, he thought he was changing things, and he was sure of his reasons. Today, he stands in an empty room and does nothing, talking to a phone balanced on his shoulder. He thinks of cops and the radios pinned up by their chins so they can confide in them like their conscience.

"Maybe you've accepted what happened back then, Jacki," he says. "And you've decided that your life was worth whatever you had to endure. So I'm sorry if I'm making it impossible to forget all over again... but I've been seeing these strange dog bites everywhere now... or maybe just tattoos of dog bites because that's what he wants me to see... and maybe this man is killing instead of raping, using his dog to cover it up... chopping down his own family tree... I know it sounds crazy..."

Miles away, Jacki sits down on the floor of the dark kitchen, paper turkey in hand, head down, phone pleading from across the room. Jack mistakes the rustling for encouragement.

"...maybe you're thinking that it's too much of a coincidence, to know all of these things and not be the villain here, or worse, the rapist. But I swear it's true, Jacki. Listen, this kind of crazy shit surrounds me. All my life I've dealt with coincidence and synchronicity and bad luck. This has happened to me in other cities, even across the ocean, but I helped all of them, even if they didn't want me to. That's all

I want to do. Help you. You know that other apartment you saw? You think that's strange? Here's another crazy apartment story for you. Different time. Different place."

He turns on the light over his head, and sits down in the center of the empty floor to imagine the police interrogation.

"One time while I was doing some Red Cross training, I met this other lifeguard by getting close in the water to perform 'cross-chest carries' all day. So we went back to her apartment one night to watch some Baywatch *and fuck around, and as the sun was coming up and the alcohol was wearing off, I looked around and suddenly realized where I was. You know where I was? I was in an apartment that I'd lived in five years earlier. How about that shit? I knew I was in the same building when we pulled in, and I even said something to her about that. But I didn't know it was the exact same apartment. And when I realized it was the same place, that I was lying in the same corner of the room I slept in back then, that I was staring at the same water tower out the window that I stared at every night half a decade earlier, I told her this, all excited. And she didn't believe me."*

Jack's neck cramps, and he switches the phone to the other shoulder. He squints up at the harsh light and wonders if the neck pain is what makes cops such assholes.

"Actually, it wasn't just her that didn't believe this. No one would believe me. So I ended up stealing one of her magazines she had tucked behind her toilet just so I could get the mailing label off of it. Then I made a photocopy of one of my old tax forms with my old address on it, that old address, and I emailed this proof to everyone who doubted me. This just made her more suspicious because now she starts to worry why I'm stealing her magazines and mail for whatever reason, even though I tell her the reason, and it's a completely reasonable reason to be stealing mail. But she gets me so freaked out that I burn one of the magazines I swiped from her in a panic because I know she's coming over. It doesn't burn nearly as fast as you'd think, so then I start worrying how weird this

is going to look, so I steal a candle from one of my neighbors'
patios to cover the smell, and she sees me do this, too. And you
know what happens after all this? You'll never guess. Everyone
started saying okay, maybe I did live there before. But if I did
live there before, I must be some kind of apartment stalker.
Like I was trying to meet someone who lived there after me.
Like maybe I wanted to impress this girl by pretending I was
psychic, maybe by mapping out the layout or walking around
with my eyes closed without bumping the walls. I should have
done that, actually…"

The light bulb finally gets to him, and he clicks it off and
sits back down, switching shoulders again.

"So she just ended up breaking up with me because it
was all too weird to believe. Or because she believed it all.
Either way. But I think she dumped me mostly because her
roommate thought I'd been watching their building for five
years, waiting for my chance to get back in there for some
insane reason. Maybe I had something stashed under the
radiator or something, she said. Maybe something horrible
happened there, she said. I tried to explain that the worst
thing I ever did in that apartment was punch through a
wall because an ex-girlfriend put up a stupid Mars Attacks!
trading cards poster. Or did she put up the poster to cover the
hole? I can't remember. I just know I wasn't stalking anyone.
And I certainly wasn't stalking a building. Of course now
that she's gone, I'm wondering who lives there, just like they
all said. And maybe it wouldn't be too insane to figure out a
way to bump into them or get inside, see what's going on. And
if anybody was going to hide something, dropping it down
into the wall and covering it up with a Mars Attacks! *poster*
might be the way to go…"

On her end of town, Jacki crawls across her floor until the
phone is next to her head. She closes her eyes, and Jack's voice
is muffled but still echoing around her skull. There's something
intoxicating about his level of crazy. Different than Anthony's
jealousy, unhinged but sort of innocent. She thinks someone

should maybe help him, so he doesn't dwell on things like this anymore. Put him down easy, like they do at the vet.

"*...so here's my plan, the dog is the key. He's using the dog to cover up the crime scenes... I'm not sure how, I just know there can't be this many bites and maulings in six years. I'm telling you, if we find the dog, we find the killer. The dog will give him up in a second. Put a dog under a harsh light and that dog will bark. You think a man is a dog's best friend? Wrong. How does the saying go? A diamond is a girl's best friend, a brick is a vandal's best friend, and, well, a tree is probably a dog's best friend actually...*"

"Goodbye, Jack."

She means it this time, but on his end of town, Jack doesn't feel it when Jacki squeezes and crumples the Thanksgiving turkey off the magnets and stuffs it down the disposal. But he does feel something when she does this to the phone.

Jacki's house. Same endless night.

She sits on the hard tile floor, some broken phone shrapnel between her crossed legs. The sickly blue glow of the television lights the wall behind her. The movie Chinatown *is on - Toni has started it over again - and Jacki watches the wall, trying to recognize the shadows of the characters. Someone recommended the movie at a video store long ago, insisted really, almost slapping it into her hand. She used to rent a movie every Friday night and was actually relieved not to have to think too hard about her selection that time. Then she made the mistake of watching it with her daughter.*

They didn't make it to the end the first time, but one night they did, and now Toni couldn't get enough. Jacki paid so much in late fees that she eventually just bought the damn thing.

Just from the shadows, she knows the movie is on the scene where Faye Dunaway starts getting slapped by Jack

Nicholson. *Jacki notices the volume dip in the other room as Toni tries to be sneaky, but they know this part by heart.*

"She's my daughter!"

Slap!

"I said I want the truth!" *Jack says.*

"She's my sister!" *Slap!* "She's my daughter!" *Slap!* "My sister!" *Slap!* "My daughter!" *Slap!*

"I said I want the truth!"

Crash.

"She's my daughter and my sister!"

"Of course she is," Jacki says, unsurprised, then she stands up off the floor and goes to get her shoes.

At the playground, Bucky Balls finally radioed for help after staring at the baffling contraption around the dog's neck for a good six minutes.

"Is it one of yours?" Bigby asked him.

"What? Are you fucking kidding?" Bucky said. "Since when are giant plastic collar bombs police issue? Looks like a game of *Mouse Trap*…"

"No, I mean the dog. Is the dog one of yours?"

"Doubt it. It doesn't seem to have much interest in its surroundings. No real training. If it *is* an officer of the law, it slipped through the academy without developing the proper respect for human life. Or authority."

"What a disgrace," Bigby sighed. Then, to the third cop, who will remain forever nameless after this night, "Go to the exit and stop those cars from leaving! We're gonna lose the kids responsible for this hoax."

"Kids?" Forever Nameless frowned. "Why aren't we thinking evacuation?"

"Just do what I said."

A skinny teenager wearing headphones crossed his path, and Forever Nameless pulled one off his ear to bark.

"Son, go find your parents!"

Drifting through the air between this kid and Nameless was Bully's sing-song, balloon-squeak of a voice, reporting an old crime which the officer mistook for movie dialogue:

"...at this point, authorities believe Mr. Bells was still convinced the bomb was an elaborate fake. No one knows why he allowed it to be locked onto his neck. Investigators theorized that he was convinced it was his alibi, and by pretending to be a hostage, he could later deny any involvement. He seems to have been somehow unaware that he was wearing the *third* such device reported sighted on the corner of Eerie and Ohio within a week. Then, at 2:01 p.m., a small key that was first mistaken as a handcuff key, but later identified to fit the lock of a child's diary was finally removed from the device, and the very real bomb began to tick. Mr. Bells seems to have changed his mind at this point. He tried to run, and a gunshot was heard by neighbors. The bullet was later matched to a police-issue .38 revolver and determined to have been fired into the nearby radio antenna, interrupting Peter Gabriel's 'Shock The Monkey' mid-chorus. This shot also stopped Mr. Bells in his tracks..."

The skinny kid ran, and the cop never made the connection. All the while, Bigby fingered the dangling snap of his weapon absent-mindedly and studied the children on the covered slide. He hated those covered versions.

Sooo dangerous.

Kids got jammed up in there and never came out with any *consistency.* It drove him nuts. He couldn't believe anyone would allow their kids to play on such a contraption. Once, he watched a covered slide at a playground for three hours straight. He could never prove it, but he was pretty sure the same little bastards that were piling into the hole on the top were not the ones shooting out of the bottom.

Because those were even worse.

* * *

Evil Boll Weevil traced a figure-eight in the dust as he waited for the ramp truck to line up behind the row of cars heading for the drive-in exit. He counted 25.

But they were long ways. Which made it more like 60.

He balanced a soda can on the boombox strapped to his handlebars and gave the accelerator a snake bite. He was going to do a practice run next to them to see what top speed he could achieve.

But a man in a wheelchair rolled in front of him, and he was forced to abort the trial run. He took his hand off his throttle to hear what the disabled man was saying.

Then he started counting the spider tattoos on the man's face with a shocked "Whoa!" and didn't hear most of it anyway.

The spider-faced man was motioning to some current action on the screen where a baby with a mouthful of fangs was screaming bloody murder.

"I can't decide what's more overused," Spider Face was saying. "The bat-like shriek every creature stops to make in every horror movie…" He cocks a thumb at a man cradling a hubcap being shoved out of the concession stand, head down in the mud. "…or the moment when the monster catches up with the hero and throws him across the room to give him another chance."

The man stealing hubcaps collected himself from the mud and ran back inside the booth.

A young woman with thick glasses and a fistful of popcorn suddenly joined them to add to the conversation.

"Ah, yes. The ol' 'You're not worth it!' moment," she says while spitting out some hulls. "The worse case I ever saw was in *Roadhouse II: The Prequel,* when the ghost fetus of Swayze says that same crap to the main villain. After both Swayzes just killed everyone in the fucking house to get to him?! Ridiculous."

Evil revved his engine to get their attention and pointed to the tow truck.

"Hey, guys? Can you move aside, please? I'm gonna jump those cars."

They all turned, nodding and smiling, eager to watch, and Evil turned up his headphones to hear Bully's voice in his ears explaining that, "'The noise produced by a single dog park can reach as much as 115 decibels, the equivalent of every car horn under every palm of the angriest cab drivers on Earth, and way too much for me!' This was an excerpt from the delivery man's suicide note, later determined to be fake…"

"Hold on, boy. You're gonna what?" The old man in the wheelchair started wheeling after him, right about when a German Shepherd blindsided Evil and upended him and his bike into a puddle. Evil gunned it to steady himself again, then the police dog bounded over the loose-spinning wheels and went for Evil's arm. Evil was able to turn his handlebars at the last second, and the dog got a mouthful of rubber instead.

Biting down, its jaws cranked the gas even harder, sending the bike, Evil, and the dog flying toward the ramp, a shitload of broken bones, and immortality.

Empty apartment. Night. Jack steps through the door, clicking on the base of the one swinging light bulb. This apartment is new but familiar, resembling every apartment he's ever infested. And he's still carrying his camouflaged bag over his shoulder as he walks to a window, opens it, and breathes in the crisp air. He sees a willow tree in the distance. He's always been able to spot them easily on the horizon, the only trees that move like some vast underwater organism, seeming to beckon other creatures into its grip in hypnotic, spineless slow-motion. Jack thinks back to when he was a boy, when he was drawn in just such a way into the huge willow tree behind his house, how he climbed it so often that he knew every big branch by heart, especially any branch thick enough to sleep nestled comfortably inside their wishbones, safer than he ever felt in his mother's arms. He climbed that willow tree so much that one day the cradle had to fall, of course, and even though the bark took most of the skin off his arms and elbows on the way down ("the epiphyseal connected to the synovial…"), that shimmering tree caught Jack's ankles right before he hit the ground, hanging him upside down for hours until his family finally came home from his brother's baseball game to untangle him, all of them laughing while he cried, the snarl of branches never letting go until his brother cracked them all easily in his fists. Sometimes between dreams, Jack could still feel the branches snake around his feet in protest, maybe to save him from hitting the ground all over again, but also to make sure that Jack stared at that ground as long as possible, if only to remember exactly how close he came to breaking his goddamn neck and how easily the world could do this to a boy as small as him.

There's the obligatory bark somewhere in the distance.

"Seize the dog!" someone yells.

"Carpe canem!" someone yells back.

The willow tree stops moving in response, and Jack holds his breath until it starts dancing again.

Hallway. Same night. Jacki stomps her way through Jack's apartment building, glancing down occasionally at the address on her blackened matchbook, checking numbers on the doors as she passes. When she finds the right one, she stops to knock, but the door flies open so fast she jumps back. A girl holding a drink and crunching an ice cube blocks the doorway, looking Jacki up and down. The girl is blonde, tall, wearing only an oversized t-shirt that reads:

"EMS: Where The Rubber Hits The Road."

She finishes chewing her ice and swallows. She seems ready to talk to Jacki, then reaches into her glass of soda and grabs another cube, offering nothing but an arched eyebrow.

"Uh, does Jack live here?" *Jacki asks her.*

"Uh, sorta?" *she mocks her, chomping and pointing to the door across the hall.* "Sorta lives there, too. And there, too, I think," *she says, pointing to a third door even further down. Jacki frowns and turns. When she turns back around, the blonde girl is holding a small cardboard box.*

"Here. Tell him this *came for him," she says, then slams the door.*

Jacki knocks on one of the doors, then another. She's bending down to leave the box in front of the third door when it swings open. It's Jack, blinking at her in confusion.

"Hi," *she says.*

"Hello," *he says, peering up and down the hall around her.* "What's going on?"

"I came to see you," *she says, holding up the matchbook and cocking a thumb at the other doors.* "But you gave me the wrong address."

"No, that's the right address, I just..." *He notices the box.* "You bring me brownies?"

"No, your roommate said this came for you."

"Oh," *he mumbles, taking it from her hand, still keeping his door half shut.*

"Are you okay?" *she asks. Then to herself,* "Who am I kidding? You're never okay."

He scratches his head and looks around some more, clearly rattled. Then he sighs, opening the door wide to wave her in. His long bag is lying in the middle of an empty floor, and the light bulb above it is swinging, its chain having just been yanked.

"Well, c'mon in if you want," *he tells her.*

Jacki steps inside and looks around. White walls. Suspicious bag. She doesn't need a roadmap. She starts to back out again.

"Are you coming or going?" Jack sighs.

"Neither. What the fuck are you doing?"

"Nothing!"

Jack follows her eyes to the bag and grabs it, swinging it around to the front of his chest. Something metal rattles, and Jacki puts an arm out towards the door.

"Wait, no," he says. "It just looks like a rifle. Watch."

"Who said it was a rifle…"

Jack unzips the bag, and a jumble of green canvas and metal rods clang to the floor. Jacki jumps back, scared. Jack reaches down, and, in a quick flurry of movement, pulls on the rods until, like a particularly well-rendered page in a children's pop-up book, a fold-out green hunting chair snaps into existence in the middle of the room. They both cross their arms to appreciate an empty room with a lonely chair dead center.

"Looks good," Jacki laughs. "Well done. Now it's a home."

"Have a seat," he says. She just stares. He tries to put her at ease with a story.

"Speaking of metal rods! The other day, this guy came in the E.R. with a 'bladder injury.' But after a little X-ray vision, it turned out there was a little more to the story. See, this guy had decided to jerk off with a metal rod shoved up his urethra. He finished that little task easy enough, but when he was done he discovered he was now a magician because the rod had poof! vanished. But after he started pissing blood two days later, it turned out the rod hadn't really vanished, of course. It had simply taken a walkabout past the seminal colliculus, around the prostatic utricle, up through the urethral crest, past the corner where old Johnson's barn used to be, around the block from where they were selling that snowmobile last Spring, and smack dab right into the wall of his bladder. They ended up operating. You know, you people have no idea *how lucky you are that you're able to urinate with such a high success rate. Open it up and you're like, 'Wait, is this a map of Pittsburgh?' Anyway, his name sounded kinda Spanish, like yours. You ever met the guy? John Colitis, Colitas, Coitus Interruptus... no, John Colandas! That's the fucker. Skinny, but kinda scary. You don't want to know him. But, yeah, the freak wanted the rod back, but thank Christ he only made a necklace out of it."*

"So, what are you doing in here, man?" she laughs.

"Long story. You really want to hear it?" She still doesn't answer, figuring one of his stories is plenty. He points, "Hey, if you're not gonna sit there, then I..."

Jacki runs to the chair to claim it.

"Okay," she says. "Tell your story standing up."

"I thought you had enough of me on the phone today."

"Guess not."

"Well, I used to live here. Before I lived over there. And there. I lived here with my ex-girlfriend-"

"Was that her chomping ice? At one of your nine apartments?"

"No, just listen. So we lived over here for awhile, but then we decided we needed a bigger place because we were always fighting. And when we were always fighting, I would go sit in the empty two-bedroom apartment across the hall. The one where I live now. See, they were painting it, and it was taking them forever, so it was never locked. Eventually things got better between us, and, when they finally finished renovating, we moved into that two-bedroom apartment. But no one's moved into the empty one yet. And now they're painting another one."

"So that is her with the ice."

"Yeah," Jack says, pacing around her in the chair. "Turned out, though, that the small apartment wasn't the reason we were always fighting after all. So then I would come back over here and sit, wondering if I'd made two mistakes now, or if hopefully the two mistakes could cancel out each other, *you follow me? Anyway, so we break up, of course, and by this time we were living with her best friend, too, to save some money. So now it's just me and her best friend. The one with the ice. Who is sort of a horrible person and wants me to fuck her to tell you the truth, probably so she can run to my ex and tell her how awful I am. Or something."*

"She was wearing your shirt."

"Whoa, Sherlock. How do you know she's not a paramedic?"

"How did you know what shirt I was talking about?"

"Whoa, Watson! Anyway, since I still had the key, the key I made my ex-girlfriend actually, I come back over here to sit and think. Or over there. Even though she's gone. I miss this smaller place especially. I just keep coming back."

"So you just keep coming back, huh?"

"I just keep coming over here to sit and think. I don't know. I'll probably keep coming over here until someone finally moves in."

Jacki starts rocking back and forth even though the chair's not built for it.

"So, what's the story with the Army 'camo' chair? You trying to hide? You're going to need some green walls or some plants for that."

"No."

"Do you hunt?"

"No. I just like this one chair. Kind of self-pitying, I know."

"No shit," she laughs. "Why don't you leave it here then? Why haul it back and forth?"

"I don't know. I don't want to leave anything here in case the landlord shows the place. And a chair in a bag looks less suspicious when I cross over the hall with it. People think I'm the exterminator or something."

"You're kidding, right? When that thing is rolled up, it's quite possibly the most suspicious thing I've ever seen a person carry over their shoulder."

"Besides another person."

"Good point. But that's your day job, ain't it?"

"Exactly."

"Whatever, Oswald." Jacki gets up to look out the window.

"Actually it was my dad's chair, okay? He did try to make a hunter out of me once. It didn't stick, but that's another story."

"Okay, just trying to follow this. So, you lived here, and hung out there, and hung out there, and now you live there and hang out here? Or there?"

Jack sits on the floor in front of her.

"Yep."

"Why?"

"I just told you!" Jack says, scratching his head even harder.

You're gonna catch something...

"When I would hang out there, when I lived here I mean, I had this hopeful feeling. I would get excited, find broken toys in the closets and bottlecaps in the corners and shit under the fridge, and I would think about who used to live there and how things could be for us if we lived here, too. But when I moved in there, and started sneaking back in here, *I started noticing pieces of the things we'd left behind. And I realized that none of that garbage you find in corners means a damn thing."*

Jacki sits back down and thoughtfully kicks at the foot rest.

"So, what happened with your dad?"

"I don't really remember," he sighs. "He took me hunting when I hit 18. But it turned out we were hunting dogs instead of deer."

"Did you just say 'dogs'?"

"Yeah, strange dogs."

"Did you just say 'strange' dogs?"

"No, I said 'stray' dogs."

"Yeah, no, you didn't," she says.

Jack frowns and looks up at the ceiling, lost in thought again. Then she leans forward to take his hand but stops when the hunting chair creaks like it's going to collapse.

"Aren't you going to open your box?" she asks after a minute. "She seemed to think it was important."

"Not in here. That would feel like moving in again." After another minute he asks, "How does that saying go? 'Don't pick up strays' or 'Don't pick up strange?'"

"Don't pick up strangers."

In her pocket is a picture her daughter had recently doodled. One of Toni's teachers had sent it home with a note describing the disruption it caused and her resulting expulsion from the room. Toni had drawn six stick figures over top of each other in a swirling vortex of copulation, and it was clear due to the ease with which she was able to illustrate this scenario with a maximum of ten or twelve lines that she'd mastered this particular diagram after quite a bit of practice. Jacki had noticed some scribbles on Toni's arms lately, but nothing discernible. Jacki was going to yell at her, at least prescribe the same amount of shame she routinely dealt on the boys who drew such things in her own classroom. But she'd stared at the drawing too long before she had a chance to discipline her daughter, and she found the world around the damp, wrinkled piece of notebook paper, particularly the perfectly circular holes between the female stick figures' legs, fading into a blur. At that moment, she decided to drive to Jack's apartment and have sex with him. To exert some sort of authority on the situation.

But some time around his third or fourth rambling story, she's changed her mind again, satisfied that she could have if she wanted to, even more satisfied that, in at least one variation of today's events which remained nestled in her brain, she had gone through with this.

And he will never know. But she tells him another story instead, which she figures should be worth more, if they were to weigh them both.

David James Keaton

"There was this speaker at my school, and he was standing
there with a cane in the middle of the gymnasium, telling us
all how he broke his neck in a motorcycle crash, but it was
a 'weird break,' and it left him paralyzed on his left half
rather than his bottom half, and we all listened about how he
compared the new division of his body to a bagel, no, he said
it was like a spaghetti squash, cut down the middle, insides
rearranged with a fork, but sewn back up before consumption.
His book was actually called Spaghetti Squashed, now that I
think about it. So he talks about all this and how, before the
ice-cream truck smacked into his motorcycle and changed the
course of his life, he was just starting to get strong. Always a
skinny kid, he was worried he'd be short and scrawny forever,
and after growing six inches in as many weeks, he only had a
good three months of 'superpowers' before the wreck. And the
first thing he asked his dad when he woke up in the hospital
was, 'Will I be able to fuck? Play hockey? Travel to the moon?'
I guess he wanted to be an astronaut, too. So there wavering
on the foul line, we get to hear how he does get married,
and is presumably able to consummate it, how he is able to
play goalie for a fundraiser at least twice, and, finally, how
he's able to travel to Moon Township, Pennsylvania, which
was close enough, I guess. And when he gets to the part of the
story where he confronts the ice-cream truck driver to forgive
him, I couldn't take it anymore. I shouted out, 'Shut the fuck
up!' or 'No one cares!' or maybe it was 'Keep that shit to
yourself!' Something like that. I was ashamed - I'm ashamed
now - because I knew it was supposed to be this inspirational
tale, of course. But it all felt so strangely performative and
off-putting. I just couldn't understand why it was necessary to
share this trauma with anyone, including the ice-cream truck
driver, especially the ice-cream truck driver, even though that
part of the story was building up to be this big moment of
forgiveness or whatever. But shouldn't the ice-cream truck
driver have gone looking for his spaghetti ass and begged him
for forgiveness? I don't know. I can't explain it. He almost fell

366

back, so visibly struck by my comments, arms all noodly on his cane. I'm sure it's still a terrible memory for both of us."

"Hemiplegia. I've never seen it myself. But a body divided vertically cannot stand," Jack jokes after a second of processing. "I wouldn't dwell on it too much though. Kids say some crazy shit when they're young."

"What? No, this was two weeks ago."

They talk in circles another few minutes or so, and she finally leaves, shaking her head and chastising herself for making the trip. A little later, now that Jack's alone, he tears open the end of the box and dumps a dirt-caked animal skull onto the floor between his knees. He quickly turns out the light and runs to close the window. It takes him twenty long minutes for his fingers to find the skull with his hands and pack it back up. Then his fingers find Jacki's glowing digits in his pocket, and he listens to the electronic simulation of a bell ringing in his ear, waiting for her to get home, waiting for her to climb back into his telephone so they can have a real conversation again.

"Where do you think the phrase 'barking up the wrong tree' comes from?"

Highway. Next day. Jack and Rick are pulling up to a car wreck on the highway where a smoking dashboard is still kicking out Red Hot Chili Peppers' "Death of a Martian."

"This Martian ends her mission, the nova is over. She caught the ball by the mission bell. Chase lizards, bark at donkeys, the love of a Martian…"

Their ambulance's broken siren is still sputtering like a backfiring engine, and it mercifully drowns out the bass slapping in the song, an instrument that Jack once heard can cause irregular heartbeats after prolonged exposure to funk. Also, Jack is driving, so the ambulance has gotten up on two wheels at least twice on the way there. Even after Rick told himself Jack wouldn't be touching the steering wheel for another year at least.

But they do get there first. The typical response time for an EMT is 12 to 15 minutes. Jack and Rick get there in six. And even though two men are stuck headfirst in the windshield of each of the cars, skulls cracked and leaking like old Halloween pumpkins, Jack is getting between the job and Rick as usual, talking his ear off and risking another punch in the mouth.

"Get out of my way, man," Rick warns him.

"Listen, I open the box, and it's a fucking dog's skull. Did you hear what I said?"

"Are you kidding me right now? We've got two-"

"Yeah, I know. And I got us here fast enough to have this conversation. So let me have it. Plus, look at these guys. They ain't going nowhere. They need the Mikes for once, not us. But listen, I open the box, and this fucking skull comes rolling out! And there's no note, nothing. So I'm thinking the skull is a message, right? I think about it all night, and I almost called the cops, but the battery in my phone is dead, even though the battery is the size of a box fan. So instead I get the address off the box and get to my computer and start messing around online..."

Rick pushes past him and moves to check the closest body for signs of life. Once he gets a good look at the first driver's head and how much of it is missing, he starts moving as slow as his partner. Jack, however, is moving faster.

"...And I find out that someone bought this skull at some taxidermist, you know, for stuffed deer heads and whatnot. Only this wasn't stuffed with anything but dirt, so it must have been the cheapest skull they had. Probably a coyote skull, actually-"

"I thought you said it was dog."

"Dog, coyote, same difference! So anyway, I'm getting ahead of myself. I start with this return address and do an internet search, find the house it came from is actually this business. But to get the phone number of whoever lives

there, I have to pay ten bucks for one of those online private-
investigator scams? But I pay it, and this internet P.I. gives
me everything: the last five owners, a map of the house from
the county assessor's office, the cell phones of those last five
owners, even a list of all the names of the neighbors within
ten blocks and which ones, if any, are sex offenders. For just
ten bucks, dude!"

"That is a bargain," Rick agrees.

"Hold on, you'll see how much of a bargain in a second.
So, I get the guy's phone number who lives there and give him
a call, pedaling to keep my phone charged. He's not happy
I have his cellphone, which is, by the sound of the motor,
larger than mine, and apparently unlisted. Unless you have
ten bucks to spend! And we get in an argument about how
he can't reveal who bought the skull because of privacy or
whatever. And I'm going, 'You're not the fucker's doctor! Tell
me the name!' And he says the person that ordered it is a 'Jack
Grinstead.' And now I'm freaking out, thinking someone
charged my credit card or something to send me a skull and
fuck with me. So I tell him, 'I'm Jack Grinstead,' and now
he's even more suspicious and says I'm trying to pull some sort
of identity theft."

"I could see that."

"So the last thing he says to me is 'Check the people you
live with. That's the last thing I'm saying.' But I keep pushing,
and he yells, 'Whoever got this for you, it was either a gift or
a gag! And they're close.' And he hangs up. So I start going
through the rest of the online info, making sure I get my ten
bucks' worth."

Sirens are approaching, working sirens, not warblers like
their own, and Rick snaps back to work. He shakes Jack by
the shoulder to steer him to the other car.

"Great, man. Tell me about it later, okay?"

"No, listen, here's the thing. I'm checking the names of the
neighbors around there, and…"

Rick shoves Jack hard.

"Enough! Get the fuck to work."

"No. You have to hear this. I'm checking the names–"

Jack expected the punch long before it arrives, and he takes Rick's fist all the way to the ground with him, still talking around the blood pooling over his bottom teeth.

"And that's when I see his name. 'Derek Bromden. Registered sex offender.' Derek. Derek Bromden. Three houses down. Ring a bell?" Jack spits red.

Rick was going to hit him again, but now the bell is ringing.

"That's right," Jack says. *"Fucking Derek. That creepy old fuck we work with who jerks off into our lunch? Well, that's apparently the most normal thing he does."*

"So he's a sex offender. So what. That's like saying water is fucking wet."

"Not 'so what.' The skull! He sends me a skull… like he knows I know…" he trails off.

"Knows you know what?"

Then there's a groan from behind them, and they're both running. Jack goes for the second car. Rick back for the kit. The sirens are about one minute away now. Jack reaches the young man half in, half out of the back seat, wearing nothing but swimming trunks, lacerations all along his bare legs. Eyes wide, Jack runs past the boy and retrieves a twenty-dollar bill flapping against the nearby curb.

He flips it over and over in his hand, recognizes the ladybug he drew in as the seventh President of the United States.

He walks back to the boy and grabs him rough under his arms, propping him up against the side of the bumper and snapping his fingers in his face for attention. The boy groans.

"Is this yours?" Jack asks him. Snap. Snap. Snap. *"Hey! Where did you get this?"*

The boy blinks slow as Rick returns to crouch down next to them. Jack grabs the boy's face by the chin, and Rick sees a look in Jack's eyes that he's grown used to already. A look he's associated with Jack not doing his job.

"Where did you get this?" Jack asks him again, louder.

The victim seems to notice Jack for the first time.

"Huh?"

"Did you notice any dogs in the area?"

"Dogs?" the victim looks terrified and tries to get up, grimacing in pain from sliced tendons in both ankles.

"Jack!"

Jack ignores his partner and keeps up the interrogation as best he can, even though he's all out of questions.

"Are you a registered sex offender?"

The victim looks down the road at the flashing lights and parade of emergency vehicles, cops, paramedics, and firemen. Jack squeezes the boy's face like he's going in for a kiss, and Rick starts to pull him away. Then stops suddenly, stands, and walks off. He kicks around near the curb where Jack found the money, looking off into the bushes, confused. Jack gets up to join him and see what's drawn his attention.

"Something's wrong here," Rick says. "There's no way she's from the crash." Rick moves a tangle of weeds with his boot.

"Who are you-" Then Jack sees her.

Curled in the brush is the severed bottom half of a female, jeans bunched around her ankles, body missing above the waist. Jack blinks at what he's seeing, remembering back to when he was young and had to draw his own pornography, like most kids who couldn't buy any.

He'd start at the bottom of the girls, like this, and he'd be so eager that he'd draw everything too big so that she ran off the page, too. Right at the belly button like her.

Jack drops the money as if burned.

The police officers are snapping photos and taping off the area, as a particularly short officer asks Jack some questions.

"And you found the money where?"

David James Keaton

"Right there in the gutter."

"Why did you pick it up?"

"What do you mean, Officer…" Jack peers at his badge. *"…'Stansberries'?"*

"I mean, you stopped everything to grab this? *They don't pay you enough saving lives or what?"*

"It's a natural reaction. You see money, and you grab it."

"I don't know," the cop laughs like he just solved everything. *"I see two guys with their heads smashed in, and I'm moving toward them, you know?"*

"We were doing everything we could do for them."

"How long were you on site?"

"What time is it now?"

The officer looks at his watch.

"It's 6:37," he says.

"I don't know. But we got here first."

The officer lets the arm holding his notebook drop and they look at each other for a little while.

"What? You want a cookie?" the cop asks him.

"Well, where the fuck were you?" Jack asks back, and the cop moves on.

As Larry pushed through the concession stand, shoving through all the players, he screwed up the all-time high scores of at least three kids on the coin-ops. Larry noted the titles as he ran, *Pac-Man, Joust, Donkey Kong…*

The arcade games all had something in common, but he couldn't quite place it.

Then he eye-balled a gray door behind the counter, right as the entrance started swarming with patrons screaming for his blood. He heard barking in the distance, too, like in a prison-escape movie, right before some asshole got caught.

Then it hit him. If it was one thing these new games had taught Larry, especially those three big ones along the wall, it was that you could run really fast out off one side of the screen and then magically reappear on the other.

So he shouldered the door and crashed into blackness. Feet still red-lining, fully expecting to catch something hard and invisible in the face, he headed for a sliver of light coming from under a crack, and he threw his shoulder into that door, too. Then one more.

He was in a long room, longer than seemed possible from the outside. It was immaculate, white like a laboratory, like heaven in the movies, with the gentle swirl of a clicking film projector in the center, spinning like a windmill that brought life-giving water up from the earth, not to drink, but to wash over the faces of weary heroes, cowboys, even dying villains.

He was in the bunker.

"At 2:07 p.m., it is assumed that Officer Dwayne "Bigbeep" Bigby pressed his hand-prints into the suspect's face. This was likely to coerce him to go along with the robbery. These prints were discovered prior to autopsy when the only son of the coroner, Joseph McNutter, who was angry that he was forced to work the holiday, used a ballpoint pen to turn the outlines into two Thanksgiving turkeys. These turkeys were, as you all know, later matched with the sizable hands of Officer Bigbee.

"Approximately 2:10 p.m., Officer Bigbee gave Mr. Bells a purple plastic sword and told him to use this 'weapon' to intimidate anyone at the bank who balked at the colorful device around his neck. Angela Strongarm then gave Mr. Bells the nine-page note, which would put him on a scavenger hunt immediately after the robbery, where he searched in vain for clues to remove the bomb. Reassembled after the explosion, the note read, in part: 'Using your time attempting escape will leave you short of the 75 minutes needed to follow these detailed instructions.

Do not delay.' Earlier that day, a fake suicide note had already been mailed to local newspapers, claiming that Mr. Bells had lost days of sleep due to the noise of a dog park near his home. Side note: the stamp attached to the envelope displayed an obese, more mature Elvis Presley. This stamp was traced to the private collection of a local teenager named Amy Luck, whose involvement has yet to be determined…"

Evil had left the ramp, but in his head the announcer was declaring, *Evil has left the building!*

"…then at precisely 2:35 p.m., with the ticking bomb locked onto his neck, Mr. Bells drove to the ZNC Bank branch in the shopping center on Peach Street. Mr. Bells walked inside the bank, appearing oddly calm on the bank's surveillance cameras, even twirling chewing gum on his finger and attempting to blow bubbles, though his mouth was too dry. He quietly informed the clerk that he had an explosive device attached to his body, and then proceeded to show her the sword. He demanded $250,000, but received only $8,702. When Bells exited the bank, one customer followed him out, perhaps believing it was a hoax, clearly thinking something was odd about Mr. Bells' behavior, besides the plastic sword he wielded, the colorful contraption around his neck, and his inability to blow even a single bubble…"

Evil felt his headphones slipping. And even though he had a police dog clamped tight onto the handlebars of his dirt bike as he launched into mid-air, it was the loss of his true love's voice in his ears that distracted him the most, even more than what she was confessing, even more than her tone of indifference. This is what they called in sports, "taking your eye off the ball," and his landing would prove those coaches right.

* * *

"Jack's apartment building. Same night. Jacki stops in his hallway, debating which door to knock on all over again. *The girl or the lion?* she thinks. She picks the right one and gets the girl, who has mercifully switched from ice cubes to bubblegum. But working her words around the gum makes this girl's mouth stretch a little wider, and Jacki starts wishing for the ice again. Or the even the lion."

"How many times is she going to go back to his apartment?"

"Apartments."

"Apartments. It's getting ridiculous."

"It'll all make sense later. Just listen. 'He's not here,' says Bubblegum Girl, formerly Ice Cube Girl. She's wearing no pants and an oversized T-shirt again, this one with a pimped-out ambulance and the words: **'This Is How I Roll.'**"

"That's not what my shirt says."

"'Is he ever here?' Jacki asks, trying to look past her. 'Sometimes,' she says, cracking a bubble like a gunshot. 'What? You don't believe me?' Bubblegum Girl opens the door wide so Jacki can look past her. Jacki looks inside, reading the back of the girl's T-shirt instead. It says:

'Paramedics: It's Not That We Want You To Get Hurt. We Just Wanna Be There When You Do.'

"Are you going to actually write this on my shirt or what…"

"'Is this a one-bedroom or a two-bedroom apartment?' Jacki asks her. Bubblegum girl blows a bubble, but chews it up before it really has a chance to grow. 'Two bedrooms. Same as every apartment in the building. Same dimensions as a prison actually, which is crazy. Why do you ask?' 'I don't know, I just thought this apartment was bigger… or smaller… I can't remember which.' She backs up and turns away. 'Never mind. Thanks.' Then the door closes behind her, and she quickly walks to Jack's other apartment across the hall. She knocks on the door and waits. Then she tries Door Number Three. When no one answers, she turns the knob to find it unlocked and steps inside. Nosing around, she finds the second bedroom and turns on the light. Laid out on the bed are medical files, X-rays, an EMS flip-chart, and several field guides for dog breeds. Now nervous, she finds the closet and opens the door, and on the walls of the closet are rows and rows of photographs of women, mostly Polaroids, all young, attractive dark-skinned women asleep in hospital beds. All of the faces have red X's through them. Except for one in the middle."

"Holy shit."

"Right? Jacki looks closer, even though she doesn't need to, and verifies this is a picture of her, curled up in the twisted metal of the car crash six years earlier."

Crash site. Same night. Jacki is standing over her tree-stump with a flashlight. There's a ring of plants growing around the ragged edge, and she leans down with the light in her mouth to touch one of the bulbs. Not expecting the plants to move, she bites down on the flashlight when one of them does, sending it shooting out of her teeth as she jumps back in shock and almost lands on her ass.

Retrieving her flashlight, she leans over again, slower this time, and sees that the plants are young Venus Flytraps, most of them with their maws open, waving in the night air, eager for something to eat.

These things don't grow here, *she thinks.* Not without help.

Her attention is drawn to one of the traps that is closed, and she puts the bright end of her flashlight behind the bulb. The flytrap glows red, revealing a dark spot in the center of the half moon. She pinches it between her fingers, and feels the plant vibrate. It's a fly, she realizes. And even though she'd heard her daughter sing about how a fly can live for days in your belly before it's digested, unless you swallow the spider to catch it, she has to fight a scream every time it buzzes. As she calms her heart rate back down, Jacki presses the flashlight into her palm and turns it over to watch the back of it glow red, too.

She's honestly surprised to find no shadows hiding in her hand, but there is something in her belly, something that wriggled and jiggled and tickled inside her, just like the song promised.

Jack's Car. Same night. He's driving home. He's frantic, eyes practically pinwheeling in panic. A Jeff Buckley song, "The Sky is a Landfill" plays on his stereo.

"You sing in praise of suicide, we know that you're useless, like cops at the scene of a crime..."

Suddenly, he slams on his brakes and swerves to stop on a corner at the base of a grassy hill. An old man in shorts, sandals, and socks up to his knees is running a lawnmower off the edge of his lawn to spin around and head back up the hill. The old man sees Jack idling and putters to a stop, looking confused. Jack leans out the driver's window, waving and shaking his head.

"I'm sorry, I'm sorry," *Jack laughs.* "I thought you were out of control. I thought... I thought that was a baby carriage."

The man wipes sweat off his face, looking down at his lawnmower then back at Jack. He switches off the motor.

"Uh, nope. This ain't no stroller, chief. I was just running to finish this hill before it gets dark, my man."

"Sorry, the sun was going down, and I..."

"Ha! I think you've seen *The* Battleship Potemkin *too many times.*"

Jack frowns, shakes his head.

"No? How about *The* Untouchables?"

377

"Oh, yeah! The baby on the steps," Jack nods, and the old man seems slightly annoyed by Jack's recognition of one film instead of the other. "Anyway, my fault. Sorry to scare ya."

The old man smiles and reaches down for the starter cord. He sees Jack still staring.

"Don't worry, chief. This ain't an umbilical cord!" he sputters. "I don't blame ya. Every time I see someone jogging and pushing a stroller at the same time, I panic and think it's the Lindbergh baby kidnapping!"

The old man pulls the cord hard, and the lawnmower starts back up with a roar. Jack coasts away, embarrassed, changing stations on the radio until he finds an obnoxious DJ shouting out a weather report over a rock beat.

"...remember there's a sun delay on I-65 heading north..."

"What the fuck?" Jack asks the radio.

He ducks down to squint through the windshield at the sky. It's still gray and overcast, like it's been all day.

"Sun delay?" Jack says, fear growing in his voice. "What the fuck does that mean? Is the sun slowing down? "

"...so be careful rush hour drivers, if the sun is in your eyes, take it slow..."

"Oh."

Jack is worried that he's losing the ability to comprehend simple clues of his surroundings, something Rick's been telling him all week. He switches stations and finds The Who. Another fucking dog song.

"You were holding a greyhound in trap number one. Your white coat was shining in the afternoon sun..."

"Nope, too close to home, limeys."

He switches stations again and lands on Peter Gabriel's "The Rhythm of the Heat," right at the tribal drum solo part of the song. The drumming now playing catch with his brain, Jack is convinced the world has conspired to cause a breakdown. He turns off the stereo before he can argue with it anymore.

* * *

Hospital emergency entrance. End of the night. Jack walks through the double doors looking more like a patient than an EMT. He sees the two Mikes leaning against a wall in the middle of a loud conversation and heads towards them.

"...that's where the phrase, 'You can't teach a dead dog new tricks' comes from," Little Mike is saying.

"What's up, men," Jack interrupts, not really interested. "Seen Rick?"

"Ain't my turn to watch him," Little Mike says. "Hey, you're early for once."

"No," Jack sighs, rubbing his head. "I just couldn't remember if we were on or off tonight. I've been getting my schedule screwed up lately. Speaking of, what the hell are you two doing here?"

"Haven't seen Rick around at all," Big Mike says, ignoring the question.

"Hey, I'll go with you!" Little Mike offers, suddenly excited. "All you need is a getaway driver, right? You can do all your usual nasty stuff in the back."

"Yeah, no, thanks. That's kinda illegal," Jack laughs. "Wait, what stuff in the back?"

"What do you care about illegal?" Big Mike asks, sharing a glance with Little Mike.

"No seriously," Jack says. "What the hell are you guys doing here? Did you get a call? Any dead dogs on the road? Any dogs in your truck..." Jack trails off as he notices Derek working on some vomit in the corner of the emergency room with his mop. Big Mike turns.

"That's right," Big Mike laughs. "Take a good look. That's your future, homey."

"More like your futures," Jack says. Then, "What did you mean?"

"He used to work here, didn't he?" Little Mike asks no one in particular.

But Derek is suddenly there in front of them in three big steps before anybody can answer, finishing Little Mike's thought for him.

"That's right. I used to be one of you. I'm a motherfuckin' cautionary tale," Derek laughs. "Back when things were different. They only needed one of me for every two of you assholes."

"Bullshit."

"Yeah, you're right," Jack says. "Who needs two assholes?"

"No bullshit," Derek says, missing the joke, getting in Little Mike's face. "There was only one medic per vehicle, instead of a 'pair' of them like ya got now."

The Mikes roll their eyes at this.

"I'm telling you," Derek goes on. "It was hard back then, when you had to do it all. Give 'em mouth-to-mouth, check their, uh, blood pressure, play with the sirens, use black tape and rope instead of band-aids, all the while driving with our knees because our hands were so busy. It was a bitch. You ever see one of those street musicians playing the guitar with one hand, a tambourine with the other hand, a drum with his kneecaps, and a harmonica strapped to the front of his head like a football mouth-guard?"

"I love those!" Little Mike shouts.

"Well, that was me. That was all of us. And the ambulances were a lot smaller, too. Had a side-car like a motorcycle where you put the bodies."

"Shut the fuck up."

"They have something like that in England actually," Jack concedes, but no one hears him. He thinks about how recklessness has forever overshadowed true motorcycle skills.

"Anybody can jump a motorcycle," Evel Knievel himself once said. "The trouble begins when you try to land it."

That walking X-ray was a sage, he decides.

"Yep, it was a juggling act back then, that's for sure," Derek says wistfully, looking off into the distance, even though there's only blood and vomit and white walls.

"You are so fuckin' full of it," Little Mike says, head shaking. "You never were no paramedic. I remember your first day. Three years back. You were walking into the wrong rooms, bumping into shit with that same mop bucket. I thought you were drunk. It took a week before I realized you worked here. Twice I tried to put you on a gurney."

"Fuck you," Derek hisses, poking both Mikes in the chest in turn. "And don't think I don't know what you two are up to. I know you guys have been following me."

"What are you talking about, rummy?" Big Mike scoffs.

"I seen you. I seen you both. You were parked behind some pine trees, just down the street. I could see both your shadows. One big. One small."

"Uh… right," Little Mike says, turning to Big Mike and trying to pick up where they left off. "So, anyway, I bet the guy…"

Derek slaps their shoes with his mop to interrupt one last time, then wanders off, disgusted with all of them. He catches Jack watching him go and forces an expression of mirth that's something like a smile after a stroke. Jack just stares, lost in thought about what he'd found online about Derek in the sex-offender registry, trying to forget the face in the mugshot, frowning so hard his forehead looked injured. He remembered when he first heard Evel Knievel say, "Chicks dig scars," and how he was disappointed he wasn't saying, "Chicks dig cars."

The scars would have to be within reason, *he thought.* Like tastefully applied by the special-effects girl just around the jaw line, or the cheek bones, one sexy line through the eyebrow. Really, good luck with the chicks if half your nose is gone and they're reading your sinuses like tea leaves when you sneeze.

After a minute, Big Mike smacks Jack's shoulder hard to get his attention.

"Wake up!"

"So I bet the guy…" Little Mike is still saying to Big Mike. "…how much to make a dead dog shit?"

381

"You know what?" Jack claps his hands to stop him. "I need to confess something. Despite the subject matter of your conversations, you two walking disasters inspire me. You really do. For some reason that I'm sure is my fault and my fault alone, I find your babbling ripe with symbolism. Deep shit that usually applies to whatever I'm dealing with. You help keep my head on straight. It's like your fucking job!"

The Mikes look at each other, smiling but baffled.

"Except today," Jack continues. "Today, you win. Today I have no idea what in the holy hell you're talking about. But it doesn't matter."

Jack walks away.

"Hey! They can't all be gold!" Little Mike shouts after him, then turns back to Big Mike. "So, naturally, I'm knuckle deep in this Rottweiler's ass, right…"

Jack calls back over his shoulder.

"Hey, tell Rick I need to talk to him. Please."

"Outta gas, eh?" Big Mike smiles. "Told you the job ain't forever."

"Just not up for it tonight."

"Why not?"

"Don't you guys listen to the radio?"

"Nope."

"Nope."

"The sun isn't coming up tomorrow."

Then he's gone.

VIII.

The Last Projectionist – Special Weapons and Tactics –
Watching a Lumberjack Contest for the Wrong Reasons
– Henny Penny – Where the Rubber Hits the Road Is
Everywhere – Tony Baloney Has Eight Lives Left – The
Rap Is The Thing – To Protect and Serve Man! – Tastes
like Chicken Shit with a Badge – Remember That Dream
with the Ribcage and the Rubber Ball or Whatever? – Stick
a Needle in Your Blood and Your Blood's Gonna Scream
– Dyslexic Paramedic with a Dog Complex – Quadruple
Walker – Hell Comes to Heck Town – They Eat Kids like
Crackerjacks – Skins Vs. Shirts – The Biggest Shadow
Animal of All Time – Bardstown Therapist – More
Like Waiting for Godon't! – Evil Gets the Girl – Catches
Dreams… and Swallows – Redrum Makes the Best Ribs
– A Plastic Infinity – The Broken Siren Is Finally Back to
Normal – Daddyunclegrandpabrother – Bully Celebrates
Veterinarian's Day in the Hospital – Doppelgänger Radar
– Larry Steals Evil's Dirt Bike – Green Wire and Purple
Bubblegum

"I'm gonna stomp your head in the ground
if you don't stay out of my hen house
You dirty old egg-suckin' hound"
—Johnny Cash "Dirty Old Egg-Suckin' Dog"

"How did I get here?" Larry asked nobody in particular, shifting his movie to another arm so his nose won't bleed on it.

Along the white, concrete walls were movie posters. Huge, "four-sheets" they called them. He traced the word "Fly" but didn't recognize the name on the marquee below it. He knew the original and its sequel, of course, but this poster was too green.

"'David Cronenberg?'" Larry whispered. "Must be foreign. Or a different kind of *Fly*."

"Sort of foreign," came a voice behind Larry that rebounded off the poster. "He's Canadian. Which normally means nothing. But this guy is real different."

"Are you in charge here?" Larry asked the monster green fly like a madman.

"What do you mean?"

Now the voice was coming from the whirling mechanism in the center of the room. Larry stepped towards it right as a man appeared from behind the projector wheels. Larry gasped and clutched his reel to his chest like a Teddy. The man was big, wearing overalls and a leathery face, built like someone who did hard work with his hands. But he smiled like a grandpa.

"Where am I?" Larry asked.

"Where do you think you are?"

"I was playing *Joust*," Larry shrugged. "I guess I ran off the screen."

"No kidding," the leathery man said in a voice that made no judgments. "*Joust*, you say? Is that one of those games out there in the lobby, where they're riding the horses? I've played that one, I think."

"No, they're riding birds."

"Right. Birds. I've played that, too."

"You have?" Larry's ear for dialogue was listening close. He wanted to soak up every word, find or force all the meaning he could. "Did you win the game?"

"Nah, just wasted a quarter. I mean, what's that game all about anyway? I can't believe that these guys don't stop all this madness and step off their ostriches and…"

"And talk seriously about how weird it is that the borders of their world keeping sending them back to the same place?!" Larry finished his sentence, excited to be on the same page.

"Uh, right. Or maybe just shake hands and be friends," the leathery man laughed. "So, do you like my posters?"

"Oh, yeah. But the only movie of yours I've seen is *The Thing*," Larry admitted sheepishly.

"Ah, yes. I'm going to have to frame that poster one day," the leathery man said. "In fact, John Carpenter himself was in town doing a Q&A at the more reputable drive-ins, claiming that particular movie was an AIDS allegory. But we know better than that. Don't let that hot wire test fool ya." Then he whispered like it was a secret, "To tell you the truth, I was going to have Mr. Carpenter sign this poster, but I didn't want him to touch it. I'm a bit obsessive about them."

"Did you think he had AIDS?" Larry asked, panicked, thinking about green monkeys and green flies and that motherfucker Ronald Reagan doing nothing about it, and most of all, every movie he and Ronnie made but wished they hadn't.

"No," the man laughed. "But he had these yellow fingers. I'll bet he smokes. Hell, have you ever seen him? It looks like he's made of smoke!"

They stared at each other a moment.

"Can we all just put down our lances for a second?" the leathery man finally said.

"Can we?"

"You bet. Hey, can I ask you a question though? Is that movie you're holding onto for dear life from Mr. Gold? I heard we were doing a switchover, but I didn't think it was happening just yet."

"Switchover? What? The speakers?"

"No, you know," he said from the corner of his mouth. "The dirty movies."

"Um, I think so."

"Well, we're always the last to know!" the leathery man smiled, disappointed but unsurprised. "And I'm the last to go. Most people forgot about us, this noblest of vocations. And they forgot about this building, too, the guts of every operation. In all those old photographs of drive-ins, you never, never, *never* see the bunker. Everyone ignores the bunker, where the movie *comes* from, dang it, in favor of the screen. Right here is where the real-live movie gets spit out! It's just like everybody's obsession with those big cooling towers on nuclear power plants, the least important but most visually interesting part of the system. But the ugly little bunkers on both of these sites really hide the 'reactors,' the power source, and that's where the real danger lies." He stopped suddenly, reaching for Larry's movie reel. "So, that's for me then?"

Larry hugged his movie close, like a baby, but then held it out.

"Maybe. Sort of. Not really. More for me really. So… who are you again?"

"I'm the last projectionist. Don't be afraid, son. You see that screen out there? It doesn't have many nights like this left in it."

"What do you mean?"

The Last Projectionist's voice got a little deeper.

"If you shine too many movies on a drive-in screen, they'll burn into it forever. Like silhouettes at Hiroshima. So if that's gonna be the last movie, it better not just be some dirty movie. It better be goddamn good."

Larry offered up his baby, relaxing his grip. He knew it was more than that. But Larry's hands were empty, and the movie was already gone.

Then he felt like confessing stuff for some reason, and he told the projectionist his version of everything that had happened to him that day. His version left out the murders, of course, and maximized the rights over the wrongs. Maybe it was his years of directing commercials, but, impossibly, Larry sold him.

So the Last Projectionist told him his real name, something unremarkable really. And he told Larry that he didn't really need Larry's movie, that he already had Jack's copy. And he told him about the movie he'd just missed. *Spunkwater,* it was called. Takes place in the near future, he told him, but also years ago. About a guy who rapes three women, a mother, her daughter, and her daughter. "Mother sisters everywhere," he explained. And he told Larry how he thought it was going to be the last movie anywhere ever, so he took a pin and scratched his name into the credits so he could be in it, too.

"Look," he said. "Right there where it says, 'Derek the Orderly.' That's me. Seemed like a good name to chose. If it's one thing I am, it's fucking orderly."

Larry felt a little safer, blinked slower. Like his hard work was done.

"How did you do that?"

"I guess I'm more of the Last Projector than the Last Projectionist, if that makes any sense."

"Not really. You mean you think other people are as uniquely fucked up as you?"

"What? Are you saying you're just like me, boy?"

"Uh, no, not really. Not all all."

"Fine. I'll put your movie on," the Last Projectionist said.

"I thought you already did," Larry said, not feeling so safe again. He stared at the man, waiting for him to put his thumbs into his overalls like they did in the movies sometimes, but he never did. Instead he reached out and grabbed the reel spinning on the machine with one giant, red hand. It squeaked in protest as The Last Projector tap, tap, tapped one of the cells.

"There's your name, too. See that, Jack? You're one of the paramedics."

"I was a paramedic once. How did you know?"

"Were you good at it?"

"I'm better at this."

"I can see that," The Last Projector said, letting the reel spin again.

"Seriously. Pornography is important. Did you know that porn is the reason for the vast majority of our technological advances? The first thing printed on a printing press was the Bible. The second thing was porn. It's why you have a job."

"And what a job it is. I thank you for that. Can you think of any other place on Earth besides a movie where such a crowd will not only sit in silence, not only sit in reverence, but they won't think of anything else or wiggle in their seats? Churches can't even make that claim. And what church lets you stay in your car? Until they start doing that, a drive-in will have everyone beat. Judging by the noise outside, though, maybe it's not always going to be like that forever."

David James Keaton

"Yeah, no, it's fucking pandemonium out there. I think the reverence days are over."

"But you were good at your other job, too, weren't you, Jack? There's always that."

"Well, you've heard of doctors with a God Complex, right? I was the first paramedic with a Dog Complex."

"But not the first with dyslexia."

"Nice."

"I love it."

"Are you really going to put on my movie?"

"I said I'd put it on. And I'll put it on. I'll put on all your movies. It's my last day anyway," he shrugged.

"It's everyone's last day."

Three years ago. Jack's apartment.

Jack and some EMS trainees are having a party. Two guys on the couch are taking turns on Grand Theft Auto: Vice City, *trying to beat each other's time in the stolen-ambulance mini-game. In the corner, two girls argue over crossed arms. The* Scanners *soundtrack is on the record player, and Jack keeps scratching the needle back to the beginning.*

There's a heavy knock on the door, and Jack gets up to answer. One of the trainees on the Playstation tucks a joint into his pocket as Jack opens the door, and several men in SWAT-team uniforms quickly enter. One of them carries a long rifle with a scope, and this man closes the door gently behind him. One of the other men puts a hand on Jack's shoulder to hold him secure while he nods for the others to spread out, studying the walls of all the immediate rooms. Someone pauses the videogame during a destructive high point - the ambulance in mid-air, the protagonist running amok, fire everywhere.

"We need to map out your apartment," one of the SWAT team says.

"What?" Jack says. "Why?"

390

"There's a potential suicide across the hall, and we need to know how this apartment is laid out in case we have to go into that apartment fast."

One of the girls gets in his face, arms still crossed from her earlier argument.

"This is completely unacceptable," she begins. "I need to see some kind of–"

"All the apartments in this building are identical," another officer forcefully interrupts. "This won't take long. We're trying to save a life here."

"I can see that," the girl scoffs, tapping the bottom of her glass for the last stubborn ice cube. "With all your life-saving equipment and all."

Jack steps between them and gives the SWAT team a "go ahead" shrug. They continue their visual mapping of Jack's apartment, pointing out corners and making notes on the same kind of notepad Jack used to use for his horrible poetry back in undergrad. One stops to admire the scene on the television screen.

"I hope you get inspired to run around my street in your underwear with a chainsaw," the officer sneers. "Watch what happens."

Jack blinks in surprise.

"Are you talking to the television, sir?" he asks the officer sarcastically, and the SWAT member quickly walks away.

After they map out Jack's apartment to their satisfaction, there's apparently some time to kill, and three of the SWAT team stand in the middle of the party and begin practicing restraint and submission techniques. As they pretend to disarm themselves over and over, everyone at the party watches with confused half-smiles. Finally, one of the officers answers a call on his radio, and they quickly gather their gear to leave.

"What the fuck was that all about?" Jack laughs.

"Those motherfuckers watch too many movies about themselves," the girl with the ice cube giggles. Jack notices her for the first time, and smiles.

"Who is across the hall committing suicide?" she asks, clearly not concerned.

"His name is Larry something," Jack says.

"Now that's a terrible name," she laughs.

After an hour or so of waiting for some sort of action in the hallway, the party-goers get tired of peeking out the door, and the party winds back up. The guys from the couch start imitating the SWAT guys disarming maneuvers, every so often barking cop voices at the videogame avatar to "watch its attitude" when it pauses to ignite digital police officers with a flamethrower. Then, after rewinding their song one last time, Jack goes to lock his front door, just in case there are any more surprises. And that's when the sound of a gunshot smacks him in the face like a fish. He looks around and realizes no one else heard it. The needle scratches backward on the LP without Jack touching it, Howard Shore's string section in mid-frenzy.

Another gunshot, then a rip and a thud, not unlike someone's grocery bag bursting open. After a moment, Jack turns up the music.

The next morning, Jack tip-toes through the sleeping revelers and finds himself standing in front of the door across the hall, now covered in a mad tangle of crime-scene police tape. He checks the door, finds it unlocked, and steps inside. He relishes the feeling of the yellow criss-crosses snapping around him like a finish line.

The apartment is completely empty, except for a television with a broken screen sitting on a milk crate. In the shattered glass of the screen, Jack sees a flash of the girl from the party, the girl with the ice from the night before. She's filling the open doorway, naked, but when he turns, she's gone.

On his way out, his foot bumps a rolled-up canvas bundle in the corner. It looks something like a child's sleeping bag, but across the side, white stenciled letters spell out, "S.W.A.T." Jack throws the bundle over his shoulder and jumps when something metal clangs inside. Heart pounding, he reaches inside and pulls out the jumble of rods and crumpled *canvas. He shakes his head, embarrassed when nothing more dangerous than a small chair springs into existence at his feet like a disappointing magic trick.*

He leaves the chair in the center of the room and walks out.

Three years later, no one ever comes back to get it.

Jack leans back in the chair, kicking the bag out of his way. At some point, he changed the word "S.W.A.T." to "T.W.A.T.," which still gives him a laugh, but otherwise the apartment is exactly as the police and former tenant left it that night of the party.

Jack stands and walks to the closet. On the floor inside are several hospital charts and files: results for allergy, blood, and paternity tests. And stuck to the inside of the closet door are the photographs of about twenty dark-skinned women sleeping in hospital beds, names scrawled on some of them. One is labeled "Jacinto Ramirez."

All the faces have X's through them, except for Jacki's. The remaining pictures cover the walls completely, except for two squares where photos are missing. Jack touches the empty spaces with a confused expression. Then he slams the door and quickly walks across the hall to his other apartment, the real apartment.

Once home, he puts some tomato soup in the microwave, then jams six pieces of bread in the toaster and two more on top. Jack owns the largest toaster in production, but it's barely enough for the carb-loading his high-stress, high-energy job routinely demands. Due to this diet, and especially the action-versus-inertia ratio, paramedicine was one of the least healthy professions.

A girl comes out of the bedroom rubbing her eyes, a lathered toothbrush sticking out of her mouth.

"You still live here?" she asks around a mouthful of foam.

"*Sort of,*" Jack mumbles, still staring at his toaster. He considers moving it across the hall with his T.W.A.T. chair. "You done in the shower?"

"Yep! Pity though. I get all of my best ideas in there. Guess what I decided to do!"

"Shut up. Everyone always says that," Jack sighs. "And if that were the case, why is it all I ever come up with in the shower is trying to turn my dick into a wristwatch?"

"That's the one thing I miss with you always gone these days," she laughs. "Not the 'watches,' but your long showers. Oh, and all the soap sculptures you'd end up leaving in there."

"You liked those, huh?"

"I liked your series of Laryngoscope blades you'd make, back when you were still quizzing me for the tests."

"Pediatric, infant, and neonate! The differences were subtle, too. Well, about as subtle as you can get with soap. Good eye."

"No, they were perfect. You helped me pass the test. To be honest though, they looked a bit like those old Magill blades the vets use, but, hell, it was fun when the soap was still asking me questions in the morning before the quiz. Kept me sharp."

Caught up in the memory, Jack puts his hand on hers. Her hand is cold, as always, even when she's not eating ice. She moves her hand away and grabs a handful of envelopes off the top of the refrigerator.

"Here, your mail is piling up."

"Thanks." Jack tries to avoid her eyes.

"Don't you want 'em?"

He says nothing.

"Well, maybe you should take a peek, Jack," she says. "Besides not paying shit on any of our bills, looks like you owe money across the hall, too."

"What?"

The toast pops up like a gunshot, and Jack finally looks at her, startled. He snatches the bills away and chews on a piece of bread while she pushes past him to spit in the sink.

"No wonder you aren't paying us," she says. "We thought you were squatting over there, but the landlord stopped by and said he talked to the bank and, based on the credit card number you gave to put a hold on that suicide apartment or whatever, he figured out you've been using different credit cards and different names to hold these units indefinitely. Something about backing out at the last minute so it never gets rented?"

"What? No, I-"

"Sounds like the worst scam in history! Why would you even do it?"

"I'm not. I mean, he's wrong. That's not why." *Jack spits a piece of stale bread past her into the sink.*

"The landlord also said you must be doing this to store something over there because you're never going to actually move in, or move out, or move on or whatever the fuck it is you're doing."

He walks to the sink to flush down the bread, and she turns him around by the shoulders. "Jack, everyone wants to know exactly what the fuck you're doing."

He shakes loose.

"So what is it?" *she asks.* "You building a mountain out of chicken wire and mashed potatoes to land a spaceship? You got meaningful quotes all over the walls? Heads in the freezer? One of those serial killer shrines with newspaper clippings and candles and yearbook photos of your third-grade girlfriends?"

Jack tries another corner of toast to buy some time between questions.

"No?" *she asks.* "Am I close?"

He chews and stares at her. He eats almost the whole thing, and when she's walking away, he finally speaks.

"Hey, thanks for fixing the letters on my bag, by the way. They were fading."

She turns with her hands on her hips, mirroring his smile like infants learning social skills. Jack slaps the bills back on top of the 'fridge, causing a tower of dog breed books and field guides to trees to tumble over. Still staring at her, he reaches into the freezer and takes an ice cube out of the tray to suck on. She shakes her head, puts her toothbrush behind her ear, then takes the ice cube away from him.

"Make sure you fill those up. I'm the only one who ever does."

She smiles and walks into the living room to turn on the TV. The bizarre lumberjack championship is on again. Jack laughs, still crunching ice.

"Holy crap, this shit has been on all week. How the fuck do you win? Does anyone ever win?"

On the screen, two women are standing on logs and furiously chopping through the wood between their own feet. His roommate peers around the corner for a look.

"How come they don't chop off their toes?"

"Would you care?"

"Sort of."

"You'd watch until you saw someone loose a limb at least, right?"

"What? Why do you care?"

"You're doing it for the wrong reasons," *Jack says, sounding uncertain.*

She barks a laugh.

"Wait, wait, wait. I'm watching the lumberjack contest 'for the wrong reasons?' And what are the right reasons? You sound like those assholes who defend NASCAR saying, 'If you're waiting for a wreck, you don't deserve to be a fan!' Well, who doesn't?" *She's laughing louder now.* "And now you're back over here after being missing for weeks, all like, 'You are not a real lumberjack tournament fan!' Fucking nuts, dude."

"Forget it," *he says.*

"No, please, tell me, what are the right circumstances to view this contest?"

396

Jack turns back to the action, watching husky women swinging their axes faster and faster. He doesn't hear the chopping or his roommate anymore as the motion of their chopping grows too blurry to follow. Then she reaches past him to change channels, and Jack snaps back to reality. The TV ends up on one of the animal channels, and three dogs are running on logs in a swimming pool. Jack rubs his eyes.

"Jack, one question," she asks, not laughing anymore.

"Huh."

"Who's the girl? She keeps coming by, looking for you."

Jack says nothing.

"She's not your type."

Amusement Park. Same night. Jacki is sitting in the dark, back on the fake Model-T they rode for Toni's birthday, the same day Anthony disappeared, the same day of the big brawl that ended up on the news. She reaches into her purse and pulls out two small flashlights, the kind you buy for your keychain, and she places them on the ends of the wooden dashboard, pointing them off into the dark, down the track. She clicks her new headlights on and off, watching the rays cut through the fog as she thinks about driving too fast and songs on radios ending too soon. Then a figure walks between the beams, giving her heart a punch in the chest.

It's Jack, walking fast towards her. She's still gasping when he leans on her window, grinning.

"What are you doing here?" he asks.

"What are you doing here?" she asks, heart still hammering.

"I asked you first."

"I came here to be alone."

"Me, too! How did you get in here?"

"Good question," she says. "You first."

David James Keaton

Jack opens the door to climb inside, reaching forward to angle one of her little flashlights so that it points to the tops of some nearby trees.

"What are you looking for up there anyway? Is the sky finally falling?"

She doesn't answer, instead trying to think of Chicken Little's real name. She remembers it has money in. He points the light at the nearby fence instead, looking for holes.

"I thought these were real headlights for a second. I actually thought you were going to drive away in this thing. Like in a real car. Did you try to start it…"

Jack is fumbling with the fake dashboard instruments, just like Anthony did, and Jacki slides away from him on the seat, sick to her stomach.

"Did you follow me, Jack?"

He doesn't answer.

"You can sit here," she says. "But only if you don't talk about-"

"Listen," Jacks interrupts. "I know you don't trust me, but I need you to hear this. I think that there's a rapist out there, and he's both you and your father's daughter. I mean, you and your daughter's father. Something like that. Do you have an abacus on you? Motherfucker's nuts, is my point."

"Stop. Just stop. You can sit here if you don't talk about my cursed family tree for five seconds. If you don't sound fucking crazy for a whole minute."

"Fine."

Pause.

"Okay, I'm all wound up though," he says, unable to stop himself from ruining things. "So how about I talk about me instead? You want a story where you can judge me, so we're even? Okay, here's one where I look bad, but it's for a good cause. Just like now. Long time ago, a couple girlfriends ago, me and whoever were driving on a night like this, and while she was screwing around with the knobs on the radio, she hit this kid on a bicycle. Or maybe it was a tricycle. Whichever

398

is worse. Either way, one minute she's messing with the static between stations, next minute, boom. A bike rolls over the hood, tire squeaking across the glass, spokes scrape the roof, and then the kid's gone. She was all hysterical, of course, so I jumped out and found the bike glowing red in the taillights, everything facing the wrong way, tire still spinning. The kid was nowhere in sight, but we were right next to this ditch, you know? So he likely got knocked down there. And that's when she got out, too, and I thought our date would be ruined if she saw. I had a great night planned, and we still had an hour before we were even close to the party. So I kicked the bike under the car. Then I ran over to the ditch and acted like I was watching the kid ride away. I was like, 'Damn, tough little bastard. Not even a limp!' I mean, 'Not even a flat tire!' And she believed me, not knowing the bike was right by her feet while I'm saying this, and the kid was probably right down there in the drain water, steam still chugging out of his mouth. And when she calmed down, we got back in the car, and I thought, 'If I pull this off, I swear I'll tell the truth someday.'"

"Did you tell the truth someday?" Jacki asks, barely listening.

"Right about then, the back tire rolled over the handlebars. If she knew, she gave no clue."

"She knew."

Jack keeps going. He's got the details down pretty good now, like a good, practiced joke.

"I was gonna write a story about it," he says. "Get it off my chest. But it would be my first story ever, and she'd know something was up."

"I don't believe a word of that," Jacki says after a minute.

"Why not? That wasn't easy to admit, you know? How do you not feel closer to me right now?"

"You should have someone write a short story about someone writing a short story about this. Then you'd be in the *clear. You know, getting it off your chest. Then no one has to listen to it again."*

"Yeah, maybe."

Jacki shakes her head at him then straightens out the flashlight Jack moved.

"Sorry. Okay, what else ya got? You know, this is the most I've heard you talk about yourself since-"

"Well," Jack says, excited, interrupting. "I was thinking that maybe this rapist was originally attracted to your mother, then later to you because of the resemblance. It makes perfect sense if you look at this..."

Jack frantically digs a photograph out of his pocket. Jacki spins her tiny flashlight on it. It's Jacki's mother. She snatches it from his hand.

"I told you to give that shit a rest! You know, the only thing creepier than your theories is when you tell me one and POW! you suddenly pull a picture of my mother out of your pocket like a fuckin' rabbit."

"Funny you should say 'rabbit...'"

"Get out."

Jack is genuinely confused.

"I'm just trying to save-"

Jacki puts both flashlights back in her pockets where they continue to glow.

"You're really getting scary. At first I thought — You know what? Forget it. You keep talking about the same shit *no matter how many times I ask you to stop. You follow me out here with this mission to 'save' me from-"*

"I'm sorry!" he pleads. "It's just... I'm noticing things I've never noticed before. On the job. Things that could have been there all along. These things have gotta be connected."

Jacki opens her door.

"I'd love to be a fly on the wall at this job of yours, Jack. While someone's coughing up blood under a tire, you're probably poking a dead frog saying, 'This is all wrong...

someone get me my fingerprint kit and the astrology page. Anyone know what today is?'"

"What is today?"

"You're nuts, Jack. Stay the fuck away from me. I mean it."

"A fly on the wall," he mutters. "At my job, sometimes there are hundreds of flies on the walls…"

She gets out of the Model-T, and he follows her.

"Jacki, wait. You don't really want me to go, do you?"

"Let me ask you this," she says. "While we're still talking about 'flies,' do Venus Flytraps grow around these parts? I mean, on their own, wherever, like Kentucky, Florida, Pennsylvania, anywhere in the wild?"

"I have no idea," he frowns. "Hollywood maybe? Shit's weird out there. But I'm not convinced you don't believe this stuff I'm telling you. This stuff about Toni. You already told me you remember what happened at the wreck. If that's true then why don't-"

"I don't know what I remember anymore!" Jacki says, patience gone. "Except one thing. I remember one thing from that night." She stabs a finger in his chest. "I remember you."

"Of course you remember me. I was the one who took you to the-"

"'Three more minutes and it never happened.'"

"Yes. That was me. We've been all through this. But I told you that was me. It's so simple. It really is." He's begging now. "I covered up the evidence of your rape. I thought I could make it so it never happened. What's wrong with that? Nothing."

Jacki is walking away, and Jack climbs back into the car to try and start the engine.

"I didn't ask you to do that!" she yells. "If that's what you did. And if that's what you did, you probably also destroyed any chance of anyone catching this monster for good, this man that only you swears is still out there."

"But I'm so close," he says. "If I could just-"

David James Keaton

"Jack, I don't give a shit. That's what you don't realize. You think you saved me, but I didn't need saving."

"You did. You still do."

Jack finds the starter cord and gives it a yank. Jacki's backing away as the lawnmower engine starts popping. She gets one of her flashlights out again, and aims it at his face. He holds up a hand, squinting.

"Let me ask you a question, Jack. If you had the choice, if you could choose whether your girlfriend or wife or mother or daughter or any female in your life was raped or killed, what would you do?"

Jack squirms in his seat. It's a question no man should answer. At least not quickly. Which is exactly what he does.

"Raped! But I don't understand what-"

"Raped, huh? Okay, now, would you rather she was raped or had one of her hands cut off?"

"Raped?" Jack says after a second. *"What's your point?"*

"Shhh. Last question. Would you rather she was raped or had one of her fingers cut off?"

Jack hesitates. Then he hesitates some more.

"That's exactly what I'm talking about," Jacki says, clicking off her light and turning away.

"Hold it!" he yells. *"Do I get to pick what finger?"*

"Bye, monster."

Jack steps on the accelerator, and his Model-T rebounds against the rail, sending him in the wrong direction.

"Hey, are these 'bumper' cars? Or can we take this thing on a real road?"

"Bye, Jack!" she yells over her shoulder. *"Think about what I just asked you sometime."*

Jack fights against the steering wheel, still trying to follow her, still trying to get the last word.

"Seriously, which finger?! You realize humans don't even use their little fingers anymore? In a hundred years they'll be gone completely. We'll have three fingers and a thumb, just like in the cartoons. That's the only reason I got that one

402

wrong. I was trying to figure out if you were talking about the little finger. That's why I hesitated! 'Cause losing that one is like losing your little toe… meaningless really…"

As Jacki wrestles with the hole, she bends to crawl under the fence and Jack is still rambling in the dark. She shines her flashlight through the cracks between her fingers, studying her blood in the glow, looking for cuts, looking for answers.

"How many times do I have to say this shit?" she asks no one, clicking off the light, leaving Jack to fight the car like Anthony did.

At home that night, Jacki struggles to close a broken window blind, hoping her daughter doesn't see their newest cat, "Tony Baloney," rubbing his head on the glass and begging to be brought inside. Toni is directly under the window, taking batteries from the television remotes to power her yellow and black "Blurby." It was a fuzzy, electronic creature, not quite a cat, not quite a dog, certainly not one of those ridiculously expensive Furbys. More like a bumblebee crossed with a monkey if anything, and it never shut up once it got going. Deciding the cat is the lesser of two evils, Jacki tries to take the hideous mechanical gremlin out of her daughter's hands before it begins its indecipherable chatter. But it's too late. The creature stirs, heavy-lidded eyes opening.

"Doo-moh ay-ay kah!" it practically screams. Outside, Tony Baloney howls.

"Fuck," Jacki says.

"Loud sound! Doo-may-ta!" it warbles.

She tries to stop her, but Jacki's daughter is already letting in ol' Tony Baloney, the latest stray they'd been feeding, apparently to increase the likelihood of more random cat attacks in their home. The mewling Blurby, however, Toni only "fed" about once a year, when she noticed or nudged it. This "feeding" consisted of letting its horrid plastic beak suckle a finger tip, a ritual Toni loved.

And the yellow beak is pulsing on Jacki's little finger before she can stop it, and instinctually, Jacki spikes it like a football. The Blurby squawks, seemingly in pain, but in all English this time instead of Blurbish, a carbon copy of Furbish, really, the only thing the counterfeiters got exactly right.

"Aah! Worried!"

Toni gasps, then starts to cry. But instead of stopping the toy's whelping, the outburst causes the toy to make even more horrible sounds. And the cat locks onto this abomination rolling across the floor, motors spinning the ghastly ears like radars, buzzing loud like hornets, and Tony Baloney poofs out to twice his size, proving the only thing a cat hates more than a Furby is apparently a cheap-ass knockoff. Toni goes to step over them both, and the cat's ears flatten as it hisses. Toni panics, and it begins to back her against the television. The toy seems to find this amusing.

"Kah toh-loo loo-loo!" it giggles.

Jacki studied the Furby Phrase dictionary online when her daughter first got the damn thing, so she understands this particular phrase. "Big fun," is what it is saying. And this is enough for Jacki to decide today is as good a day as any to stomp the beast forever into silence. She brings her heel down hard, feeling first the mechanism snap that registers a child's fingers pressing into its fuzzy belly, then the damaged toy stops speaking any discernible language at all and just starts warbling nonstop.

"Wah-wah-wah-wah-wah-wah-wah-wah…" it burbles, one eye closed, one half open, beak quivering. This is all too much for the cat, and when Toni tries to run to save the toy, a panicked Tony Baloney locks onto the pink meat of her leg, teeth and claws flashing.

Toni screams. Jacki stomps. And the toy just hums and hums.

Then something clicks in her daughter, and she kicks the cat free with one foot and raises the other high.

"No!" Jacki shouts, just as Toni brings her small foot down

on the cats spine, snapping it with an ugly twist of her heel. Tony Baloney begins to run for the open door, screeching, dragging its back legs as its urine splashes, and Jacki runs after it, tipping a bag of groceries near the door. The cat disappears under the porch, hissing in the dark, and Jacki comes back inside, not knowing what kind of meltdown to expect from her child. A can of shredded chicken rolls lazily across the floor.

A little chicken? The sky is falling! *she thinks, trying not to laugh as she picks up the split paper bag.*

But Toni is quiet. She's rubbing her leg absently, silent tears already drying on her cheek. The toy sits on the floor between them. Broken but still talking.

"I like to dance, too," it offers as a solution.

Jacki doesn't know how to turn it off, and she collapses on the floor in defeat, crying freely now. This is the first time her daughter has seen her cry, and she's ashamed, helpless. Jacki wishes she could be relieved when her daughter calmly takes the toy into the other room and does something to stop its electronic voice and clockwork heart for good.

But she's not.

Evil only saw the tail end of what looked like a mangy cat robot being murdered on the giant screen, but he heard enough children crying about it, and it started to get him rattled. Picking up speed and weaving through the parked cars, he reached past the snarling dog still hanging on by its mouth and pushed play on his stereo. It was Billy's tuneless croak that began rapping over his scene, and Evil almost didn't recognize it.

"I pour whiskey in computers that try to get greedy... got icicles in my beard like R.J. MacReady... wear my cowboy hat sideways on the bottom of the world... crazy fuckin' Swedes throw grenades like a girl..."

Then Larry crashed through a door directly in front of Evil's dirt bike, head on a swivel, trying to regain his bearings, as a cop was suddenly stuck to Larry's shoulders like a magnet. Impossibly, all of them were near the playground now, and the man piggybacking the officer plowed through a gaggle of mothers gathering up their broods when a bubblegum machine surprised Larry's knees out of nowhere and the glass ball imploded into shards and rainbows. This wave of color washed over Larry's shoes like he was a giant in a children's ball pit. Then the two of them pedaled in midair for a split-second like a cartoon, and Larry realized it wasn't bubble gum they were ice-skating through after all, but Super Balls.

Oh, shit.

Evil saw all of this in his peripherals, and he would have applauded if it wasn't for the dog and the deadlines and the girl he still had to impress.

With all this action around the playground, no one was really watching the big screen anymore. So when the movie finally went black altogether, there were no howls of complaint, no car horns honking. Instead, the remaining people that hadn't headed for the bottleneck at the exit started their engines and turned their headlights onto the action near the monkey bars. The spectators were torn between this sudden double-feature of a cop riding a man like a horse through a wave of bouncing rubber balls, and a kid on a dirt bike tearing ass through the chains of the swing set with a growling German Shepherd hanging off his handlebars.

Most watched the kid and the dog. He had the better soundtrack.

"...*watching* Let's Make a Deal *too many times to count... fuck this tape, I know how it turns out... all that's left of my posse are bloody shirt labels... don't dump spaceship parts, you'll scratch the pool table...*"

But Evil's bike was beginning to sputter in defeat as the dog bit hard enough to throttle his rubber grip back down. Evil was considering bailing out at the sand box.

But then he saw the ramp again. And now it was lined up perfect.

And above it all was Bully.

Evil saw her standing tall, taller than she'd ever been, up high on that weird concrete bunker with the fluttering eye of the film projector dancing between her feet. Her hands were at her sides, and he knew, even with the insanity going on around him, that for the first time, she was only watching him.

Evil grabbed the dog's snout and cranked it forward on the throttle. The dog yelped, and teeth peeled back the rubber on the handgrip, exhaust shrieking like pertussis and billowing like a swamped outboard, and stones fishtailed high into the sky behind him. He was amazed how disciplined the K-9 officer was. It still hung on tight. In fact, now it was chewing the rubber, sawing off chunks into its jaws, and Evil figured he had only a couple seconds before it ate his whole damn bike.

Officer Bigby, who had been laying low and letting the dogs do all the work, suddenly recognized Evil and realized he was about to lose his quarry. So he headed him off on the other end of the slide, then got lucky with the dog distracting him and snagged Evil by the face, a thumb finding his nostril and a pinky finding his ear. Bigby started to lift him up off his seat, and the bike's back tire swerved in protest, losing its grip on the road. Bigby threw an elbow to smash the stereo and stop the boy's song, but he elbowed the dog instead. It chewed faster.

"...on Commodore 64's watchin' cells get devoured... back in the kennel, dog splits open like a flower... stick a needle in your blood and your blood's gonna scream... stick a needle in your blood and your blood's gonna scream... someone in this crib ain't what he seems..."

Watching the dog, Evil could see what teeth and a little dedication could do, especially teeth as clean and strong as Evil's after his new regime of mouthwash five to seven times a day (he still never left his house with it swishing in his mouth, however. That would be like running out the door twirling a loaded gun). Evil waited until Bigby's forearm started sliding down for the chokehold, and he aimed for the tattoo, but missed by about a foot, chomping down tight to answer the eternal question:

How hard is it to bite through bone?

It turned out it was the easiest thing in the world really. That night, Evil discovered the only reason people thought bones were strong was because we were afraid to bite our own fingers hard enough to snap them off. Evil found out bones weren't shit. Shit was much harder to bite through. He sang along with Billy, even though it was muffled around his meal.

"...someone creepin' 'round and trashed the bulldozer... keep your enemies close but your aliens closer... the only bitch in the movie likes cheatin' at chess... that puddle on the floor? 'It ain't Fuchs,' I guess..."

He bit through three of the cop's fingers, the three good ones a cop needed. And as his teeth sunk in, and his mouth overflowed with copper, he imagined Bigby, years from now, struggling not just to hold his gun, but to even make a pretend gun with his hand. Bigby bellowed, and his forearm slipped and he rolled off the side, hot metal cracking him upside the eyebrow. Suddenly free, Evil got control of the bike, and the back tire finally bit the ground, and Evil headed for his ramp, chewing all the way. Tasted like chicken shit. Chicken shit with a badge.

He weaved through a couple more cars, heading for the tow truck near the exit. The congested line reminded him of summer construction on the highway, when every vehicle was idling and miserable, and he'd zip along them in the ditch while they glared. Sometimes he tried to imagine which driver was the angriest. He knew that somewhere in that line of a hundred steaming cars was one person gripping their steering wheel harder than anybody else.

But today that was every car. And now they were getting out, a mass of humanity pressing in, blocking his path. A sweaty crowd of screaming spectators, thick as mayflies used to be on the highways. They grabbed at his head, his arms, his new favorite dog who he swore was singing, too...

"...*Palmer smokin' blunts big as a brick... that shit on the poster ain't in the flick... ain't gonna rest till we burn down the whole station... Quaker Oats shrugs, 'That ain't dog. That's imitation...'*"

A little boy tried to climb onto his seat, and Evil caught the child's face in his hands and yelled.

"Run, kid! Tell everybody! The Police Training Manual? *To Protect and Serve Man?!* It's a cookbook! It's a cookbook!" Then he laughed so hard he choked on it.

No, it was just more hands in his mouth. But way too many to eat, and his bike was stopped cold in the dust as they swarmed him, still a good thirty feet from the finish line.

On the other end of the playground, Bucky Balls, still stuck tight to Larry's back and trying for the ol' L.A. choke hold, too, stopped fighting for a second to watch the action over Larry's shoulder. He saw an old man in a wheelchair, skinny arms pistoning his way into the fray, and Bucky's eyes went wide when he noticed the spiders all over his face. The wheelchair bumped into Larry's ass, and Bucky tried to ask him a question.

"Wait a minute, sir," he started. "Aren't you..."

Then most of Bucky's head exploded into chowder from the ears on back, christened by Officer Dwayne B.

Bigby (last name pronounced "big bye"). His first lethal bullet. First any bullet.

Another bullet flipped a child's swing over and up like a duck at a shooting gallery. Then another bullet flipped a child. Bigby had all the medals to prove his marksmanship in case anyone ever asked, but while shooting at Evil's disappearing dirt bike, he'd just discovered what happens when you try to operate a gun with your two smallest remaining fingers.

It affected some stuff.

More gunfire erupted, and at first Larry thought it was more cops. But the bullets were coming from the cars, and the arms coming from the cars were tattooed. Homemade bullshit mostly, illegible, except for one, a rash splatter of black ink surrounding a sketch of a broken arm in a sling, advertising something called a 'podcast,' which was very strange, not just because it sounded like some sort of horticulturist's splint and neither of the bearer's thumbs were remotely green, but also because when the body was exhumed decades later for reasons unrelated to this incident, an investigator would become convinced this tattoo referenced a form of entertainment derived from technology that wasn't widely available until 20 years after the man's death.

Out of time or not, these men behind driver's-side doors were here now, protecting their families, sliding along hoods like pros from half a decade of *Dukes of Hazzard* reruns, gunfire popping off in all directions, even a compound bow or two.

Larry was suddenly convinced that the new John Carpenter remake of *The Thing* was much more popular than the bad reviews suggested because, in their panic, people seemed to be targeting every goddamn dog in the place. These emotions were infectious, ongoing, and very easy to maintain in the midst of so many bouncing rubber balls.

But Larry decided Bigby must have been a big *E. T.* fan instead, because he was keeping his shit together a little better. In fact, like a lazy bolt of lightning, Bigby seemed to be moving more steadily, almost as if he was seeing everything unfolding in slow-motion, finally, after years of abuse from fellow officers, recognizing the intricate and idiotic workings of the two young terrorists' plan to simply make all branches of law enforcement look foolish. It wasn't that complicated. There was no bomb. There was never a bomb.

That was it! Bigby thought. *I'm a real detective!*

Then he heard his name, pronounced wrong as usual, coming from the curly hair of a child near his boots, and he commandeered the boy's headphones. In his cauliflower ears, Bigby heard the helium voice of his original suspect describe his every movement... in a very judgmental tone:

"Officer Bigbee watched the entire incident with binoculars from his nearby squad car, and when the call came over the radio, he sped home, empty-handed. But at his residence, Angela Strongarm waited, and when Dwayne Bigbee returned without the money, she assumed Bigbee had double-crossed her and simply hid the cash along the route home as he feigned distress over his missing K-9 unit, 'Gretel.' Officer Dwight C. Bigby was questioned as a possible accomplice to Bigbee, due to their dogs' resemblance, but both were subsequently released. Angela jumped into the squad car and headed toward the bank, driving erratically, occasionally stopping to search weeds along the median. Witnesses notified authorities, and as Angela Strongarm searched for the money and Officer Bigbee ran down the highway, presumably after his car, Mr. Bells' life continued to tick away. Or so he thought. Using the nine-page letter as a guide, Bigby tried searching for clues. After the bank, his first stop was a nearby McDonald's drive-thru, where he thought the first item in the scavenger hunt would be the prize in the second of three Happy Meals he would purchase. But in an attempt to save time, he only bought two such meals, which he consumed. It is then that we believe Officer Bigbee began constructing his own device out of guilt..."

I didn't do that...

Horrified, Bigby began to understand that just because one bomb was a fake, it didn't mean the others were, too.

He held the headphones tight against his head and ran to the nearest car. He smashed the drive-in speaker through the driver's side window, then reached in to press the heel of his hand against the horn. He needed everyone's attention, even civilians. He could explain it all to everyone right now, if they'd just stop fighting. He honked and honked to calm himself. A horn still felt like home to Bigbeep, and he even tried tap, tap, tapping out a message in Morse Code, a message from his childhood which, as always, explained every goddamn thing that was happening if people would just bother to listen.

Sadly, everyone was already honking their horns even harder than his, either stuck in the exit line or angry at Bully's gigantic, happy-dancing legs now blocking the projector beam of the movie. Even though the movie was over, everyone hated shadows on a screen. Bigby turned up his headphones as he honked faster.

"...at 3:00 p.m., Mr. Bells was spotted at a particularly long traffic light, trying to remove a key from the back of a toy robot and periodically holding a cheeseburger up to the sun. When they removed him from the car at gunpoint, they saw the device on his neck and were reminded of the hoax the week prior. He wielded a plastic sword..."

Then a little girl in lime-green pajamas slipped from her parents' grip so she could chase one of the rubber balls. She caught up with a red one, and she put it in her mouth.

And she choked. For a second, this changed everything.

* * *

The screaming subsided a bit, civilians putting down some weapons. Spectator's hands untangled from Evil's face, his arms, the scruff of his new dog's neck, and they let his dirt bike's back wheel touch the ground again, pick up speed, aiming for the elusive ramp as the crowd ran to help the little girl instead.

The dog was still locked tight on the accelerator, but now it was helping.

"I am the last gladiator," Evil mumbled.

Evil was riding so fast he swore he broke the sound barrier. But it was just the cassette getting caught on the tape heads for a moment. He smiled, remembering his dreams of the rib cage and the red rubber ball, finally understanding what it meant. He turned his dog's head harder on the throttle, but stroked its fur lovingly at the same time. The dog snapped like a gator to get better grip, and its tooth caught a meaty chunk of his thumb. Evil didn't even blink. Sirens screamed in the distance, and Evil kept petting away and singing along.

"...*hot wire test not really scientific... head be turning into something really horrific... one gun in the camp and Childs wants to keep her... Jesus Christ, dude, can you cut my thumb any deeper... stick a needle in your blood and your blood's gonna scream...*"

And he made it.

Evil wrenched his arms and the dog up and back, lifting the front tire to cover the gap between the ground and the tow truck's ramp, a stuntman's age-old confidence technique that convinced his body into believing it had more to do with the launch than it really did.

"Did you see the weather channel on that TV back there?"
  "Back where?"

413

"At the gas station," Jack says. "There was a big-ass red spot coming at us, but the TV feed froze."

"Not a cloud in the sky."

"How do you know it was Doppler radar or whatever? Maybe that red spot was something else."

"Don't start," Rick says.

"Just take it easy on the corners when the storm comes. We're still missing some tread on these tires."

"We're fine."

"Fifty bucks says you roll this thing."

"How are you doing back there?" Rick yells to the old man on the gurney.

"I'm fine," the old man says, annoyed.

"We know you're fine," Jack says. "You're always fine. That gurney is for people who aren't fine, not for a free taxi service so you can go to the gas station and get cigarettes."

"Come on, Jack…" Rick says, in good spirits for no reason, like the early years, when his partner was doing everything right.

"Come on nothing."

Jack reaches to turn off the siren, but Rick stops him.

"You know when it's time for a paramedic to quit?" Rick asks.

"When?"

"When they start losing… patients!"

"Zing!"

"Get it?"

"Oh, I get it. I don't need the word spelled different to get it."

"Good."

"The siren will get us there faster," Rick says, reaching for it again, holding onto the memory of them doing their jobs like men.

"It's bullshit," Jack says. "Ten dog attacks today alone, and we're carting around this fool."

"Don't worry," the old man says. "I'm sure there will be plenty more. And just because you drive this meat wagon around in circles all night don't give you the right."

"What?"

"You shouldn't talk to us like that."

"Like what?" Jack asks.

"Like you're down here with the rest of us."

"What's that supposed to mean, you miserable old fuck?"

"That's enough, Jack."

"There's a reason the Russians put a dog in space while we used a monkey," the old man says after a couple blocks.

"And why's that?" Jack asks.

"I didn't say I knew what the reason was, but you can be damn sure it was a good one."

Jack remains unconvinced.

"So, what's up with all these dogs anyway?" Rick asks, really asking just this once, to see what happens. He watches the old man walk into the emergency room, turn around and walk out again, then light up a smoke, not even trying to fool anybody.

"We're gonna find out tonight. Once and for all," Jack says, putting the CB back in its holster. "Hit it."

"Don't you want to go in and get your hand checked before we finish up tonight?"

"Barely scratched me! That old bastard wasted his last tooth on my ass. An old man's fingernails are a lot more dangerous than his rotten mouth. Hold on, did you say check my head or my hand?"

"Well, you shouldn't have shoved him," Rick says, not answering Jack's question. Then he turns on their siren and stabs the gas.

"If this was a movie and I ignored a bite like this, I'd be so fucked," Jack laughs.

415

Rick shakes his head and, for the first time in weeks, watches his partner with something like sympathy. It feels like their last day on Earth.

"We've got what, twenty bites in as many hours? I think people are confusing dogs with something else."

"Like what." Rick is long past caring about the answer. So Jack doesn't answer. He's blowing on a stethoscope and checking his own chest instead. Jack taps his chest over and over, then starts laughing.

"You're the first dyslexic paramedic with a Dog Complex," Rick sighs, throwing stones and swerving through traffic. He checks the sky for rain and sees nothing, so he takes the corners harder.

"Hey, you know how they say dogs start to resemble their owners, or people start to resemble their dogs?" Jack asks him. "You've heard of doggelgängers, right? Maybe that's what's happening."

"You make no sense."

The girl on the gurney starts convulsing, but Jack does nothing to help her. Rick turns around, livid.

"What are you doing, man? Check her pulse."

"Doesn't matter."

"What?!"

"No pulse."

"How do you know?"

"Because I don't have one either."

After a moment, the girl stops moving, and Jack crouches down next to her. He pulls a sheet over her face so there might be something to fall to the floor if she sits back up like they do in the movies. He hopes this will scare Rick enough to finally roll the ambulance on the next turn.

* * *

Hospital entrance. Next day. Jack is walking back to their lockers. Rick is walking behind him, glaring over his bottle of lemonade.

"You don't work here anymore," he says.

"She's fine. She was fine. I was just fucking with you."

"I don't care, man."

Derek the janitor runs up behind them before Jack can answer, tapping Rick on the shoulder, his mouth slack and hanging. Rick smacks his hand away.

"Yes, I know," Rick says. "It's piss. Yes, I'm drinking your piss. I've gone crazy. You got me. Now fuck off, Eric."

Derek turns to leave.

"Wait, I'm sorry. Is it 'Eric' or 'Derek?' I can never remember."

"It's 'Derek.' I can never remember either," he admits. *Then he's gone.*

"I think you finally broke him," Jack says.

"Just saving time," Rick says, then, "Don't talk to me."

"You know, if anyone should remember that fucker's name, it should be you."

"Why's that? You're the one who stalks him online like you're in love."

"No, you. Because you've got half his name," Jack smiles.

"Right." *Rick opens his locker.* "So, am I gonna have to kill you by lunch or quit or both?"

"I don't know. Did the sun come up today?"

"Probably?"

"Don't worry then. I'm good."

Rick finishes his lemonade, still skeptical.

"We'll see. After that bite, you got Old Man Crazy Juice running through your veins."

"Nah, he didn't do shit. Old fucker's teeth were soft as chalk."

Right then, Big Mike and Little Mike walk by, talking loud as usual. Rick and Jack share a look like they can't believe these guys are still slinking around the hospital.

"So I took my dog to get the shots," Little Mike says, "Getting him immunized for the 'hunta' virus, you know, and I gotta hold him down every time because he goes bonkers. And I get a hold of two handfuls of fur right behind his head, got a good grip on him, right, and the doc says 'ready?' So I go 'ready!' And the doc sticks the dog. But the needle goes through a fold in the fur I'm squeezing and comes out the other side… and it stabs me right in my fucking hand."

"Aaaaah! Fuck!"

"And the doc doesn't even see this. Just jams the plunger down and injects the whole needle right into my hand. I felt so stupid I didn't say nothing. Just stuck my hand in my pocket like an asshole."

"You realize what this means, right?" Big Mike says.

"What? It means I feel so dumb I'm probably going to pay a bill for dog shots the vet gave me by accident? Just so I never have to tell anyone?"

"But you just told everyone," Jack says quietly, but they ignore him.

"No!" Big Mike bellows. "It means you're immune to the hantavirus now, too!"

"You ever hear of a man getting it?" Little Mike asks everybody.

"Nope. But that don't mean nothin'," Big Mike says. "Maybe there's a lotta people that got shots by accident. Maybe what happened to you happens more than we know."

"Shut the fuck up, Mike," Rick sighs. Then, "Wait. What did you mean by 'too?'"

"Huh?" Little Mike frowns.

"You said, 'You're immune now, too.'"

"Oh. 'Cause now we're both immune."

"But why are you immune to the… you don't even have a goddamn dog that… I mean, the chances of the same thing

418

happening to you that happened to me are... fuckin' forget it," Rick says, slamming his locker. "Okay, Mike and Mike, have a great day!"

"What's up with all the names around here anyway?" Jack suddenly wants to know.

"What do you mean?" Rick asks.

"They're all the same."

"How do you mean?"

"Like doppelgängers?" Little Mike offers.

"Do you even know what that word means, Little Mike?" Jack asks.

"Hell, yeah."

"What?"

"It's German for 'double walkers.'"

"Do you know what *that means?*"

"Well, it sure means something to you," Little Mike smiles. Jack doesn't argue. "And don't call me 'Little Mike' no more," he adds.

All four of them are heading for the exit when a young, bouncy candy striper walks up, handing out baseball caps. Both Mikes excitedly grab a handful from her, putting two on each, one forwards and one backwards. Jack is visibly alarmed by what he sees above the visors.

"It's okay," the girl chirps at him. Then to everyone, "You can wear them any way you want. It's up to you!"

"Who are the hats for?" Rick asks her.

"The family of the girl attacked yesterday, that girl you brought in, I think? They had these made up and sent to all the schools, churches, and hospitals in the area. To warn the kids."

"When I first got out of film school, I made a movie on that baseball diamond by my house."

"Let me guess," Rick says. "It was called Third Base."

"Nah, nobody liked to see anyone get to third base, even in the movies. It was called, There's No Crying in Baseball."

"Of course it was. Same thing, really. Didn't you know that the 'bases' mean different things to different people?'" Then, "Hold on, when did you make movies?"

Jack doesn't answer, instead reaching to take a cap as Rick pushes him past the girl and out the door.

Later that day. Massive car wreck. Fire, blood, screams: "a sandwich with the works," the first responders call them. Three ambulances are lined up like they're going to race later. Jack and Rick see a pile of men already working on a trucker next to his upended semi, so they run for the other vehicles. They find the worst of them, a smoking Buick Regal folded almost in half, and a bloody and bruised couple fighting with police and paramedics inches away from the steam of their hood. Rick joins the melee, as Jack attends to three young women crying near the curb.

Next to the Regal, the woman is calmer than her husband, and she allows Rick to treat her wounds. Rick gets to work, watching Jack out of the corner of his eye. Jack seems all business at first, securing necks, tying off wounds, checking pupils while whispering instructions and reassurance into ears instead of the wild conjecture he'd been partial to lately. Moving off to help restrain the husband, then watching for them to crack the car open and get to the baby that was trapped inside, Rick thinks back to how good Jack used to be at his job before shit started to slip. Jack was the best before the slippage, it was true.

Then a fire truck roars in at an awkward angle, stopping to block every ambulance's line of sight. Jack sees this and runs over to raise some hell.

"Hey, move that thing forward, man!"

"Just do your job. We'll do ours."

It's a Mike saying this to Jack. He's not "Big Mike" or "Little Mike," really, but a different Mike altogether, one who's kind of in the middle today without his partner. If this was Goldilocks, normally this would mean he was "just right," but this clown was anything but. Jack and Rick hardly recognize him without Big Mike and a dog pole in his hand. He'd washed out of the firefighting trade like the Big Mike, but had somehow wrangled his way back in.

Among the things that Jack and Rick never knew, was that Little Mike had finally hit Lieutenant that week, after only a decade and a half, and he'd been trying real hard lately to get the other men to call him "Crow," short for "Crowbar" because he carried one around even when he was just going to see a movie.

"Just in case," he'd say.

But worse than all that, he was one of those assholes who, despite being a hateful, vindictive, judgmental sort, never, ever used swear words. No profanity crossed that smirk for years, at least while he was awake. He was also the kind of guy who joined the Fire Department instead of the Army after that B-25 bomber hit the Empire State Building in 1945, exactly the kind of glory hound that gave them all a bad name. The other firemen couldn't remember a single encounter where Crow didn't explain to anyone who didn't know any better how he "never asked to be a hero." They all called him "Heck" instead of "Crow" sometimes. Mostly because when they did this, they sounded just like he used to.

"Heck, why do we gotta go through this every time," one of the EMTs says. "We don't park in front of your hydrants. Pay us the same courtesy."

"Move aside, Jack! We need a hose line set up here. Let's go!"

"Dang it, huh?" Jack says, already furious, looking to the other men for sympathy.

"The bigger the wreck, the bigger the Heck," they'd say sometimes. Which meant, the bigger the wreck, the more Little Mike, formally "Crow," formally "Heck," tried to throw his weight around.

But for once, his trusty crowbar was going to come in handy, as Rick and another police officer had been struggling with the crumpled passenger's side door for so long the fire below them had started melting the rubber in their shoes.

"Good thing it wasn't a Pinto," someone says, an old joke that might be funnier if it wasn't so hard to conclusively identify what model it was before the 18-wheeler centerpunched it.

"I got this," Little Mike announces, slipping his hooked end into a space around the hinges. He pushes hard, and that's when something strange happens. The door pops out and up, fast as a dog door, almost flipping the fireman into the car headfirst.

It only takes an almost imperceptible nudge from Jack's elbow to erase the rest of Little Mike's balance and dump him all the way inside.

He lands like those babies in the home videos, face plant right before a steady wail builds up in the backs of their mouths. Feeling foolish, Little Mike starts laughing right when the door slams shut, almost on his glove. He always wore gloves long past their expiration date, plastic burnt so bad it was almost impossible to make a fist.

"What the heck?" he asks the car.

Abandoning the girls on the curb completely, Jack runs back to try reaching inside a broken window and loosens the car seat with the screaming baby. He pretends to be shocked when finds himself face-to-face with Little Mike instead.

"How did you get in there, Houdini?" Jack asks him.

"No idea," Little Mike laughs, kicking at the door with his boots. The fire is popping like high-end, gourmet popcorn as the electrical system under the car sparks out, and people start moving away, even the ones in the uniforms. Little Mike coughs and buttons the top button on his slicker for the first time in his life as he kicks harder. But the heat has welded the door firm, and, more importantly, his crowbar is lost somewhere under the backseat, buried in black smoke as the oil burns from the engine block.

"Hey, while I've got a captive audience, do those look like bite marks to you?" Jack asks him, pointing to the seatbelt.

An old fireman, gray hair curling out from under his helmet, pushes past Jack to get the baby loose.

"Back up," he says.

Before Jack can argue, the car seat breaks free, and the baby is pulled through the hole. Then both of them are running the bundle to the side of the road to unbuckle her, gagging on the gas as the rubber burns off the exhaust system. As a fireman cuts the straps, Jack notices a bloody half-moon tear in the baby's jumper and starts working to pull down the child's pants, shaking the rolled cuffs, when another fireman throws him to the ground with an arm across his throat. Rick pulls the fireman off and prepares to fight, but the fireman loses interest as the rest of his brigade starts to circle the inferno.

Little Mike is punching the windshield, screaming as the black tips of his gloves ignite, and that's when an airbag detonator blows, the bag already burning from taking that big drink of oxygen. It envelopes his face like a jellyfish, filling his eyes with embers and the diamonds of glass that sprinkled the dashboard. The flames inside the car have already gone from gas-grill cookout to couch-burning party size, and Little Mike is finding it harder to punch, blinded with the skin running off his knuckles and out the bottoms of his gloves like barbecue sauce.

The other firemen all know a B.L.E.V. fireball is imminent (a.k.a. "Blev-ee," a.k.a. "boiling liquid expanding vapor blah blah blah…") with the gas tank cooking as long as it has, and they're pulling back. No one outside the movies tries to walk away from one while looking cool. And no one stays to stare through the window except for Jack and Rick.

They study the burning face of a man who swore to Jack once how much he was gonna hate Backdraft when it finally came out ("How does a movie not have an axe fight when the villain's name is 'Axe'?!") then asked him if he wanted to try to sign up as stuntmen for it. This was the same fool who told

423

Rick how years earlier he'd written letters to Ron Howard, the young director of Grand Theft Auto, *about how fire and explosions never made animal noises, and to "save that shit for when you're playing* Twister *while simultaneously trying to surf a Toronado." Of course, Jack had heard him trying to sell that same line of bullshit to a couple girls at the annual fundraiser where they torched everyone's old Christmas trees, pretending like the growls* weren't *coming from the side of his mouth.*

"It's a real live monster," he'd said, pine trees and ribbons burning over his shoulder and loving it. "It's got teeth, claws, and a voice. Sounds like the MGM lion, I swear…"

But that's the thing about Heck. He always swore. And it never meant shit. Not until today.

Rick turns away, thinking Little Mike sure picked a hell of a day to get his job back as a firefighter, but Jack breathes deep, smelling the cornucopia of flavors coming off the bonfire of the man's body. The copper scent of his blood, like a mouthful of pennies, was first. That blood was the only thing that kept a burning human being from smelling exactly like meat on a grill. There's a reason animals are bled out at the slaughterhouse.

I don't know how we taste, but we sure don't smell like chicken, *Jack realizes.* More like liver and spare change.

And when the rest of his hair burns away, the keratin and amino acids fill the air with another unique smell. But one that's familiar. Now Jack is backing up. It's the smell of the underworld, a chemical combination that Jack suddenly is convinced might be responsible for all the myths throughout history involving damnation and bodies sentenced to the stake. Pure sulfur.

Then, for dessert, comes the fabled hot perfume of foaming cerebrospinal fluid. He'd heard about it from veterans, possibly smelled it once before at a factory blaze. It's a musky, inviting scent that's always struck Jack as almost lonely.

As a pheromone, how could you ever offer the equivalent in return? *he thinks.* This is exactly what it smells like down there under my feet.

Impossibly, Jack can still hear the man screaming inside the smoke as he cooks away into memories, swearing to the fire that he'll change his ways, try to avoid running over animals on the way to the fires, swearing he'll at least button that top button.

But it's too late for him to start swearing, and everybody knows it.

Jack stops to watch a large dog run through a field on the horizon. His face pinched and distracted, he gets as close to the burning husk of the car as he's able, then turns to a fireman and asks the question again, quietly so Rick can't hear.

"Did those look like bite marks to you?"

"What the fuck are you doing?" *the fireman hisses, teeth clenched, waiting for their chance to get the dead man from the wreck.*

"Something is wrong here," *Jack says, not noticing the fireman's "No shit" look he's giving him. Then the fireman has a handful of Jack's collar as Rick is running over, cops and onlookers following. Rick shakes his head as a police officer breaks them apart.*

"What's wrong with you guys?" *the cop asks. The fireman points at Jack, but before he can speak, two police cruisers and another ambulance pull in. Jack recognizes one of the dispatchers pointing him out to a stocky, brown-shirted officer. This Sergeant bridges the fifty yards between them in what seems to be three large steps.*

"Is your name Jack Grinstead?" *he asks.*

"Yeah, why?"

"You need to come with me."

"For what?"

"Attempted rape."

"What?"

425

"He was undressing the baby!" the older fireman yells. "That's the guy! I heard about this motherfucker. He's gone nuts."

"Wait a minute-" Rick starts, and the Sergeant holds up a hand, then holds up identification. It reads, "Joseph Stansberries. Robbery/Homicide."

"Back off," the Sergeant says. "After receiving an anonymous tip this afternoon, our department has reviewed the video from the back of your ambulance and discovered that… you know what? Just come the fuck with me."

"They didn't have cameras in the back of ambulances six years ago," Jack says.

"Six years ago, huh?" Stansberries says. "We're not talking about six years ago. But thanks for the tip. Now come with me."

Jack takes a couple seconds to crack his knuckles, wondering how they could have gotten him on videotape. He isn't too surprised really. One thing he's learned on this particular adventure was any movie that existed at any time on VHS has always existed on VHS. And that includes himself.

"What?"

He realizes he's said most of that crazy shit out loud.

"From the '80s until now, videotapes are always with us."

"How's that?"

"It's the nature of the tape," Jack smiles. "More specifically, the nature of any moment you can rewind or fast forward with your finger."

"Uh huh."

"There's a trick though. You ever try to rewind a VHS tape without hitting the button?"

"And how would I do that?" Stansberries asks.

"Just close your eyes, fool."

With that, Stansberries shoves him to start walking.

"What did they see on the tape?" Rick asks, walking with them.

"What did who see?" Jack asks.

"Your old partner, Mike 'Johnson' Johnson. 'Little Mike?' Come on."

"Wow. Really? You, too, huh?" Jack looks back to the smoking car and the men still trying to crack it open. "You should go talk to them. You two have a lot in common."

"Me, too, what?"

The officer doesn't wait for an answer and reaches for Jack's arm to keep him moving.

"Forget it. You'll have plenty of time to-"

"He thought a dog molested her or something," the old fireman interrupts.

Jack brushes gravel from his hair, trying to appear calm, as he tries to remember who he is today, and if Larry is questioned under a hot lamp, can he remember if Jack was a paramedic who turned to porn or porn director who turned to paramedicine. Ultimately, he decides it won't matter.

"That's not really what I said," Jack says, as Rick steps up between him and the officer.

"Listen, we have to get these people to the hospital," Rick says. "We'll have to figure this out later."

"Damn straight he needs a hospital!" the old fireman says, and Rick shoves him aside.

"That baby doesn't have time for this shit. Neither do I."

The stocky cop gauges the climate of the eyes around them.

"Go," Sergeant Stansberries says. "We'll finish this later."

Jack runs to the ambulance and climbs into the back, closing the door behind him. Rick climbs into the driver's seat and starts their warbling, forever-busted siren. The crowd turns to look at the source of the horrible noise as Rick tears off down the road. No one seems surprised by the sound anymore.

Ambulance. Hours later. Jack is resting on the gurney in the back. Rick is driving.

"Just take me home if you don't want to hear what's really going on."

"I am taking you home," Rick says. *"Dude, I've known you a long time, and that's the only reason I kept you out of jail today. But as far as the job goes, we're through. Once I drop you off, I don't ever want to see you again."* He looks around the cab. *"Where's the cameras?"*

"I've never mounted a camera in here, but I did put a fake phone booth in the back of the ambulance once. Of course, back then it was half a phone booth, lightweight so it could quickly get stuck to any wall, with bubblegum if need be. And back then my name was Larry."

"Right."

"The booth was leftover from my film-making days, and along the inside read 'In case of plot problems, break glass.' Which, of course, meant 'drop a dime.'"

"Stop."

"Basically, back in the days before cellular phones, when a character needed information to move a story along and they couldn't afford or improvise or 'afro-engineer' an essential sequence, as Glen would call it, Larry would have his actors just slap the phone booth up on a wall, or hold it up with one hand if they had to, and they'd make an imaginary phone call. In their best Children of a Lesser God, *one-sided phone call, the actor would announce to the viewer with some ridiculously obvious exposition just what the fuck was going on."*

"Like you being this 'Larry'?"

"'What do you mean I only have ten minutes to get to the dock and fuck the baroness before the bomb goes off?!' You see, quite perversely, Larry still used the fake phone booth in his more respectable gigs, not while being a paramedic, 'cause that might have been first, but at least during his 'artier' films. See, instead, the makeshift phone-booth conversations would leave it all up to the audience's imagination, like every piece of shit at Cannes."

"Where?"

"'What? Yes. No. No. I will.' Click. You get it? You might think this makes all fake-phone-booth, back-of-ambulance expositions utterly fruitless, but at least they remind Larry of better days, better work."

"This movie sucks," Rick says.

"Okay, if a rapist is faking dog attacks, too…" Jack winds back up. "…then how fast can you give someone a dog-bite tattoo…"

Rick interrupts him. "I saw what you did back there. To Little Mike."

Jack says nothing.

"I didn't know he was your partner," Rick says.

"Long time ago. He was annoying as hell. Even worse than he is now. Was…"

"Don't you mean 'annoying as Heck'?" Jack misses the joke. "And another thing," Rick goes on, shaking his head. "If you ever turn up on the side of the road, sniffing asses at a car wreck again, looking for signs of Milkbones or mystery molesters, I will fuck you up then call the cops."

"…all you would have to do to fake it is leave a couple dog hairs," Jack is saying. "…put a dog's favorite chew toy in someone's shorts so that he'll dig for it. That's enough."

"You sound like an asshole," Rick sighs. "You know what you're doing? You're the oldest story there is. You're inventing crimes and characters to stop it. You're like the firebug standing with the crowd to watch them put out the fire. Or watch you do it. Only there's no fire. Or something."

"Good analogy. Can you run that by me one more time, numb nuts?"

"Shut the fuck up."

"Okay, listen to this, you know how a dog always sticks its nose between a girl's legs the first time it smells her…"

The sound from the siren crackles and cuts out, then comes back on louder and more erratic. A car that was easing into traffic from a side-street suddenly lurches forward and takes out a mailbox. Rick reaches to turn off the siren, but the button isn't working any more. The sound grows even louder. Rick yells over it.

"You realize that the only one who thinks about shit like this is someone who does shit like this, right?"

The siren emits an almost human shriek, then coughs. Jack isn't hearing Rick anymore or vice versa.

"…well, once I was hiding a squeeze toy behind my back, and my friend's Rottweiler just about bit off my nuts trying to get at it… wait. Turn right here."

"Where are we going?"

"I know a shortcut."

Rick turns hard onto an onramp, almost taking them up on two wheels again.

"You know what, Jack? At first I thought you just raped her and covered it up. Now I think it's got to be worse somehow."

"…but if we can X-ray this dog, we'll find the answer to the… whoa. Turn left here."

"Jesus fucking Christ. You know, you describe this theory about this man and his dog and his balls because it's the nastiest thing you can think of. It's the limits of your imagination because we've seen too much horrible shit. And you know what's so fucked about that? You're like the Holocaust survivor telling a story that you've heard before, that I've heard before, and you don't think I'm paying attention, so you start searching your little brains for the nastiest thing you can think of. But you're not very good at this game, dude. That's the problem with our job, man. Out here we have seen and heard and smelled it all. So quit trying so hard with ghost stories, it doesn't work on us, remember?"

"What do you mean 'lack of imagination?' Have you thought of something worse? Tell me about it. But turn right here…"

Rick takes a harder right turn. The siren is almost deafening now. Rick can only hear random words that Jack mutters.

"...'cause dogs are man's best friend... not woman's... turn left... dogs... actually smarter than dolphins... also known to rape... turn right there where they used to be selling that snowmobile..."

"Jack, I saw a reality show the other day, and the girls couldn't wait to get their rape stories out. This one chick was telling her story and you could tell, even though she had really been raped, that she was making it more dramatic and more interesting for the television, and suddenly I didn't care anymore."

"That makes you a horrible person."

"No, we're talking about you."

The siren stops, and the silence is almost painful. Jack sits up, the sheet sliding off his face. They say nothing for a mile. Then:

"Do you believe me that there's a rapist, Rick?"

"No." Pause. "I don't know." He punches the dashboard in frustration.

"Stop!" Jack yells. "Right here!"

Rick slams on the brakes, and the ambulance slides and rocks on its tires. They're at the entrance of the amusement park. Rick looks around confused.

"Why?"

"I want to check the scene of the crime."

"Fine. Get out. And realize this is the last time I'll be seeing you. I'm not risking my job because of your delusions. This is where you get off, know what I'm saying?"

Jack steps out of the ambulance.

"I'm going, I promise. But you didn't answer me. Do you believe there's a rapist out there?"

Rick stares straight ahead. Jack walks away backwards, reluctant to leave without getting an answer. The park is still open but thinning out, and Jack aims for the boy at the gate who's handing out samples of elephant ears on toothpicks. The boy is frozen at the sight of the ambulance, scouring the

431

horizon for an accident. Jack backs into the kid, then takes a sample and eats it. Rick puts the ambulance into gear.

"It doesn't matter anyway," Jack says, smiling around his toothpick. "You wouldn't know him if you were sitting right next to him." *Rick just shakes his head.*

Jack laughs and walks past the boy, then he quickly turns around.

"Rick! Watch this!"

He spins his baseball cap to face forward and walks past the boy for another free sample.

"See that shit?! Watch it again."

He turns on his heels, spins his baseball cap around backward again, and then takes another hunk of elephant ear. The boy is understandably confused.

"I could do this shit all day. And this kid doesn't even recognize me. If I had a fake mustache, I'd never buy groceries again."

Rick is driving away.

"Rick! Hey! Watch your back, Rick!"

Jack spins his baseball cap around one last time, then flips up the visor. He plucks one more cube of powdered, greasy dough off a toothpick, then smiles at the boy.

"Sorry. Just making a point. So… you see any dogs around here today?"

"Dogs aren't allowed on the rides," *the boy frowns.* "They aren't tall enough."

"Good thing. They eat kids like Crackerjacks! World's best kept secret. Ask anybody with a new baby."

The boy looks up at the words on Jack's cap. A stitched cartoon dog grins and reminds him:

"Beware Kids! Not All Dogs Are Friendly!"

Amusement park ride. Minutes later. A long line of Model-T cars are backed up on the ride, and it's pandemonium. Children are crying, balloons are popping, and parents are hanging out of their cars and hollering, fake radios blaring, some even slapping the heels of their hands against horns that have never been functional. Jack is at the front of the line, refusing to move forward. Every family screams abuse at him from their cars, leaning almost far enough to fall, but so far afraid to step out as if it's a traffic jam on a real highway. Jack sits calm, lost in thought, both hands behind his head and nowhere near his steering wheel, pretending this is where it happened, this is where it all went down, and he was the driver who crashed that car.

Larry tried to roll out from under the dead man on his back, and he somehow came up with a .38 Special. It had fallen from a holster that one of the officers had unsnapped way too early in the action in a sad attempt at intimidation. From the meager safety of the sandbox, Larry fired back at Bigby, who dove for the covered slide in fear. A shirtless, spiky-haired kid trailing popcorn and blood ran between them, and Larry saw what he mistook for tattoos of dog bites along the boy's ribs.

What kind of idiot gets a dog-bite tattoo? he thought, taking aim. *Here, let me draw some bullet holes on you, too.*

But the trigger wouldn't budge. The safety was on. Normally .38 Specials didn't have safeties, but when cops made clicking noises with their mouths, it served the same purpose. Somewhere in the world, a cop made that noise. So Larry squirmed like a snake backing out of its skin, and the dead man still hung on awhile, finally tearing away the last shred of Larry's shirt before he dropped.

Larry stood up in the glow of a hundred headlights, shirtless and trembling. Everyone could see him now, as well as the images covering his body. He panicked and began scratching long strips of skin free from his shoulders, arms and torso, like the ragged fringe of notebook paper, but more like marbled bacon. He stripped layer after layer until he'd uncovered every tattoo lurking in his bloodstream.

These were mostly movie tattoos that had burst forth inexplicably from Larry's body, shimmering and shifting and taking shape in his seeping wounds. Movie fans would recognize them as tattoos from their favorite flicks, every one of them scribbled in washable ink, since there was no commitment to body art in the fiction of films. Once upon a time, these markings buried inside Larry's trunk had been drawn on the shanks of actors by men and women with no dedication to the reality of their moment. But now, in this scene, with no explanation at all, they had stained Larry's skin forever.

He wasn't too surprised.

It was the usual suspects crawling on his epidermis, but this time he knew their real names. There was Kurt Russell's cobra on his belly, last seen in *Escape from New York*, now doing battle with Nick Nolte's devil tongue from the prison musical *Weeds*. Rows of Mel Gibson's "Z's" from *The Bounty* covered the ridge of Larry's collarbone, where his knuckles, inked with Robert Mitchum's infamous "Love" and "Hate" from *Night of the Hunter*, of course, rubbed and rubbed like they were trying to start a fire. Even Axel Jodorowsky's huge eagle had landed, now draped across his chest like it was in the import *Santa Sangre*, a movie where a violent, primitive tattooing ritual was quite convincingly faked. A Geisha and a dragon from a Chinese New Year parade rode across Larry's back, just like the one Maude Adams had to endure against her will in *Tattoo*. And "Death" tickled his toes, the same toes that Vince Gil stabbed the gas pedal with when he portrayed a surprisingly easily rattled *Mad Max* villain. Nicolas Cage's (and Randall "Tex" Cobb's) Mr. Horsepower logo from *Raising Arizona* made an appearance, the same bird that still got confused for Woody Woodpecker on a daily basis, two of them actually, smiling high and proud over Larry's bicep and his black heart. Circling Larry's spine were Rod Steiger's lions and rockets and Mars ("Oh, my!"), still glistening like they did in that film, where they'd clearly been applied about five minutes earlier in the makeup trailer of *The Illustrated Man*, just in time for the leading man to start sweating. And, finally, on Larry's shoulder, for *Fantasy Island* fans, there was even a tattoo of "Tattoo" on the shoulder of a tattoo of Ricardo Montalbán.

It made sense if you saw it.

It should have been enough to grab everyone's attention. But their indifference to Larry was a glimpse into the future, when Hollywood would one day begin experimenting with CGI for hardcore sex in mainstream films to maintain the integrity of the stars, and how they'd accidentally stumble onto some of the real reasons behind the fading criticisms that everyone hated computer imagery and 'would never *never* mistake it for reality.' And in spite of the dwindling porn industry being the only voice of reason in this dystopia, when they one day organize a naked march down Rodeo in protest of this technology, including a leathery, 75-year-old Jack with nary a picture anywhere on his body, the mob would be universally ignored, especially on television, where true nudity would be dismissed as a particularly unrealistic special effect.

Larry was dead-center in the burn of two hundred headlights now, with all that crazy shit all over his body, dramatically clicking off the safety of his weapon, but it still wasn't enough to keep everyone's attention when a real girl entered the spotlight.

Jacki's car. Toni is watching her frustrated mother work to pass a slow-moving ambulance. When the other lane finally clears, Jacki speeds up to go around it. But once they're finally in front, its flashers light up their world, and Toni puts her hands over her ears at the choked, turbine warble of its siren. Still clutching her head, she climbs up on the back of the passenger's seat to read the blood-red, backwards writing painted on the hood.

"'*Ecnalubma*'..."

"*What?*"

"*What what, mommy?*"

"*What are you talking about?*" *Jacki asks her, distracted by her rear-view mirror. The ambulance driver's face is shadowed by a ballcap, and Jacki slows to let it pass, peering in vain to see if it's who she thinks it is. Then she looks over at Toni and sees her hands still tight against her head, eyes pinched shut now, and Jacki thinks of the toy screaming as she stomped it to death.*

And the thing Toni did right after that.

She tries to calm her daughter down.

"*You can put your hands down now, baby. Hey, you know what you look like? Do you? You look like the 'See No Evil' monkey!*"

Toni makes a face somewhere between a smile and a frown and drops her arms. Then she takes out a red crayon from her Hello Kitty *purse to write some backwards letters on her hand in her shaky childish script.*

Oh, no, Jacki thinks. Not that again.

Toni had gotten into the habit of writing backwards on her hands ever since she caught a certain horror movie on cable looong past her bed time. She always drew the letters with the red crayon, and she called them her "Redrubs." Jacki never translated the word in the movie for her. She knew this would take the fun out of it.

But as she slows for a red light, Toni is cupping her hand to conceal what she's written, and Jacki realizes it's the first time her daughter has ever hidden anything from her. Then their car is suddenly bumped from behind, and she turns around to see Jack at the wheel of another *ambulance, frantically waving for her to pull over. Jacki adjusts her mirror so he can't catch her eyes as she debates running the light. Jack inches forward to bump their car again. After a third nudge, he flashes the lights and gives a quick burst with the broken siren.*

They all sound like that, *she thinks.*

Toni starts to cry, and two burly men who are watching from another lane climb from their cars and run over to Jack. They start pounding on the ambulance window, and he rolls it down a couple inches, smiling.

"Hey, fuckface, what the fuck are you doing?" *the first man yells, spittle making Jack blink.*

"Guys, relax. I know her."

"Then why is she looking straight ahead?" *the second man asks.*

"Please, this has nothing to do with-"

The light turns green, and the first man turns to run back to his car. The second man waits a moment, then punches off Jack's side view mirror and spits on his hood.

"You're lucky you're driving that thing, motherfucker. It might save time later."

Jack sits idling, shaking his head, and the cars behind him start piling up and honking. He finally rolls out and catches up with Jacki's car at the next light, pulling up on her left to roll down his window and talk. She's rolling hers back up.

"Hey!" *Jack shouts.* "Just listen!"

Don't say it, *Jacki thinks.*

But he says it.

"I'm trying to save you!"

Jack gets out and runs around her car, Jacki watching in disbelief as he pounds on her windshield. Amazingly, Toni stops crying and watches him with interest, still drawing in her hand.

"I'm not lying to you," *he pants.* "But I have a few more questions. Like... how exactly were you fucking that guy when you crashed your car six years ago? I can't picture it."

437

Jacki runs the light, her bumper cracking Jack in the knee and spinning him onto the road. She watches him rolling around in pain as she gets out her cell phone.

"Hello? I'd like to report a murder."

She looks at her own eyes in the mirror.

"And a rape."

Then she rolls down the window, breathes deep.

"One question for you, officer," she says as she speeds up. "Which one do you think is worse?"

Empty apartment. Later that day. Derek the janitor is making a snow angel in his plush orange carpet. His shirt unbuttoned, a pair of binoculars rocks on his sweaty stomach. All around him are wires and pieces of a police scanner that he's disassembled. Rows of glass soda bottles on the floor line every wall, filled to the brim with cloudy fluid. He's staring at the ceiling where photographs and magazine pages of hundreds of dark-skinned girls have been tacked and taped, all ages, toddlers to middle-age. He stops making his angel and puts the binoculars over his face, turning the dial to focus on one girl in particular.

It's Jacki's daughter.

Next to his head is a small tape recorder crackling with a muffled conversation from Jack and Jacki's date.

"...ever dress as something particularly creepy for Halloween and then no one talks to you for a year? Back in EMT school, me and a couple friends did 'Father, Son, and the Holy Ghost' for a costume, and my roommate, she just wore a sheet with holes in it, but me and my girlfriend, I mean my roommate, we dressed like a typical boy and his father, her wearing a Little League outfit, and me in a tucked-in Hawaiian shirt, mom jeans, big cell phone in a holster, and a Jimmy Buffet trucker cap. It's ironic, but nothing makes you look more like a dad than mom jeans. So that was all creepy enough, but I think it was how I kept saying to her, 'You remind me of your mother,' while putting my tongue down her throat that threw everyone off for so long. Well, I thought it was funny anyway…"

"So do I," *Derek says as the tape runs out on his hamburger and he clicks a stop button shaped like a tongue of tomato.*

Jack's face is also visible in the photograph, as well Jacki's leg that Toni used to hide behind. But it's Toni that fills the frame, hiding from Jack but smiling at Derek as he snapped her picture, a smile that no one caught but him.

Jacki's house. Same night. Jack runs up to Jacki's front door and knocks with the authority of someone with good news to deliver. Toni opens the door a crack, peering out through the space under the chain. She's sniffling, tears in her eyes.

"Mommy ain't home," *she pouts.*

"What's the matter?" *Jack asks, crouching down.*

Toni looks past him and sees the ambulance parked in her driveway. She frowns and wipes her nose.

"What's 'eck-nail-ub-muh' mean?" *she asks.*

"Huh?"

"Right there. On the front. What's that mean? Sounds Spanish."

Jack turns to look.

"That's just the word 'ambulance.'"

Toni shakes her head and holds out her hand.

"Unh-unh. It's Spanish."

Jack looks down at the red letters scrawled in her palm.

"Yeah, that says 'ambulance,' honey. It's just backwards."

"No, it doesn't."

"Yes, it does. It's the truth. It's written like that so you can read it when it sneaks up behind you. It's not backwards in a mirror. You can check in your bathroom."

"I know all that! So, why were you chasing us?"

"Chasing you?"

"That truck was chasing us. And it was screaming."

"Screaming? Oh, you mean the siren? Yeah, sometimes our sirens are a little off."

"It sounded like it was hurt," Toni says, eyes down.

"Well, that siren wasn't me. That was a different ambulance. They all say 'eck-nail-ub-muh' on them," he smiles.

Toni looks skeptical.

"The siren works fine on mine though, I promise."

"Prove it."

"What?" Jack is surprised by her challenge.

"Turn it on and prove it."

"I can't, Toni. It would scare the neighbors."

"Why are you driving it when you're not at work? Is that where you live?"

"Pretty much," he says, weary of her questions and checking the windows for her mother. *"We leave the keys in them for everybody. And it has a special radio I like to listen to. Toni, why were you crying?"*

"I stepped on a spider and killed it," Toni whispers, hand over her face. *"I didn't mean to kill anybody."*

"Don't cry," Jack says gently. *"I'll bet you didn't really kill it."*

Toni peeks out between her fingers, looking hopeful.

"Really?"

"Really. You might think you killed it, but you can't really tell with spiders. They've been around for a long, long time, and they know how to curl up and hide in between the treads on your shoes. You look down and think it's dead, but it's just waiting for you to keep walking."

"It had stuff coming out," Toni says, doubtful again.

"No, that's just a trick they play," Jack says, shaking his head. *"They spit when they see you coming."*

Toni's eyes are wide and clear. She seems relieved.

"You know. The same thing happened to me once, Toni. I hit a beaver with my car, and I was all upset. But when I

got out and looked around, the beaver was running away. I thought for sure it was dead, and it wasn't even limping. I think I saw it jump up and eat a lightning bug on its way out…"

"Beavers don't eat lightning bugs."

"They don't? Maybe it was a possum then."

"They don't eat bugs neither. And they sure can't jump!"

"How do you know? You ever throw one a Frisbee?"

"No. Sounds scientific though."

Jack blinks. He didn't think a child so young would have such a mastery of sarcasm.

"So you didn't throw one a Frisbee."

"No."

"Didn't think so. Now go squish another spider, killer."

Toni slams the door, and Jack starts to leave. Then the door opens and she steps out, hopping as she puts her shoes on. She takes his hand and leads him down the steps to look under the porch.

"Can I show you something?"

Jack's heart jumps, then he's disgusted with himself for being scared of a little girl.

"What is it?" he asks.

"Under there. You think it's still alive?"

"Think what's still alive?"

"The spider!"

"Oh," Jack says, relieved and checking the windows again. Then Toni reaches into the dark and pulls out a dead cat, fluid pouring from its mouth, back end flopping like a wet towel. Unnerved, Jack backs up so fast he falls on his ass. Toni just smiles, holding it at arm's length.

"Think this one can jump?" she asks.

He practically runs back to the ambulance and turns up the police scanner to listen, almost burning rubber to leave before the little girl gets to his door.

* * *

At any drive-in built in the '70s, the cement bunker that housed a projector was kind of like a real bunker. And because the beam was so low to the ground, some places put up barbed wire to stop you from stuffing something into those flickering peepholes, just like they stopped the Allies at Normandy from stuffing something into those machine guns. And until they started making what the drive-in veterans called a "Glory Hole" higher up off the ground, if you were the kind of kid that wasn't afraid of getting your clothes torn or leaving a little bit of blood in your popcorn, you could hop that fence and walk face-first into the firefight, 20,000 lumens of blazing lighthouse to be exact, and you would effectively disrupt everyone's movie. Hell, you could make giant shadow animals in that beam if you had the balls.

And that's exactly what Bully had. And that's exactly what Bully did.

The Last Projectionist had just switched over to Larry's film, and he really did have his thumbs in his overalls like some sort of blue-collar hero for a good minute or two while the movie started threading through its extra bit of tail. But no one would ever see this. The Last Projectionist had already received notice that he was losing his job for good and this would be his last weekend, so tonight he'd brought something special when he stole a nip from his bottle. He'd brought a set of wooden goblets recently carved on the spinning lathe in his garage, the finest drinkware he'd ever crafted. He used green wood this time, so he could carve those edges paper thin, not quite as transparent as glass, but good enough to hold up to the sun. And he wanted to hold them up to the sun just once, for a toast. But it had been a gray, miserable week. They were right when they said the sun was usually Kryptonite to a drive-in (translation, "Kryptonite to a projectionist"), but lately he'd craved the sunshine more and more. He even found himself day-dreaming of the worst thing in the world for his chosen profession, a day the sun never went down. Hell, even an extra hour would be a drive-in disaster.

So when the sun ran to hide, he took his two wooden goblets to the "Glory Hole" to catch the living light of the beam, to see if he'd carved them thin enough to disappear.

He'd gone through quite a few prototypes, and settled on the two goblets that had warped the least, the only two that didn't explode on the bell of the cup's flower like the rest of them, always splitting into rivers of cracks just after drying. These were the only two that had survived the process, and he planned on filling one with a bit of rye and toasting a job he'd done for twenty goddamn years, hopefully sharing a drink with someone. Or not. Didn't matter really. He was going to ask that crazy fucker who brought the last movie, but he'd ran off way too fast.

So he held his drink high.

But the beam was wrong. It felt too hot on this end, shook his cup, as if the light was… bulging, or like someone was pinching off a vein just as their heart sped up.

He put down the rye and glanced at the reel in a panic. There was still plenty of movie for the projector to eat. So he got on his toes to look out through the peephole and see what was clogging the works.

It was a naked girl. And she was overshadowing the other naked girls on the screen. The last movie Larry had given him was probably Larry's best film, but to everyone at the drive-in that night, it would have looked as unremarkable as interchangeable oceans of skin, fucking away their indifference on a monolith that was grayer and bigger than the one that educated the apes in *2001*, only this monolith was laying on its side, with nothing left to teach us.

But something weird was happening with Bully's shadow dancing in front of all this. Although an Amtrak-size cock was leveling, steadying, and getting prepared to penetrate an asshole the size of the largest production trunk (one day, that would be a 2008 Pontiac Grand Prize, and Larry would own it), Bully's shadow somehow made these alarming images acceptable. Reasonable. Oddly touching? Poignant. All words Larry dreamed as blurbs one day adorning his posters.

The pornography was a surprise to everyone. Even Larry had forgotten he'd shot this scene. This was Larry's masterpiece, sure, and finally flickering up there on the big screen was his life story, his monument, and this would be the magnum opus to redeem him in the eyes of respectability.

But for the popcorn eaters, there was always gonna be some butt sex.

So the train went through the tunnel, bending a little in the middle to maintain the best visible angle, as tunnel-bound trains in the movies are wont to do, and Bully danced. And she wasn't really naked, as the spectators first assumed. It just seemed that way with all that light shining through her as she spun around. Out on the playground, knee-deep in battle, she seemed especially naked to Larry, who pretty much saw the world as naked anyway. Larry had seen so many people in the nude that he was like a walking, talking exercise in imagining that hypothetical naked classroom in order to feel more relaxed during a presentation. Except it was just the opposite with Larry. In porn, you had to imagine people wearing a lot of clothes when you really needed to focus.

But this was not necessary with Bully. Larry could see her body was as covered in ink as his own.

He was in love.

During his second career, Larry had worked around pointless portraits on people's bodies before: album

444

covers, dead nephews, marginally famous people. But as he strode through the headlights and exhaust fumes towards her, gun now swinging impotent at his side, this giant, naked girl seemed to be covered utterly with the cast of second-tier supporting actors.

That was weird.

When she spun around, twirling and dancing in the spotlight, it was like an entire yearbook of *Variety* second-fiddles were adorning her back with their earnest "put me in your movie!" mugs. Larry imagined the roll call for their feature film, *Awesome-When-They're-Angry Character Actors Stuck in an Elevator*:

"Now starring! Ronny Cox, James Spader, Jon Polito, Brad Dourif, Fred Ward, David 'Not Keith David' Keith and vice versa, Donald Moffat, Brian Dennehy, Michael Ironside, and William Atherton, with Terry O'Quinn as the Voice of Reason. Coming soon to the bottom shelf of a video store near you!"

All men and psychodramas? Larry noted. Then, unable to shake his old recruiting habits, *So she's got daddy issues, eh?*

But those guys weren't alone on Bully's body. He could see she was covered in movie titles, too. Every horror flick that had a baby in it. All the movies Bully had watched from her window, on the flickering drive-in screen in the distance, like the forever earthbound watching taillights blink across the night sky. But Larry couldn't know this, of course. He was just amazed how complete her collection was. Mostly '70s stuff like *Rosemary's Baby, Basket Case 1, 2,* and *3. Rosemary's Baby II?* What? She had a sketch of the *It's Alive* crib across her ribs, of course, because those words rhymed. There was *American Gothic,* which looked more like the poster for the 1974 movie *The Baby,* that short-lived trend of having full-grown assholes acting like infants. But, hey, she had that poster, too! Right by her hip. That movie used to make Larry furious, until he realized it was far easier to suckle a full-grown man than it was to train a goddamn child to act. Every filmmaker eventually learned that children had no business working with adults. Was there any other profession in the world besides film where you'd let a fucking child do the job? No, no, not "children fucking," of course. Yeesh, Larry did have some integrity.

But, yeah, he'd trust a child as an air-traffic controller before he'd allow one in front of his camera.

Which is why the parade of bleach-blonde moppets from *Village* and *Children of the Damned* across her belly almost made him gag. And there was the ol' four-sheet from *Who Can Kill a Child?*, Chucky from *Child's Play* getting choked out by Gage from *Pet Semetary*, the little princesses from *The Bad Seed* and *The Pit* all over her shoulder blades (although those "kids" always looked to Larry to be about 30), the terrifying *Look Who's Talking* crew, the snowmobile-suit wearing, beaked rage babies of *The Brood*, and, dangerously close to her bathing-suit areas, *Peopletoys*, a.k.a. *Devil Times Five*, a.k.a *House on Horrible Hill*, a.k.a. *Tantrums*.

Watch 'em. Learn 'em...

It seemed like an awful lot of tattoos, but he was suddenly sure she had four arms to carry them, just like his Mary.

"Oh, shit."

Larry thought he could just barely make out the squealing, limbless thing from *Eraserhead* and its dozens of tadpole brothers and sisters.

"Did she really watch all of those from her window?" he asked a family pressed up against their car's windshield, which made zero sense because there was no way he could know that. "And all those movies about babies? Is her stomach swollen in that shadow or is that just a 50-foot optical illusion?"

But Larry didn't need to ask. He had no doubt that viewing so many movies about killer babies from the comfort of your bed would knock anyone up. Luckily, Larry had racked up that year and a half in film school and could recognize such obscure movie references, and recognize when something was out of order. Maybe this helped him know things he shouldn't. Maybe her body would mean little to anyone else's eyes.

He pitied anyone who saw nothing but skin, but envied their confusion, as well.

And there were those tattoos on her thighs, too. Not as interesting to Larry as the movies about babies, but revving their engines from Bully's knees on up were cars of every make and model. Right under some Old English script bridging both knees that shouted, "Remember Our Vets!," the fleet of vehicles was all stacked in formation to lean out their driver's side windows and watch the show starting on the tiny black monolith, well, more like a monorail actually, that was now cruising between her legs.

That's where the movie would be.

Larry tried to picture her receiving all these tattoos, the artist at the parlor leaning in close with black gloves and the hum of a needle and anticipating exactly what to draw on that tiny black screen down there. Larry was surprised by the movie he saw. Impossibly, it depicted this exact moment, the naked girl standing on a bunker at D-Day, with another tiny screen between her legs, and another movie flickering down there, too. And another, and another, all the way to infinity until they were too small to see without really getting your nose in there like any good director.

She tapped an invisible microphone to get the crowd's attention, and he was finally angry for the first time since the credits. That was his job, not hers.

* * *

Jack's apartment building. Later that day. In the hallway, Big Cop and Small Cop run up on Jack's door, rainwater dripping off their guns and noses. Small Cop knocks with the authority of bad news, ready for delivery. He knocks harder than Big Cop's previous partner, Little Cop, who has called in sick, specifically "sick of this shit." Small Cop is mumbling the lyrics to Nick Cave's "Messiah Ward," although he has no way of knowing this, and Big Cop mistakes it for some sort of pre-game psych-up, even though the future hit single is actually a post-op psych-out chant back from Jack's Red Cross training days.

"They keep bringing out the dead now, and it's easy just to look away. They're bringing out the dead now, and it's been a strange, strange day..."

He beats on the door for another minute or two but gets no answer. Then Big Cop steps forward with his shotgun, and with two cocks and two blasts, there are now two holes where the hinges used to be. He kicks the loose door onto the floor and steps over it with his partner, both their gun barrels tracing lines of fire from each doorway and corner. Then Small Cop shares a frown with Big Cop and he lowers his weapon.

The apartment is empty. Not just nobody home. This place is a shell. No furniture, tables, TV, nothing. Well, almost nothing.

*Small Cop walks over to a camouflage bundle leaning in the corner of the living room. He frowns as he spins it to reveal the words "***T.W.A.T.***" stenciled in white on the canvas.*

Lightning crashes outside.

"Where the fuck is he?" *Big Cop sighs.*

"I don't know. This is the number the landlord gave us. And his name is on the lease."

"Whose name?"

"Are you kidding?"

"Just who do you think we're dealing with here?"

"What do you mean 'Who?' You know who."

"Not the Bardstown Rapist?"

"I'm just saying, the last time we saw him, there was a storm coming, just like today. We saw it on the fucking radar remember?"

"You think a storm front on the radar brings him to town?"

"I think it brings some kind of weird shit to this town."

"Didn't we solve that crime over in Lexington?"

"Not really. Same letters, just slightly rearranged. The man's sign read 'Bardstown Therapist'. Actually, I think that was just an unlicensed dentist we busted."

"Ah! That's right. The Jaw Carpenter!"

"Who would go to a dentist with 'Jaw Carpenter' on the sign?"

"Plenty of people apparently."

The rest of the SWAT team flows into the apartment, pushing past them. One of them grabs the bag and upends it and starts shaking it around.

"Careful," Small Cop says. "Could be dangerous."

The officer reads the word on the side and laughs.

"Yeah, no shit. I wouldn't stick my hand in there unless I wanted it bitten off."

Jack's other apartment. Seconds earlier. Jack sits up fast from reading his library book on rare dog breeds when he hears two shotgun blasts across the hall. He quickly walks out his door, fighting the urge to run, sliding past the police filing up and down the stairs and barking orders at him to get the hell back inside. He doesn't look back, doesn't look up. Never notices Derek outside on the sidewalk, back against a suspiciously ratty phone booth, hiding his face in a hoodie.

Derek steps inside the busted booth, and after a flurry of motions that could only be the result of substantial dimes being dropped and buttons being popped, Derek makes what certainly looks to be a very important phone call. The kind of call that ensures everyone ends up at just the right place at just the right time. This call appears to be even more crucial to the plot when Derek lets the receiver fall from his hand, and it bounces out through a hole in the booth, rattling and rolling off the sidewalk and into the yellow grass, never having been connected to anything at all. A new man, Derek exits, does a little spin, then follows Jack to his car.

Jack's heart is pounding so loud, he opens the driver's side door but doesn't notice Derek open the passenger door at the same time. Both men slide into the car like men in a mirror, even slamming their doors in unison. It's only when Jack's police scanner under the dashboard squawks and Derek leans over to turn it down that Jack finally sees him.

"Hey!"

"I got the same one in my car," Derek says. "No, wait, mine's an older model-"

Jack sucks in most of the available air.

"Jesus fucking Christ, what are you doing? How did you-"

"Sorry to scare ya," Derek says. "Door was open. Can you give me a ride?"

"I got things to do. But how did you-"

"That would be great," Derek says, talking over him. "Because I figure, with the cops up in your apartment right now, ready to bust in the other apartment, too, we're both in kind of a hurry."

Derek sits back, arms crossed. Jack starts the car and pulls out.

"Where do you live?"

"I didn't say I was going home. Just drive. I'll tell you when to turn."

Jack drives past the police cars on the curb, trying not to duck down and look suspicious. They drive a couple more miles in silence, then Derek starts slapping his leg to punctuate some directions.

"Left here…" Slap. "Straight awhile… right here…" Slap. "Right here?" Jack asks him, almost smiling.

"No, not 'right here,' turn right *here… shut the fuck up."*

Jack's loved that joke since he was a kid, climbing around the back seat of a rusted-out Jeep Cherokee and annoying the hell out of his mom. He sees the sign for Interstate 65, and he thinks back to how he used to ride with her from Louisville to Chicago when she was interviewing for a better job to hopefully move Jack and her out of the "Goddamn Red States" for good. And on those rides, Jack would practically wait with his nose against the glass in anticipation of those endless fields of windmills on 65 that rose on the horizon, an army of metal flowers. At first, he would count the ones that weren't spinning. Then he'd count the ones that needed a new coat of white paint. Then, after it finally hit him what they really *resembled, Jack rode that half hour in silence, mesmerized.*

If you blinked your eyes during the rotations, those windmills were actually stick figures, like the ones you'd draw for a game of Hangman, but all lined up on the edge of a pool, arms above their heads, diving sideways and into the invisible waves, one at a time. Then they were standing back up and starting that dance again and again. And when the wind got them all spinning just right, it was almost impossible not to be hypnotized. His mom thought they were a godsend the way they kept kids quiet, but Jack used to wonder why that stretch of 65 wasn't a pile of accidents with such an incredible distraction every possible way you looked.

Then his mother did get into a wreck on 65, when Jack wasn't riding in the Jeep to bother her, and he didn't wonder about this anymore. He hadn't seen those windmills since, and these days he really didn't give a shit what they were doing or if they'd ever find the wind or water they were reaching for.

A couple more miles with Derek's hand on his knee, and Jack adjusts his mirror again. They both go for the radio and conjure up Dolly Parton's "Cracker Jack," the "best friend she ever had, but he was more than that..." *and they're both into it for a verse or two. Then they're horrified that the song is about a dog, like every other song in the world these days. They fight to turn it off first.*

"You know," Derek says. "I've overheard some of your theories back at work, and I wanted you to know that I, for one, believe you."

"Great."

Derek leans forward and reaches behind his back, and Jack takes his foot off the gas anticipating a weapon. Instead, Derek comes up with a photograph of a woman and her daughter.

"You've seen this picture, right? We're in this together."

"What are you talking about?"

"I think we're both trying to save the same person. What do you see here, Jack?"

Jack doesn't have to look, but he answers anyway.

"I see a girl and her mother."

"No, the real question is this, 'Is that Jacki and her mom, or Jacki and her daughter?'"

Jack says nothing, and Derek laughs.

"I know, right?! I can't tell anymore either! Turn right here."

"Proceed to eighteen seventy Walnut Street... seven eleven in progress."

A couple miles later, and Derek is still laughing when the police scanner crackles. Jack turns the volume back up to drown him out.

"What's a 'seven eleven'?" Derek asks.

"Dog attack," Jack says without hesitation.

"You sure?" Derek says, mockingly. "I think it's code for 'dry-rub ribs.'"

Jack stares ahead.

"Naw, you're right. Those are the only two police codes I can remember, too. 'Seven eleven' is a dog attack, and 'one eight seven' is murder. I remember 'em because one is the exact price for a hot dog and coffee, and the other one… is where you buy it!" Derek leans out the window and sighs. "So what is it, Jack? What is up with all the dog attacks this summer? You'd think more people would be paying attention instead of just the two of us. I guess it's gotta be bears or sharks to make the news. Or maybe it's the locations. But we do what we gotta do."

"Well, a shark attack on a playground would cause some panic," Jack agrees. "Even if it's not a slow news day."

"You know what I mean, smart-ass. Turn here."

He turns.

"Okay, now stop the car and get out. And relax. I can hear you humming from here," he says, palms out. "See that? Not armed. You have nothing to worry about from me."

"Yeah, right," Jack mutters. "Until you tell me I'm related to you, too."

They step out of the car, and Jack is not surprised to see that they're back at the scene of his crime, parked in front of the tree where both of Jacki's boyfriends died, back to the place where Toni was conceived after the crash.

Derek walks toward the point of impact, the tree stump. Ground Zero. Patient Zero. Jack follows him. They circle the stump, and Derek's fingertips brush a ring of dying Venus Flytraps planted in the rotten bark around the edges. The stump looks evil to Jack, like a shrine, a place of rituals, bad memories, and stagnant black rain.

Derek squats down by his plants.

"I don't know what's going wrong here. Seeds should grow anywhere."

"Why are we here, Derek?"

Derek brushes the fuzz on the lips of a bulb, trying to get it to move. He brushes it again a little rougher, and it twitches *feebly. Then he flicks it in frustration, and it lolls on its stem like it has a broken neck.*

"You know, the first time I ever saw one of these things, it scared the shit out of me," he says. "It's hard to get your mind around the fact that a plant is moving where there's no breeze anywhere, you know what I mean?"

"Nope." *Jack thinks about how people typically look for the exits in a bad situation. Outside in the open, with too many options, he finds it impossible to visualize possible escape.*

"My little sister was growing them in her room, right next to her bed. And for the longest time, I thought they were dangerous. Especially growing next to your fucking bed, right? I remember watching her feed 'em dead spiders and flies, and that was crazy enough. But the thing I remember most was the hamburger. She would actually drop little bits of burger or roast beef or turkey, and it would gobble 'em up. Of course, back then when I was young and hearing everything all wrong, I thought it was called a 'Venus Mouse Trap,' and I coulda swore that's how hard they snapped shut. But now I realize it's a much more graceful snap, a smooth, almost sinister motion, kinda like those expensive soft-eject cassette players."

He suddenly grabs Jack's arm like a cop.

"Are you listening to me? Don't you understand how weird it is for your sister to be feeding a plant scraps from her dinner, like she was feeding a dog under the table?"

"What's your point, man?"

"The point is, a little kid starts wondering what exactly they'll eat. You drop all sorts of shit in there to get a reaction. Pennies, rocks, staples, cigarette ashes. Hell, one time I actually drew a picture of a fly and tossed it in there to see what it would do. Then, when my sister went off to school and left those crazy plants behind - this is right around when I'm turning 13 or so - I start to wonder what else would make them snap shut. So, yeah, maybe I pissed in it a little bit."

"Oh, boy. Of course you did."

"But nothing happened! So I shit in it."

"Why not."

"But that flattened them. Killed half of them, I think. So then I figured it out. I jerked off into one. Squirted right into that mouth. Nobody can tell me they weren't made for that."

He nudges Jack like they're buddies.

"I know it looks like another part of the body with those eyelashes on there, but it's definitely a mouth, trust me."

"Christ."

"And slowly, slowly it closed around me as gently as any woman."

Derek pulls Jack down to a sitting position next to him, tapping one of the largest plants on the stump. The green half moon at the end of its stalk stands taller than them all.

"Why did you come back here, Jack? What were you waiting for?"

"Waiting for Godot."

"Who?"

"Forget it."

"You see that?"

Jack looks close and sees a dark spot in the center of the closed leaves where the fading sunlight can't shine all the way through. Even though it's no longer struggling, the shadow of a fly is visible. The teardrops of the wings, the head, even the snout are clear.

"See that bug in there? That exact thing saved my life. And years later, it's what gave me my purpose. You want to know how?"

"Cannot wait," Jack says, clapping his hands and getting comfortable.

"It was a day like this, about twenty years ago, living alone, just moved to the Coast. The sun was coming through the window like a laser one morning when I noticed it. There was this dark spot inside the Flytrap on top of my television. At first, I was amazed it had captured its own dinner, you

know, 'cause I'd been feeding it Taco Bell like my sister taught me to. But then I started to think about what the plant looked like to me at that moment, that shadow inside and what that was trying to tell me..."

He strokes the plant lovingly and it seems to recoil.

"...see, back then, I had been getting this pain in my left testicle every day for a couple months. And I just assumed it was from riding a bike or taking a car door in the balls or leaning on my mop or something like that. But when I stood there that day, with the static of the television screen tickling against the hair on my stomach, thinking about how many times I masturbated into that yawning green mouth, I reached down, grabbed my balls and pulled them tight, and that's when I found the tumor."

He adjusts his crotch a bit for effect. Jack gives an empathetic smirk before he can resist.

"I could feel it rolling around in my fingers," Derek goes on. "Like a pebble stuck under a skinned knee. So I pinched a handful of skin and stretched the sack all out under that ray of morning sunlight. I was like Superman with X-ray vision, seeing right inside my body. I didn't need all your bullshit fancy machines that you drive around in those trucks. I could see the veins radiating from this dark spot inside my very core, stuck in there like a bullet that had pierced a bat's wing."

Jack pulls away, wincing in disgust. He starts walking to see how far he'll get.

More like *Waiting For Godon't*, he thinks.

"I wasn't sure if I was being punished for what I'd been doing," Derek explains, standing up to follow. "Or maybe rewarded with this knowledge. Rumor has it that they send signals to the cell phones of sex offenders all day long to chemically castrate them. It's in your pocket all day, you know? So I threw out my phone. Cracked it in half and threw it away for good. But the Flytrap showed me this shadow for a reason. It showed me that my seed was destined to die and

I didn't have much time left on this planet. That was a long time ago, though. Maybe I had more time than I thought!"

Jack walks towards the woods, looking to the sky through the leaves for answers.

"So let me get this straight," he says, turning back to Derek. "You're tellin' me that the reason you're this crazy-ass rapist is because you got turned on staring at fuzzy plants as a boy, and you started thinking of them as green little Martian pussies or some such bullshit?"

"I just want my family tree to go on!" Derek yells. "Is that so hard to understand? Just one more generation will be enough, I think. At first, I thought I could just store some seeds for later. And I did that. I stored it everywhere I could. Underground, under any loose brick in the road, in prescription bottles, at work in the break-room freezer. Yeah, that's right. I'd even drop some in someone's drink, so they could carry me around for the day, just in case."

"In case of emergencies, huh?"

"By the way, if you ever see him again, tell Rick you should never, never steal someone's lunch. That goes double for me. 'Cause technically, that's fucking kidnapping! Anyway, I thought maybe a part of me could wait for Toni, too, and if I couldn't live inside her for more than forty-eight hours, hell, maybe it didn't matter. The Guinness Book of World Records says the youngest pregnancy case on record is nine years-old. Nine. So there's a chance, you know? Maybe it's always been possible and not such a strange thing, just no one ever takes that chance until there's no other choice."

"But there is a dog right? Those dog attacks? That's all you, right?"

Derek hangs his head, suddenly ashamed.

"I'd never kill anyone. At least not before I found the second tumor."

Jack starts running.

"I know I've made mistakes," Derek is still explaining. "My dog... my Smokey, he helps me keep things straight in my *head. Still, I probably killed nobody. Somebody else is doing that shit. It's been a weird summer..."*

Evil had spent three long seconds with the wheels of his dirt bike still on the ramp when he saw Bully's shadow start dancing in the corner of his eye. That sad, lonely asshole "Billy" was still singing, all proud of the horrible song he'd written for her. The dog biting his handlebars whined, almost seeming to sing along between its teeth.

"...with a flamethrower, Russell ain't no slouch... Garry ain't spendin' the winter, tied to this fuckin' couch... fat bastard's belly ate our defibrillator... wait, how the hell did we climb outta that crater..."

Amazingly, Evil had seen most of the movies drawn all over her body, too. At least the faces looked familiar. But maybe it was just the beam, the excitement of seeing her on the big screen. The biggest screen.

Even more incredibly, Evil wasn't afraid. If it was one thing growing up in the era of 80's blockbusters had taught him, it was that deadpan under-reaction to insane or life-threatening situations was required. Billy was entirely too passionate and probably should have been born decades later. But not Evil.

Then the tape coughed and clicked, and another voice was talking. Somewhere out in the world, at the end of a long table in a glass room, a cop was revisiting his worst day in the glower of Internal Affairs:

"The collar that held the bomb to the victim's neck was as weak as a child's toy. It could have been pried away with little or no effort. The device appeared to be sophisticated, but Federal agents discovered it was constructed with, among other things, a partial Girl Scout's bracelet that could have been easily snapped, given a significant amount of pressure. One investigator at the first of several press conferences famously compared it to a Native

American 'dreamcatcher.' 'What's that?' the reporter asked, that single question recorded before cameras were abruptly turned off that day. 'Bunch of shit hanging off a hoop,' the Erie, Pennsylvania Chief of Police answered impatiently. 'Catches dreams.' At 3:28 p.m., the Chief was proven wrong as two bombs exploded…"

Then the beat of the song was back on, and Evil now was flying, and Bully was dancing, and Larry, he was down there fighting again. Fighting hard.

Larry fought harder than he ever thought he was capable. He was convinced it was the nakedness that allowed this. Naked people always fought harder, of course, even if his new tattoos had blurred the rules of the game. He turned the .38 back on Bigby, firing three wild shots at the cop as he ducked down inside the covered slide where the kids were crying and vanishing forever.

Officer Bigby would never be seen alive again.

So Larry turned his gun on the shadow of the girl, who held her arms a mile wide, just like the Journey song, showing off the remote control to everyone who was still paying attention to the movie.

And Evil, he was still flying. A good hundred feet up, he felt gravity bringing him back down to Earth, so he took his hands off his dog, turned down his music, and opened his shirt to reveal the smeared names and logos of his sponsors, rivers of Magic Marker dripping down the sweat of his chest.

But did she see him? She had to see him. He was *flying*, for fuck's sake.

Larry didn't see him, but he could still hear the song. He'd seen the movie, but the lyrics still made no sense to him at all.

"…*can you drag a man by his face? I got some misgivings… a pimp ties up the dead along with the living… man with diabetes wants to come back inside… builds a saucer in an hour? No way that shit flies…"*

Back in the beam, Bully had her thumb back on the button. The same thumb that had wrestled Evil into submission the first time they met. She saw the second-to-last dog left in the world, still tied to the slide, surrounded by the screaming families scooping up their children. The second-to-last dog had bright lesions on its nose from trying to get out of her trunk earlier in the day, and she felt a moment of pity, and her thumb wavered.

Then she saw a little girl yelling and running toward the animal, shouting a word indistinguishable to everyone but Bully, whose veteran drive-in eyes could read her lips easily.

What are the chances of that? she thought when she deciphered the dog's name. *Well, no time for reunions…*

Then she pushed the button.

Six years ago through the reflection in a dog's eyes. The smoke and fire of a burning car reveals a shadow dragging a girl's body toward a stump. The dog knows the shadow and cowers from it, trying to make itself small.

"Aren't you hungry?" the shadow asks. "You have to be thirsty."

Every word is like a hard tap on the dog's head, and it flinches with each one.

"Come here!"

This command impossible to resist, the dog takes a few wary steps toward the voice. When it reaches the stump, it begins to lap up cold black rain from inside the ring of wavering plants. Then a vicious kick sends the dog rolling into the brush with a yelp. The shadow looms over it as it offers its belly.

"Don't ever do that."

The dog slinks away, miserable in its confusion, averting its eyes but trying to be ready for what its master may expect. It hears the sound of a zipper and finally relaxes its shoulders. It associates this sound with moments of reprise. Calm before the storm. The dog looks up, whimpers.

A long time ago, the shadow tried to teach the dog to sing, starting with a particularly easy one, 5-year-old wunderkind Nellie McKay's "Dog Song."

"I said, 'Woof, be mine,' And you gave a wail, and then I was no longer alone…"

The lesson ended with the dog as miserable as he was after a kick.

"Here it comes… open wide…" *the shadow says to the plants. The dog howls almost reflexively, but he knows this command is not for him. Then the dog sneaks another look, brown wet eyes following the rain of white, ropey tendrils that begin painting the open mouths of the young plants. The bulbs ache towards the ejaculate, until they are covered and falling around the ring like dominoes, snapping shut like baby birds.*

Jack Grinstead stares up into the sky, his body swaying with the treetops while he shakes his head, thinks about everything he's just been told.

"You can't treat a dog like that, you know? You can't force a dog to do things like that and still expect to keep it around. They're smarter than you think. Okay, they can't make you an omelet or anything, but emotionally? They are fuckin' complicated."

Derek raises a gray eyebrow.

"Clearly more complicated than you," *Jack adds.*

"What I am doing is the most natural thing in the world," *Derek's voice is quiet, serene.*

"No, that dog will turn on you eventually. Trust me. Think I'm lying? Trying jerking off into your dog's mouth and

461

see what happens, you crazy fuck. Wait, I'll bet you already did that."

There's some crunching underbrush behind him, and Jack spins to see Derek is gone. He quickly runs back to find the Flytrap with the black spot in the center, and he tears it open, suddenly desperate to save the fly for no good reason at all.

The shredded plant falls from his hands, and he sees that it's empty after all.

Derek's apartment. Later that night. Derek is lying on the floor again, looking at his ceiling with binoculars, studying each photograph for several minutes at a time. He has a phone balanced on the side of his face.

"Hello? Toni? This is Jack, your mommy's friend. Hey, I have a secret to tell you. You wanna hear a secret?" Pause. "Good. You can't tell anyone, but I'm going to tell you who I really am. Now, this is a secret just for you. And it takes only four words to tell you this secret, so listen close. You swear you won't tell?"

He balances the binoculars on his forehead as he waits for her to swear.

A whimper comes from the closet, and he blinks slow, disgusted. He's not sure when he became so impatient with dogs, but he thinks it has something to do with growing up in those alleys, with all those cats. After all those felines orbiting his feet, looking for food from his hand and nothing else, he always found himself hating the intelligence he'd find in a dog's eyes. And if a dog looked at him worried or miserable? Forget about it.

If Derek was the kind of person to attach meaning to incomprehensible events, he would have reflected on what happened to his ears 30 years ago, when something went wrong at the local radio station during a freak thunderstorm, when there was a huge, red, mercurial blob on all the local weather radars, and for nine long months, the only thing the two little woofers in Derek's eardrums could pick up were songs about dogs. Desperate, he'd tracked down the station's tall, blinking towers, but no matter how many plugs he pulled, flashing lights he smashed, antennas he bent, or boomboxes he destroyed, it was all dogs, all the time. These days, he remembered hearing dog songs back then that hadn't even been written yet, and, of course, no one believed such incredible reception. He'd heard of a shoestring nephew picking up Springsteen in his fillings once, but none of those were dog songs, as far as he knew. And that incident was over mercifully quick. But for Derek, it was nine straight months of music echoing around his brainpan, and never one dog song repeated. That year, Derek realized there were a lot of dogs in the world, and even more songs written about the beasts.

Doctors were of little help. One of them even peered judgmentally down her otoscope and shamed him for jamming magnets into his ears as a boy, as if every kid didn't try it at least once.

Then one day, the dog songs stopped, as if the canid-obsessed musicians had finally run out of ideas.

He was relieved there were never any long-term psychological effects.

"Okay, you got your crayons? Good, just hide this after you write it down. Yes, write it on your hand. That'll be the easiest thing to hide. Are you ready? These four words are important, our secret. They mean I'm everything to you..."

Toni's bedroom. Minutes later. Jacki walks in and turns off a late-night talk show. She sees Toni hiding something from her mother behind her back, and Jacki smiles and playfully wrestles her hands open. Scrawled in crayon is red gibberish that spells:

"*Rehtorbapdnargelcnuyddad.*"

"What is this?" Jacki asks, and Toni surprises her by bursting into tears. She thinks back to when they both sat through a Citizen Kane *and* The Shining *double feature, and how afterwards, Toni started writing "Rosebud" on everything, but backwards. It was better than "Redrub," she decided at the time.*

Toni is crying harder, so Jacki lets her go, unplugging the television on the way out and vowing to get her some books.

Highway. Next day. Rick is driving with his new partner, Jess. About half a mile back on the highway is Jack, trailing them in another ambulance.

Before Rick can notice him in his rear-view mirror, he pulls a U-turn and heads in the other direction, lights flashing and siren blaring. Rick's siren is now clear and normal. He leans over to share a bag of peanuts with Jess, but she refuses, so he throws the bag out the window.

"What the hell?" she says.

"What?"

"Don't throw that shit into the street, man." *Jess is young, black, muscular. Speaks with authority, confidence, even on her first day at work.*

"You didn't care when I was throwing the shells," *Rick tells her.*

"That's 'cause those are natural."

"Well, so is plastic."

"The hell it is."

"What do you mean? You see plastic in bird's nests constantly these days. Just like any leaf."

"Yeah, and you see it wrapped around a turtle's face, too."

"Exactly!"

She shakes her head in disgust. "Once, I saw a turtle with one of those plastic rings from a six pack squeezing its shell. It turned the shell into a big-ass question mark. Tell me that

464

wasn't a message from somewhere telling us to get our shit together."

"You'd think those rings would squeeze a shell into a number eight."

"What's your point," she asks.

"That's like infinity. Can't be all bad."

The radio crackles.

"What did dispatch just say?" Rick asks.

"He said something about Greenbury Road?"

"Greenbury Road? There's nothing out there. That voice didn't sound right. Do me a favor. Try calling 'em back."

She eats a stray peanut from the crease of her pleats, wipes her hands on her pants, then clicks the CB.

"Dispatch. Come in, dispatch."

She drops the receiver and shrugs.

"Now it's dead."

Rick ducks down to check the equipment, teeth grinding as he pulls up a handful of loose wires.

"What the fuck?"

While he's leaning over, Rick doesn't notice Jack driving past them in his ambulance. But Jess does, and she taps on her window as he zips by.

"Now where was he…"

Then Jack swerves and does a quick wobbly U-turn to follow them, and she turns back around, assuming he's on the same call.

But Jack exits before they do, so that he can get there first. Jack still has routes in his head. Back in England, he used to have the routes on his walls. Sometimes he even drew them on his arms. If he'd have kept that job, he might have gotten them tattooed. But now his head would have to do.

Rick sees the car wreck on the horizon, the twisted body of a woman visible on the road.

It's Jacki.

He hits the brakes, and they both jump out just as Jack runs past them, bumping his shoulder into Rick's and rebounding him against the side of his truck.

Jack's heart is jack-hammering as he recognizes where they are, of course, near the woods again, back to the scene of Jacki's first crash, the stump, the Flytraps, everything. Suddenly, he ducks around their ambulance, out of Rick's sight.

Rick freezes, back against the truck, and Jess stops and tugs on his shirt.

"What's going on?"

"I don't know. Just stay where I can see you. I'm calling the cops."

Rick climbs back into his vehicle and comes face to face with Jack opening the passenger door and reaching for the ignition. Jack plucks the key, and Rick grabs Jack around the throat.

"You crazy fuck. I'm going to-"

The threat is squeezed off like a valve as Jack's hand turns white under Rick's chin, too. Then a third hand reaches up to help choke Rick harder.

Then a fourth.

Rick's hands slump.

Confused by the math with all those hands, Rick falls backwards out of the ambulance, catching a glimpse of someone pulling Jack out of the passenger door. Through the haze of his circulation pumping back into his brain, Rick see Jess helping him to his feet, but he pushes her away and runs back to the second ambulance, looking for Jack and the owner of those extra hands. He does a lap around it, stopping to stare at huge, jagged childlike letters spray-painted on the back doors.

"Time Machine."

"Stop running in circles!" Jess screams. "What are you looking for?!"

"Where did they go?" Rick pushes past her, frantic. "Did you see him?"

"Who was that? Come on, she needs our help."

Rick hesitates.

"I don't know."

He turns back toward the woods, motioning for her to follow.

"C'mon. He took the keys."

"Wait, aren't you forgetting something?"

Jess points back to Jacki's body on the side of the road.

"No. This is more important. It's probably a trick. She'll be fine."

They climb into Jack's ambulance, and Rick floors it, his tires throwing up a fishtail of dirt and dead leaves on his way out. The siren is choked and strangled.

Back to normal, *Rick laughs to himself.*

When the dust from their tires clears and they're long gone, sunlight and insects start to penetrate the smoke and light on Jack's body, bloody and inert between the tire tracks. In the distance, a shadow crashes through the woods, breaking branches for no reason.

Later that night. Derek is standing back in front of Rick and Jess's ambulance with his dog, a huge, hairless blue Doberman.

Toni standing next to him.

She's holding his hand, smiling at the word "Ambulance" reflected in the mirrored sunglasses he's wearing. She tugs on his arm and uses her tiny hands to angle his head so she can read it clearer. Then she holds her palm up to Derek's face. Written in the color of every broken crayon in her box, but only legible in the reflection of his glasses, are the words:

"Daddyunclegrandpabrother."

Derek smiles and helps her up into the passenger seat. The dog jumps over her and into the back where it curls up under the shelves. Toni laughs and follows the dog. She seems nervous but not scared, interested in the equipment, the animal, and all the cartoon warning signs surrounding her. Derek reaches for the dashboard, brushing aside all the loose wires, a Frankenstein combination of radio/police scanner/tape player that's been rigged under the steering column. Derek rewinds a tape, then pushes play. A very official-sounding woman's voice is heard, sounding every bit like a dispatcher reporting injuries.

Then, after a long pause, the woman sniffles and the fear is her voice is revealed.

"Will you let me go now?"

He rewinds and plays it again.

"Dispatch? We got a 'seven eleven' over."

No, it ain't over, *he thinks, looking to the body of the woman in the road.*

He removes the tape, putting in another one. The drums of Peter Gabriel's "The Rhythm of the Heat" begin to pound. Toni climbs back up front.

"Why are you driving Jack's car?" *she asks.*

"It's not his car," *Derek says.* "It's not a car. And it's more mine than his. Or any of those bastards playing doctor. I played doctor. You played doctor. Who hasn't done that shit? Who are they kidding…"

Toni frowns. She hasn't played doctor.

"See, they leave the keys in them all the time. For anyone who really needs one," *he adds.*

"Why?"

"They're for everybody!"

"I don't believe you."

"They leave the keys in any vehicle that has a siren. Even leave 'em running, too, sometimes. You'd be surprised."

The dog is growling at its own tail, and now Toni is looking scared.

"It's just like in those videogames. Fire trucks, cop cars, ambulances, all the tools of First Responders are there for the taking! Don't believe me? Listen to them in an interview. They didn't 'ask to be a hero.' You don't have to either…"

The dog's growling rises with Derek's voice, and Toni shrinks in her seat. Then the dog is panting and smiling again, and she's up and playing with the defibrillator paddles. She holds one up to the side of her head and starts messing with the buttons. Derek turns to watch her, ready to warn her to put it down, but interested to see how far things will go. She flips a switch that makes the machine power up with a rising hum, and Derek's eyes widen in anticipation, both him and the dog now cocking their heads curiously. But before Toni can push another button, Jacki suddenly opens the driver's side door and pushes her way inside. Surprised, Derek moves to the passenger seat, happy to see what's going to happen next. He watches, amused, as she puts the ambulance in gear and starts driving. Lines of blood streak her forehead like a ragged American flag. A long canvas bag marked "T.W.A.T." is draped over her shoulder, and a long, military-style rifle is resting against her leg.

"Hi," *Derek says, warmly.*

"Don't talk," *Jacki says.* "We're going to the scene of the crime, the same place you were taking her."

"I thought we were already here."

"Mommy!" *Toni yells, dropping the paddles.* "Where are we-"

"Quiet honey, we're going for a drive."

The ambulance leans hard to the right as it slides around a corner too fast, picking up speed as she straightens it out. Derek looks nervous, his hands scratching at his legs.

"If we have some time," *he offers.* "I'd like to explain-"

Jacki swerves harder through traffic, tipping him into the aisle.

"Heard it already. Don't bother."

"How's your head? I didn't realize I hit you that hard."

She ignores the question but wipes some blood from her brow.

"Did you see how they left you? And that's their job. I wouldn't have left you."

469

"Quiet."

"The only thing worse that playing doctor is playing God."

"And if a tree falls on a car and no one lives to see it, does it make a sound?" she laughs. Then she honks and dodges more cars.

"So…"

"Don't give a shit," she says, bringing the rifle up to tap Derek's chin. "Stop. Fucking. Talking."

"We have a connection," Derek practically whines. "You can't deny that. One look at your daughter and you must realize this. If you could do anything different, if I could do anything different, would you even want me to? If I didn't do what I did, she wouldn't exist. You wouldn't exist. And her daughter won't exist. Meaning you."

"Your family tree is fucked, whoever you are," Jacki says, and Derek leans towards her.

"Why deny these things? Why interfere in something that's perfect?"

She stomps the gas, and Derek sits back down. He hits the ghastly siren to warn oncoming traffic out of their path.

"Please, just relax," he says. "You're scaring our daughter."

She buries the gas pedal.

"Where are we going? This isn't where we were going, Jacki."

"You okay back there, honey?" Jacki yells over her shoulder.

"No!" Toni yells back, defibrillator paddles over her ears in fear.

"What's with all the fucked-up sirens?" Jacki says, looking around. "Why the hell does it do that anyway?"

"Just watch the road," Derek says, face pinched. Then, "Okay, I made it do that. To keep Jack unbalanced. But to tell you the truth, I don't understand why it's doing it now…"

Jacki takes another hard turn, and the song "The Rhythm of the Heat" is reaching its frantic climax of drums. Derek has a foot on the floorboard between them, ready to attack. Another hard turn, and the sun visor flops, dropping a

470

fluttering piece of paper onto Jacki's leg. She flips it open with one hand. It's one of Jack's crude, crayon drawings of a baby flying headfirst through a windshield, a red circle with a line through it. Apparently it's something you shouldn't do.

Jacki squints as an idea seems to occur to her, and she yells back at Toni again, forcing a smile.

"Baby! Get up here and sit in our daddy's lap."

Derek looks at her in surprise and smiles back, touched, when Toni does what she's told.

"Let our daddy strap you in with him," Jacki says, trying not to cringe at the sound of all this.

"But he's my daddy," Toni pouts.

"That's true. Let your daddy strap you in. There's a sharp turn coming..."

Derek welcomes her onto his lap, adjusting his crotch before she sits. Then he carefully pulls the seatbelt over them both and wraps his arms tight around her shoulders. Stone-faced, Jacki stares straight ahead and starts counting to ten.

"Please. Where are we going?" he begs. "We aren't going to where she was conceived. We just left there."

"No, we are. We're going to the place where you made us all."

Then she turns the ambulance too hard one last time.

Across the parking lot, Evil finally touched the ground on the other side. All of the cars behind him were still honking, not just from the violation of the dirt-bike jump, but mostly furious they'd been tricked into sneaking their children into a triple-feature so vile. When he hit, Evil's front wheel caught the last cop, who had still been working the traffic jam, square in the face, plowing his whistle through four incisors, but even worse, breaking his neck and killing him, if not instantly, then very soon after that. Evil's new dog, the second-to-last dog in the world, soon to be last dog, finally released its grip on his handlebars and slammed into an El Camino. The weight of the dog broke an elderly man's shin, and, seeing a dog in distress, dozens of people who knew immediately how movies worked, forgot about everything else, even stepping over the cop's body to cradle it, weeping and stroking its fur.

Evil, he went headfirst through a windshield, body twisting so bad that the first paramedics on scene would be confused as to whether or not he'd been driving that Fiero (they weren't really the best paramedics in town, budget cuts increasing the competition between hospitals, not the best at identifying cars either). Evil's boombox, however, was thrown free and landed on its feet, pretty much unscathed. It kept playing awhile, continuing to sing of a more lovestruck Billy, a poor imitation of evil.

"...*walks and talks like us without taking classes... all we know for sure is it spits out your glasses... stick a needle in your blood and your blood's gonna scream... stick a needle in your blood and your blood's gonna scream... someone in this crib ain't what he seems...*"

Then there was a moment of silence between the screams and tinkling glass, and the crowd looked to the shadow of the girl on the screen, almost ready to ask her what they should do. But the girl was pinwheeling her arms and kicking her legs in wide circles, seemingly swimming between and free of the huge, projected thighs, big as Redwoods, bent at the knees and spread up and wide. This birth came almost instantly after the hazy giants had stopped fornicating, and the crowd was in awe of the miracle of creation. Then...

Boom.

Just as the little girl touched its tail, the bomb on the collar of the second-to-last dog in the world exploded.

And the drive-in screen came tumbling down. In a cloud of dust, it ruptured and rolled over itself like a closing fist, piling onto the playground, right overtop of hundreds of bouncing babies and balls of every color. Bully had seen enough movie explosions to know what she was supposed to do. She turned from the fire and smoke so that it all filled the sky behind her like a spinning, monstrous blood orange, and she walked as slow and calm and stern-faced as possible across the roof of the bunker, like any action star should. She even tried out a catchphrase:

"Happy Veterinarian's Day, motherfuckers!"

Then a piece of shrapnel caught her in the back of the head, right above the ear, breaking her jaw and upending her into a garbage can full of rotten popcorn.

Months later, when they plucked out the thirty tiny spiders stitched across her cranium, she cursed through her wired smile the entire time.

Thirty years ago? Hot, hazy day in Florida near the beach. Peter Gabriel's song "Intruder" is playing deep in someone's headphones. There is a young man sitting on a bench near the ocean, wearing a baseball cap and sunglasses. He turns the cap around and lifts his head. It's a teenage Derek. Just over his shoulder is a large sign with a grinning cartoon dog. The dog's eyes seem to be watching everyone. And everyone is leading a dog, of course.

"All Dogs And Their Owners Welcome!"

Behind him is the dead screen of a drive-in theater, waiting for the sun to go down.

Derek cradles a small potted seedling like a baby. After a while, an attractive Chicana girl walks by.

"Can you please tell me what time it is?" he asks her.

Fast forward through several dark-skinned girls walking by Derek's bench and answering his question in Spanish. There is a dismissive, impatient tone to the parade of responses. No one notices how amazing it is that a young, blind man only interacts with pedestrians possessing a certain look. *Clearly a preference, or a profiling, is going on. No translation is necessary with a rapid-fire list of rejection:*

473

"El tiempo para usted comprar un reloj," says the first girl.

"Joda Lejos," says the second.

"Cogida apagado," says the third.

"Vete a la mierda," says the fourth.

"Coja eso," says the fifth.

"Varfunculo," says the sixth.

Derek raises his head sharply at this last response. Certainly some kind of rebuke, but not Spanish. He's angry not understanding what the girl said, as he's clearly gotten used to a steady stream of Spanish "fuck offs" and learned to let them roll off his back.

Finally, a small Mexican girl smiles and stops to answer him. Their connection and the friendly tone of the conversation is obvious. Derek's apparent blindness also puts her at ease.

"No puede decir ested por el sol?" says the Mexican girl, number seven.

"Usted madre no lo dijo para nunca contestar una pregunta con una pregunta?" he asks.

"Eso no es lo que usted acaba de hacer?"

"Eso no es lo que usted acaba de hacer?" he asks, smiling.

The Mexican girl moves closer.

"Yo no recuerdo a mi madre," she says.

"What's all that noise down there?" Derek whispers in English. "What are they doing by the water?"

"I'll show you…" she starts, then stops, embarrassed. "I mean… let's see."

She steps toward him, taking his arm. He's surprised and almost drops his plant. Gently cradling it, they both walk toward the water where a pier is under construction. Suddenly, a thundering pile of tree trunks rolls out of the back of a truck and crashes onto the sand. The noise startles at least a dozen sunbathers, several of them sitting up on their towels, sliding down their sunglasses and frowning and looking around. The Peter Gabriel song climaxes, the chorus of screams resembling the hollow cries of the ice-bound alien in The Thing:

"Intruder come... intruder come and leave his mark... leave his mark. Leave his mark."

"Feel the sun on your nose?" Jacki Ramirez's mother asks him. "It's noon. To answer your question, that is what time it is. See how easy we did that?"

"Thank you," Derek says, in love again.

"You didn't answer me back there," Jacki's mother says. "I asked if your mother ever told you not to answer a question with a question."

"No, I asked that. But I guess she didn't. But one time, my father said that if I threw enough rocks off that pier..." He nods toward the construction. *"...I would eventually hit a duck that deserved it!"*

"What were you trying to hit?" Jacki's mother asks, suspicious. "How could you even see to-"

Derek holds up a hand to stop her.

"Don't you mean to say, 'There wasn't a pier here until today?'"

His voice fades as they walk on together. Smiling wide with his nostrils flaring, Derek turns to the ocean. A dog's ragged ball rolls in front of his foot. And even though the ball doesn't bump his shoe, he quickly kicks it away as if he sees it coming. He takes a deep breath, hiding his urge to kick the dog along with it.

Somewhere in the dark, he carves another heart.

The small dog quickly skids to a stop and alters its course to run down the ball, and Jacki's mother doesn't notice the quick kick. After the dog catches the ball, it trots back towards a boy wearing headphones. Halfway there, the dog stops, then turns to stare at Derek, its head cocked to one side. Just like Derek's.

"Was ist los?" the boy with the headphones asks in German. Then, *"What's wrong?"*

The dog ignores its master. It slowly opens its mouth and the sand and saliva streaked ball drops and is stolen by the surf.

* * *

As the concrete screen came down around him, Larry found himself closer to any movie than he'd ever been before. As a boy, he'd put his nose to the crackling TV tube and watched images burst into colorful fireworks like a disease under a microscope, but he'd never gotten his nose up against a drive-in screen before. And now that he was inside of it, he saw the strange green circulatory system within and recoiled. But not too much recoil, really. Sort of the recoil you'd get from a .38 when you stopped the bad guy. In other words, manageable.

But the recoil was there.

The movie kept rolling, projected onto a storm of rock and debris, projected onto the screaming mob, even projected onto the distant harvest moon when the dust cleared. Larry watched the movie on the lunar surface awhile and thought about how you might not need a helmet up there on the moon after all.

He heard someone shout, "Those kids did this!" and Larry looked around in vain for the culprits. But he thought these words made all the sense in the world. When he was shooting pornography, there was a well-known rule in the business regarding the number of teenagers you should have in any one particular scene. The rule was never, *never* two kids together. Four was the magic number for adults, but only one teenager per scene and that was it. Some directors even insisted on a one-teenager-limit per film. Mostly this was because two teenagers couldn't fuck with any degree of certainty, and for Larry it was sort of like watching paraplegics play basketball. Meaning, they were probably still better at the game than any civilian, and he'd still be rooting for them and all, but someone out there on the court needed their sea legs to keep things professional.

476

So, yeah, one teenager per movie is the limit. Two fucks everything up and down. Like tonight.

When the smoke lifted a bit, Larry was shocked and excited to see the only thing still standing amid the carnage. It was a dirt bike, engine still hiccupping, pinned upright by something horrible and bleeding, a combination of man, dog, and cop.

Two legs good, eight legs bad, Larry thought.

He mounted it, smiling, remembering his training across the ocean all those years ago, where paramedics rode on two wheels instead of four. Where he could get to an accident before it even happened.

As Larry dreamed of when he was Jack and tore off through the new holes in the fence, The Last Projectionist held his wooden goblet up to the flames, watched the cup vanish in his hand and the liquor dance in midair. A week ago, he'd known the concrete screen was on its last days when he saw the weeds and wildlife prying it apart at the seams. Then, a couple nights prior, after the movies had faded and the drive-in slept, he saw the shadows of a young couple, giggling and chasing each other around the support beams. Later, he crept up to the foundation with a flashlight and traced the weeds with his light until he realized these particular weeds were kind of different. These were red and blue weeds mixed in with the green, and some of them were connected to small bricks of a sticky substance that reminded him of that strange, purple bubblegum he used to push into his walls as a kid, the stuff he'd stamp big thumbprints into when he decorated his bedroom with movie posters. Ironically, *Duel in the Sun* had been his favorite poster. Favorite movie, too, which was weird since sunlight was a drive-in's worst enemy. As a kid, he never had a chance to see that one on the big screen, or the biggest screen. He'd only been to the drive-in about a dozen times, but he remembered each time like it was the only time. And he remembered always praying for rain so he could roll up the window and lock out all the sounds, the water smearing away any face that came looking for him. But for some reason, he never remembered the movies at all.

But this strange, purple bubblegum that he remembered so well had been given to him by a crazy uncle, fresh home from Vietnam. There were bricks of this gum tucked behind some open plumbing in the bathroom wall, but even if The Last Projectionist had stolen some corners to hang his posters, he'd never dare to blow a bubble with it. Then one night, the purple gum disappeared, and even the corners of *Duel in the Sun* had been ripped away.

That night after he saw those kids running around, The Last Projectionist studied the strange new bricks in the support rails under the screen. And he studied the weeds and mushrooms growing in every crack, straining like the blinded Samson to weaken the will of the world. He thought of the mushrooms the most though, imagining running a razor across them every morning instead of his chin, clipping them at the base with almost a knuckle-cracking sound and a puff of blood instead of spores. He imagined shaving the entire screen until it ran red, and it was oddly satisfying.

But even though he knew the green wires would bring it all down some day, it was the red and blue wires that scared him the most now. And the wires were everywhere. How long had they been multiplying? He didn't know. He wondered if they'd been always hidden behind the roadmap of Creeping Charlie that reached higher and higher every year.

The only projectionist older than him had told him once that, kind of like a heat lamp, you couldn't shine the warm glow of too many movies on any surface, including concrete, or it would eventually get infested.

"Everything *turns* eventually," he told him. "Just watch."

Now he wondered if he'd really said "infected" instead.

The Last Projectionist drank deep from his wooden goblet, then began to walk home through trees that seemed to bend and creak out of his way. He'd seen old drive-ins from the sky before, in library books or every time he flew home for a funeral. So he knew they left a mark on the landscape, like ragged crop circles, as if the UFO actually crashed checking out the prank.

He looked at his rows of cars one last time. Tried to ignore the screaming that was ruining his moment. He worried that the cars didn't need drive-ins to gather anymore. Soon they wouldn't even need movies.

IX.

"For the dog that chases its tail will be busy
Un-tied dog in telematic society
ain't your average huckleberry hound
Why must I feel like that?
Aw, why must I chase the cat?"
—George Clinton "Atomic Dog"

In the distance is the screen of a drive-in, a sunset and a beach scene filling Jacki's windshield with the promise of a spectacular wreck. She turns her ambulance straight for the movie.

Walking her hands across the top of the steering wheel, the ambulance leaves the road sideways, its headlights exploding through a sand dune, a beach someone had filmed in Toronto, pretending it was California, specifically the intersection of North Hollywood Boulevard and Pennsylvania Avenue, now projected onto Kentucky Street. A wall of sand blankets them as the family rolls down this beach, rebounding off a dune, all wheels flying over a sunburned boy leaning on his Jeep, finally crashing into the lumber supports under the pier. Distracted by the little girl on his legs, Derek doesn't see the trusses and unmilled tree trunks coming at his half of the windshield until it's too late. Glass showers his face, and blunt chunks of wood fly over and under Toni's body to pummel him in the chest and groin. Behind them all, the boy reaches into his vehicle and turns up the volume on his Peter Gabriel cassette. Then he folds his arms like he's doing everyone a favor.

"Down at the ocean lies a body in the sand. Big woman sits beside, head in hand. With heat from her skin, and fire from her breath, she blows hard, she slows deep in the mouth of death... burning, burning with the kiss of life..."

Then all the songs no one can hear anymore end, and all cassette tapes unspool and curl up their dashboards like snakes. Derek is doubled over Toni, trying to catch his breath as Jacki reaches over to unbuckle her daughter and pull her out the driver's side door with her. Hissing through his teeth in pain, Derek picks red cubes of windshield from the corners of his eyes. Then he stumbles from the passenger side, one hand squeezing his heart, the other squeezing his crotch. The ridge in his pants from his fractured erection now resembles a fistful of something from the deli counter, bleeding through the wax paper. His dog, uninjured, whimpers and scratches at the back doors.

Derek's rage builds, and he starts to lurch toward them when a second ambulance plows down the beach, Rick jumping from the driver's door while it's still cruising. Rick runs at Derek, and he's almost on him when the dog crashes out of the back doors and intercepts Rick instead.

The wrecked ambulance starts to burn. It burns easily, like they were meant to burn, like the vulnerable rolling room of a home they always resembled.

The dog goes for Rick's throat, like a good dog, knocking him onto his back with his arm clamped in its jaws. It snaps at his neck, and Rick finally gets a grip on the dog's snout, at the cost of most of the webbing near his thumb, then Rick gets his own mouthful of fur as he bites its neck right back. The dog's teeth stabbing through the love line on his palm, then moving down to his life line, Rick struggles to bring his thumbs up and into the dog's pinballing eyes. His thumbs push down and in, and the dog yelps and kicks, fight gone, now struggling to get away. Rick stares at its face in his hands for a moment, hesitating to apply enough pressure to rupture its eyes and blind it for good. Instead, he struggles to his feet and dumps the dog back into the burning truck and slams the doors behind it.

Instantly, Rick regrets his move as the dog crashes back out through a shattered window and knocks Rick down again, smoldering fur filling his nose. Rick gets a mouthful of burning snout and bites harder. The dog screams and backs off, now submissive, tail curled under its balls. It slinks under the pier and is gone.

Toni runs to follow the dog and disappears into the dark. Derek turns to follow them both, but Jacki grabs his arm and spins him around easily. He's still hunched over, weak, one hand squeezing the red ruin between his legs. Bloody and dazed, Rick stumbles over to them.

"Who the hell are you?" she snarls at Rick. "I don't need any more of you crazy fuckers."

Then Jacki steps past him and punches Derek in the face. When her hand comes down to swing by her hip, Rick sees she was holding a jumble of keys in her fist, the ignition key protruding from her knuckles. Derek screams and grabs his face, and one of his thumbs slips into the hole where his eye used to be and his scream climbs so high it's inhuman. Jacki looks down to see most of his eye, deflated and dripping, hanging from the key, and Rick changes his mind again a third time about blinding the dog.

Jess is there now, too. Rick points to the pier, and she runs after the child, faster than he can. After his eyes adjust to the shadows, he finds all three of them where the beach meets the wood, petting the injured dog to comfort it.

"Hello?"

Toni peeks out from behind a pole under the pier like she did when she was hiding behind her mother's leg as the dog buries its bleeding snout in the sand to cool it down. Jess gently examines the child for injuries as Derek keeps screaming in the distance, but now it sounds more like words again.

"Don't you understand?!" he's asking Jacki. "Every man you've ever met, without exception, is a piece of shit. Think of yourself sitting in front of a slideshow with their faces, one after the other, clicking on the screen. Think about how every one of these creatures that you've encountered has disgusted

you or failed you or fucked you over in some way. Think about it!"

Jacki figures "fuck it," and does what Derek asks. She sits in the sand next to him and closes her eyes. In her head, she's sitting at a desk in a classroom, and behind her are the sounds of a slide projector humming and clicking through the images:

The first pictures are of her mother, walking with Derek under the pier all those years ago. Then Jack. Then her grandmother? Jacki looks to the projector in the back of the room, and isn't surprised to see Derek is teaching this class.

"...first, you have the ones that have had a tragedy in their lives. Look close how they want to make the death of their mother or father all about them, *and how they think, maybe without even knowing it, what money, attention or "Get Out Of Jail Free" cards they accumulate because of this. Think about how every good deed is for a selfish reason, and anyone who helps you only helps themselves..."*

The next slides are two cops, one big, one little, smiling side by side.

"...next are the accusations..."

Then come the two rival paramedics, Big Mike, and Little Mike. But this slide turns into a movie, and the Mikes are jawing away, Little Mike going on about the first books he ever read:

"...and I was losing interest in all the Mothman Prophecies bullshit, until it got to Louisville's contribution to the sightings. It reads as follows. 'According to the Louisville Kentucky Courier-Journal, *July 29, 1880, two men, C. A. Youngman & Bob Flexner, reported seeing "a man surrounded by machinery which he seemed to be working with his hands." He had wings or fans on his back, which he was flapping rather desperately to keep aloft. The startled men watched him flutter unsteadily out of view.'"*

"Did you memorize that?" asks Big Mike, looking around Little Mike's hands for a book.

"Yep. Someone has to pass it on to the next generation."

"Your Mothmen suck," says Big Mike. He's from Pittsburgh and very defensive about the origin of the creatures.

"Bite your tongue! Our Mothmans might not be scary, but they work harder than yours. Are we moths or men?!"

"Should it be 'Mothmen' or 'Mothmans'? Why does 'Mothmans' sound so much more accurate?"

"Do they even know what movie they're in?" Jacki asks no one in particular.

Then a storm rolls in out the classroom window. Something starts falling from the sky. She hopes it isn't frogs. Derek's voices continues.

"...now think about how people in power wait for an emergency to ask you something that they never would in a normal situation. A cop asks a rape victim if she was a virgin, just because he wants to know. Maybe they don't do this consciously. Maybe it's such an essential part of being human that they don't even know they're doing it..."

The next slide clicks. It's Jacki's father.

"...see that man? Okay, I don't know whose slide is up in your head right now, but I do know, whoever it is, he wronged you. You can always make that bet."

The next slide is the doctor sneaking up on her daughter with the needle.

"See that man? I don't know who he is either, but I know he lied to you, too..."

Another slide clicks into place, and Jacki stares at the face on the screen a moment. Then gets up from her desk and leaves the classroom. It's raining in the hallway. Hailstones in the rest of the lecture halls. She turns the light off and slams the door behind her, in her head, her feet sinking into the damp sand outside the classrooms, and Derek's voice turns desperate.

"Where are you going?"

Jacki opens her eyes and sees Jess leading Toni back to her mother, and all three of them start walking down the beach.

Derek, sand and glass crusting his remaining eye, is now blind for real, and forgets all the behaviors he'd memorized when he faked it. He falls after two steps.

"Who's there?!" he cries.

"Who do you think? That's my daughter."

"That's right," Derek laughs. "She's your daughter. And that means she's halfway to me!"

Jacki stops, drops Toni's hand, and walks back to Derek. She's still clenching her fist around the keys in her left hand, and she punches him again before he can react. It's a straight-on shot that punctures the one good eye he had left. Derek drops to his knees, head down, both hands over his face now, and Jacki asks just one question. More of a riddle really.

"If you can't see me doing this to you," she asks, sincerely. "Did I really do it?"

Derek stumbles around, trying to grab anyone he can, flailing around for his family.

"Without me, you're not even here!" he screams. "Not just somewhere else, you and your daughter are not even alive. Jacki, no, please, you're half me, and she's three quarters me. One more generation and the child will be all mine. Check the math…"

He lets this insanity sink in, and Jess looks to Rick. Rick holds up a hand that promises to explain everything later, but he doesn't look too confident that it would be possible. Then Derek stops bumbling and raging and slumps into the sand, head down, arms limp. Blood drips like tears, and he grabs his head again, mumbling, barely audible.

"You ever wonder about why you're with the three of us, Jacki? Why all our names are the same? Derek? Eric? Jack? Rick? These aren't even names. 'Jack'? More like verbs, all of them. This is no accident they almost rhyme. We all keep going back to what we know, even if it has never worked, like a dog to its own sick. You know why? Because it's delicious."

His finger comes out of his eye with a POP! like a toddler's thumb being pulled reluctantly from his mouth.

"*…where's my dog…*"

He tries to whistle for it, blood bubbling through his lips instead, but the dog doesn't come. Derek finally collapses, face sinking into the beach like a sand crab after a wave.

Jack walks up behind them all, rubbing his head in the distance, carrying some equipment like he's ready to do his job.

"*Did I miss anything?*"

Seconds later, cop cars are piling in, too, blue and red dividing everyone's faces.

And as they all run toward Jack, he waits until their hands are on him, or on the conducting metal flank of the ambulance so the electricity can handcuff them together. Wired together forever. Then he reaches inside his toolbox and hits a button.

"*Clear?*" *he asks, knowing they're not.*

"*At some point after that, there will be a brawl. Resisting arrest? Lots of arrests to resist. Everybody will have a head full of electricity from Jack's defibrillating, and they will be seeing things a little differently. Big Rick and Big Cop maybe even have a battle to the death. Big Mike will jump in, too, while the Big Cop reveals he killed Anthony, thinking it was Jack, thinking it was The Bardstown Rapist. It would have confused everyone at the drive-in if they didn't have their own problems to contend with. No one will even care about all these loose ends.*"

"'*Why did you kill the girl?!*'"

"'*Who?*'"

"'*The babysitter with the money! The ladybug for President!*'"

"'*Oh, her! To smoke you out?*'"

"'*Really?*'"

"'*I don't fucking know. Ask him.*'"

"Cut. Okay, good. Now Small Cop will tell Jack that he can appreciate his urge to make all their stories overlap. But get this. He can't! And even his roommate will be there, because Larry wanted one of those final scenes that tied a nice bow around everything. The roommate will be his wife, of course, maybe, chewing ice as usual. She'll be in uniform, an EMT-P, the highest rank of first responders. Jack won't be able to look at her because that's right about the time she and Jack started having problems, when she started to outrank him. And Larry will hire Rick to play Jack because awhile back he smelled semen in the back of the ambulance and realized that Rick had been renting the truck out for some Gonzo pornography, that is pornography with someone dressed like Gonzo from The Muppets…*"*

"Why do you keep saying, 'Big Cop, Small Cop'? Don't you mean Good Cop, Bad Cop?"

"Shut the fuck up."

"Cut!"

"What did you call me?" Rick laughs.

"…just have Rick as Jack open those double doors and get a big ol' whiff of Pyrus Calleryana, *those white-petaled trees that used to be all around his first girlfriend's brownstone, an earthy smell that Jack would try desperately to ignore when he'd come and pick her up, at least until her brother, always perched on the top step, flared his nostrils one night and laughed, 'Careful, sis, the Come Trees are in bloom!' This distinct odor will be radiating off the hot metal and sticky equipment, just like it is now, and Larry, I mean Jack, is furious. This is when he realizes that for all his self-righteous bullshit, Rick was using the ambulance for clandestine porn shoots, and that's why he disabled the camera. Until recently, Larry would have thought it was unusual to go from a career in medicine to a career in pornography…"*

"You know what rhymes with cut?"

"What?"

"Exactly."

"*…and even stranger than Larry hiring Rick to play Jack is the fact that Joe Fuck, now playing Larry, will insist on calling himself 'Joe Luck,' his given name, perhaps the strangest revelation of them all…*"

"Wait, who the fuck am I now?"

"*…and during all the fighting, the Girl Who Loves Ice Cubes will have to bite through something to help someone, and the audience will realize that all that chomping gave her the strongest teeth on the planet. Joe Luck as Joe Fuck as Larry as Rick as Jack as you as me will probably watch her snap through police officers' fingers like breadsticks, remembering the day they met in the hailstorm that cost $2,500 worth of damage to his car, and all five of them will fall in love all over again. The hailstones had shaken the car harder than the bass of her new DMX single, a song which declared, 'This one time I'm-a let a dog be a dog,' which will be good advice really…*"

"That day, she ate every hailstone she caught in her mouth. Still did."

"The crew shuffled around, staring at their feet."

"Damn right we did."

"And then later, all the cops, they'll be out on patrol, and everywhere there's a dog attack they keep hearing these kids saying, 'Eck-nail-ub-muh!' and pointing off down the road. But the cops they're fuckin' racists, so they just shrug and think it's Spanish or ghetto slang. Not realizing these little witnesses are giving the audience the biggest goddamn clue of all time!"

"If you have any extra clues, I could use one."

"You guys ready to shoot this? Come on, are you 'lubri-can'ts' or 'lubri-cans'?!"

"That has never made any sense."

"So, let's do it. Clear?"

"Clear."

"Larry, I hate to fuck up this movie, but I'm not going to do any of that."

* * *

Hours later. Sun coming up over the beach. Big Mike is being interviewed by a little cop. They make a great pair. Bystanders linger. Someone nearby listens for a minute or two, then comments how much the interrogation reminds him of listening to mental patients stuck in an elevator. Then someone else asks how he ever heard that before to make such a comparison.

"I'm getting like ten different versions. Maybe you can clear some things up."

"...so, here's how it went down, I'm holding my finger up under the light," *Big Mike says, holding a finger up under a light.* "And it's glowing green. I turn to Mike, and I'm like, 'See, I told you something was wrong with that girl!' and he's like-"

"I'm like, 'Everything is glowing green, dumb ass,'" *Big Mike says, interrupting himself from behind his own shoulder, with a black and burnt finger now playing the role of the recently roasted Little Mike.* "Cause it's one of those blacklights in the room, and he's standing under this poster of a panther that's glowing like Three Mile Island and he doesn't even notice..."

"Let's get back on track," *Little Cop says, understandably confused by a black finger pretending to be a dead man pretending that the finger is green.* "You knew this janitor?"

"Oh, hell, yeah, we knew him," *Big Mike says.*

"Do you remember how tall he was?"

"Huh?" *Little Mike Black Finger answers for him.*

"*His* height," *Little Cop goes on.* "We've got a measuring stick from an amusement park in evidence, and a witness who seems to remember a suspicious man who was... three feet tall?"

"No, Derek's a big dude."

"Don't you want a description? Or a last name?"

"What the fuck do you think this is? Literary fiction?"

"Just the facts, boys," Little Cop coughs. "And please, no amateur sleuthing necessary."

"You laugh," Little Mike Black Finger says. "But stranger shit has happened. You know how they're saying Derek was pissing and spitting on people's food? Well, I used to live with this asshole who put a big black pubic hair on my pizza slice in the 'fridge. After four days, the hair was twice as long. Explain that shit, Detective."

"Think about that," Big Mike says. "Is it the 'fridgeration? Is it the pizza? Boggles the mind..."

"Naw," Little Cop says. "That's a myth. It's like when they say fingernails keep growing after someone dies."

"They don't?" Big Mike asks, looking at his fingernails. "I swear I've seen that."

"No, he's right. It's just the skin on the fingers shrinking back after you're dead."

Little Cop slams his book shut.

"Precisely! Okay, I think we're about done here-"

"Wait! Did you hear about how I got immunized for the 'hunta' virus?"

"No."

"True story. I'm holding down the dog for the vet to give the shot and the needle goes through-"

"Hold on. Same thing happened to me!" Little Cop says.

"Bullshit"

"No shit?"

"No shit."

"Me, too!" Little Mike Black Finger is going nuts to be part of things.

"No. Shit."

"What did you do about it?"

"I go back every year to get another shot. Just in case."

All three of them laugh.

* * *

Hours later. The back of an ambulance with a strong, steady siren blaring.

A paramedic with a baseball cap covering his face is working on Derek's. Captain Beef Loaf's "Electricity" is playing loud on a small portable cassette player. Then the song is interrupted by Derek giving a fake radio dispatch.

"Please respond to dog attack on the corner of... fuck, that doesn't sound right..."

The paramedic laughs and pulls back his cap. It's Rick. He fast-forwards the tape to get back to the song. Jack hovers over Derek on the gurney.

"Hey, asshole!"

The muscles that used to hold Derek's eyes try to pinwheel.

"Ever heard anything by the band, Penis Flytrap? Me and Rick bet five bucks that's where most of your ideas come from. Pretty sad."

"Why is it taking so long to get there?" *Derek asks through a mouthful of sand and blood.*

Rick turns off the siren. Captain Beefheart is now the only thing howling.

"Good question," *Jack laughs.*

"I'm just trying to remember my buddy Jack's philosophy," *Rick says.* "Or was it yours?"

He rips off the tape covering Derek's empty eye sockets.

"What was it you said? 'If you can't see it, then it didn't happen'? Or was it, 'If you can't hear it'?"

Derek's empty eyes blink out of reflex.

"Never said that," *he mutters.*

"Question for ya," *Ricks says.* "Is it true? I mean, all that crazy shit about the dogs? Did you really do those things with the dogs? Or was Jack chasing shadows these last couple days? Or should I say, chasing his tail?"

"I'm sorry," *Derek says, groggy, lost in thought.* "I never did anything like that."

"What do you mean?"

"Smokey just follows me around, like any dog would. It's as simple as that."

"Smokey?! We're not firefighters, fuckface."

"He follows me, I swear."

"Impossible."

"Your partner put so much time into his theory. I don't know. It seemed so important to him, to let him think he was right about everything."

Rick puts a hand over Derek's mouth.

"I knew it. That fucker was crazy. I fucking knew it."

"He's only like twenty-five percent crazy," Jack says. "Thirty tops. The rest really happened. And this motherfucker did the worst of it."

He stops laughing, considering the crimes.

"He did the worst, and he deserves worse," Rick says. "All of this really happened. Sorry I doubted you, man…"

Jack stares into Derek's sockets.

"Yeah, it happened," he says. "But it won't as soon as I flip the switch on this Time Machine…"

"Wait," Derek pleads. "I was just trying to…"

"Shhhhh," Jack whispers. Rick turns to watch.

"Hey, you ever see those three monkeys?" Jack asks him. "The 'See No Evil, Hear No Evil, Speak No Evil' little bastards?"

"No. But for the record, Tommy sucked," Rick says.

"Well, there you go."

"Your attempt to blame all this on the butler is laughable, Jack," Rick says. "Transparent. It sounds… fishy."

"Sounds?"

"Smells fishy."

"That's not what we are. We're the janitors."

"Butler, janitor. Doctor, director. Same difference. Everyone knows more than doctors. For example, I didn't make that joke about fish. Because one man's forgotten colostomy bag learned me long ago that fish means you're smelling piss, not pussy. Point is, you did this. You did it all."

"No, he did."

Jack flips a switch, and a climbing whine fills their ears. Derek pinches his sockets closed, and Rick looks around the back of the ambulance one last time, stopping to focus on Jack's baseball cap, the Georgia Bulldog watching him close. It's a weird feeling. He squints at the baseball cap drawn on that bulldog and wishes there was a dog on that one, too.

Then Jack brings the two defibrillator paddles up to Derek's ears. Derek doesn't really struggle but seems to know what's coming.

"Relax," Jack says, knee in his chest. "Hear no evil, right, brother?"

"That's right," Rick says, eyes on the road. "Fucking do that shit."

Jack hesitates.

"You know, I never realized what 'Timber' meant to a lumberjack until someone said it sarcastic and all quiet-like," he tells Derek. "Just a 'timber?' you know? Telling everyone what's coming. I think that's the same with 'Clear.'"

The metal walls echo like a submarine as the charge reaches its peak.

"Clear?" he asks, softly.

Then there's a hollow smack like someone swatting an insect too hard against their ear, and the waxy childhood magnets deep in Derek's head are humming now, making his head shimmer around the edges like a tuning fork, causing the cassette to stop and the heads of the old player to begin eating the tape. The song "Plush" by Stone Temple Pilots plays next regardless. It's about dogs. When the band gets big one day, Rick's wife will call them "Stone Temple Toilets," and the premonition causes him to click it off after just one lyric:

"When the dogs begin to smell her, will she smell alone…"

The electric whine starts to climb the metal walls again. Blood trickles from Derek's cored out eye sockets and nose.

"These are gonna make you a new man. No, seriously, someone else entirely."

Jack rubs the paddles again.

"Clear?"

They're sitting at a red light. Rick looks both ways for traffic.

"We're all clear."

Jack looks at Derek one last time.

"Three more minutes and you never happened."

The blast wave ripped a flyer off the teeth of the windshield that held Evil's ribs tight. The hot breeze carried it at least half a mile, and it rode the heat until it finally stuck, slapping and flapping against a tree trunk, miraculously upright. The flyer read:

"**Lost Dog**" and "**Answers To 'Skinny Elvis.'**"

Speaking of, back at the blast, someone was crooning.

"…he wants to come back inside… too bad his head died… he wants to come back inside… too bad his head died… he wants to come back inside… too bad his head died…"

Bully's voice kept clickclickclicking the refrain of his love song out of the wrecked radio, even as response teams started sifting through the rubble for survivors. Billy had way too many lyrics for that song, but that was back when he was still Billy. And they'd all argued over the title, too. To compromise, Billy wanted "The Rap's *The Thing* (To Catch the Conscience Of the King)," but Bully was really into the much simpler "Your Blood's Gonna Scream." Evil didn't have an opinion.

So she won. She always won. But even though she mocked him mercilessly when he was taping this song in the garage, she'd snuck back to add a few extra lines of her own. She wanted the song to be good. She guessed it was because she was still rooting for him. She couldn't help it. A first kiss at the movies was still a first kiss at the movies.

Nearby in the smoldering crater, faint but unmistakable, hard but tiny, Bully's voice was still coming out of half of some fuzzy headphones, going on and on about something else, always something, but this something sounded a lot like a full disclosure at a deposition:

"…a small blonde female was recorded on several police cruiser dashboard cameras, running along the concrete divider with a gym bag over her shoulder. She came upon the scene of the delivery man in the circle of dead police officers at 3:35 p.m., just minutes after detonation. Her whereabouts are currently unknown. Tragically, Officer Bigbee did not notice the extra weight in his bulletproof vest until it was too late. His head was launched from his torso, rebounding between the wheels of traffic for a good 15 minutes until it became pinned into a lowrider's exhaust… wait, I've told this story before. How about this instead? On March 15th, at 3:27 p.m., surveillance cameras will record a pizza delivery man walking into a local bank. Around the man's neck will be a basketball hoop, which is no way to make a reliable explosive device. These events will be transcribed onto a small audio tape, later to be discovered in a discarded bag of pepperoni because all pizza is Greek to me. The small blonde female was later identified as Amy Luck, a.k.a. 'Any Luck?' Birth name 'Toni Ramirez,' nickname 'Bolita' or 'Boli,' renamed 'Tully,' tragically mispronounced as 'Bully.' She was state-raised by the Luck family following the suicide of her mother. Or was it her sister. Either one…"

There was some rustling in the recording, then Bully's voice softened for the first time in her life.

"…Billy, I'm sorry about the tape bomb. It wasn't supposed to rat you out, I promise. It was supposed to be discovered after we leveled the drive-in. To take credit after we did our thing. But your confession became the perfect manifesto. I think we were following the wrong cop, too. Awkward!"

And then her voice stopped for good.

After eight hours of sonar and search teams and sifting bloody rocks and blocks of the void where The Spotlight Kid used to stand (now more like Beefheart's *Clear Spot* instead), rescuers discovered that when the screen had come crashing down, the crushed playground was mercifully empty after all.

Well, almost empty.

After some struggling in the dust, one lone, raggedy chunk of concrete flipped over in the rising sun, and the men stepped back to reveal a smoldering covered children's slide, now just a twisted lump on the ground, flattened except for the grotesque bulge in the center, like an anaconda that had just choked on a pig.

Epilogues

Rat Chases the Cat – The Last Project – Hard Ralph's Café – (Spoiler Alert!) – The Worm Turns and Eats the Worm – Bugs Bunny Paradox (or See No, Hear No, Speak No Evel Knievel) – Suitably Dramatic Removal of the Chicken Skin – Signing the Cast (The Scene in Which Our Hero Finally Kisses the Girl after It Doesn't Mean Jack Shit Anymore) – Turtle Cake Turns Turtle Tank – Warning Signs – The Best Scene of the Red-Faced Bastard's Career – Snap Snap Snap

"They find their own way in
And they rip up everything that I believe in"
—Pulp "Dogs Are Everywhere That I Go"

Years later. Jack will be sitting in an apartment, a frayed baseball cap shading his eyes. The apartment will be empty except for a crappy black-and-white television on a cinderblock, a small potted plant drooping on the windowsill, and a black rotary telephone on the floor by his knee. On the screen, the credits will be rolling on Eric Bogosian's *Sex, Drugs, Rock & Roll.* Unprepared for such a sight, he will quickly rewind it to the middle.

"I saw this tree, this beautiful tree. They dug a hole and put it in the sidewalk. Every day I come to say hello. And this guy was backing up his truck. The truck was making that beep sound, 'Beep beep beep beep' right over the tree, 'cause, see, the tree can't hear that…"

The phone will ring, and he'll fumble it a bit because of a broken thumb.

"Hey," he'll say. "Hi." Pause. "How did you get - nothing. I'm surprised you called."

Long pause.

"Come on up."

He'll walk in circles, flattening imaginary grass until the knock at the door. Opening it, he'll see Jacki standing impatient like she always was, and he'll finally lift his cap to let in the light. He heard somewhere that cowboys did that when they were finally ready to talk. His left eye will be covered with a scabby bandage. Jack's new dog, Derek's

503

old Dobie, will trot up to the door behind him. It will stand obedient, peering out from behind his left leg. Jack will absently scratch its bobbed bat-like ears.

"Say, 'Hi,' boy. He's my new eye," he'll laugh. "I seem to have lost my peripheral vision."

"Or maybe you got it back," Jacki will offer.

"Huh?"

"Nothing. So... I just wanted to say... I don't know. Something," Jacki will sigh. "I'm not really sure why I'm here."

"That's fine. Makes perfect sense to us."

Jack will hold his door open wide to coax her inside, and Jacki will look past him to the TV screen. The credits will be back, and a valve in Jack's heart will hiccup in fear. He still won't be able to keep the credits at bay for long.

"Wanna come in?"

"No. What movie were you watching?"

"No idea. There was a dog in it though. Or someone pretending to be a dog."

"Of course there was," Jacki will say with a long blink.

"It all evens out," he'll say, rubbing the Dobie's ears flat. "When this dog here dreams, I think he dreams of being a cop. He loved our movie, too. Right up until the drive-in blew up."

"Mm-hmm." Jacki will walk in toward the television, interested in something.

"Dogs are good for us. Did you know I hit a dog with my car the first day I got my license? That's what made me want to be a paramedic..."

"Please," Jacki will interrupt. "Not that story again. I can't take it."

They will stand silent a moment, until she tap, tap, taps the heavy glass of the TV with her toe.

"So, do you still get an empty feeling when the movie is over or what?"

"Not really. Maybe."

He'll walk to the window and look down to see an El Camino parked in front of the hydrant. There will be a tiny hand drawing on the glass from the inside, exhaust chugging out the tailpipe. When Jack realizes the car is still running, his muscles will slump a bit in disappointment. Then he'll jump, startled at the sound of his television tipping over.

"Sorry," she'll say. His lack of peripheral vision will make it easy for her to pocket some things that had caught her eye as he works to set the TV back on the cinderblock.

"Do you remember when I told you my dad made me catch stray cats in the junkyard with him?" he'll ask her.

"I don't know. Yes? I thought you said it was stray dogs though."

"No. It was cats, we'd catch cats hiding in the tires in the junkyard. Living in the rain water like otters. Ten more generations and they'd have flippers."

"You ever read *Tom Sawyer*?" she'll ask.

"No."

"No?"

"Probably. You ever heard The Byrds 'Old Blue'?"

"Please, no more dog songs, Jack. There can't be any left, right?"

"*We lowered him down with a golden chain, and every link, we called his name...*" Jack will sing.

"Well, I think you'd love *Tom Sawyer*, Jack. Long time ago, I read it, and Toni just started reading it to me at bedtime these days. And it turns out I remembered it all wrong. 'Spunkwater' wasn't the cure for warts. It wasn't the cure for anything. It was the chant Tom Sawyer said *after* he stuck his hand in the stump."

"Okay?"

"And it was a dog not a cat. And Tom said, 'The dead cat chases the dead, and the warts chase the cat.' Or maybe it's the dead cat chases the rat. Either way."

"What the hell are you talking about, Jacki?"

"I don't know," she'll admit again. She will say this a lot. "Toni skips a lot when she reads."

"My dad made me hunt stray rats once," Jack will say.

"I thought it was cats," Jacki will say through her teeth. "How can there be such a thing as 'stray rats'?"

"Spunkwater doesn't cure anything, huh?" he'll say, sounding too interested. "If it did, you wouldn't need guys like us."

Jack will be able to tell by her eyes that this is not a bad prospect.

"Never mind. Look. I gotta go."

"Goodbye, Jacki."

She'll start to turn around.

"Hey!" he'll say. "Sorry about whatever I'm supposed to be sorry for."

"But you're not really sorry, are you?" she'll say, turning back again.

"You shouldn't have cheated on me," Jack will shrug.

"And you never should have punched me in the stomach."

"That wasn't you. At the time."

Jacki will be furious at this, and it will be like three hours have passed instead of six years.

"I cheated on a dead man, you crazy fuck. God damn it, it had nothing to do with you."

"Same thing. And, yes, it did. Ever think about why you didn't tell anyone about it?"

"I know, I know, because it wouldn't have done any good. You ever think about who else besides me Derek may have... any other projects he may have, uh…"

"Not anymore."

"Just thinking, you know?" she'll say. "So, what about you?"

"What about me what?"

"Any obsessions, a righteous cause? Pulling flies from webs or cats from dogs' mouths…"

"Well, there was this one thing," he'll say, smiling and stepping a little closer. "See, there's this procedure we had at the hospital, and you might have also seen this sticker on the door at most retail stores, calling it 'Code Adam'? Well, that's also what you're supposed to say over the loudspeaker whenever a parent is missing a child. And the parent is then asked by security what color shoes the kid was wearing. So then every employee can watch so no kids leave and they look for any child wearing those color shoes-"

"What's so important about the shoes?"

"The theory is, an abductor might bring a change of clothes, might even bring another coat and hat, but the abductor wouldn't know what size shoes to bring, get it?"

"I get it. Okay, so, always remember the color of Toni's shoes? Gotcha. Anyway..."

"Here's the problem, Code Adam doesn't take into account the easiest way to abduct a child."

"Which is how?" she'll ask, suddenly worried.

"By spanking them. You spank the child you're abducting and then no one looks twice when Adam is crying or fighting back. Or put a Halloween costume on them. Kids wear those all year round... and, of course, take off the shoes. I need more time to continue this research though. Small price to pay for the lives I'll save."

"Don't they call those things 'Amber Alerts'?" Jacki will ask, moving away from him. "But it sounds like a plan, Jack. Really."

She'll head for the door, and he will follow. Following her will feel good, like old times.

"Let me walk you out!" he'll say way too loud, like old times.

Jack and his dog will follow Jacki down the hall, then down some stairs. Jack will be unsteady on his feet, his left hand never far from the back of the dog's neck. Outside in the parking lot, Jack will nod toward the idling car.

"Could I say goodbye to her?"

"Why not," she'll say, not really asking.

"You know," he'll say, "I tried to write it all down once, but every time I typed the word 'dog' my fingers typed 'god' instead. After the hundredth time, I finally ripped the damn keyboard loose. I still type on it, even though they won't let me back in the library."

"Great story, Jack."

"How did you know my name was 'Jack'?!"

They will both laugh at the old joke, then Jack will lean over as Toni rolls down her passenger's window. Toni will reach out, and, mercifully, the dog will lick her hand instead of his.

"He's a good boy, ain't he?" Jack will say.

"I get to have one when I can keep my fish alive!" Toni will offer.

"They're easier than fish actually," he'll tell her. "A fish can't sniff out its own food and feed itself if you forget about it."

"Where's your ice cream truck?" Toni will ask. She will be old enough for jokes now, old enough for a lot of things.

"Oh, I don't drive those anymore."

"I saw one last night. It's so weird! Lights were on inside, in the back. It looked... like someone's bedroom driving by."

Jack will smile.

"Yes, that's exactly what it is."

Jacki will get into the car and close the door. Then she'll reach across Toni and roll up her window while Jack's finger traces her handprint from the outside.

Minutes later. Jack's dog will be leading him around the room, seeming to be looking for something it lost. In spite of its terrible life so far, the dog will get better at figuring out when things have changed. Or are missing. But it will have no way of communicating this with its new owner. Then Jack's attention will be drawn to a flash of movement on the windowsill. He'll walk over to find his Venus Flytrap closed tight, but sagging in an entirely new position. He'll hold it up to the light and see the outline of a fly twitching inside.

After a second or two, he won't be able to help himself, and he'll suddenly grab the plant and rip it apart to set the fly free. Then he'll drop the shredded leaves, pot, and crumbled wings to the floor and close his eyes, realizing he's killed everything during the rescue.

Days later. Jacki will be walking through a quiet neighborhood with a matchbook and a photograph in her hand. She'll read the matchbook again as she comes to a certain mailbox to confirm she's found the right house. Holding the photograph up to her nose, the sunshine will illuminate a young, dark-skinned girl very similar to Jacki. And her mother. And her daughter.

The picture will have an "X" through it, like the rest of the small, framed photographs in Jack's apartment that will be balanced precariously on his crappy television.

Jacki will take a deep breath and stare at the front of the house. A little girl will be peeking out one of the windows, sounds of laughter inside. Breathing deep, she'll walk up to the door and knock hard and with the confidence of someone delivering the worst news of all time.

A different little girl will open it.

Jacki will smile, but the little girl will cross her arms defensively.

"Hi. Is your mommy home?"

"Why?"

"There's something that I need to..."

But she'll trail off, smile slipping from her face. A woman will be coming down the hallway, and Jacki will notice the round melon of her stomach protruding from under a "Hard Rock Café" T-shirt. Both her daughters will run for her legs. A closer look, and Jacki will see the woman has been suckered into buying a shirt that read "Hard *Ralph's* Café" instead.

Suckered twice, she'll think, checking out the belly again.

"Can I help you?" the woman will ask.

Jacki will just stare, and the woman will look up and down the street.

"Are you looking for Eric?" she'll ask Jacki.

"Who? No, I'm sorry. I've got the wrong house."

Jacki will turn and quickly walk away from the woman and all those daughters. She'll head down to the end of the block, almost tripping over a small mutt chasing nothing. Then she'll turn a corner and stop at a splintered tree lying in her path. A worker in an orange helmet will smile and wink, then fire up his massive wood chipper. Jacki will jump from the deafening roar, and reach into her pocket for her headphones. She'll put them on and sing along to Sisters of Mercy's "You Don't Exist When You Don't See Me." The worker in the orange helmet will do a double-take when he notices the wire from the headphones dangling down her arm is plugged into nothing.

She'll walk straight through the exhaust and debris billowing out of the wood chipper's chute, ignoring the panicked shouts and warnings of the worker. Smoke, dust, and wood will blow out all around her, walk with her, filling her eyes with the welcome sting of splinters and fire.

Seconds later, a decade earlier. 45,000 feet above sea level. A siren warbles as if dying, then a voice crackles on the speakers.

"*Ladies and gentlemen, this is Captain Pete Heart speaking. I regret to inform you that we'll be arriving fifteen minutes ahead of schedule and will have to cut the in-flight movie short. I can, however, tell you how it ended.*"

Jack looks around to see how upset everyone is to have the story ruined like this, but no one seems to care.

"*So, here's what happened. The man was punished,*" *the Captain continues.* "*The woman was punished. The villain got away with it. And the dog, oddly enough, did not survive the explosion. I'm sorry, just a second…*"

The sound of an "overspeed" alarm was beeping in the cockpit and coming through the speaker, and now the passengers were looking around at each other in shock.

You never fuck with a dog, no matter how grim the film, *Jack thinks, not understanding it wasn't the alarm that was upsetting them.* Not unless you want to lose the audience for good.

"*What did I miss?*" *a passenger on his elbow asks.*

"*Well, if you really give a shit about these things. See that guy? 'Stan'? Well, 'Stan' was actually 'Dan,' which means he was Sam all along. And 'Larry' was 'Jerry,' meaning 'Dick' was 'Nick,'*" *Jack explains.* "*But this revelation is muted by the fact that, even if DNA can't conclusively prove they are the same person, they've now done all of the same things by reenacting their pasts with more effort than they ever lived their lives.*"

"*What movie are* you *watching? What about the talking dog?*"

"*I'm sorry,*" *the Captain interrupts.* "*I'm being told that our flight path has been rerouted because of the storm. The movie will resume shortly. Did I ruin anything? Sorry about that!*"

* * *

Jack stopped one block short of his home, bike sputtering as his toes tapped the crossroad near the stop sign by Mary's house.

She was waiting for him, and she didn't say a word as he calmly dismounted, walked over, kicked her loose from the dirt, plucked her like a 60-pound sunflower and carried her under his arm across the street to home plate. He thought back to some script doctoring work he did before his porn gig. His 37th occupation. He would chop typos and clichéd hard-ass speeches from other people's screenplays with an abandon he could never muster for his own, all the while humming along with Robert Palmer's "Bad Case of Loving You" or Harry Nilsson's "Coconut":

"Doctor, doctor, gimmie the news, you got a bad case of tough guy blues… I said, 'Doctor, ain't there nothing I can take? Doctor, to cure this spelling ache…'"

Or sometimes he'd talk to the script like it was there for its annual checkup:

"Listen, you, we got to get you down to one cigarette per scene. Not every character needs to smoke or flick one to punctuate every dramatic moment."

There was about half a radio hanging from Evil's handlebars, and Larry walked it over to the diamond, checked the dial on the way. He listened for dialogue from the drive-in he just left behind, settling for Don Henley's "Building the Perfect Beast," a surprisingly deep album cut for A.M. Even more surprising on half a radio.

Yeah, there were too many cigarettes in those movies. Almost as many explosions.

He wished there was a way to force a movie to keep smoking until it got sick, so it would never smoke again. He remembered when his mother did that to his brother. Years later, when he was getting drunk at a seafood buffet at his own wedding, he shouted, "Hey, Mom, you know that thing you did to me with cigarettes? Please do it to me with shrimp!"

But when he was being a humble script doctor and only dreaming of pornography, there was one overused prop he was never able to chop.

He always left in scenes with tequila, especially the worm.

He was enamored with the worms. Maybe because he never drank one before. Ate one. Whatever you did with them. In porn, you could always use a bottle over and over, but he still hadn't taken a nip, even when the bottles were still being used on the right end of his talent, still performing the task they were created for.

He looked up and down the street. He loved being out and about at this time of night. It was around 3:33 a.m., give or take a minute. This was the launch window where the least amount of humanity was always roaming. It was easy to pretend it was the end of the world. In apocalyptic, last-man-on-Earth movies like *The Quiet Earth*, *Omega Man*, and, yeah, even *Last Man on Earth*, they always depicted this sort of scenario as misery. But it always looked utterly intoxicating to Larry. Bliss. Speaking of...

He pulled his bottle and flicked some leftover porn fur from the cap. There was still the worm to consider. There was always the worm.

Until the worm has turned.

He tipped back the bottle, and he swallowed. He heard the worm showed you things sometimes.

Evil was in the back of an ambulance, struggling to talk to the paramedics. They turned off the sirens to play music instead. He heard the words "That was a deep, deep, deep cut!" and got scared. Then he realized that they were talking about a Billy Squier song.

513

"You know, a deep album cut?" one of them said. "Something that shouldn't be on the radio, but is…"

"Whew. I thought you said something else and we were going to have to do real work."

"…album cuts, b-sides, flipsides, the song you request from the DJ knowing he'll never play it?"

"Yes. I get it. What about 'em?" the other one asked.

"Take this song. Maybe you don't notice it on the radio because you have the album, and you know it well?"

"Okay."

"Well, that's proof that you're just like that Bugs Bunny cartoon with that giant pencil just drawing shit around you as it goes, making it up on the spot."

"Huh?"

"When you hear a deep cut that would never be on the radio, that's the writer up there, in the zone, cranking music in the background."

Evil pondered this a moment, then tried to tell them that he shouldn't have to be listening to Billy Squier in *every* scene for the past few days, especially this scene, just because his name used to be "Billy." He tried to say a lot of things, get in on the discussion, but it was hard to talk with the bones in his jaw mostly sand. Someone switches stations. A low, Elvis-like croon comes from the speakers as "Messiah Ward" plays again.

"They're bringing out the dead now, and it's been a strange, strange day…"

"Is that the crazy motherfucker from The Birthday Party? When did he go solo? How new is this?"

"That's what I'm trying to tell you."

"If they don't want us to drive like maniacs, dispatch shouldn't put songs like this on."

"Put *my* song back on."

"Okay, like this song! No *way* that's on the radio right now!"

"This song? This has got 'hit single' written all over it. A girl running? It's a tale for the ages."

"It was nine songs in on *Emotions in Motion*. Never hit the airwaves. I'm telling you, there is some sort of future manipulation going on. To somebody up there, this song is nostalgic. This shitty bit of album filler that's like two songs from the end of the second side, that's a *memory*. That's why a radio only plays the hits, get it? It's a loop! A smokescreen!"

Evil thought about his poor smashed boombox, and he tried in vain to ask where they got their special radio. He'd heard of these new antennas, the ones that actually picked up songs from the past, too.

"What year do you think this is? 1988?"

"Try 1999."

"See?! Time travel."

"Dick, listen…"

"That's not my name."

"Close enough."

Then the paramedics talked about the other explosion, years ago, when the other drive-in went down. Evil knew it was Bully, and he would have loved to tell them all about it. But what Evil didn't know was it happened the day The Butch Cassidy switched to over to porn, too, just like the Spotlight Kid. Then the paramedics talked about all the dogs. And all the songs about dogs. There were a lot of them. But they mostly talked about the injured police dog that the crowd at the Spotlight Kid had tried to get them to take in the back of their ambulance.

"They get that behavior from the movies," one of them said. "It's ridiculous. Fuck people. You have to hurt a dog in a movie these days to get an audience emotional."

"Why do you think that is?" the other one asked.

"You tell me why."

"I'll tell you why. Dogs are so effective in movies because everyone has lost a pet and will tear up instantly.

515

Even a goldfish. Not so many people have lost a dad. There is a cure for this though. Give more people real, live, dead loved ones to grieve over."

"I'm on the case."

Evil didn't understand how they'd help remedy this, but he couldn't ask.

"Kind of like that little girl?" one of them said.

"What little girl?"

"The little girl who was choking."

"Exactly! All those people putting away their guns for a second, working it out, getting together to save her. It might have been one of those heartwarming moments if one of those dumb fucks actually knew the Heimlich Maneuver, of course."

"I'll bet they can do it on a dog though."

"Even a smack on the back might have helped! Assholes."

"What happened back there anyway?"

"What do you mean what happened? Didn't you see the screen?"

"Yeah, I've seen that movie a million times."

"What movie?"

"Doppelbängers."

"Ha! Nice name. What is that? A porno where people fuck anyone that looks like their ex-wife?"

"No, anyone who looks like themselves. Masturbation fantasies."

"Of course. Play that shit at a drive-in where they're already jerking off and..."

"Boom."

"No one will try that again."

One of them turned up the music.

"Okay, think about it," he went on. "If you're hearing a B-side on the radio, it means you are important enough to exist in the imagination of some other creature. That or you should try to make yourself more important pretty damn quick before you're written out. A B-side like this on the radio means that the author is up there spinning old records, looking for a hero…"

"What the fuck is all over this kid's body?"

The voice was close, and Evil could smell the burger on his breath. He tried to sit up. Tried to ask who stole his girl, or who stole his bike.

"Worst tattoos I've ever seen."

"More like an infection. Give me a needle."

They were making sense to Evil now, and he kept trying to sit up, all the way up until he slipped underwater. He didn't hear them change tapes and put in more popular music for the long drive.

After the worm slid down his throat, Larry tore his sleeves down to the elbows and scratched even harder. He scratched as hard as he used to scratch the rental stickers off the corners of his videotapes. And those suckers were on like cement. Harder than anyone dared to scratch living tissue, that's for sure. Almost as hard as a young man's cock, the young man he used to be anyway. His fingernails stripped the gray hair off his arms, along with the wrinkled husk of his pale exoskeleton, past what a paramedic might call the epiphyseal bone connected to the synovial bone, past the hyaline cartilage that sent the bump of bee stings all over the funny bones.

And underneath, there was another layer.

One that split easy, with barely any pressure at all, then finally slipped away like spoiled, wet chicken skin with just that sting he used to get as a kid when his new blisters hit the air. He felt about a foot taller, and the new skin underneath was glistening, smooth as a boiled frankfurter and just as angry. Larry didn't see the patterns at first since he was so close to the experiment, but as he ran his fingers over the rapeseed crop formations of hives on his arms, shoulders, chest, stomach, he didn't have to see it from the clouds. He'd seen them all so many times now, he could read them like Braille. Larry's stains were always childlike, the same bullshit a little boy would doodle into his school books...

Race cars, monkeys, and dragons covered his arms. Gators, hummingbirds, ivy, roses, unicorns, unicorns listening to boomboxes, unicorns having trouble with their headphones, the ol' cat showing its ass where Larry's bellybutton would be, lions and tigers and bears, all carrying an assortment of guns, guns, and more fucking guns like the little boys loved, barbed wire, telephone wire, an entire cemetery of headstones and dates, Jesus on the cross, an alien on the cross, Jesus playing basketball, loading a musket, riding a goddamn dinosaur, a spider web and an angel trapped inside, the hedge maze of tribal nonsense on his tricep, a Rosetta stone of indecipherable languages and fonts on his bicep, the dual snakes of caduceus on each wrist, a symbol of thievery, instead of the single snake on the Rod of Asclepias, just because those idiots in the U.S. Army Medical Corps sewed the wrong one into their uniforms back in 1902, the hoary ol' ouroboros sucking itself off forever, the buckshot scatter of five-pointed stars on his shoulders, sharks and fire, sharks on fire, and, finally, the names of everyone he knew that had died. With every fucking name misspelled. Just like his given name, "John," that everyone always got wrong before he changed it three times.

You can't be around them that long… his wife's singsong voice in his head. …*you're gonna catch something…*

He remembered her first tattoo, a ladybug on her thigh. She said it gave her infinite wishes. Then she fucked it up with a ladybug as the President on a fifty-dollar bill.

When they did tattooing in real tribes, they didn't have an electric needle. Larry saw this on a show once, or maybe it was the movie *Utu*, something about the Maori tribes of New Zealand using this tiny hammer and chisel, and they would trace the lines of your chin, your brow, and bang channels into your face to soak up the stain of octopus ink, berries, or your own blood.

Tap. Tap. Tap.

In his hospital bed, Evil stared at his arm and leg suspended high over his head. Sleeping on his purple cast-covered toes was a stuffed green monkey with a bright red bow. No card.

Sometimes, when he drifted in and out of consciousness, he would see the blur of someone in the room with him, someone with a patch over her eye when she leaned in close for a kiss. Maybe it was a him, not a her, but the kiss never came. Sometimes, he would see the crowd from the drive-in pile into his room, and he would scream in pain when they fought to sign his cast. They would push too hard with their names and doodles and their very own monsters, but his voice would still be underwater, or at least underground, buried in six feet of blood and bandages.

"I haven't seen a cast this big since Marlon Brando broke his leg line dancing…" Evil slurred, unheard.

They would draw on him all through the night, not realizing they were pressing the red fire of broken bones against metal pins they'd used to rebuild him. They'd wrestle and scribble, covering him in Mothmen and the lyrics to *The Monster Mash* and maps to the stars. After a while, he stopped trying to scream. He stopped trying to communicate with sign language or a fluttering eyelash. He even abandoned his half-remembered Little League baseball signals soon after that. It was no use.

When you're the star, the cast did the signing, not the other way around.

* * *

At the funeral reception, Bolita Ramirez kicked and rocked her body around some lazy figure-eights on a child's swing. She let her feet drag every fifth spin or so to keep her orbits just slow enough to seem distraught, while all around her swam a backyard of mourners, respectfully silent. But most of the children, particularly the ones that were the same age as the deceased and therefore much more likely to talk freely about his short life and lack of legacy, were gathered around the plastic playground with her. Boli felt a kinship with 9-year-olds, or at least that particular mentality, as she understood the difficulty of imitating rational adult behavior the minute she became one.

The boy they'd buried that morning had been killed in a car accident, collateral damage from Boli's latest crusade against wanton roadkill. Even though her newest scheme involved 100% fewer explosives, the boy had been thrown from a car that had made the mistake of swerving to hit one of Boli's "turtlecakes," a counterfeit Carolina Terrapene she'd crafted from cereal bowls, spray paint, a gutted Pound Puppy, and a bit of garden hose which, when compressed by a car tire, revealed a porcupine of carpenter nails almost guaranteed to result in a blowout and a ton of frustration. Fatal accidents afterward were a surprise, and a bonus.

Boli had originally started out with a World War II helmet that her boyfriend had scavenged from an Army Surplus. She had this thing about vets again lately, and he swore he was heading for veterinarian school after he shook off all that National Guard bullshit. But she quickly discovered they just didn't make things like they used to, or make cereal bowls like they used to make steel infantry helmets anyway, because even an 18-wheeler wouldn't crush a soldier in her box-turtle infantry.

Colanders and popcorn bowls were too big, too, even though the popcorn seemed especially appropriate while waiting in the bushes for the trap to spring. But there was something about any turtle bigger than breakfast size that made people start worrying for their tires, and they wouldn't take the bait. And indeed, during her research, she'd read news reports of turtle shells piercing the white walls of some asshole's Lincoln when the driver exercised his God-given right to flex his *Great Santini* Syndrome (people didn't have to see that movie to understand that, yep, "It takes a mighty brave man to run over turtles!"). But a regular-size cereal bowl held the porridge that was just right, spot-on dimensions of the familiar box turtle, the perfect target that people steered towards on the roads the vast majority of the time.

Her New Boy, fresh home from Afghanistan, was no stranger to funerals, of course, but he wouldn't come near this one, for good reason. He was feeling way too guilty about what they'd done, even though it was probably him that had given her the idea to begin with. Okay, him and seeing that creature lying burst open next to his mailbox where her letters had piled up unread, bloody string of intestine and Ping Pong balls trailing off into the gutter. Maybe she suspected he squashed it, who knows. Everyone blamed the mailman for everything. But her projects would always get complicated, intentions forever blurred in favor of effect. It was the cat that really set her off though. Her New Boy had this cat, a sluggish obese calico with the markings and fur pattern that was very similar to a turtle, but even more similar to a cake. In fact, Bolita's boyfriend started calling her "Turtle Cake" rather than her real name, some idiotic movie reference that never stuck in Bolita's brain for even the length of a heartbeat (although she did hear him call the little fatty feline a "turtle tank" once). For fun, when it was the New Boy's birthday, Bolita even tried to balance some candles on Turtle Cake's back. Turtle Cake wasn't amused. And she also wasn't burned too bad really, as the candles fell off before anyone had a chance to blow them out. But after that there was just no getting the image out of her head, a cat, turtle, pancake, porcupine or whatever the fuck combination, all those burning candles sticking up out of its shell. This image sort of morphed into a daydream, then smack dab back to fantasy. Until one day, maybe on her birthday, evolution would finally gift mankind a turtle that could safely flatten out under compression, rather than die squirting out a streamer of aborted omelets. Instead, drivers would get a bevy of secret spikes that would punish any motherfucker who swerved to run a poor critter over. All the fantasizing and fat cats led to the fabled *ding!* and a light bulb went off over her head. Well, maybe more like a *boom!* really. But definitely the blowout she was looking for.

A girl half Bolita's age, but twice her height, joined her on the swings, and it didn't take long to get her to talk about the dead kid they'd buried in the box. How he lied, bent stuff, broke stuff, stole stuff, generally how he put his fingers where he wasn't supposed to, and Bolita felt a lot better and stopped dragging her feet on the swing as much. She certainly would have been happier if the driver who'd swerved to crush her precious turtle bomb had been the one who flew through the windshield, neck snapping somewhere along the journey, ending up dead with bare feet swinging lazy figure-eights from that willow tree, but she was always destined to work within an imperfect science. Eggs would get broke and all that.

She swung faster and faster in the plastic swing, black shiny shoes tapping the clouds. She didn't feel bad at all anymore, not that she ever did really, but this would surely put her New Boy's mind at ease. And now she was confident they could step things up very soon. A relationship had to move forward, right? This was the real reason behind every funeral reception. Attendance cleared consciences. Justified all the plaster casts and fatalities in her wake.

She knew that soon she could ask her New Boy, probably pacing right now in his half-empty apartment, memorizing dog diseases and ear mites, finally back home in the States and finally forgetting about that leg he left in the teeth of an I.E.D. in Panjshir Province.

There on a swing set that wouldn't last three summers before it disintegrated, a poor substitute for the immortal swings at every dying drive-in the country, munching on funeral shrimp and thinking of her newest boyfriend, she realized only a psychotic hopes for a car wreck when someone does something as foolish as running over reptiles. Certainly there was room for improvement here. Wouldn't a driver's survival be favorable? Maybe. If the crash also left someone with a loss of limbs resulting in the most turtle-like appearance, of course. A turtle that was tucked down in fear inside its shell. This would be the preferred outcome. Something to shoot for.

She'd start working on a more lethal birthday cake any day now, when she got back to the empty apartment she shared with her New Boy. Something more like the mechanical roadkill that ate his leg for dessert in a desert halfway across the planet. Now that would be a turtle tank to reckon with when it got pancaked. The rabbits could still win all the races, but they'd fucking pay for it.

Next night. The driver searches the rear-view mirror as a line of streetlights pulse through the back windows of the ambulance. He's alarmed to see his new partner, Jack, holding defibrillator paddles up to the sides of his head.

"What are you doing?"

"Locking shit down so it doesn't slide," Jack tells him.

"Well, I'd keep those away from your dome. Unless you wanna forget the alphabet. Can't you read the warning label?"

"What if it's actually a warning for us, if we use 'em too much?"

"Huh?"

Jack ignores the question.

"It's like those babies through the windshields."

"Are you all right, man?"

"Come on, you haven't seen 'em? The warning signs are everywhere."

"Everywhere, huh."

"Yep."

They're on a dark stretch of road, and Jack is lost in the shadows again.

"Not too many streetlights in your country, huh?" Jack says, looking out the back windows. Then a red hotel "Vacancy" glow reveals Jack rubbing the paddles together thoughtfully.

"So, maybe these warning signs are just warning us not to put these next to our heads so that..."

"They warn us not to put them on our patient's head!" the driver almost shouts.

"...so we don't try it ourselves," Jack finishes. "You know, out of curiosity. Just to see what would happen."

"Who would try that?"

"Maybe it's harmless," Jack whispers, moving closer. "Maybe it just changes the color of your eyes. Clears your head. Are you clear?"

"What? What are you doing?"

"Maybe it makes us smarter. Are you clear?"

"I guess not. Why don't you give me a jolt?" the driver laughs nervously.

"Clear." Jack says again, sincerely. Then he leans over and pushes both buttons, marked "apex" and "sternum," and electricity arcs from the paddles through the metal frame of the driver's glasses. The whip crack of a thousand volts freezes *his eyes in surprise, teeth bared like a dog. The driver sucks in one last breath as if through a straw, both feet suddenly concrete, stomping the gas and brake at the same time. The engine screams in protest while the ambulance slows, slows, then stops.*

A week later and another partner is adjusting the steering wheel to his height while Jack organizes the equipment in the dark.

"Hey, man, you sure you want me to drive?"

"Yeah," Jack says. "But we should eat early before calls start coming in."

"Cool. I heard this is the most stressful time of the night."

"Some can't take the stress. Coronaries ain't uncommon."

"Don't worry. I just had my physical."

"So, what do you wanna eat?"

"Let's hit the drive-thru. Hey, what are you doing back there anyway?"

"Tying everything down, in case you take a bad turn." Then, *"Drive-thru, huh? Haven't you seen the warnings?"*

"On the burgers?"

"No," Jack sighs. "On the drive-thru. Right next to the speaker. A cartoon of what happens when someone leans out too far pulling up. Dangerous world, man…"

The driver tilts the rear-view mirror around to search the shadows behind him as an electric whine worms into their ears.

Jack and Mary got drunk as long as they could while he told her all about his promising young career as a film major at the University of Pittsburgh, which led to a short career as a paramedic, both in the States and overseas, which led back to movies with a whole new idea, like a dog to its own sick, but only if that sick was delicious.

He told her how he'd once studied people like Sergei Mikhailovich Eisenstein, Eadweard J. Muybridge, (otherwise known as "Ed*weird*," in all his notes, but actually born Ed Muggeridge), even some Samuel Taylor Coleridge. All were perfect names for Oscar posters. Or porn. He told her how he once wrote, directed, and chopped an award-winning short called *Engaged/Enraged* where a nurse's engagement ring got tangled in the chest hair of a man who'd come in for a little innocent EKG, and how it ended in jealousy, infidelity, and a little murder.

He was going to be the stunt hand, but his finger was too hairy for the contrast. Jack's wife once told him that a ring on Jack's finger "looked like Keith Richards' headband." She wanted him to shave his knuckles for their wedding ceremony, but he refused, having already shaved his ears and figured that was already a demonstration of his commitment. Her idea of commitment was to get "Ecnalubma" tattooed on her arm where she'd written it a decade earlier. Jack knew she'd done this just to upset her mother.

No, not "Ecnalubma." It said "Escanaba," that little burg in Michigan where we met, both doing our Red Cross training together, patching people up outside the casino, and chomping ice cubes on the bumper of the ambulance when the sun came up, messing around in the back of the ambulance when the sun went down, remember...

But the ring through the chest hair? He couldn't remember whose hand they ended up using. But it was a good scene.

Jack and Mary got drunk, drunk enough to stay Jack for awhile and not go back to being Larry. They all got drunk until the sun came up and her grandson came out.

It had been a busy day, but Jack still needed to prove his theory. That a skinny, cement Virgin Mary whose feet came to a point was clearly constructed for one purpose and one purpose only. No, not a vibrator.

A baseball bat.

Jack's grip sunk in under Mary's chin as if she was made to be cradled by Babe Ruth himself. Jack had been hoping to give the red-faced bastard one more chance to yank on his hood ornament, pull the pin on his Grenada so to speak, but Jack surprised the red-faced bastard outside the safety of his car, right when he burst out of his grandmother's screen door, ham hocks white-knuckled and clenched. Still, Jack's first swing whiffed over the man's head, dusting off his UFC cap. But the second swing connected low, right where he would have been labeled "breadbox" in the game *Operation* he'd had as a boy, marked "beatbox" in young Larry's modified version, when he was still "John."

Jack swung again. And again. And he heard the game's buzzer and watched his nose light up with every shot. When Jack's arms were tired, he moved the red faced, now dead-faced, bastard's limbs around, feeling every joint pop like dry Buffalo wings, amazed how a human body finally did everything he wanted for once in his career, followed every direction, bloody shoes pointed perfect, arms and legs hanging in the air where he posed them as if suspended on invisible wires.

Jack managed to prop him up on an elbow, balanced so that anyone driving by, anyone catching his actor at just the right angle and ignoring the leaking, deflated weeks-after-Halloween pumpkin that used to be his head, they would think someone freeze-framed a baseball game right when the Red Sox were sliding into home.

Back on his new dirt bike, Jack pulled his shirt over his new girl so they could share it, something he saw the kids do once. He kickstarted the engine, then turned his head to kiss a nose cold as bone.

Even though there was no antenna for miles, songs lingered in the sky for a lifetime, and every one of them was skipping now.

ABOUT THE AUTHOR:

David James Keaton's award-winning fiction has appeared in over 50 publications. His first collection, *Fish Bites Cop: Stories to Bash Authorities,* was named *This Is Horror's* Short Story Collection of the Year. He grew up within sight of a drive-in, and in his spare time creates soundtracks for sequels that do not exist. This is his first novel.

ACKNOWLEDGEMENTS:

Thanks, as always, to my beloved reading machine Amy Lueck, who devoured this book in one marathon, sixteen-hour session. That's at least six movies she missed. Thanks to my family, especially my brother for allowing me to edit *The Crow* down to 30-minutes. Thanks to my past-and-present paramedic friends, Jamie Bono and Sean Ferguson, who answered crazy questions about EMT dog-attack protocol and what happens if you put defibrillators on someone's head ("It'll arc through your glasses! Don't!"). Any paramedical errors were made by my characters, not my consultants. Thanks to editor J. David Osborne for believing in this book after a rapid-fire description on a crowded roof under a plastic supermoon; Joel Vollmer for his brilliant artwork and ability to translate suggestions like "the *Megaforce* poster, but with the Virgin Mary" into the beautiful cover you now hold; Rachel Johnson for co-writing our doomed *Spunkwater* script back in the day, which ended up as the gooey heart of this novel; the songwriters who helped craft "The Rap is the Thing (or Your Blood's Gonna Scream)": Rachel, Mike, Matt, Mark, Nate, and Cryptozoology 101; and fellow writers, readers, and artists: Erin Keaton, Jedidiah Ayres, Chuck Kinder, Simon Jacobs, Glenn Gray, Dyer Wilk, Alec Cizak, Patrick Wensink, Sal Pane, Jason Stuart, Maggie Hannan, Sean and Jessica, Robb and Livius, and A.J. Hayes, everybody misses you already.

And finally, special thanks to the drive-in theater out our back door when I was growing up, which opened in 1949, burnt down in 1958, then was rebuilt and renamed "Butch Cassidy" in 1982, the year of *The Thing*. It was sold and demolished in 1990. A tornado took out its partner, the Sundance Kid, last year.

www.ingramcontent.com/pod-product-compliance
Lightning Source LLC
Chambersburg PA
CBHW071012280326
41935CB00011B/1324